Essays In Honor of Professor Stephen T. Zamora

A LIFE BETWEEN MEXICO AND THE UNITED STATES

Essays In Honor of Professor Stephen T. Zamora

A LIFE BETWEEN MEXICO AND THE UNITED STATES

Alfonso López de la Osa
Escribano

and

James W. Skelton Jr.

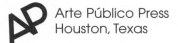

Arte Público Press
Houston, Texas

Publication of *Essays in Honor of Professor Stephen T. Zamora: A Life Between Mexico and the United States* is made possible with support from the Center for US and Mexican Law at the University of Houston Law Center and the North American Consortium on Legal Education (NACLE). We are grateful for their support.

Recovering the past, creating the future

Arte Público Press
University of Houston
4902 Gulf Freeway, Bldg 19, Rm 100
Houston, Texas 77204-2004

Cover design by Mora Design

Cataloging-in-Publication (CIP) Data is available.

TABLE OF CONTENTS

v

DEDICATION

This book is dedicated to the honor and memory of our dear friend and colleague, Professor Stephen T. Zamora (1944-2016), who was a brilliant lawyer and law professor in the fields of international and comparative law. Steve was deeply respected and admired. He was always upbeat, kind, thoughtful, pleasant and helpful, and that kindness, which took the form of good humor and generosity, came to him so naturally and effortlessly that he made everyone he met feel important and valued. His open character allowed him to create an international academic network of colleagues who quickly became his friends. He was a team player with a strong sense of community, a consummate gentleman, a great professor, and an inspirational leader. Always well prepared for his classes, he shared his knowledge with enthusiasm, and helped his students whenever he could.

We also dedicate this book to Steve's loving wife, Lois, confirming the saying that behind every great man is a great woman, and to their children, Camille and Peter, faithful mirrors of his charisma. Professor Zamora's professional life was very important and fulfilling to him as his numerous achievements showed, but it constituted a small part of what made him such a great man. Steve was primarily a dedicated family man who relished the fulfillment of his principal roles as a loving husband, father, brother and grandfather.

To Steve, thank you for combining academic gravitas and expertise with your unlimited talent for friendship.

PREFACE

It is with a profound feeling of both sorrow and pride that we offer this collection of scholarly essays in memory and honor of our dear friend and colleague, Professor Stephen T. Zamora. We still miss our treasured friend terribly because he was larger than life and one of the greatest and kindest men we have ever known.

The initial goal in putting this anthology together was, of course, to gather a group of substantive articles about international and comparative law matters from among Steve's friends and colleagues. Alfonso began the process on January 27, 2017, when he sent an email message to a list of potential participants inviting them to participate in an anthology that would connect with Professor Zamora's contributions through an essay related to our common legal fields of interest. The idea was to compile articles for a Festschrift honoring Professor Zamora's intellectual and institutional dedication to US-Mexican understanding that would demonstrate the respect, admiration, and affection we had for Steve. Indeed, Festschrifts are excellent ways to commemorate either the retirement or passing of excellent scholars. While we know Steve would have never asked for honors or personal recognition, we believe he would have enjoyed very much celebrating life with fascinating legal topics and his academic and professional colleagues, who quickly became friends. All the articles are an excellent example of Steve's vision, versatility, and talent for friendship. Most of the articles also include a few lines about a situation, a moment, or a remarkable anecdote the authors lived with Steve.

When the project started, Jim responded immediately, saying that he would be extremely honored to contribute an essay or an article to the anthology. In June 2019, during a meeting of the International Law Section of the State Bar of Texas in Austin, Alfonso and Jim spoke about the delays concerning the submission of a few articles for the Festschrift. First, as an author and afterward as an editor, Jim became, during the process, an invaluable ally to this book, being of tremendous help with editing responsibilities and contacting authors who had agreed to write an article, and persuading others. Thanks very much to Jim for his time and dedication.

Although many of Steve's friends and colleagues agreed to participate, many of them were unable to adhere to the timeframe for submitting the first drafts of their articles due to other pressing commitments. *No están todos los que son, pero si son todos los que están*, following the Spanish idiom stating that *Not all the needed are here, but the ones here are very much needed*, and we would like to express our gratitude to all of them. We keep in our thoughts and prayers, especially Amalia Mena-Mora and her family. Amalia was a young and promising lawyer that Steve mentored, who also left us too early in December 2019. Amalia had the time to submit her article a few months before her passing, and Alfonso and Jim had the privilege of exchanging messages with her several times. We are sure she would have also enjoyed seeing this book published in memory of Steve.

Alfonso and Jim worked closely to coordinate their efforts, and slightly more than a year and a half after forming their editing team, they had most of the articles fully edited and ready for publication. We were even able to gain the agreement of two more participants from among our contacts. By the end of November 2020, we had a total of nineteen chapters ready for the publisher, and assembled the final manuscript for submission to Arte Público Press. Without Jim's thoughtful editing work and the authors' outstanding contributions, this Festschrift in memory of Steve would not have been possible.

We hope readers will enjoy this book remembering Steve, as much as we have enjoyed working closely with his friends.

The Editors, Alfonso López de la Osa Escribano and James W. Skelton, Jr.
December 2020

INTRODUCTION

PROFESSOR STEPHEN T. ZAMORA: A VISIONARY AND GENEROUS SOUL

By Alfonso López de la Osa Escribano[1]

On July 8, 2016, Professor Stephen T. Zamora suddenly passed away in Mexico City. His good health, active life and clear mind never gave the slightest sign of such a terrible event. He died "con las botas puestas"—with his boots on, as the Spanish idiom has it. He was full of energy and had many projects in progress.[2]

Professor Zamora was Leonard B. Rosenberg Professor of Law at the University of Houston Law Center, which he joined in 1978. An international authority in his field, he received the Decoration of the Order of the Aztec Eagle Award from the Mexican Government in 2006—the Mexican government's highest award given to a foreign national in recognition of his dedication to Mexican law, education, and the promotion of U.S. and Mexican cooperation.

Professor Zamora's paternal family originated from the Spanish Basque in a fishing village known as Lekeitio, which is a province of Biscay in Spain. Emigrating to the United States, the Zamora family settled in Los Angeles, California, where Professor Zamora was born in 1944. He was the second of seven children and always remained close to his family in California. He also constantly maintained his bonds with his cousins in Spain—whom he often visited—feeling proud of his Hispanic-Basque origins; pride that he projected in his beloved Mexico.

---

[1] Dean of Law and International Relations and Professor of Law at Nebrija University in Madrid, and former Director of the Center for U.S. and Mexican Law at the University of Houston Law Center. This article was originally published in the *Houston Journal of International Law*, Vol. 40, No. 3 (2018), and is reproduced with the permission of the *Houston Journal of International Law*.

[2] I came to work with Professor Stephen T. Zamora in August 2015, joining the Center for U.S. and Mexican Law as an Affiliate scholar to undertake and develop research projects in comparative law between the US and Mexico in the fields of energy, health, immigration and corporate law, among others. From our first meeting, I was taken by the intellectual capacity, warmth, energy, and good will of Professor Zamora.

Professor Zamora was fascinated by Mexico and its complex history and society—especially by Mexico City, also known as the City of the Palaces, with its rich pre-Hispanic and colonial culture.[3] He particularly loved the *plaza* and *iglesia* of San Jacinto in San Angel, a neighborhood in the southern part of Mexico City where his remains are today, and where for twenty years, Professor Zamora and his wife had an apartment they loved. To walk the area of San Angel, with its ancestral cobblestone streets, and colonial buildings, beautifully preserved in the middle of frantic Mexico City, is like being tele-transported in time to the Mexican past. Just as Professor Zamora was proud of his Spanish roots and an admirer of ancient cultures and popular traditions, he was also immersed in modern Mexico. San Angel was the perfect spot for him, replete with historical echoes and family memories, his beloved Lois, his children, and friends.

Professor Zamora enjoyed spending time with his friends at the Chapel of the Capuchinas near San Angel, a chapel designed by the Mexican architect Luis Barragán that truly is an architectural gem and was designated by the UNESCO as a World Heritage Site. This chapel may also be said to reflect Professor Zamora himself. The set of lights is amazing: light enters the chapel from above and mixes golden and red shadings on the walls, creating an imposing effect in a space of pure light and line.[4] So, too, Professor Zamora's personality was imposing but clear, radiating a charismatic aura that inspired students, colleagues, and friends to share his vision of international understanding and cooperation.

I. Professor Zamora: A Visionary

A visionary is a person with the capacity to project himself or herself into the future, to foresee possibilities with broadmindedness and intelligence.[5] Such a person intuits what *needs* to be done, what *can* be done, and *how* to do it. Professor Zamora was a visionary, and also a realist. He knew what steps had to be taken, day by day, year by year, to realize his vision: "Lo cortés no quita lo valiente" or "Courtesy detracts not from bravery," as we have it in Spanish. Actually, this popular say-

---

[3] CHARLES LA TROBE, THE RAMBLER IN MEXICO: *1834*, COLL. HISTORY OF COLONIAL NORTH AMERICA, Ed. British Library, 2011. In this very instructive text of manners from La Trobe—an expert in that type of anthropological works—we can appreciate in a very descriptive way the customs and the everyday life habits in Mexico City. Besides these descriptions, La Trobe mentions recurrently in several passages the numerous and outstanding palaces existing in Mexico (*see* § 109, 118, 122 or 127, among many other examples) after which he named the city.

[4] Luis Barragán: Capilla en Tlalpan/México. Fotografías de Armando Salas. Ed. Capilla y Convento de las Capuchinas Sacramentarias. Tipografias editoriales, p. 15.

[5] Adjectives found in the definition of visionary, see https://www.merriam-webster.com/dictionary/visionary.

ing could very well illustrate another of Professor Zamora's character traits: He constantly combined courtesy and bravery, kindness, and expertise. His colleagues at the Law Center and in Houston's legal community remember this characteristic in particular: "He didn't even know how to be unkind;"[6] he was enthusiastic, listened to students and "offered them a helping hand whenever he could;"[7] "he was always natural, genuine, and never pretentious."[8]

Professor Zamora's fields of expertise were international trade and investments, international banking, conflicts of laws, international economic relations, Mexican law, and U.S.-Mexican relations. His book, *Mexican Law,* co-authored with José Ramón Cossío Díaz, Justice of the Mexican Supreme Court, and three other authors, was conceived as an introduction and overview for U.S. lawyers, and was published by Oxford University Press in 2005.[9] Professor Zamora also wrote about Mexican constitutionalism, and peso-dollar economics,[10] NAFTA,[11] and most recently about energy reform legislation initiated in Mexico in 2013.[12] Additionally to cite a few of Professor Zamora's contributions to various areas of international law, there are his articles on international monetary law,[13] liability for damages in international transport,[14] and judicial review in Latin America.[15]

Building international programs at the University of Houston Law Center was central to Professor Zamora's vision. When he was Dean from 1995 to 2000, he

---

[6] Professor Sandra Guerra Thompson, Alumnae College Professor in Law and Director of the Criminal Justice Institute at the University of Houston Law Center, http://law.uh.edu/news/summer2016/0711Zamora.asp.

[7] Counsel Bradley J. Richards, partner at Haynes and Boone. Prof. Zamora that served as Of Counsel for Haynes and Boone for more than 15 years. *See*: http://law.uh.edu/news/summer2016/0711Zamora.asp.

[8] James W. Skelton Jr., Member of the Advisory Board of the *Houston Journal of International Law*.

[9] Stephen Zamora, S., Cossio, J.R. (*et al.*) *Mexican Law,* Oxford University Press, 2005.

[10] Stephen Zamora, *Peso-Dollar Economics and the Imposition Of Foreign Exchange Controls in Mexico*, Am. J. Comp. L., 32 (1984).

[11] *See* Stephen Zamora, *A Proposed North American Regional Development Fund: The Next Phase of North American Integration Under NAFTA*, 40 Loy. U. Chi. L. J. (Fall 2008); *see also*, Stephen Zamora, *Rethinking North America: Why Nafta Laisser Faire Approach to Integration is Flawed, and What To Do About it*, 631 Vill. L. Rev. 56 (2011).

[12] Tony Payan, Stephen Zamora & J.R. Cossio, *Estado de Derecho y Reforma Energética en México*, Tirant lo Blanch (2016).

[13] Stephen Zamora, *Sir Joseph Gold and the Development of International Monetary Law*, 23 Int'l L. 4 (1989).

[14] Stephen Zamora, *Carrier Liability For Damages or Loss To Cargo In International Transport*, 23 Am. J. Comp. L. 3 (1975).

[15] Stephen Zamora, Judicial *Review in Latin America*, 7 Sw. J. L. & Trade Americas 2 (2000).

promoted a strong international dimension at the Law Center, considering this to be an essential part of today's legal education.

Professor Zamora created the North American Consortium on Legal Education (NACLE) at the time of the establishment of NAFTA in January of 1994. The principal objective of NACLE was (and still is) to promote professional cooperation and comparative legal education in North America. Thirteen law schools in Canada, Mexico and the United States are member institutions of NACLE. This program is more relevant than ever and will continue to be promoted in the Center for U.S. and Mexican Law, which Professor Zamora created in 2012.

The contribution to the internationalization of the University of Houston Law Center began much earlier, in 1979, when Professor Zamora was invited to join the Advisory Board of the *Houston Journal of International Law* (HJIL). He also became, along with Professor Jordan Paust, who had joined HJIL in 1978, a faculty advisor to HJIL. Professor Zamora believed in the relevance of international law in every U.S. lawyer's education, and thus aligned himself with the philosophy of John O. Brentin,[16] as documented by James W. Skelton, Jr.—one of HJIL's most avid supporters and sponsor of HJIL's annual Skelton Lecture Series—in his text celebrating the thirtieth anniversary of the HJIL.[17] Professor Zamora joined this team and helped, among other things, to obtain articles and to receive them on time—not an easy task in the world of academic writing.

Professor Zamora's vision of strong international programs was grounded in experience. After clerking for Justice Raymond Sullivan at the California Supreme Court in 1972-73, he received a postgraduate fellowship in international law and arbitration at the University Consortium of World Order studies in Geneva, Switzerland. He shared wonderful memories from that period, and he pronounced the French he learned and refined during that time with an almost perfect accent. But it was Mexico that was closest to his mind and heart.

Upon arriving at the University of Houston in 1978, then Dean George W. Hardy III asked him to direct the University of Houston Law Center's Mexican Legal Studies Program—a summer program for law students from the University of Houston Law Center and other law schools, which he then organized for fifteen years. This program not only provided hundreds of students an understanding of a different legal system and legal culture, but it also contributed to building a solid reputation for the University of Houston Law Center. Today, under the leadership of Dean Leonard Baynes, the University of Houston Law Center is widely recognized

---

[16] First Editor in Chief of HJIL.

[17] James W. Skelton, Jr., *The journal at 30: An Insider's view,* 30 Hous. J. Int'l L. 618 (2008). In the words of John O. Brentin in his Editor's Foreword, "Given the phenomenal pattern of growth Houston has been experiencing in international business and commerce, the Journal will become an important medium of communication for practitioners, students, and scholars within the international community."

in Mexico for its LLM program for Mexican lawyers and diplomats, and for its programs offering internships to University of Houston Law Center students in Mexico, which the Law Center's current administration continues to develop. To this date, both programs have been in operation for more than twenty-five years. Thanks to Professor Zamora's vision and persistence, the University of Houston Law Center is more than a point of reference for American legal education in Mexico today.

Professor Zamora's initiatives over thirty-four years (at that time) have increased "the understanding of Mexican laws and legal institutions in the United States, and of U.S. laws and legal institutions in Mexico,"[18] and in 2012 led to the establishment of the Center for U.S. and Mexican Law (US-MEX LAW). Today, US-MEX LAW is the only center in any U.S. law school dedicated to the independent and critical study of Mexican law and its interactions with U.S. law.[19] The special standing of the University of Houston Law Center on the national scene with respect to diversity is enhanced by US-MEX LAW, as is its standing in the international legal community. I use the term "international" in relation to Mexico and the U.S., though the Center also envisions the integration of North America not only in trade, but also through intergovernmental cooperation in technology, employment, security, and immigration aspects. Supranational cooperation, distant from the international one, is advantageous to neighbors who are naturally inclined to find common solutions to close common issues. In the Center for US-MEX LAW, we are working in this direction, following Professor Zamora's legacy because *"L'union fait la force."*[20]

Professor Zamora appreciated the fact that the University of Houston Law Center believed in the future of U.S.-Mexican relations. The Law Center facilitated his creation of externship programs with institutions in Mexico, including the *Secretaria de Relaciones Exteriores de México* (Mexican Foreign Ministry, Mexico's State Department), Petróleos Mexicanos (PEMEX), and the *Comisión Nacional de Hidrocarburos* (National Hydrocarbons Commission). Professor Zamora arranged summer externships in Mexico City for students at the University of Houston Law Center—an experience that is professional, cultural, and personal. Still today, University of Houston Law Center students spend up to two months during the summer working in Mexico City, learning about legal, political, and economic relations between the U.S. and Mexico. The program with the Mexican Foreign Ministry began in 1991, when Professor Zamora signed an inter-institutional agreement with the Ministry. It is to the credit of the University of Houston Law Center, as well as Professor Zamora, that this externship program has been on-going for twenty-seven years.

---

[18] *See* Mission Statement of the Center for U.S. and Mexican Law, https://www.law.uh.edu/mexican-law/mission-statement.asp.

[19] *See*, https://www.law.uh.edu/mexican-law/mission-statement.asp.

[20] Translate "Unity is strength."

This agreement encourages Mexican diplomats and lawyers to take an LLM degree at the Law Center. Their residence in Houston varies from one to two years and results in a comparative understanding of two different legal systems and legal cultures. Similar agreements exist with PEMEX and the Hydrocarbons National Commission. International mobility of law students was for Professor Zamora a must. He wanted students at the University of Houston Law Center to have intercultural and comparative legal experiences in Mexico, knowing that this would lead to enhanced understanding among lawyers in both nations.[21]

II. Professor Zamora: A Generous Soul

Generosity is manifested in different ways. It might be material help, an amount of time dedicated to others, an interest shown in them, or an intellectual generosity of shared ideas without expecting anything in return. A generous person is ready to give "something larger than usual or expected,"[22] and one who is "characterized by a noble or kindly spirit."[23] Professor Zamora conforms to both definitions. He was moved by shared ideas and the desire to do good for others.

Professor Stephen Zamora was married to Lois Parkinson Zamora, a mirror of him in many aspects. She, too, is a professor at the University of Houston. Her field is Latin American literature and art, with a particular interest in Mexico—an obvious complement to Professor Zamora's dedication to Mexican law and culture. Both were Deans at the University of Houston at the same time. As Dean Leonard Baynes points out, Professor Zamora's "tenure as Dean was notable for two reasons: First, he was the University of Houston's and the Law Center's first dean of Hispanic origin; and, second at the same time his wife, Lois, was dean of the then-College of Humanities, Fine Arts and Communication at UH, making them quite unique in academia."[24]

They are the parents of two children, Camille and Peter, and grandparents of Nate and Landon. For Professor Zamora, his family was a high calling and he devoted the scarce time he had outside of his work to them. His family was always on his mind, as anyone knows who spoke to Professor Zamora for more than ten minutes.

Professor Zamora's generosity also took the form of sharing his experience with others and giving useful advice. He spent time with my wife Marie-Sixtine and me after I accepted an affiliate scholar position with US-MEX LAW in February of 2015. After our meeting, we talked about our families, and I mentioned that my wife

---

[21] *See* Dean Leonard Baynes' words at: http://law.uh.edu/news/summer2016/0711Zamora.asp.

[22] *See,* https://dictionary.cambridge.org/us/dictionary/english/generous.

[23] *See,* https://www.merriam-webster.com/dictionary/generous.

[24] To learn more about Professor Zamora's life and legacy, please read how the University of Houston Law Center colleagues remembered him: http://laaw.uh.edu/news/summer2016/0711Zamora.asp.

was outside waiting for me. He did not even think twice before he took us to a place near the Law Center for a cup of tea, and explained to us Houston's residential areas, using a map of the city. This openness was quintessential to Professor Zamora. He spent time with us, knowing how to make foreigners new to Houston feel at home.

Professor Zamora's global vision led him to build bridges, promote synergies and alliances, and seek ways to solve legal issues and controversies. He was never divisive but rather the opposite; working to get things done for the sake of the community. He was patient, persistent, and devoted to his students. His high academic profile in both research and teaching underpinned the supervision of his students. Far beyond the hours of class, he was always available to encourage them to excel. While he was Dean, Professor Zamora remained personally involved with HJIL, offering advice and direction to student editors and contributors.

From 1967 to 1969, Professor Zamora lived in a village in the coffee-growing area of Colombia with his wife in a Peace Corps program of "acción communal."[25] The communal and generous spirit that I have highlighted in Professor Zamora is reflected in this experience. Even today, the information of the program fits Professor Zamora's personality: "The Peace Corps is a service opportunity for motivated change-makers to immerse themselves in a community abroad, working side by side with local leaders to tackle the most pressing challenges of our generation."[26] Could we find a better description of Professor Zamora?

Professor Zamora worked to fund scholarships for Mexican LLM students through US-MEX LAW. Together with the Advisory Board of US-MEX LAW, he institutionalized financial support for these students. In his will, Professor Zamora designated a certain amount of money to this end. The Stephen T. Zamora Scholarship Fund has been created, and we look forward to raising funds year after year to allow Mexican students to study U.S. law at the University of Houston Law Center.

In US-MEX LAW, we are working to maintain Professor's Zamora's legacy. We are expanding our research projects, applying for multidisciplinary grants, increasing our internships agreements with Mexican institutions, and working toward legal and economic understanding between Mexico and the U.S. through seminars, lectures, and professional training programs. The task is not small and the responsibility is great, but we are sure that the results will be positive. We strive to replicate the effort Professor Zamora so enthusiastically put into everything that he did.

Thank you, Steve, for your example.

---

[25] Translated as "rural community development."

[26] *See* https://www.peacecorps.gov/about/.

CHAPTER 1

DISCERNMENT IN PUBLIC LAW: A COMPARATIVE LAW PERSPECTIVE BETWEEN SPAIN AND THE UNITED STATES OF AMERICA. FROM GEORGE FLOYD'S DEATH TO THE RIGIDITY OF CERTAIN RULES: WHEN COMMON SENSE IS LACKING

By Alfonso López de la Osa Escribano[1]

Introduction

On May 25, 2020, George Floyd was killed by a police officer who was performing a chokehold that may have lasted eight minutes and forty-six seconds[2] while he was in custody. The brutal action done by the officer had a significant impact worldwide, questioning the protocols police officers had to apply, the action's proportionality, life's threat notion, law enforcement certifications and training, brutal treatment, and police expertise, among others. George Floyd was not representing a life threat, although he received the most brutal treatment possible for someone, who, even if he had committed an infraction, and may have been under the effect of drugs,[3] did not endanger the persons surrounding him. Judgment and discernment lacked in this action.

Discernment is a quality, a capacity that we attribute to human beings that allows us to distinguish rationally between different situations. Latin *Discernere* is a verb composed by the prefix *dis* (to separate through different paths) and the root *cernere*

---

[1] Dean of Law and International Relations and Professor of Law at Nebrija University in Madrid, and former Director, Center for U.S. and Mexican Law, University of Houston Law Center, Adjunct Faculty, University of Houston Law Center.

[2] *See* about what the symbol "eight minutes and forty-six seconds" have become, although the exact time of chokehold still is unclear: https://www.nytimes.com/2020/06/18/us/george-floyd-timing.html.

[3] *See* about the controversy on the methamphetamine and fentanyl found in George Floyd's autopsy: https://www.newsweek.com/george-floyd-was-fentanyl-medical-examiner-says-experts-dispute-cause-death-1507982 ; *See also*: https://www.npr.org/sections/live-updates-protests-for-racial-justice/2020/06/04/869278494/medical-examiners-autopsy-reveals-george-floyd-had-positive-test-for-coronavirus.

(which means to sort, to isolate), namely, to sort among several options. The word discernment is, in turn, formed by the Latin verb *discernere* and the Latin suffix, *mentum*, which means medium or instrument. Thus, having a discernment capacity would imply having the means to choose the best option from among the many that would exist. It also means to have the intelligence to understand, a term etymologically coming from the Latin *intellegere*, which would define the capacity to read between the lines, "to read through" the situation that is in front of us. In this sense, discernment and intelligence could be considered as being, in a way, synonymic terms. It means understanding quickly, not delaying too much in the explanations, adapting rapidly to the present situation.[4] One can measure the level of intelligence as being inversely proportional to the time it takes for someone to adapt to a new situation.

As far as public law is concerned, discernment would be the ability of police officers, bodies, and persons belonging to the Administration[5] to adapt to reality with their intuition and training, and by applying relevant legislative or regulatory texts. As well, in the absence of a specific text, they would take a decision that will solve wisely and fairly the problem, without generating friction or alarm, or by creating the least possible. In addition to the content of laws and regulations, it may be necessary to go beyond the regulated authority of the Administration so that public officials make the decision. Those officials, entrusted with the executive power, would decide among the many existing legal options, using their discretionary power in the best interest of society, as persons belonging to the Administration (not as a private person or with a private interest).

Discernment capacity for law enforcement officers is also a necessity, and its absence can also be detected. The recent tragic event of George Floyd's death is an unfortunate example. Mr. Floyd died by asphyxia, caused by a police officer who kneeled on his neck for an unacceptable length of time; Mr. Floyd was not supposedly offering any resistance and had expressed several times during custody that he could not breathe. The result showed an arbitrary abuse of power, a disproportionate action. The police needed to respect law and order in that situation, but in doing so, the action was not at all adapted to reality. It seemed that either no protocol existed, or the existing one was not accurate. Police officers at the scene lacked discernment, especially the one performing the chokehold, and the others helping him.

Public agents represent and personalize the Administration. In doing so, they should always be acting in respect of the principle of legality, choosing the best option (the most intelligent solution) among the various alternatives available to

---

[4] According to the Merriam Webster dictionary, discernment is "1. the quality of being able to grasp or comprehend what is obscure: skill in discerning; 2. an act of perceiving or discerning something". *See* https://www.merriam-webster.com/dictionary/discernment.

[5] For the purposes of this article, Administration includes the different public bodies, agencies, and civil agents devoted to public service that are part of the Executive branch (at both the federal and state levels). These bodies are not considered from a partisan political point of view as an Administration identified with the federal or a state Government. In Codified legal traditions, Administrative Law analyzes the way public office and service tasks (of general interest or common good) are organized by the Constitution, the law and regulations, and how citizens interact with these bodies, overall considered under the Public Administration. The political dimension of the Executive power, the Government, is studied under Constitutional Law, also called Political Law.

accomplish their duty. This dichotomy between legal authority (or legal competence) and discretion when making the decision is known in Spanish law as *potestad reglada-potestad discrecional*, and in German law, as *Geregelten Befugnisse* (legal competence settled), and *Ermessens Befugnisse* (discretionary competence, situated in the context of *Rechtsfrei Raume* or *room free from the law*). Discretion, as we shall see, justifies the taking of administrative decisions with a certain margin of maneuver. These decisions are, traditionally, beyond the control of the administrative judge, but that must always be taken, obviously, within the framework of the law.

By Administration's discretionary power, we consider the existence of the mentioned margin of maneuver proper to the Administration, when laws and regulations do not specifically define everyday activity. Traditionally in Spain, discretionary decisions were not subject to a complete revision by the administrative court judge, on the pretext that the judiciary could not substitute to the intellectual judgment or rational approach followed by the Administration on this specific discretionary aspect. The judge, when exercising jurisdiction, could only control the procedural legal aspects followed when enacting the decision, the rule of law we may say, but not review the content of a specific decision.

Thus, we saw a double notch of independence of the executive power vis-à-vis two classic powers, the judiciary and the legislative. There is already independence of the executive power *per se* (it is one of the three constitutional powers). There is as well independence in the intellectual process of a decision, taken under the umbrella of discretion, which should, one would like, be taken with discernment and in respect of the rights and freedoms of all citizens. Unfortunately, it is not always the case, and law and justice must be there to remind the Administration about the most appropriate action to take for the common good, as recent tragic events related to George Floyd's death exposed.

In an increasingly global legal world, it is useful to relate the interpretation of discernment to the global phenomenon. From a legal philosophy point of view, the principle of freedom helps us in interpreting discernment. We live in a world that tends to homogenize some of the structural elements that are strongly influenced by the ultra-rational, or integral human rationality. Should it be science, technology, production, markets, or political relations, we tend to situate solutions in an ultra-rationalistic environment. Increasingly, ultra-rationalism reaches different sectors of society, leaving a small place for free, disinterested, and spontaneous solidarity. Even the notion of general interest or common good seems to be eroding and shrinking nowadays due to a desperate race to seek economic profit. The economy should move on and work, of course, to generate jobs and wealth and improve everyone's lives, but other interests are also in play. The construction of fair and humane decisions relies on lower levels of society (civil servants, and first responders, among others) who play a crucial role in this direction, and that are the first levels of the Administration in contact with citizens. These first levels may seek to avoid shocks or collisions,[6] encouraging this dialogue beyond purely private interests. However,

---

[6] J.C. Scannone, *Discernimiento filosófico de la acción y pasión históricas*, Ed. Anthropos y

these levels are not always provided with the best tools and resources to perform their work. A more humane and close Administration must set itself up as a promoter of this dialogue, but there is a lot of weight and responsibility put on the shoulders of these mentioned first levels, and they need to be trained for that.

The process of making a decision based on discernment must be associated with the respective culture of a specific country, and to its principles or values. For instance, in Europe and America, culture is based on the conditions peculiar to Judeo-Christian values, which have legally and socially shaped the legal systems of these continents.[7] Besides, to act with discernment in each case is to bring solutions following the existential, historical, and pragmatic conditions that give birth to a customary action. Beyond purely philosophical perspectives (such as the epistemological break that would reject previous knowledge in favor of new knowledge, free from the past and common sense, and in the benefice of new science to appear), the solutions to the problems will be brought by a critical and educated mind, in relation with the existing assumptions and conditioning situation in a specific culture: what we are.

The purpose of this essay is to analyze discernment in Spanish public law, which one will attempt to enrich with some notes of comparative law from a United States of America perspective. Several questions come to our mind when defining the subject: can a public Administration have the capacity to discern? How does this kind of intelligence, initially considered a human trait of character, manifest itself in institutional areas of public and administrative law in Spain or the United States, for instance? How can citizens know the intellectual reasoning followed by their Administration? Is it possible for an administrative judge to control today the judgment or criteria used by the Administration? How would that be done? What examples can we cite in Spanish and US law, and what elements do they bring to our discussion?

After analyzing the capacity of discernment perceived as the intelligence of the Administration (I), I will expose some examples of administrative actions showing the ability of autonomous discernment (II).

I. Discernment Capacity Seen as the Intelligence of Public Administration

Before taking a decision and discerning from various options which one to choose, the Administration's agents must understand the situation to determine the action that will be decisive, always supported by the rule. The human action and the law and regulation will then meet. In this same line, Ricœur was studying the existing connections between the theory of the text, the theory of action, and the theory

---

Universidad Iberoamericana, Barcelona 2009, p. 10.

[7] On this matter related to principles and values, the French philosopher Maurice Blondel, who prone the idea "to live as Christian, think as a philosopher," had reflected about the importance of roots and values in order to find adapted solutions to social needs. *See* P. Archaumbault, *Vers un réalisme integral. L'Oeuvre philosophique de Maurice Blondel*, Paris 1928, note 40.

of history,[8] which are theories that must be present at the moment of taking with discernment a decision fully adapted to its context.

Also, one would add a necessary condition to discernment, the imagination,[9] which is a quality that can be put in place when finding the best solution.[10] Imagination is also a capacity that should not be foreign, not only to the jurists but also to public officials who have to adapt with discernment to everyday situations, without becoming mere automatons. Such as when a law enforcement officer has to apply a protocol to someone who is not offering much resistance like in George Floyd's case.

In deciding with discernment, the words and their meaning have considerable importance. It is a question of doing things with words, of explaining actions with words.[11] Mastery of speech or verb is, in our view, also essential when making a clear decision taken with discernment, giving quality to the whole process.

In discernment, the normative text will become autonomous from its author, from its intention, to be interpreted by the person in his action, endowing it a specific content that initially does not exist. The author will know the initial meaning, although the decision will be detached from the text to be applied, having a specific reading, revisited by the author. The normative texts to which we refer are multisemantic and can have different meanings when no interpretation excludes the other.

This factice adaptation by the public official will have to be appropriate with the evolution of society. The "world of the text," as Ricœur calls it,[12] the world of the rule that defines all the different possibilities of being and acting. In summary, it is a question of choosing or discerning among different possible options.

In discernment processes, the explanation is critical. The administrative act becomes legal in its justification, in its motivation. It is a question of its legality and its legitimacy (when the motivation is also consistent). The act needs to be justified, explained, in order not to violate the principle of legality to which the Administration is bound. When lacking, the administrative decision falls under the scope of arbitrariness, of illegality. To avoid arbitrariness, we must justify the administrative act, explain it intellectually, deeply, and substantially. Moreover, the lack of motivation condemns, or should condemn, the administrative act to disappear from the legal order. It should become null.

Understanding the meaning of words referenced in the legal text, the education, and even the experience accumulated by the public agent, will allow enriching the given explanation. An explanation that will help to understand the choice among the existing valid interpretations. Among these options, there will be some more valid or more legitimate than others, thus the explanation of any applied choice becomes

---

[8] P. Ricœur, *Du texte a l' action. Essais d'hermeneutique II,* Paris 1986, at 161-182.

[9] *Id.* P. Ricoeur, *"Imagination dans le discours et dans l'action" (Imagination in speech and in action),* (1976), at 213-236.

[10] According to the Merriam Webster Dictionary, imagination is the "Act or power of forming a mental image of something not present to senses or never before wholly perceived in reality; 2. Creative ability; ability to confront and deal with a problem," *see* https://www.merriam-webster.com/dictionary/imagination.

[11] J. Austin, *How to do things with words,* Cambridge, Massachusetts 1962, at 7.

[12] *Id.* at note 6.

critical. Applying by analogy Ricœur's thought to the legal argumentation, the convergence of indicators or counter-indicators can show us the importance or the greater probability of a valid interpretation, which allows us to reach a high degree of certainty.[13] It is also a matter of anticipating possible outcomes, which is as well a sign of intelligence and, consequently, of discernment.

Indeed, discernment for a lawyer practicing public law will allow greater anticipation of the probable legal outcome chosen by the Administration or by the administrative judge. The lawyer will be well-versed on the mentioned theory of the rule or text, the theory of action, and the theory of history. Therefore, this lawyer will seek the coincidence of judgments and bits of intelligence to give the best legal advice to his client, whether to continue or not the procedure, for instance.

Discernment always expresses a dialectic between mental comprehension and its oral or written explanation, something those of us dedicated to teaching and writing know well. The decision resulting from the discernment's process highlights the convergence of signs (rejecting radical extremes or opposites), or the importance of tools, such as when an investigative magistrate leaves aside specific accusations to follow other clues leading to the solution. Therefore, discernment gives us greater freedom and greater justice, and also greater law enforcement actions. Discernment gives the option of attaining a higher common good, preceded by a reflection made with the necessary knowledge, appropriate baggage, or background. Discernment allows, therefore, greater human freedom, the perfect legal world.

The Administration's discernment capacity must be at the service of the common good, of the general interest, of the well-being of citizens, imposing public burdens equal to all, protecting persons' life and human dignity. Public Administration is obliged to guarantee in its actions this general interest while respecting the principle of legality.

The discernment capacity of a private person, his intelligence, will serve him to put forward his person, his professional ambitions, and his life objectives. On the other hand, the Administration's discernment capacity must seek to protect and guarantee the common good. Misuse of powers will, therefore, exist when the public Administration would use this interpretative margin of discretion for the private interest of its public officials. It would be an arbitrary act of the Administration, prevarication, with the absence of intelligence or discernment from the Administration. It would indeed be an inept and corrupt Administration.

In some situations, the law may leave no room for the discretion of the Administration, the use of its discernment; the Administration must apply the rule without reflection. It is an entitlement binding the Administration to respect it. These rules will have to be adapted to the social reality, even if we can sometimes find excessively rigid texts. In any case, these standards serve as a basis for making decisions according to the law.

We may also witness the existence of an Administration's regulations, enacted but lacking discernment and common sense. Also, we may witness regulations leaving a margin of discretion to the Administration to decide, but the latter not making it intelligently or skillfully. For example, the use of excessive force by public officials to dissolve a peaceful demonstration, or when in custody to control a person

---

[13] *Id.*

not presenting a life threat, or the confiscation of property related to a person's professional activity, due to a procedure of seizure for existing tax debt. The Administration must certainly advocate protection of the general interest over private interests, but it must not go beyond the protection of private interests for whatever reason. Citizens must feel confident that the Administration, in the exercise of its prerogatives, will provide guarantees to citizens on their interests too. To act with balance here is also to act with discernment.

We must distinguish clearly between the binding authority of the Administration and its discretionary power.

A. Binding Authority and Discretionary Power: the Prohibition of Arbitrary Action of the Administration

Binding authority and discretionary power are both at the origin of regulated and discretionary acts.

1. Regulated Acts and Their Power of Exercise

The existence of the rule of law provides for a series of specific hypotheses and their direct consequences that the Public Administration enforces through actions. These actions are generally administrative acts that are previously regulated. Actions in these cases are confined to strictly apply the law, materializing what a regulation forecast. In these circumstances where the Administration executes a binding authority, there is no margin left to interpretative freedom. The Administration's action only verifies that the case satisfies the legal or regulatory conditions necessary to enact the administrative act. We then witness the correspondent consequence: the eventual benefit or burden applied to the citizen's estate or environment (his patrimony, material or immaterial), or the interested party. For instance, when they are issuing licenses or regulated administrative authorizations, such as a driving license or building permits. Citizens expect a precise and specific action when all conditions are objectively fulfilled.

Regulated powers (or binding authority), therefore, determine the prior existence of regulation, including scenarios and resulting legal consequences. In these acts, the Administration will limit itself to applying the provision contained in the regulation without interpretation. Theoretically, as we can appreciate, the procedure is quite simple from an Administrative law perspective. These regulated powers are part of the legal regime of Administrative acts. We find them in Codified legal system such as Spain, and also in Anglo-Saxon countries such as the United States. The problem arises when these regulated powers are too strict and do not match exceptions that somehow should be considered by the law.

In the United States, there has been strong criticism, sometimes of existing excessive regulation that may render procedures burdensome. An American author, Howard, analyzes and condemns this excess of legislation, which would be killing law.[14] The famous adage which dictates "Too many laws kill the Law" turns up in

---

[14] Ph. K. Howard, *The death of Common Sense. How Law Is Suffocating America,* Ed. Random House Paperback- New York, New York 2011, p. 10 and following.

corollaries of the incapacity of the Administration to know how to manage exceptions that become very relevant. Let us see an example of it:

During the winter of 1988, the Sisters of Mother Teresa that managed the religious order of the Missionaries of Charity had agreed with New York City's mayor at the time, Mr. Ed Koch, that two buildings that were burned and abandoned in the Bronx would be used by the religious order to accommodate homeless people.[15] The transaction seemed to be easy: New York City would sell both buildings for a value of $1, and the Missionaries of the Charity would put $500,000 on their side, for renovation and reconstruction. The Sisters were looking to give shelter to sixty-four homeless people in a community context, which included constructing a refectory and a kitchen on the first floor, a large space in the second, and small rooms or cells with beds in the third and fourth floors.

Notably, the Missionaries of the Charity, following their wishes of poverty, had deliberately avoided providing the building elements of comfort in its reconstruction. They had not planned a laundry washing machine or a dishwasher; all its tasks would be done by hand by the good sisters. New York City saw the possibility of housing the homeless, managed by this religious order, for sure a Providential fact. In Howard's words it was, "a godsend."

Because it was a city-owned building, the transfer of the property was not easy due to lengthy bureaucratic procedures. For a year and a half, the Sisters of Charity, with their joyful and ascetic spirit, were touring the administrative instances of New York State at the two existing levels (at local and county level: in the Bronx and New York). In September 1989, the City of New York approved the project, and the Missionaries of the Charity began the repair work of the property.

One of Howard's criticisms in his book (and we referred above when talking about ultra-rationalism) is that solidarity does not always connect with the law. After two years of bureaucratic procedures, the Sisters learned that according to New York's building code, the buildings having several floors had to include an elevator. The Missionaries of the Charity explained that they did not want to use an elevator because it was a comfort contrary to their principles and that it would save them an additional cost of $100,000. Besides, they considered it entirely proper to climb stairs, moreover in four floors building. However, the law could not avoid overriding the existence of an elevator in these buildings. Therefore, by a too rigid law, without the installation of an elevator, the project could not prosper. Mother Theresa surrendered. The Missionaries of Charity stopped the project because they did not want to dedicate such amount of much money to something they thought was superfluous and did not help people without resources. It was a matter of principle for them considering the elevator unnecessary and not related to safety, but simply comfort. As Howard mentions, ironically, the Sisters of the Charity preferred to use this money to make soups and sandwiches for the underprivileged rather than to build an elevator.

In a correct letter written by Mother Theresa to the City of New York, she expressed her regret that the project could not be accomplished, and expressed with Holy resignation, that this case "served to educate us about the law and its many complexities." As Howard states, there are undoubtedly many buildings in New

---

[15] *Id.* at 11.

York without elevators, but the current middle-class standard in the United States requires a model of home and comfort that may not be adaptable to everyone, as it was the case here. However, the law did not allow that. Rigidly normed, with automatisms that did not consider the particularities of the situation, we witnessed a sort of lack of discernment from the New York Administration and the law, that did not allow housing for the homeless, moreover in a project that would not have been financed by it. One can only see benefits from this happening.

The Administration may also adopt discretionary acts.

2. Discretionary Acts and their Exercise Authority

The Administration dictates discretionary acts when it uses its ability to assess the utility and opportunity of taking a particular decision. When the law acknowledges the Administration possesses this discretionary power, the action falls into an existing margin of maneuver, which we expect will be used with discernment. Discretionary power is, in fact, also associated to a discernment capacity, because when we speak of this Administration's characteristic, we refer to its capacity of reflection, of adaptation, its intelligence, concerning the regulated authority (what is content in the law). There is a double lever of discernment, as it belongs to the legislator, or to the authority creating the norm (Administration in its executive orders, for instance), to exercise discernment, besides those cases in which the Administration will confine itself to applying the regulated disposition.

The Administration, when making use of its discretionary power, will adopt, with some degree of discernment, among several alternatives, the decision considered adapted to the specific case. Traditionally, an important sector of the Spanish doctrine has considered these acts as necessary and indispensable to the activities of the Administration as they may fit better the specific needs of society.

In a rather graphic way, in Administrative Law in Spain, the use of the expression "could" (*podrá*) or "must" (*deberá*) in the articles from the law or regulations is an indicator of the degree of existing margin of appreciation. A provision in which the law indicates that the Administration "could" take a concrete decision or take action opens the door to the mentioned margin of appreciation, discretionary, and with discernment. Besides, it entails a probability of the enactment of the decision. There is indeed a potentiality of this decision; it may happen or not. On the other hand, where the law indicates that the Administration "must" adopt a particular measure, the Administration has no discretion or option; it is a standard regulated act, mandatory in all its elements, and in such a way it has to be enacted.

Regulated acts are, however, always related to discretionary acts. They are both associated. Discretionary power adds to the regulated administrative power a subjective, rational, and intellectual element, but any discretionary act has inherent regulated elements that must be respected. Moreover, as we will see later, this margin of appreciation cannot be considered as being arbitrary because it exists under a law that frames it. As we know, public Administration, even when taking its discretionary decisions, is bound to respect the principle of legality, the rule of law.

Therefore, we confirm that the Administration's discernment is governed by the law, which limits its deployment in order to create several guarantees for citizens in the use of public authority prerogatives. The existence of law conditions the Administration's discernment, foreseeing the elements (formal and subject-matter based) that the act needs to respect: the public body that may exercise jurisdiction; the extension and purpose of the creation of this power; time-based limits to its exercise; the procedure set for such purpose and the legal authority of the agent, that is, his technical training or his political experience (where needed) as a public official.

By using its power legitimately, the Administration can choose the solution that best suits and complies with the interests and needs of the moment, which must always protect the general interest. The Administration may act as it deems appropriate, but, in advance, legal standards must always give authority to the administering body, while not imposing on the latter any specific conditions of action. The fact that authority is given beforehand gives a plus legally in terms of accountability and transparency of the Administration's actions.

Here again, we can cite an example of discretionary power in United States law in matters of school education, more specifically English language learners (ELLs) or teaching English as a second language (ESL) in American schools. Even as American citizens, the English language would not be for some children, their mother tongue. The educational system can detect a deficiency at this level. Teachers and students' parents should manifest it in order to allow schools to cope with this lack of knowledge.

Synthetically, ELL regulation exists at three levels: federal, state, and local levels. President Johnson's Administration passed the federal Bill that regulates the matter, the 1965 *Elementary and Secondary Education Act* (ESEA). This Bill has been amended on two occasions during its more than fifty years in effect, in 2001 and in 2011. The 2001 ESEA reform under President Bush's Administration was the *No Child Left Behind Act* (NCLB). In 2011, given the rigidity with which American public elementary school teachers applied the law using their discretionary authority, President Obama asked the US Department of Education to invite each State Educational Agency to request Local Education Agencies and school instructors to act with flexibility while applying the ESEA Standard.[16] The amended law was known as *ESEA Flexibility*.

The US Supreme Court promoted further reforms condemning the deficiencies of the American school system. In *Lau v. Nichols* from 1974,[17] a local school was sued by the parents of a Chinese child because ELL students did not receive sufficient education to learn and understand enough English in order to take courses with the possibility of success. The Supreme Court decided that these schools were to adopt the necessary measures to provide students with a learning program that would provide access to education in a manner consistent with the principle of equality.[18]

---

[16] For further information, *see* https://www2.ed.gov/policy/elsec/guid/esea-flexibility/index.html.

[17] *See* https://www2.ed.gov/about/offices/list/ocr/ell/lau.html.

[18] *See also Keyes v. Denver,* 1973, dealing with a case of segregation of African-American and Latino groups students from other Caucasian students groups. The Supreme Court forced desegregation, on the basis that ELL students could not be separated from other students speaking the language in a fluent manner. *See also Castaneda v. Pickard,* 1978, where the Court of Appeal of the Fifth Circuit declared that the district was separating the students by race and ethnicity, and that in bilingual programs students were failing school.

This flexibility was requested concerning the specific requirements of the *No Child Left Behind Act* (NCLB) when implementing action plans and program by the states to improve the educational expectations of all students, to reduce the cost of education while guaranteeing the principle of equality between them and improving the quality of teaching.

In this way, American schools had to establish a system to identify a student with limited English, as required by the US Office of Civil Rights, to be able to teach them the language in a way that suited their situation. With this procedure, students had to pass an assessment to determine whether they were categorized as *English language learners* (ELL), speaking English as a second language, or ESL Student (*English as a Second Language*). This identification procedure followed Section 3302 of the ESEA, related to parental notification,[19] following the reform introduced by the 2001 *No Child Left Behind Act*. According to this procedure, within thirty days (with some exceptions[20]) after the beginning of classes, parents should be notified by teachers that during this time, their child had been identified as a *limited English proficient child*, a learner, and that needs special language education, including adapted teaching and additional courses during recess. A *Home Language Survey*[21] allowed the evaluation and identification by an oral interview with the child and a written examination about the language spoken at home. While the results could, within a strict application of the law, be provided on the thirtieth day after the beginning of class so that teachers could start the ESL program, most of the time, teachers were aware after the first or second day of class, about the lack of English knowledge. Moreover, in undeniable cases. In those situations, teachers and instructors were strongly invited to exercise flexibility to obey this criterion and to start, even before the end of this period, to consider these students as ESL and start applying it, when, by any other additional *discerned* route, they would have identified their pupils as ESL students.[22]

---

[19] *See* section 3302 https://www2.ed.gov/policy/elsec/leg/esea02/pg50.html.

[20] If the child ever goes to school after the beginning of school, the identification must be made within two weeks.

[21] The Home Language Survey consists in analyzing a series of questions: it is a question of which language the child understands best; what is the language most often used when others are talking to the child; what is the language most used by the child at home; what is the language most often used when the child speaks to other family members; also what is the language used by the child when he addresses his friends. As a general rule, when the child answers that he uses a language other than English, the school must evaluate its level in the latter language. The fear that some parents consider that the lack of knowledge of the language could prevent their children from going to school (and for that reason they would not manifest this deficiency themselves), obliges the school to evaluate by its own means children identified as ESL. According to the case law of the Supreme Court of America, preventing a child from studying in an American public school because he does not know the English language is indeed considered discriminatory, which is why this system of instruction has been established and strengthened since 2001.

[22] Apart from the *Home Language Survey*, which would be an important step to make, the flexibility in identification of language deficiencies in English, also required state educational agencies to put in place additional means to identify their ESL students, such as interviews with parents, information given by teachers or other forms of evaluation.

Surprisingly, a large part of American schoolteachers waited for the end of the thirty days to set up the ESL education system, and this even if they had already detected the linguistic deficiencies of the child, most of the time apparent. Doing this, teachers would wait for the official delivery of the result of the evaluation (the survey) thirty days after the trial, leaving the children, future ESLs, in a sort of school learning incomprehension limbo, before the expiry of the term. The main argument was not to deliver results that were unofficial before the due date (the thirtieth day). In case ESL teachers would provide additional support to ESL students during this survey period (that they will for sure need it in the future), they would be violating the principle of equality, acting in a discriminatory way related to other English-speaking students in the class. In fact, they were considering dedicating more time to ESL students than to other regular students.

The needed Administration's discernment capacity leads to our current reflection. In our view, the argument of these public employees of the American Administration lacked discernment. It is equivalent to say, in pedagogical and educational terms, that assisting a specific student who needed more attention than others, or answering during class a student's question that would have misrepresented something and not have been asked by other students, or lingering for a few more minutes when grading one exam over others for the sometimes tricky syntactic used, would undermine the principle of equality. In our view, we witness a rigid and unproductive interpretation of the principle of equality that would only impact students negatively.

The good judgment of public officials working in school education implies that, by essence, they are devoted to students and their learning process and knowledge. Indeed, in students' learning process of the full annual program, teachers will have to associate specific assistance to those who would need it most, always keeping a balance with the whole class moving on with the program. Seeing an alleged violation of the principle of equality in the specific support of students requiring specific assistance not only supposes a rigid application of the norm but shows a lack of common sense and judgment that cannot be related to the missions and specificities of the school education sector. Teachers must attempt to ensure that deficiencies are detected, providing the child with the instruments enabling him/her to overcome obstacles, finding a solution to the identified shortcomings. The flexibility demanded by the Obama administration from a perspective of proper discernment was desired and welcomed.

In Spanish law, an example of a combination of rule-making powers and discretionary powers is related to the age of retirement for public officials. The official retirement age is sixty-five years old, but public agents will be able to be on active service for another five years, if they wish so, and if the service's operation so requires. However, from the age of seventy years old, public agents' retirement is enforced by law, fixing the actions to be taken in order to retire. As a result of the retirement at seventy years old, the Administration has no margin of maneuver, instead of between sixty-five and seventy years of age, the Administration has the authority to decide whether the departure has to occur. In this interval, the Administration may act following the different departments' needs, and those from other staffs, allowing public agents to remain on active status until they retire forcefully.

According to Article 67 of the Revised Text of 2015, adopting the law on the Basic Statute of the Public Employee,[23] mandatory retirement following the legally established age is enforced. This mandatory age retirement, according to Article 67.3, is therefore automatically declared at sixty-five years of age. This provision also may require, according to the laws implementing this Statute, the extension of tenure in active service to a maximum of seventy years (70). This article adds that: "The competent public administration will have to solve in a motivated way the admission or refusal of this extension," issuing a motivated decision, with discernment, adapted to the situation of the service.[24]

Therefore, we confirm the existence of the mandatory powers related to the maximum time in which the action of the Administration is settled and has no room for maneuver or discernment. Alongside this mandatory competence, which cannot cover all aspects of the law, there exists a margin of flexibility and discretionary capacity, always governed by the principle of legality. The discretionary power will belong only partially (not wholly) to the administrative act, and even in completing the latter with a discretionary decision, overall, the legal conditions of the act must be respected (the regulated authority). Thus, incorrect aspects such as procedural defects, misuse of power, or error of fact will always be situations condemned by the administrative court, based on the arbitrary action they will encounter, even when supposedly taken based on a discretionary decision.

In terms of age limits to access certain positions of public service, the jurisprudence in Spain is numerous, and many are the arguments used, which can be related to the judgment or discernment of the Administration. The principle of proportionality and common sense become primary vectors for considering age as a differentiating element, in addition to the principle of opportunity. This difference must be objectively justified by the nature of the functions to be performed, never undermining the principle of equality. It is discriminatory and not proportionate to impose age limits for the opening of pharmacies, as stated in the Spanish Constitutional Court in a 2011 decision (no. 117/2011 of July 4th, 2011[25]). Instead, to request a maximum age to access law enforcement academies (candidates need to be under forty-five years old) is justified by the prejudice to the public interest if older persons could have access, not only for functional reasons, but also economic, by the cost that their substitution during the performance of operational functions would produce.[26] The target is to ensure the optimal physical condition, which guarantees

---

[23] Royal Legislative Decree 5/2015, of October 30, approving the revised text of the Law of Basic Statute of the Public Employee. «BOE» núm. 261, of 31 October 2015.

[24] On the maximum age limits to allow access to the public service since right perspective of the European Union *see* J.A. Fuentetaja Pastor, *Los limites máximos de edad como requisito de acceso a la función pública desde la perspectiva del derecho europeo. Comentario a la Sentencia del Tribunal de Justicia Vital Perez y Ayuntamiento de Oviedo, de 13 de noviembre de 2014 (C-416/13).*

[25] *See* http://hj.tribunalconstitucional.es/en/Resolucion/show/6899.

[26] Judgment of the Constitutional Court n° 29/2012 https://www.boe.es/diario_boe/txt.php?id=BOE-A-2012-4321.

a level of permanence in the service, both for the Civil Guard (*Guardia Civil*)[27] and for National Police. For the latter, a Supreme Court Judgment, dated March 21, 2011, stated that age limits are justified for "specific public interests" and cannot be considered discriminatory.[28] As far as firefighters are concerned, there is a restriction to access the exam to persons under thirty-five years old, a justified objective, and reasonable decision that respects the proportionality principle.[29] For example, another argument justifying the limit of age for the police of the Basque Region in Spain would be to guarantee the stability of the personnel in the best possible conditions, aspects that are less easy to ensure for older candidates.[30]

All the decisions related to age and access to specific public service bodies coincide with the intensity or consistency of the Administration's motivation. We may find abstract motivations of public interest to justify the age limits, most of the time, annulled because of that. For instance, the decision from the Spanish Supreme Court from February 10th, 2014[31] considered the age limits introduced to access the military engineer corps as not only unjustified but as causing "serious damage to the general interest and in particular to the army forces" which cannot satisfactorily meet its operational requirements.

Besides, for civil servants in Spain, a typical example of discretionary power that takes a dimension of technical nature is used, for instance, in the selection of public officials by juries, using competitive selective procedures and evaluation charts (*see below* in section II. A.).As said, a decision taken by the Administration using its margin of appreciation and demonstrating its discernment capacity and judgment cannot be described as arbitrary when taken under the guiding principle of legality. On the contrary, arbitrariness, which is, in essence, illegal, could be described as the absence of judgment or intelligence of the Administration.

3. The Arbitrariness in the Administration's Action: the Absence of Intelligence or Discernment from the Administration and its Agents

In the Spanish Constitution, Article 9.3 expressly forbids arbitrary actions by public authorities, citing this prohibition alongside with other ground principles of Spanish law: "The Constitution guarantees the principle of legality, the hierarchy of legal provisions, the publicity of legal statutes, the non-retroactivity of punitive provisions that are not favorable to or restrictive of individual rights, the certainty that the rule of law shall prevail, the accountability of public authorities, and the prohibition of arbitrary action of public authorities."

---

[27] Judgment of the Superior Court of Justice of Madrid of 22 May 2012, www.poderjudicial.es.

[28] *See* https://www.boe.es/diario_boe/txt.php?id=BOE-A-2011-9 788.

[29] Judgment of the Superior Court of Justice of Madrid of March 7, 2011, www.poderjudicial.es.

[30] Judgment of the Superior Court of Justice of the Basque Country, of 6 October 2008, www.poderjudicial.es.

[31] Recourse n° 5837/2011. www.poderjudicial.es.

The prohibition of any arbitrary action taken by public authorities when exercising their functions goes along with important principles like the mentioned principle of legality, the hierarchy of legal provisions, and its publicity. While discretionary power implies some control of legality, even if it is diffuse,[32] arbitrariness in the Administration results from the absence of control.

For Professor Tomas Ramon Fernández, the traditional perspective of discretionary authority doctrine, criticized by another doctrinal sector, is regarded as "the unconditional ability to impose a decision in a free manner and free of all possible control or external correction,"[33] of any justification. This action should not be arbitrary, however.

Arbitrariness is the conduct of public bodies belonging to the Administration not connected to the public common good, a decision contrary to the law, taken either by misuse of power or by abuse of power. In this context, the action of public service activity does not respect the goals that it must seek and guarantee. On the contrary, it is embezzled, going beyond what is allowed by the legal system.

The Spanish Supreme Court, in its judgment of March 12, 2008 from its Administrative Section,[34] declared that arbitrariness is a condition for the judge to control "in an exceptional manner" and is within his technical discretionary power. The Supreme Court adds that the flip side of the arbitrary act is precisely rationality, advocated by Article 9.3 of the Constitution mentioned above, which could also be considered discernment. Actually, in another Supreme Court decision from May 18, 2007,[35] the specific jurisdictional control based on standard rationality criteria, therefore of discernment or intelligence, was admitted in the complaint against multiple-choice tests in exams to access public service.

Fundamental Rights and the principles that orient them are the limits to discretionary power, and when infringed, the ones that justify a judicial review. Among others, protection of human lives, or the principle of equality and non-discrimination mentioned in Article 14 of the Spanish Constitution,[36] will be a matter of judicial control. The judge can indeed control the discretionary power in those cases.

---

[32] By diffuse control we understand the incidental control exercised by a judge to a specific case. The norm that gives base to the adopted act is discarded because considered illegal but is not directly declared nulled from that time on. In the case, the norm is merely left without application and not rejected from the legal system, and the administrative act is declared null.

[33] In his Spanish version "el poder discrecional es una capacidad incondicional de imposición libre y exenta de cualquier posible fiscalización o corrección desde fuera, de dar cuenta de si misma, de justificar una palabra" (quote in English: "discretionary power is an unconditioned capacity to impose a decision in a free manner and free of all possible control or external correction, to account for itself, to justify itself in a word"), Cf. T.R. Fernandez Rodriguez, *Arbitrariedad y discrecionalidad,* Cuadernos Civitas, Madrid, 1991, p. 17.

[34] Case n° 3151/2003.

[35] Case n° 4793/2000, www.poderjudicial.es.

[36] Article 14 of the Spanish Constitution says: "Spaniards are equal before the law and may not in any way be discriminated against on account of birth, race, sex, religion, opinion or any other personal or social condition or circumstance." *See* http://www.congreso.es/constitucion/ficheros/c78/cons_ingl.pdf.

A. *Jurisdictional Control of Discretionary Power: Questioning the Discernment Capacity of the Administration*

The jurisdictional control of the Administration's discretionary power, about its rationality and discernment, seeks to avoid the arbitrariness or misuse of power and to guarantee the always existing control of legality. Criticism could be that not only should discretionary power be subject to the control of legality as such (the formal and subject-matter elements we have already mentioned), but also to complete control over the rationale or motivation about the utility or the opportunity of the decision. In sum, if we accept judicial control and the intellectual process that is followed, everyone will understand the intelligence of the Administration.

One can affirm the same, when interpreting Articles 103.1 and 106.1 of the Spanish Constitution, which respectively stipulate that:

"The public Administration serves the general interest with objectivity and acts under the principles of efficiency, hierarchy, decentralization, deconcentrating, and coordination, being fully subject to justice and the law," [and that] "The Courts control the power to issue regulations and to ensure that the rule of law prevails in administrative action, as well as to ensure that the latter subordinates to the ends which justify it."[37]

It is, therefore, to the judge to control the discretionary acts of the Administration. The judge would be able to exceptionally overrule the nullity of the discretionary act, either by non-respect of rule authorizing it, by the little motivation of its administrative act, or by the disproportion of the act. For instance, when a law enforcement officer disproportionately uses forces, it should be considered by courts illegal and arbitrary, such as what we can jurisdictionally anticipate happened in George Floyd's death. Even before knowing the custody details that may be exposed in the upcoming trial, the death of George Floyd awakes a feeling of clamorous indignation, should the person be under the effects of drugs or not. As we will reiterate, law enforcement training on how to deal with intoxicated persons is also an aspect that needs to be emphasized.

Besides this mention of the substantive-matter control of the administrative acts' discretionary nature, we will set out how the administrative court can control the administrative acts dictated based on the discretionary power.

For instance, in Spain, judges apply the discretionary powers judicial control general theory for public agents, which is done in four ways:

The first way is the control of *vague or undefined legal concepts*, dealing with the legal terms mentioned in a law or regulation, but whose definition or content would have to be defined explicitly by the Administration according to each particular case. Therefore, the Administration would have chosen, related to the undefined legal concept, one of several valid and legitimate options to give a sense to it. If a controversy turned up on its legality or its adaptation to the facts, the judge would have to interpret the legal concept applicable in that case. The Administration fre-

---

[37] *See* http://www.congreso.es/constitucion/ficheros/c78/cons_ingl.pdf.

quently shows judgment in diligently adapting these legal concepts to the reality of the situation. During the controversy, among the various existing options, the administrative judge will, in turn, either corroborate the Administration's interpretation, or choose one of the options, which the judge will consider the only valid one in the specific case; a decision that may not align with the content the Administration would have given to the concept. Some examples of undefined legal concepts are *public order*; the diligence of *good father* or *good paterfamilias* (or a *reasonable person* in France after the 2014 reform of the Civil Code[38]); the *public interest*; the *public good*; the *good governance* administration, among others.

The second way is the one that controls the *regulated elements of discretionary power*. As has been stated, the control exercised over the acts dictated by the Administration under the discretionary power would be made on the legal or regulated aspects of the act, namely the aspects related to the Administration's regulated authority or legal capacity. The judge would have to supervise the correct *exercise of power*, the *legal competence*, the *extension* of it, and the *goal* sought, to decide about the regularity of the act. If the existence of none or few of them could not be confirmed, the administrative act would be tainted with nullity, regressing actions to the moment before the illegal act was taken and compelling the Administration to take a new administrative act.

The third way is the *control of decisive facts*, done by the judge when controlling the analysis and valuation of the acts taken by the Administration, in their objective reality. We understand by decisive facts, the objective elements existing before taking or dictating the administrative act. These elements can be legal grounds or fact grounds, meaning the specific analysis of facts that gave rise to the said act. If *de facto* the ground or justification is nonexistent on the facts, the administrative action could be tainted with illegality.

Finally, the last way is to control the *general principles of law*, the law, written and non-written from the Spanish legal system. This reflection is, moreover, the interpretation of Article 103.3 of the Spanish Constitution, which we quoted beforehand when it referred to the block of legality and stated that the Public Administration "fully subjects to justice and the law," distinguishing *justice* and *law* clearly. This block of law is formed of principles such as equality, freedom, and more recently (and given the specific legislation related to the Administration), the principle of legitimate trust (*confianza legítima*). Administrative judges become, therefore, the defenders of those principles and play a critical role when they have to control the discretionary power of the Administration through these principles, which sometimes find themselves between *legal principles* and *vague legal concepts,* good Administration, or nature of things, among others. These essential principles operate within the bounds of the discretionary powers of the Administration and serve to check on arbitrary powers, for the Administration to respect the principles forming the legal system in Spain.

We must not forget that the legal motivation of the administrative act remains essential to correctly understand the discernment or intellectual process of reasoning

---

[38] Reform introduced by Law n° 2014-873 of 4 August 2014 for the real equality between women and men, OG 05/08/2014.

used by the Administration. It is this motivation that will be reevaluated by the administrative judge in the different cases brought to his attention.

II. Some Examples of Administrative Actions Demonstrating an Autonomous Discernment Capacity

1. The Discretionary Power of the Administration, the Technical Dimension in the Access to the Spanish Public Service

The right to access public service under conditions of equality and non-discrimination is a right of legal configuration, meaning that its recognition does not in itself guarantee access, but that in each competition it will receive content. If there is a controversy, the court must determine its content to guarantee equality in a specific manner. Thus, the equality of all candidates will be considered, checking first if they meet the conditions necessary to apply for the competition or exam, and, therefore, who will be able to participate in the selection. The organization of tests and exams must, of course, not leave room for discrimination. It must only be based on candidates' merits and capacities, according to Article 23 of the Spanish Constitution.[39]

The Administration will also need to make proof of discernment when evaluating candidates, by following the regulated aspects of the procedure to choose the best profile for the vacant position. In this area of competitions, there may be a more significant value given to the evaluation of knowledge and the number of points awarded to each question correctly answered. A framed margin of maneuver, of subjectivity, might exist, however. The relationship or dichotomy between technical aspects (e.g., the maximum number of points awarded to each question) and discretionary decisions (e.g., how many points the candidate receives) can take two forms: an external form and another internal form. The external form consists in the exercise of discretionary decisions based on technical data; the internal form refers to the technical rules and their relativity, meaning their possibility of modulation.

In a public agent's selective process, the control over the motivation of the decision choosing the ideal candidate has traditionally escaped the judge's control, based on the argument that the judge could not substitute his technical appreciation for the technical appreciation of the jury's exam—a sort of remnant of the *imperium* or command of the Administration. There was an understanding that the Administration would have acted with discernment. Furthermore, it was considered that the administrative judge still had control over the legality of the jury's exam actions. Nevertheless, the Spanish Supreme Court has reminded, on several occasions, that discretionary authority is not an arbitrary action for the Administration. On the other hand, we will add, discretionary actions should not be the excuse to escape the law and take arbitrary decisions, or act against the law.

---

[39] Article 23.2 of the Spanish Constitution: "I. Citizens have the right to participate in public affairs, directly or through representatives freely elected in periodic elections by universal suffrage. 2. They likewise have the right to access on equal terms to public office, in accordance with the requirements determined by law."

The specific prior training or education of the competition's jury enhances the technical component of discretionary powers and is the main argument for the technical judgment of the Administration to escape judicial control; a kind of exorbitant privilege similar to the traditional political acts or government acts theory, where citizens could not initiate legal action against them. This jury's knowledge, education, and training is precisely the ground to enact reliable decisions and ideas, with judgment and intelligence; it is the technical, academic, or professional knowledge of the jury. The administrative judge wishes to detach himself from scrutinizing this technical component, under the pretext that his control would be only legal (based on a manifest error of assessment, arbitrariness, or misuse of power, as we know), and based on the judge's limit to get the knowledge and technical background necessary to each member of the jury. Omniscience that judge does not hold. The exception to this principle is when the technical judgment impinges on the legal framework or the regulated matter. For instance, the legality above mentioned. We disagree with the frontal exclusion of this Administration's discretionary power from judicial review, even in technical aspects. For instance, if the judge says justice can also be assisted by technicians and experts (such as in any other technical field) when there would be controversy on how a specific question or exam would have been graded or evaluated.

In some cases, the judge has agreed to exert particular modulation to limit discretionary decisions, based on the presumption of reasonable grounds, or the certainty of the administrative action and the partiality of the administrative bodies having authority to evaluate and grade candidates. Spanish Constitutional Court jurisprudence, in the decision no. 353/1993,[40] accepts that this presumption *iuris tantum* (admitting a piece of contrary evidence) can be reversed if the jury's breach or lack of knowledge is demonstrated reasonably, either by the misuse of power, an arbitrary action, or the lack of possible justification of the decision taken. The Constitutional Court recognizes that while zones of immune power do not exist for the Administration, this control is not absolute regarding competition and exam juries. We find ourselves in an area of discernment whose access and control by the judge is still difficult, which remains *de facto* "immune to judicial control," quoting the same expression the Constitutional court often utilizes.

Indeed, this traditionally recognized parcel of immunity in these Administration's decisions remains, however, subject to the requirement of a justified administrative decision. An act that will not respect the duty to express the arguments justifying it should be void. A decision lacking motivation or justified grounds from an objective perspective would not be valid. The same would happen if this decision lacked authenticity or rationality. With fair criticism, the decision's rationale must be consistent and taken with discernment and intelligence, leading, where appropriate, the judge (and any other interested party) to understand and analyze the legal component of the rationality of the decision, without substituting himself in the jury's decision.

To this Spanish Supreme Court and the Constitutional Court doctrine, we find two kinds of administrative acts when grading exams or competition: on the one hand, those who evaluate scientific knowledge of candidates; and, on the other hand, those who evaluate by applying a scale or objective criteria, mathematically fixed. The latter is included beforehand in the call for applications, as they need to be

---

[40] Judgment of the Constitutional Court No. 353/1993, Legal Basement 3.

known in advance, to grant transparency in the grading process. In the first case, as seen, the judge could not revise grades, except when there would have been an infringement of specific aspects related to call for applications' content. In the second case, the judge's control will relate to the use of the evaluation's scale, which is, in our view, not compatible with a discretionary judgment, and where the control could be absolute (for example, following a mistake in points' calculation). This scale will be subject to the rules exposed in the call for applications.

A Spanish Supreme Court Judgement from January 18th, 2010 seemed to channel the action of the Administration reminding the use of its discretionary power, but being always "under surveillance" by the judge: "It is true that one assumes the legality of the acts of the Administration and that the decisions of the juries of exams, by the specialized knowledge of its members and the objective and impartial notes which must preside their action. These are presumed considerate when these juries exercise the technical discretionary power peculiar to them. However, it is also true that it is a presumption *iuris tantum*, denatured using a probationary activity, which clearly shows its error."[41]

It is as well critical in terms of public order and security, the ability of the Administration and its public officials to act with discernment.

2. The Discernment of the Administration in Public Order and Security

As we have mentioned, the notion of public order from a legal perspective is a *vague legal concept*. Each particular case will see its content specifically established. We can define public order as the set of rules presented in a preponderant social consciousness, necessary for an orderly civic cohabitation. Hence, we identify public order as the enforceable (positivistic law approach) legal order associated with the general principles of constitutional law, which would implicitly limit the legitimate exercise of fundamental rights.[42]

The final criteria to be considered with regards to public order are the following two components: 1) public safety and security; and 2) public peace or public tranquility, as a clause that empowers public authorities to act, always subject in their action to the principle of legality preserved in the national Constitutions. We can also add public sanitation or public health and also the protection of human dignity as elements intrinsically associated with public order.

For instance, human dignity can be what law enforcement must be seeking to protect persons in custody when they use reasonable means to grant the necessary security, and not using chokehold techniques that would be disproportionate to the target pursued, such as what caused George Floyd's death.

In this way, when analyzing the judgment with which law enforcement and police officers should react (beforehand) or would have reacted (afterward) to a situation endangering public order, we could analyze the criterion of relevance or per-

---

[41] Judgment of the Supreme Court of 18 January 2010, Third Chamber, Seventh Section, Appeal No. 4204/2006, Legal Basis V.

[42] *See* I. Agirreazkuenaga Zigorraga, "State and autonomous competitions in matters of public and private security; Is there any change in the new Statute for Catalonia? Catalan Journal of Public Security" (RCSP), 16/2006, p. 62.

tinence. To act in this way, the doctrine of the Spanish Constitutional Court wanted to highlight the following elements, which can serve as a possibility to analyze the legal entitlement and authority to intervene for local, regional, or national police. These elements related to the relevance of the action are set forth below.

- The current level of life threat has to be related to law enforcement intervention. It is a matter of security controls intended to prevent crime by altering and reorganizing the cohabitation of people in society.
- The absence of another action (a more specific title of intervention) would reduce or eliminate danger and its consequences. For example, in a broad sense, the existence of a law enforcement authority to deal with the lack of a title of intervention to controlling a specific sector: road traffic, health,[43] transportation,[44] or capital flow (for money laundering crimes).
- The existence of an emergency, shifting the authority from a public official to others: e.g., police officers at the regional level to law enforcement at the national level. The Administration's action through its law enforcement bodies seeks to guarantee security measures due to the exceptional circumstances that require urgent intervention at the national level. Regular law enforcement inspection mechanisms would not solve the situation (for example, for the control of narcotics concerning the Administration of Justice[45]). Public order and public peace or tranquility are at the origin of the actions of the law enforcement authorities who must, with discernment, protect the rights and freedoms of citizens.

As parallelism to the United States situation, in July 2020, President Donald Trump expressed his intention of sending the National Guard integrated in the US armed forces, to the states where George Floyd's protests had become out of control and violent.[46] While George Floyd's death proved how deadly lack of discernment from law enforcement could result, and how justice and the rule of law has to be applied consequently, public security of all citizens and their rights must be kept and protected. In our view, violence cannot be the solution in our legal system. Justice, on the one hand, and appropriately trained law enforcement on the other, must keep on structuring society and protecting law and order. We need to avoid anarchy and chaos to take advantage of the situation. To pour oil on fire cannot be the solution.

In Spain, the law integrates civil protection and public security notions,[47] and it guarantees people's and property's safeguarding during periods of risks, disasters, or calamities. The Administration and police officers will interpret these legal concepts to adapt to reality, in a correct and discerned way, and to mobilize the necessary

---

[43] Spanish Constitutional Court decisions: SSTC 33/82, 54/90, 329/94.

[44] Spanish Constitutional Court decisions: SSTC 59/85; 181/92; 203/92; 2/93.

[45] Spanish Constitutional Court decisions: STC 54/1990.

[46] As an example of the many press articles written about it, *see* https://www.npr.org/2020/06/01/867063007/trump-calls-governors-weak-and-urges-them-to-dominate-violent-protesters.

[47] Spanish Constitutional Court decisions: STC 123 /1984 y 133 /1990.

resources and services.[48] The law was reformed in 2015 to update and improve national coordination when national action is in place.[49] This legislative reform mentioned two aspects in its preamble that are related to the discernment capacity of the Administration and, in general, to public law aspects.

On the one hand, first responders and emergency management matters and the crucial coordination at national coordination, regional and local level in this field, remains one of the most critical issues associated with public order. The Spanish legislators aimed at developing rational structures through action protocols and training programs that can put in place rapid, coordinated, and efficient responses. We are very much aware of those aspects in Texas due to the recurrent hurricane seasons, and after what Houston experienced with Harvey.[50]

A fair judgment of the Administration, the proper discernment of its public officers, requires more effective training and continuous education in its activity sectors. Training adapted to the requirements of each administrative body, from school to technical, academic, professional education, and as well as empirical upbringing. In the United States, after the death of George Floyd, several steps should be taken by the Administration to update and monitor the risks of avoiding such events from happening again. There must be a necessary link between technical knowledge requisites and "on-the-spot" learning, adapting this knowledge to reality to make informed, discerned, and reasonable decisions. That is, to make decisions a reasonable man would take. Knowledge and education remain the basis of a decision adopted with discernment.

The Spanish legislators considered the education of public officers a critical aspect when it introduced by the 2015 Bill an aspect not existing in the prior Bill,[51] the importance of training the human resources of the Civil Protection National Sys-

---

[48] *See* Organic Law No. 4/1981 of 4 June 1981 *on the state of the alarm, exception and siege*, through which all police forces of the State, coordinating human resources, will be mobilized; Also materials resources. Overall by the national police force, when the situation is of such magnitude.

[49] 2015 July 17, 2015, Civil Protection Bill, BOE (JO) n° 164, July 10, 2015.

[50] The Center for U.S. and Mexican Law is a co-founder of the Texas One-Gulf Consortium. Texas One-Gulf is a RESTORE funded consortium of nine top state institutions led by the Harte Research Institute (HRI) for Gulf of Mexico Studies at Texas A&M University-Corpus Christi with wide-ranging expertise in the environment, the economy, and human health. This project was paid for with grant funding from the Texas One-Gulf Center of Excellence. On July 2020, they finished a research project called: "RESTORE Centers of Excellence: Hurricane Harvey Decision-Support - Resilient Environments and Communities (1RCEGR480001/TCEQ 582-15-57594/GAD 91613)" 2018-2020. This project was paid for [in part] with federal funding from the Department of the Treasury through the State of Texas under the Resources and Ecosystems Sustainability, Tourist Opportunities, and Revived Economies of the Gulf Coast States Act of 2012 (RESTORE Act). Part of this project was published under the title: "Texas Disaster Law Guide—Legal Consideration for Emergency Responders and Managers," Arte Público Press (APP), 2020.

[51] Bill No. 2/1985, January 21, 1985 on Civil Protection, remained into force until January 10, 2016, after being repealed by 2015 bill.

tem (*Sistema Nacional de Protección Civil*). The education and training aspects are indeed essential for the proper functioning of the national security system. It must be a priority for Administration's law enforcement bodies. Their training in the mid and long term, giving ordinary, necessary skills to all law enforcement members, seeking better coordination, is critical. Ultimately, a better ability to discern the adaptation of the means used to the goals pursued.

Standards and rules seeking to provide public-safety responses in a general way[52] should complement standards targeting specific sectors, from health, as we have recently seen with the COVID-19 crisis and law enforcement measures, to motor and vehicles traffic, and the human rights associated (such as the right of association and freedoms in general).

In any case, civil protection and public security actions must respect the following principles: the principle of legality, the principle of subsidiarity (to avoid, where possible, displacing the decision-maker authority from one level to another, making the decision closer to the target or person benefitting or bearing the consequences), the opportunity principle (if the decision is needed) and the principle of proportionality (adapting means to the target sought).

The principle of legality related to public security positively links the action of the Administration to the law. In doing so, the action finds its limit in every citizen's rights. Any coactive action needs a prior legal provision. To act with discernment means to have, at first, a good knowledge of this legal provision and to know the extent of the action that may be taken by police officers and security agents belonging to the Administration. This discerned action should make it possible to avoid the commission of a criminal act, by preventing it in advance, or by stopping it when it has already begun. In the case of George Floyd's death, not only police officers should have known in advance what to do to a person in custody that was not resisting, but they must have had the discernment of stopping any use of force when the late Mr. Floyd expressed his distress because he was suffocating. Besides the specific legal procedure to follow, we can already anticipate the principle of legality's infringement by the feeling of scandal and indignation that this death caused. The principle of legality in the law enforcement area of administrative intervention provides greater legal certainty to citizens, putting in place a system of guarantees and respect of every life. Police officers must know their duty, exercising their actions in full respect to human life actions. Their actions must fall into a legal margin of maneuver, into the framework of legality.

The principle of subsidiarity guarantees that law enforcement citizen's security protection does not interfere with any other Administration's powers exercised by other competent public authorities. An example is the general exercise of local law enforcement authority, besides firefighter's intervention, and besides other Administrations bodies that would be competent in terms of security (national security, border patrol, for instance). The principle also encourages empowering agents to take decisions closer to the area directly either benefitting from or suffering the consequences, unless there is a superior authority, more knowledgeable and competent for

---

[52] They are norms that will allow the fulfillment of the rights and freedoms of people living in society, by means of preventive, corrective or repressive measures, as well as inspection or surveillance, possibly limiting the exercise of rights or administrative co-operation.

it. The responsibility of a fair decision on the situation caused by Mr. George Floyd's custody had to be dealt with by the officers on the scene. There was no possibility in real-time to escalate it to higher authorities.

The principle of opportunity implies three aspects: the use of discretionary power or margin of appreciation, which leads to intervention, the recipients or beneficiary, and the means to be used among the existing legal alternatives. One of the most controversial aspects of discretionary powers in the field of public security is, in our view, how law enforcement and public officials give content in real-time to the opportunity to act, defining *in situ* terms such as "live threat," "suspicion," "threat" or "imminent threat," "risk," "emergency" or "danger" to a specific situation. The decision on the opportunity to intercede is predefined by the essential rationale of public security, which must be to protect citizens' human rights and freedoms while attaining public peace and tranquility. Actually, in the opinion of the Spanish Supreme Court, when Administration public officers (such as the police) would not act "when there is a suspect, and the causes of this suspicion are not verified, the authority's officers would be failing their duty of inquiry."[53] To grant the latter, positively, the Administration must intervene when needed, but certainly, this needs to be done proportionately.

The principle of proportionality allows us to assess the capacity of discernment the Administration must have. In Spain, this principle is the materialization of the constitutional principle of prohibition of arbitrary action of public authorities. Moreover, for the Spanish Constitutional Court, with respect to "the constitutionality of any human rights, a restrictive measure must be established respecting the principle of proportionality."[54] Its compliance with the law primarily monitors the principle of proportionality. The actions taken to grant public security must always comply with the law, especially as mentioned when they introduce limits to human rights. The application of this principle helps to assess law enforcement's legitimate interventions, in a field in which vague legal concepts are sometimes numerous and need to receive a content justifying the action taken, balancing proportionally to beneficiaries, on the one hand, rights and freedom, and on the other the means used. Proportionality assessment or judgment is necessary to verify what the enacted decision is likely to achieve; the result sought (the opportunity or pertinence); if the intervention is necessary; or if there is a more moderate action to be taken allowing to effectively achieve the result (confirming the necessity appearing). As well, analyzing if the measure is proportionate and balanced, bringing more benefits to general interest than harm to other values in conflict—the notion of proportionality in its pure essence. In any case, the judgment of proportionality in an action or decision restricting rights must be justified so that the addressees understand the reasons that led to punctually limit or burden their rights. To act with discernment respecting the above principles is necessary not only in the action of the Administration concerning public security but also in any action of any public power.

---

[53] Spanish Supreme Court decisions SSTS of April 27, 1994 and November 11, 1997.

[54] *See* Judgments of the Constitutional Court n° 55/1996, 207/1996.

Conclusion

One can judge the Administration's capacity to discern by the ability to adapt its decision to the reality of the situation. As it happens with persons, the more the Administration will be adaptable to a current context, the more intelligent it will be. If this intelligence is shown through the human intelligence of its agents and public officials, the Administration will have a larger capacity of discernment. The Administration manifests discernment in its fields of action in which there is no automatic or systematic application of the law or in a fully regulated authority or process. In the latter regulated case, it is the legislator who has proven beforehand discernment by profoundly regulating the Administration's action. The Administration will be merely applying the rule. The discretionary power that allows *Rechtsfreie Räume* actions (following the German doctrine), so actions as spaces or *"rooms* free from the law," must, however, be always respectful of the principle of legality.

The discretionary power of the Spanish Administration remains impenetrable for some. The Spanish doctrine does not find a consensus on the elements that must escape the judge's control when they are technical. If for some, the discretionary power must remain outside the judge's control, empowering the Administration even more, for others, and we adhere to this position, the Administration must be able to demonstrate to citizens and eventually to the judge, the justification of its decision, even where there are many equally valid solutions but choosing only one. It should be possible to know the intellectual process or rationale followed by the Administration, by even asking experts to assist the judge. Some courts in Spain have even resorted in an innovative way to the doctrine of the *veil-piercing* or *veil lifting*, by the removal of the immunity veil that jurisdictionally seemed to cover the Administration's technical discretionary power.[55]

While we have seen how easy it is to question an Administration's discretionary decision based on numerical or mathematical scales, we have also seen the difficulty of substituting the technical judgment of the Administration when assessing knowledge. How can we prove to the judge an Administration's manifested error of appreciation? Through a broad majority opinion expressed by the scientific community? Through experts brought by the parties with the corresponding biased opinion? Through experts impartially chosen by the judge? The task remains complex.

If a scientific community's general majority opinion can modify the Administration's discerned decision, then we must question ourselves how this opinion is formed and how their knowledge is acquired. We will have to assess the authority this opinion would inherently have, in the sense of *auctoritas*, known in ancient Rome as a socially recognized knowledge. This *auctoritas* held by experts would have been acquired empirically but also by training and education. Promoting training, education, and learning remains essential to enact discerned decisions, not only by experts or majority opinion but also to any Administration's public officials. Indeed, it is critical to educate and train civil servants, law enforcement, and any public official in using tools the Administration provides them to attain the common

---

[55] For an interesting synthesis on the discretion of technical order, *see* Cf. P. Calleja Pueyo, *Las siete vidas de la discrecionalidad técnica,* http://www.legaltoday.com/practica-juridica/publico/d_administrativo/las-siete-vidas-de-la-discrecionalidad-tecnica.

good. Training is paramount, so horrible events such as George Floyd's death, by the total lack of discernment of a police officer in the use of force, will not happen again.

We need an intelligent, flexible, and adaptable Administration that would act with discernment. An Administration's intelligence will manifest not only in the requirement of justifying any act but also in the consistency and coherence of this justification. In the absence of it, we would be facing an Administration's arbitrary action, lacking intelligence or discernment, therefore against the law, and it should be responsible for it.

The judgment of the Administration would also be assessed by citizens knowing with transparency what have been the criteria and arguments used in a decision-making process. Clarity and precision define these criteria. Public officers must know them beforehand (that is why, again, the importance of training and education), and afterward by citizens (that would have eventual access to them where and when necessary), in order to understand, within the Administration's existing margin of appreciation, the reasons that prompted it to take the decision.

Indeed, it is not easy to establish an infallible system to question an inappropriate technical evaluation of the Administration based on its discretionary powers. We face the most human dimension of the Administration that we would like to be rational, but that remains inherently debatable. What we can for sure establish is a system that trains and educates public officials to use common sense and proportionality in any action they would take, acting with discernment when using force when human rights and lives are in danger. Every life matters, and we should limit tragic events, such as George Floyd's death, so that others will not ever happen again.

CHAPTER 2[1]

REGULATING LAWYERS: NORTH AMERICAN PERSPECTIVES AND PROBLEMATICS

By Richard F. Devlin[2]

In most modern societies lawyers—both individually and as a collective pro-fession—are identified as playing significant social, economic, cultural, and politi-cal roles. Lawyers are implicated in almost every aspect of our lives: they frequent-ly influence and draft legislation that regulates—among various other things—the roadways and our behaviour on them, how our houses are built and maintained, the conditions under which we can offer our labour; lawyers provide advice on multiple matters including family relations, exchange relations, taxation matters, domestic trade, and international trade; they help us establish relationships (both familial and commercial) and help us resolve disputes when they break down; when social rela-tions fray, they litigate on behalf of citizens and commercial entities; they defend or

---

[1] Chapters 2-5 constitute a Mini Symposium that grew out of a panel discussion sponsored by the North American Consortium on Legal Education in Monterrey, Mexico in March 2015. The papers by Professors Devlin, Roussy, Urquiaga and Lutz are dedicated to the memory of Steve Zamora, the "founding father" of the North American Consortium of Legal Education, and a lifelong champion for the cause of greater North American co-operation and collabo-ration. Each contribution of this Symposium was originally published in *The International Lawyer*, Volume 50, Issue 3, and each is republished with the permission of *The Interna-tional Lawyer*.

[2] Richard Devlin FRSC is a Professor at the Schulich School of Law, Dalhousie University, Nova Scotia, Canada. Most recently he has been a coeditor of three books *Regulating Judges: Beyond Independence and Accountability* (2016), *Lawyers' Ethics And Professional Regulation* 3d (2017), and *Canada and the Rule of Law: 150 Years After Confederation* (2017).

prosecute alleged criminals; they advocate for the equality rights of disadvantaged and minority groups; they protect us from abuses of police power and from state interference in our private lives (and advise the state how to successfully interfere in our private lives). In short, lawyers exercise enormous power and influence.

Because lawyers have access to and exercise such significant power, it is often said that they have a social contract with society. In return for the privilege of being a lawyer, the responsibility of every lawyer, and the profession, is to promote and protect the public interest. Others go further and claim that because of their privileged status, lawyers and the legal profession are fiduciaries.

The inevitable questions, of course, are as follows: how do we ensure that lawyers fulfill their side of the bargain, how do we guarantee that they will faithfully and effectively live up to their fiduciary obligations? Do we adopt a "trust us" approach, or do we establish norms, institutions, and procedures to frame and, where necessary, enforce lawyers' obligations? The core concern is not so much that lawyers are bad (although there are, of course, bad lawyers in multiple senses); rather it is that there are structures, incentives, and temptations that might distract lawyers from their contractual obligations with, and fiduciary obligations to, society and the public interest. On one level, there is the materialist concern that both individual lawyers and the legal profession generally will put their economic interests ahead of either their clients' interests or society's interests. On another level, there is the social capital concern that like many professions lawyers will give priority to matters that advance or protect their privileged social status. Third, there is the ideological concern that lawyers will articulate, advance, and even enforce their particular worldviews, which may not be generally representative of society.

One potentially fruitful approach to addressing these problematics—indeed these conundrums—is to turn towards the contemporary regulation theory.

I. Contemporary Regulation Theory and Practice[3]

In the last three decades there has been an explosion of theoretical analyses and empirical research on regulation. This work has been driven by the insights and interactions of multiple disciplines including (but not limited to) economics, sociology, psychology, political science, law, public policy, anthropology, criminology, political economy, philosophy, history, mathematics and international relations.[4] There have been regulatory investigations of almost every realm of human interac-

---

[3] For a fuller exploration of the relevance of regulation theory to the legal professions see Richard Devlin & Adam Dodek, eds., *Regulating Judges: Beyond Independence and Accountability* (Edward Elgar, 2017).

[4] John Braithwaite et al, *Regulation and Governance Make a Difference*, 1 REGULATION AND GOVERNANCE 1 (2007) [hereinafter *Regulation and Governance*]; Robert Baldwin et al. eds., *The Oxford Handbook of Regulation* (2010) [hereinafter OXFORD HANDBOOK].

tion: political, economic, social, cultural, bureaucratic, "public" and "private."[5] Regulatory research has been focused on micro,[6] meso,[7] and macro-level[8] relationships and has targeted local,[9] national,[10] and international dynamics.[11]

Because of this diversity and richness, it is not possible to provide a definition of regulation that would command the agreement of all its interlocutors. In this sense, regulation is an 'essentially contested' concept[12] and practice. But for the purposes of this Symposium, we adopt a working definition and suggest that there are four key themes that are particularly significant. By way of a working definition, Black et al. have suggested that:

> Regulation is a dynamic exercise in collective problem-solving . . . the sustained and focused attempt to alter the behaviour of others according to standards or goals with the intention of producing a broadly defined outcome or outcomes which may involve mechanisms of standard setting, information-gathering and behaviour modification.[13]

Building upon this skeleton, a review of the literature suggests several key themes.

Regulation is an inherently normative and programmatic exercise. While there are undoubtedly difficult technical and practical aspects to every regulatory initiative, in the end, all regulation is driven by a desire to improve the public good.[14] Inevitably, there are different—even competing—conceptions of what is meant by 'the public good,' but there can be no avoiding the normativity of any regulatory

---

[5] *See generally Regulation and Governance, supra* note 4.

[6] *See generally* Hugh Collins, *Regulating Contracts* (2002).

[7] Neil Gunningham & Peter Grabosky, *Smart Regulation: Designing Environmental Policy* 6-7 (1998).

[8] *See generally* Mark Findley & Wei Lim, *Regulatory Worlds: Cultural and Social Perspectives When North Meets South (2014).*

[9] *See generally* Christopher Hood & Martin Lodge, *Pavlovian Innovation, Pet Solutions and Economizing on Rationality: Politicians and Dangerous Dogs in Regulatory Innovation: A Comparative Analysis* (Julia Black et al. eds., 2005).

[10] *See e.g.,* Jacinth Jordana & David Levi-Faur eds., *The Politics of Regulation: Institutions and Regulatory Reforms for the Age of Government (2005)* [hereinafter *The Politics of Regulation*]; G.B. Doern et al., *Rules and Unruliness.*

[11] *See generally* John Braithwaite & Peter Drahos. *Global Business Regulation (2000).*

[12] W.B. Gallie, *Essentially Contested Concepts* 56 PROCEEDINGS OF THE ARISTOTELIAN SOCIETY 167 (1956).

[13] Julia Black et al. eds., *Regulatory Innovation: A Comparative Analysis 11* (2005).

[14] OXFORD HANDBOOK, *supra* note *4,* at 563*; see generally The Politics of Regulation, supra* note 10.

enterprise.[15] Importantly, even if there is no dispute as to the ideal values, there is usually more than one value at stake in the pursuit of the public good and these various values may be in tension or even in conflict. Regulatory interventions need to be aware of, and responsive to, these normative challenges and dilemmas.

Regulation is complex. Once upon a time 'regulation' was conceived of as an essentially prescriptive, pseudo-Austinian phenomenon: it was the command-and-control model whereby one party would mandate rules and enforce compliance through sanctions.[16] Regulation in this model was hierarchical, monological, deterrent-driven and 'hard.' Contemporary conceptions of regulation acknowledge that command and control prescriptions are one form of regulation, but argue that, descriptively and normatively, regulation is more encompassing. Because command and control approaches have their weaknesses and limitations—ineffectiveness, expensiveness, bluntness, and inflexibility—the realm of regulation has been expanded to identify and endorse other forms of regulation that are more collaborative, more persuasive, more co-operative, more accommodative, more dialogical, and 'soft.' These have been variously described as 'responsive,'[17] 'smart,'[18] 'meta,'[19] 'really responsive,'[20] 'risk-based,'[21] 'principles-based,'[22] or 'outcomes-focused.'[23] Such approaches, in turn, generate an additional set of inquiries into the meaning, nature and dynamics of (non)compliance.[24]

Regulatory analysis is highly contextual. Because the realms of social interaction are so diverse, and because the regulatory objectives, goals and values can be so distinct, it is neither possible nor desirable to seek universability of regulatory

---

[15] *Regulation and Governance, supra* note 4, at 1; Christine Parker, *Twenty Years of Responsive Regulation: An Appreciation and Appraisal* 7 REGULATION AND GOVERNANCE 2 (2013).

[16] *See generally* OXFORD HANDBOOK, *supra* note 4.

[17] Ian Ayres & John Braithwaite, *Responsive Regulation: Transcending the Deregulation Debate* 4 (1992).

[18] Cunningham et al., *supra* note 7, at 1.

[19] *See generally* Christine Parker, *The Open Corporation: Effective Self-Regulation and Democracy* (2002).

[20] Robert Baldwin and Julia Black, *Really Responsive Regulation,* 71 MODERN L REV 59 (2008).

[21] Bridget Hutter, *The Attractions of Risk-Based Regulation: Accounting for the Emergence of Risk Ideas in Regulation* (2002).

[22] Christie Ford, *Principles-Based Securities Regulation in the Wake of the Global Financial Crisis*, 55 McGILL L. REV. 257 (2010).

[23] *See generally* Andrew Hopper & Gregory Treverton-Jones, *Outcomes-Focused Regulation: A Practical Guide* (2011).

[24] *See generally* Christine Parker & Viebieke Nielsen, *Explaining Compliance: Business Responses to Regulation* (2011).

analyses.[25] Rather it is preferable to identify a particular realm of inquiry, articulate appropriate guiding values, and then interrogate and assess whether those values are being achieved through the prevailing structures, institutions, processes, actors and dynamics.[26] Such contextualism requires us to pay attention not only to what regulators try to do, but also how the regulatees respond.[27] Viewed in this light, regulation is a craft, a problem-solving art.[28]

Change, Flux, and Innovation. Many analysts of regulation argue that because of the inevitability (and rapidity) of social, economic, political, cultural, and technological changes, regulatory norms, processes, and instruments must also be dynamic.[29] Regulation is, therefore, always a work in progress.[30] To be effective, regulatory thinking cannot be frozen in time, and regulators must be open to innovation, revision, recalibration, reconstruction, and experimentation. Reflexivity and imagination are core capabilities for both regulatory actors and institutions.[31]

It is important to emphasize, however, that regulatory imagination and innovation are not to be understood as ends in themselves. Rather, any assessment of such changes must be directly related to the norms and values initially identified, and the outcomes desired. This is simply a re-iteration of my initial observation that regulation always has an irrepressible normative underbelly.

II. Applying Regulatory Theory to the North American Legal Professions

In this mini-symposium, which grows out of a North American Consortium on Legal Education (NACLE) workshop in Monterrey, Mexico in 2015, three scholars from Canada, Mexico and the United States apply some of the insights of regulation theory to the legal professions in each of these jurisdictions. A comprehensive analysis of the regulation of the legal professions in each jurisdiction would, of course, require a significant volume. Therefore, to make the project manageable, we have identified three key dimensions that are particularly challenging at the current moment: legal education, lawyer regulation, and transnational lawyering. We have chosen legal education because control over who gets permission to enter the pro-

---

[25] Ayres and Braithwaite, *supra* note 17, at 110; Robert Baldwin et al, *Understanding Regulation: Theory, Strategy and Practice* (2nd ed. 2011) [hereinafter *Understanding Regulation*].

[26] *See generally The Politics of Regulation, supra* note 10.

[27] Parker and Nielsen eds. *supra* note 24.

[28] *See generally* Malcolm Sparrow, *The Regulatory Craft: Controlling Risks, Solving Problems and Managing Compliance* (2000).

[29] *See e.g.*, Ayers & Braithwaite, *supra* note 17; *The Politics of Regulation, supra* note 10; *Understanding Regulation, supra* note 25.

[30] Julia Black, *Learning from Regulatory Disasters,* 10(3) POLICY QUARTERLY 3 (2014).

[31] Black, *supra* note 13, at 11.

fession (and by what criteria such decisions are made) has determinative impact on the delivery of legal services in each jurisdiction. Second, we have chosen lawyer regulation because, in the last decade, there have been several significant controversies in each of the jurisdictions on who, or what, should be regulated, and by whom? Third, we have chosen transnational lawyering because the combination of globalization (and in particular the desire for greater North American integration) and technological innovation suggests to us that the historic national boundaries that have traditionally structured the regulation of lawyers are eroding, with the result that this is an immediate and pressing challenge that cannot be ignored. Each of the essays presents a careful and insightful analysis of some of the most currently significant regulatory challenges in each of the three jurisdictions, and each can be read on its own. But collectively, they also illustrate the four key regulatory themes discussed above.

Regulation is an inherently normative and programmatic exercise. All three contributors clearly illustrate the normative and programmatic nature of regulation. For Professor Lutz, the goal of regulating "inbound transnational lawyers" to the United States is to ensure competency and competition, while the goal of "regulating outbound transnational lawyers" is to facilitate trade in legal services and building the rule of law in the world. For Professor Urquiaga, the normative agenda for the regulation of Mexican lawyers must be to ensure the provision of competent, accessible, and professionally responsible legal services. For Professor Roussy, the currently dominant normative imperative is to provide uniform quality in legal education and the ethics standards of the Canadian legal profession.

Regulation is complex. While the circumstances of the United States, Mexico and Canada are different, each of the authors agrees that the regulation of the legal profession is a highly complex exercise. In Mexico, the sheer numbers of law schools, legal associations, and lawyers makes coherent and cohesive regulation an enormous challenge. In the United States, regulation is plagued by the tension between the forces of globalized openness on the one hand, and localized protectionism on the other. In Canada, the federal nature of its legal professional framework has created historic barriers to national mobility and uniformity, and has required the Federation of Law Societies of Canada to engage in a slow and patient (but very determined) reconstruction of the regulatory regime.

Regulatory analysis is highly contextual. The essays also reveal the highly contextual nature of lawyer regulation. The economic, political, social, and cultural traditions of Canada, the United States, and Mexico are radically different, and this has a manifest impact on the prevailing regulatory challenges in each jurisdiction. Mexico seems to be struggling to establish some of the rudimentary elements of an effective and efficient regulatory regime for its legal profession. Canada is maneuvering to move beyond its checkerboard historical regulatory practices to constitute a more uniform—and hopefully fair—governance system. The United States is exploring and experimenting with a variety of mechanisms to ensure that it remains a central player in the increasing globalization of legal practice.

Change, Flux, and Innovation. All three contributors demonstrate that change and flux are unavoidable realities of the contemporary legal services marketplace. They all agree that the dynamics of globalization and the emergence of new technologies will inevitably have an impact on the regulation of the legal professions. Furthermore, they also agree that access to justice—to the extent that it dovetails with access to legal services—is an increasing challenge in every jurisdiction, and that the regulators of the legal professions need to respond to this fundamental challenge to the legitimacy and integrity of their legal professions. But the three jurisdictions seem to vary in their willingness to engage in innovation. While none are particularly radical (compared, for example, to what is happening in Australia or the United Kingdom) the United States is seeking to re-orient legal education and become more responsive to transnational lawyering. In Canada, the major innovation is the centralization of power and authority in one national umbrella organization with the express desire to get things done. In Mexico, despite attempts at significant regulatory reform to improve the governance structures of the profession, there has been tough (and seemingly effective) resistance.

III. Conclusion

Professors Urquiaga, Roussy and Lutz have identified significantly different contemporary challenges for the regulation of the legal professions in Mexico, Canada, and the United States. On the one hand, this indicates that it would be unwise, or at least premature, to espouse the idea (or ideal) of a North American legal profession. But at the same time, the essays illustrate that there is increasing awareness of the global and regional forces that are having an impact on the obligations of the regulators of the legal professions. While the problematics and perspectives (and even the aspirations) in Canada, Mexico, and the United States might be different, there is consensus that the regulation of the legal professions is a work in progress and that, if anything, the challenges may be getting even more difficult.

CHAPTER 3

LAWYER REGULATION IN CANADA: TOWARDS GREATER UNIFORMITY

By Alain Roussy[1]

Canada is a federation comprised of ten provinces and three territories. Each of these jurisdictions has a law society (or two, in the case of Quebec),[2] governed by lawyers, that is mandated to regulate the legal profession in the public interest.[3] Some of these law societies are older than Canada itself.[4] Law societies are explicitly recognized by provincial and territorial legislation as the sole self-regulating authorities of the legal profession within each jurisdiction.[5] Among other things,

---

[1] Associate Professor and Vice-Dean of the French Common Law Program, Faculty of Law, University of Ottawa, Ottawa, Canada. The author would like to thank then-student Rebecca Porter for her research assistance.

[2] Quebec is Canada's only jurisdiction with a civil law system. It also has a clear distinction between lawyers and notaries, each profession having its own area of practice and each being governed by a separate law society—the "Barreau du Québec" for lawyers and the "Chambre des notaires du Québec" for notaries. *See* Fiona M. Kay, *Intraprofessional Competition and Earnings Inequalities Across a Professional Chasm: The Case of the Legal Profession in Quebec, Canada,* 43 L. & SOC'Y REV. 901, 904-05 (2009).

[3] *See, e.g.,* Law Society Act, R.S.O. 1990, c L.8. § 4.2 (Can.). The regulation of legal services is one of provincial (as opposed to federal) jurisdiction under the Canadian Constitution. *See* Constitution Act, 1867, 30 & 31 Vict., c 3 (U.K.), *reprinted* in R.S.C. 1985, app VI, no. 92 (Can.).

[4] For example, Ontario's law society, the Law Society of Upper Canada, was created in 1797, well before Canadian Confederation in 1867. This explains the society's historical name, "Upper Canada," which was the former name for Ontario. *See History,* LAW SOC'Y OF UPPER CAN., http://Isuc.on.ca/with.aspx?id=427 (last visited June 17, 2017).

[5] *See, e.g., About the Law Society,* LAW SOC'Y OF UPPER CAN., http://Isuc.on.ca/with.aspx?id=905 (last visited June 18, 2017); Law Society Act at ss 4.1, 4.2, 5.

they decide matters of admission, competence, and discipline.[6] Few have questioned their existence or authority.[7] Aside from matters of tradition, there are a number of reasons that explain adherence to such a self-regulation model, including efficiency, expertise, and independence from the bar and the judiciary.[8] Though law societies have been working in a much more concerted fashion in recent years, each law society remains an independent body with full statutory authority to regulate the legal profession within its jurisdiction.

The Federation of Law Societies of Canada ("Federation") is the national "coordinating body" for Canada's provincial and territorial law societies.[9] From its humble beginnings in 1972, the Federation's influence has grown enormously.[10] The Federation is involved in a number of national regulatory initiatives that are substantially creating more uniformity among the law societies.[11] The increasingly important role of the Federation cannot be overstated. In fact, it could be said that, at least in some instances, the law societies are "uploading" their traditional and fundamental responsibilities to the national entity.[12] This is a remarkable development, particularly when one notes that it is not being driven by an angry public or a controlling government, but rather by the law societies themselves.[13]

Part 1 of this paper will briefly discuss the self-governing model for law societies in Canada and provide an overview of the Federation. Part 2 will focus on the role of the law societies and the Federation in regulating legal education in Canada. Part 3 will examine various developments in lawyer regulation in Canada spearheaded by the Federation. Finally, Part 4 will address transnational lawyering in the Canadian context. The overarching theme of the paper is one of increasing national regulatory uniformity.

---

[6] *See* Alan Treleaven, *Moving TowardNational Bar Admission Standards in Canada, 83* BAR EXAMINER *17, 17 (2014),* http://www.ncbex.org/pdfviewer/?file=assets/media_files/Bar-Examiner/articles/2014/830314-Treleavenpdf.

[7] *See e.g.,* Richard Devlin & Porter Heffernan, *The End(s) of Self- Regulation?,* 45 ALTA. L. REV. 169, 171 (2008); Jeff Roberts, *Time to Streamline the Societies?,* CANADIAN LAWYER, Jan. 1, 2009, http://www.canadianlawyermag.com/468/Time-to-streamline-the-societies.html.

[8] *See generally,* ALICE WOOLLEY ET AL., LAWYERS' ETHICS AND PROFESSIONAL REGULATION (Markham, Ont.: LexisNexis Can. Ed., 2d ed. 2012).

[9] *See From Conference to the Nation's Capital,* FED'N OF LAW SOC'YS OF CAN., http://flsc.ca/about-us/yesterday-and-today/ (last visited June 18, 2017).

[10] *See id.*

[11] *See National Initiatives, Fed'n of Law Soc'ys of Can., https://flsc.ca/national-initiatives/* (last visited June 19, 2017).

[12] *See generally From Conference to the Nation's Capital, supra* note 9.

[13] *See id.*

I. Part 1: The Regulatory Model

A. *The Provincial and Territorial Law Societies*

The universal model of lawyer regulation in Canada's provinces and territories is that of self-regulation by which we mean that the regulation of lawyers is largely the domain of lawyers. The law societies that started appearing in the country at the end of the 18th century, generally modelled on British Inns of Court, already had a high level of independence. Education of aspiring lawyers and the accompanying control over admission to the profession were fundamental powers of the law societies. As the years went on, the level of independence and self-regulation of law societies grew to encompass the enforcement of codes of conduct, the handling of complaints against lawyers, the power to discipline lawyers (including the power to disbar a lawyer),[14] the creation of mandatory insurance programs,[15] the regulation of continuing education standards,[16] and the power to make various other rules and regulations for the governance of lawyers and law societies themselves. These have been the hallmarks of self-regulation in Canada for at least a half century.[17] In return for shouldering the burdens of self-regulation, lawyers are granted an exclusive statutory monopoly on the provision of legal services within each jurisdiction.[18]

Self-regulation has received judicial encouragement in Canada. In a unanimous decision by the Supreme Court in 1982, Justice Estey wrote: "[t]he independence of the Bar from the state in all its pervasive manifestations is one of the hallmarks of a free society."[19] In a very recent case, the Supreme Court declined to rule on the question of whether self-regulation should be recognized as a constitutionally protected principle of fundamental justice. But the Court reiterated "the central importance to the legal system of lawyers being free from government interference in discharging their duties to their clients."[20]

---

[14] *See* W. Wesley Pue, *Cowboy Jurists and the Making of Legal Professionalism,* 45 ALTA. L. REV. 29, 36-41 (2008).

[15] *See e.g., Professional Liability Insurance,* LAW SOC'Y OF UPPER CAN., http://lsuc.on.ca/For-Lawyers/About-Your-License/Professional-Liability-Insurance/ (last visited June 18, 2017).

[16] *See, e.g., Continuing Professional Development Requirement,* LAW SOC'Y OF UPPER CAN., https://www.lsuc.on.ca/CPD-Requirement/ (last visited June 18, 2017). In March 2017, the Supreme Court of Canada held that the Law Society of Manitoba's suspension of an attorney who failed to complete twelve hours of mandatory continuing professional development was both reasonable and within the scope of the society's legislative mandate. Green v. Law Soc'y of Man., 2017 SCC 20 (Can.).

[17] For a more detailed overview of self-regulation of law societies in Canada, *see* WOOLLEY ET AL., *supra* note 8.

[18] *See, e.g.,* Law Society Act, R.S.O. 1990, c L.8, s 26.1(1) (CN.).

[19] A.G. Can. v. Law Society of B.C., [1982] 2 S.C.R. 307, 335 (Can.).

This is not to say that there are no other actors who play a role in shaping the legal profession. Education of aspiring lawyers, for example, has largely been overtaken by university law schools. When law societies initially arose at the end of the 18th century, lawyers were principally trained through years of hands-on work in apprenticeships with experienced lawyers. Today, law societies have not completely abandoned the principle that on-the-job training should be a requirement for admission to practice. An apprenticeship period (usually called "articling") between six and twelve months is still a requirement across the country.[21] There has been an ongoing debate, particularly in Ontario,[22] about getting rid of the articling requirement, but so far, no jurisdiction has dared to make the change. Over the last two centuries, however, legal education—like education generally—has become more formalized and the general trend has been a shift away from relying solely on training in the workplace towards an emphasis on a more academic legal education. A three-year law degree from a recognized law school is now the standard requirement. Apart from Quebec, a four-year undergraduate university degree is generally necessary for entry into law school,[23] which means that most lawyers in Canada will have at least seven years of university-level education by the time they start practicing. But law societies have not completely exited the business of training lawyers. Some law societies still offer courses that must be successfully completed after graduating

---

[20] Can. (A.G.) v. Fed'n of L. Soc'ys of Can., 2015 SCC 7, para. 97 (Can. B.C.); *see also* Andrews v. L. Soc'y of B.C., [1989] 1 S.C.R. 143, 187 (Can.); Pearlman v. Man. L. Soc'y Jud. Comm., [1991] 2 S.C.R. 869, 887 (Can.); Finney v. Barreau du Que., 2004 SCC 36, para. 1 (Can.).

[21] *See* Treleaven, *supra* note 6, at 19-20.

[22] This was part of an ongoing debate regarding ways to address the "articling crisis" in Ontario that dates back to 2008. *See* Michael McKierman, *Articling Crisis Set to Grow,* LAW TIMES (June 6, 2011, 1:00), http://lawtimesnews.com/201106061875/headline-news/articling-crisis-set-to-grow. The Law Society of Upper Canada opted to create an alternative pathway to the legal profession so that one could choose between the traditional route of a longer articling period and the new route of coursework followed by a shorter articling period. *See* Simona Chiose, *Call to End Articling Alternative for Ontario Grads Sparks Controversy,* GLOBE AND MAIL (Sept. 28, 2016, 9:41 PM), https://www.theglobe andmail.com/news/national/education/call-to-end-articling-alternative-for-ontario-grads-sparks-controversy/article32121475/. The Faculty at Lakehead University follows an entirely different model, approved by the Law Society of Upper Canada, in which the articling component is incorporated into a law degree, allowing graduates to bypass the usual articling requirement. *See Integrated Practice Curriculum,* Bora Laskin Faculty of Law, LAKEHEAD U., https://www.lakeheadu.ca/academics/departments/law/curriculu./ipc (last visited June 18, 2017).

[23] *Canadian Law School Guide,* POWERSCORE, https://s3.amazonaws.com/powerscorepdfs/lawschool/guides/Canadian/Law/Schools/Guide.pdf (last visited June 18, 2017).

with a law degree and all law societies also have mandatory bar examinations that are accompanied by particular study materials.[24]

Apart from universities, other actors also help to shape the legal profession. Courts do not play the direct role they sometimes do in the United States when it comes to lawyer discipline. Courts do, however, act as inevitable final arbiters in such cases. The reason is simply that law society discipline tribunals are treated as any other administrative tribunal, so the losing party can request a judicial review of the initial decision.[25] But when undertaking such reviews, courts are very deferential to the factual and legal conclusions reached by the discipline tribunal in accordance with general administrative law principles.[26] The same is true for other decisions that are made by law societies, such as the denial of admission of a particular applicant. Those decisions are also subject to review by the courts using a deferential approach.[27] In addition, clients can sue lawyers for professional negligence by way of a civil trial. Issues addressed in the context of those lawsuits, such as competence, will often be similar to and may even overlap with issues before law society discipline tribunals. Although the outcome of civil cases will always be a decision as to the financial liability of the lawyer to the client (and not as to the appropriate discipline, such as disbarment), courts nonetheless help to shape the regulatory and disciplinary analysis and can, thus, have a direct impact on the conduct of lawyers.

Despite the many pronouncements related to the importance of the independence of the Bar from the state, as noted above, provincial, and territorial governments do play a role in the regulation of lawyers. The nature and scope of law societies' powers are defined by provincial and territorial statutes.[28] Such statutes can, of course, be amended at the whim of those governments. For example, the Law Society of Upper Canada's statute[29] was amended in 2006 to include a duty to act at all times "so as to facilitate access to justice for the people of Ontario."[30] This arguably restricts the law society's regulatory freedom. At the same time, the Law Society of Upper Canada was given the power to regulate paralegals within the province,[31] thereby increasing the ambit of the law society's powers. Most provincial governments have a more direct say in the decision-making process of law societies in that they have guaranteed representation on the highest-level boards of directors of the

---

[24] *See* Treleaven, *supra* note 6, at 18-19.

[25] *See* Amy Salyzyn, *The Judicial Regulation of Lawyers in Canada,* 37 Dalhousie L. J. 481, 504 (2014).

[26] *See id.* at 503-04.

[27] *See id.* at 506.

[28] Treleaven, *supra* note 6, at 17.

[29] Law Society Act, R.S.O. 1990, c L. 8 (Can.).

[30] *Id.* at § 4.2(2).

[31] *Id.* at § 2(2)(d).

law societies. In Ontario, for example, this board is governed by paralegals, attorneys, and laypeople, all referred to as "benchers."[32] Benchers come together "most months in a meeting called Convocation to make policy decisions and to deal with other matters related to the governance of Ontario's paralegals and lawyers."[33] Convocation is composed of 40 benchers elected by members of the law society and eight lay benchers appointed by the government of Ontario.[34]

Despite peripheral roles played by other actors, the core elements of lawyer regulation remain within the sphere of control of law societies in Canada. Law societies decide who gets admitted into the profession, what standards they have to comply with while members, and how to discipline members who contravene their codes. Up to this point, Canada has not experienced the diminution of self-regulation that has occurred in other common law countries, such as the United Kingdom and Australia.[35] Self-regulation is still alive and well in Canada.

B. The Federation of Law Societies of Canada

As noted above, the Federation of Law Societies ("Federation") is the national coordinating body for Canada's fourteen provincial and territorial law societies. The Federation was not created by provincial or federal statute. Its inception can be traced back to 1927, when the law societies first came together to form the Conference of Governing Bodies of the Legal Profession in Canada.[36] The primary purpose of that body was to allow the law societies to consider "matters of common interest."[37] In 1972, it became what is now the Federation, which was "established as a non-profit corporation" and has been based in Ottawa, the nation's capital, since 2006.[38]

The Federation's vision statement is: "Acting in the public interest by strengthening Canada's system of governance of an independent legal profession, reinforcing public confidence in it and making it a leading example for justice systems around the

---

[32] *See Governance,* LAW SOC'Y OF UPPER CAN., http://www.Isuc.on.ca/with.aspx?id=673 (last visited June 18, 2017).

[33] *See id.*

[34] Law Society Act at §§ 15(1), 23(1). Ontario's statute was the first to formally include this type of public oversight, but most other provinces have now followed suit. *Benchers,* LAW SOC'Y OF UPPER CAN., http://www.Isuc.on.ca/withaspx?=1136 (last visited June 20, 2017); Alice Woolley, *Rhetoric and Realities: What Independence of the Bar Requires of Lawyer Regulation,* 2011), https://papers.ssrn.com/so13/papers.cfm"abstract_id+1920921.

[35] For a general overview of developments related to self-regulation in those two countries and elsewhere, *see* Devlin & Heffernan, *supra* note 7, at 1, 5.

[36] *From Conference to the Nation's Capital, supra* note 9.

[37] *Id.*

[38] *Id.*

world."[39] The Federation has also adopted the same core mandate as the fourteen law societies—to serve the public interest.[40] It is involved in various endeavors, including managing the Canadian Legal Information Institute (CanLII), a free online search engine for Canada's laws and decisions,[41] assessing internationally trained lawyers who wish to move to and practices law in Canada, providing continuing legal education programs, and generally being the voice of Canada's law societies.[42]

But the Federation's various national regulatory initiatives have transformed the body into a major agent of both change and unity. As further discussed below, these initiatives impact both regulation of legal education and regulation of lawyers.

II. Part 2: The Regulation of Legal Education

In October 2009, the Federation undertook an initiative on behalf of the law societies "to develop national standards for admission to the legal profession in Canada."[43] Key goals of the initiative were "[c]onsistency in admission standards and candidate assessment."[44] This initiative was a logical, and perhaps inevitable, extension of a previous initiative, further discussed in the next part of this paper, regarding lawyer mobility between the various provinces and territories. Almost ten years prior, law societies started to sign on to the National Mobility Agreement, which allowed lawyers to move "with relative ease" from one jurisdiction to another within Canada.[45] It was natural to address the question of national admission standards in order to establish a certain consistency between lawyers called initially in a given province and lawyers arriving from other provinces.

---

[39] *Our Vision Statement*, FED'N OF LAW SOC'YS OF CAN., http://flsc.ca/about-us/our-mission/ (last visited June 18, 2017).

[40] *What is the Federation of Law Societies of Canada?*, FED'N OF LAW SOC'YS OF CAN., http://flsc.ca/about-us/what-is-the-Federation-of-law-societies-of-canada/ (last visited June 18, 2017).

[41] *Id.* Other countries have similar legal information institutes. *See, e.g.*, CORNELL LAW SCH. LEGAL INFO. INST., https://www.law.cornell.edu/ (last visited June 18, 2017); BRITISH AND IRISH LEGAL INFO. INST., http://www.bailii.org/ (last visited June 18, 2017).

[42] *What is the Federation of Law Societies of Canada?*, *supra* note 40. The Federation's handling of a recent Supreme Court case between itself and the Canadian government is an example of how the body serves as the national voice for Canada's various law societies. *See* Can. (A.G.) v. Fed'n of L. Soc'ys of Can., 2015 SCC 7 (Can. B.C.).

[43] FED'N OF LAW SOC'YS OF CAN., NATIONAL ADMISSION STANDARDS PROJECT: PHASE 1 REPORT 1 (2012), http://flsc.ca/wp-content/uploads/2014/10/admission3.pdf.; *see generally* Treleaven, *supra* note 6.

[44] *Id.* at 1.

[45] *See id.; see also* National Mobility Agreement, Federation of Law Societies of Can., Nov.7, 2002, http://flsc.ca/wp-content/uploads/2014/10/mobility1.pdf.

The first phase of the initiative had two goals: first, to identify essential competencies "required [of applicants] upon entry to the legal profession" (National Competency Profile); and, second, to establish "a standard for ensuring that applicants meet the requirement to be of good character" (National Fitness and Suitability Standard).[46] In September 2012, the Federation released its National Entry to Practice Competency Profile for Lawyers and Quebec Notaries.[47] The document is divided into three sections—substantive legal knowledge, skills, and tasks—[48] and is essentially a laundry list of things that, according to the Federation, any new lawyer should know or know how to do, from general principles of contracts and torts to more specific items like drafting demand letters and using time tracking systems. The substantive legal knowledge section of the document is clearly aimed at law schools because those institutions provide the bulk of such knowledge. The National Competency Profile has been adopted by thirteen law societies across Canada, "on the understanding that adoption [was]" subject to the development and approval of a plan for implementation.[49] The second phase has proven to be more complicated than originally anticipated,[50] as has the adoption of a National Fitness and Suitability Standard, which is still a work in progress.[51] Nevertheless, there is increased recognition and willingness to standardize entrance requirements even though various law societies may have different views on how to assess the required competencies.

The above initiative, dealing generally with education of aspiring lawyers, has an indirect effect on the operation of law schools. Another related initiative of the Federation has had a much more direct impact on law schools. In 2009, a Federation task force recommended that Canadian law societies adopt a uniform national requirement for entry into their admission programs.[52] Whereas the initiative dis-

---

[46] PHASE 1 REPORT, *supra* note 43, at 2.

[47] FED'N OF LAW SOC'YS OF CAN., NATIONAL ADMISSION STANDARDS PROJECT: NATIONAL ENTRY TO PRACTICE COMPETENCY PROFILE FOR LAWYERS AND QUEBEC NOTARIES (2012), http:// flsc.ca/wp-content/uploads/2014/10/admission4.pdf.

[48] *Id.* at §§1.2(a), 1.2(c), 3.1.3(i), 3.1.1(d).

[49] *National Competency and Good Character Standards,* FED'N OF LAW SOC'YS OF CAN., http:// flsc.ca/national-initiatives/national-admission-standards/ (last visited June 18, 2017).

[50] The ongoing debate about the future of articling, mentioned previously, is certainly not helping.

[51] *See* Treleaven, *supra* note 6, at 25. Some have criticized the use of a "good character" or "suitability" requirement for admission to law societies as being unworkable and unfair. *See, e.g.,* Alice Woolley, *Can Good Character Be Made Better? Assessing the Federation of Law Societies' Proposed Reform of the Good Character Requirement for Law Society Admission,* CAN. J. ADMIN. L. & PRAC. 1, 40-41 (2013), http://papers.ssrn.com/sol3/papers. cfm?abstract_id=2262863.

[52] FED'N OF LAW SOC'YS OF CAN., REPORT OF TASK FORCE ON CANADIAN COMMON LAW DEGREE 4 (2009), http://docs.flsc.ca/APPRTaskForceReportOct2009.pdf.

cussed deals with standards for entry into the profession, the Federation's "National Requirement" initiative deals squarely with competencies that are expected to be acquired while in law school. The National Requirement[53] became effective in 2015. Law schools must now be reviewed annually to ensure they comply with the National Requirement and must be accredited by the Federation in order for their graduates to be eligible for law society admission programs.[54] This is not to say that law schools did not have to go through an accreditation process previously.[55] But the new process is centralized under the umbrella of the Federation and the standards it utilizes are uniform across the country. The National Requirement specifies the various competencies that must be demonstrated while in law school. These include numerous skills including research and communication, an understanding and awareness of ethics and professionalism, and substantive legal knowledge.[56] Several law schools have already had to modify their curricula in order to ensure compliance with the National Requirement, particularly regarding the mandatory ethics and professionalism component.[57] Though some may see the National Requirement as an encroachment on traditional law school turf, its implementation has generally—though not entirely—been rather smooth.[58] This is likely due to the fact that law school deans had been consulted on the drafting of the National Requirement, law schools were generally given leeway in choosing how to teach the various competencies, and for the most part, complying with the National Requirement did not require a radical change to the curriculum.[59] The National Requirement does, how-

---

[53] *Canadian Law School Programs*, FED'N OF LAW SOC'YS OF CAN., http://docs.flsc.ca/national-initiatives/canadian-law-school-programs/ (last visited June 18, 2017); NAT'L REQUIREMENT (FED'N OF LAW SOC'YS OF CAN. 2011), http://flsc.ca/wp-content/uploads/2014/10/National-Requirement-2011.pdf.

[54] *Id.*

[55] *See generally* LAW SOC'Y OF UPPER CAN., CONSULTATION REPORT OF THE LICENSING AND ACCREDITATION TASK FORCE (2008), http://www.lsuc.on.ca/media/licensing.pdf.

[56] *See* NAT'L REQUIREMENT at §§ 1.1-1.3, 2.1, 3.1-3.3.

[57] *See, e.g.,* Kent Kuran, *Law Societies Introduce New Requirements*, ULTRA VIRES (Oct. 30, 2013), http://ultravires.ca/2013/10/law-societies-introduce-new-requirements/.

[58] For criticism of the competencies outlined in the National Requirement, *see*, Constance Backhouse, *The "Approved" Common Law Degree*, 3 CAN. LEGAL EDUC. ANN. REV. 141 (2009); Annie Rochette et al., *Respone to the Consultation Paper of the Task Force on the Canadian Common Law Degree of the Federation of Law Societies of Canada*, CAN. LEGAL EDUC. ANN. REV. 151 (2009), https://papers.ssrn.com/so13/papers.cfm?abstract_id=2102596.

[59] *See generally* FED'N OF LAW SOC'YS OF CAN. TASK FORCE ON CAN. COMMON LAW DEGREE, CONSULTATION PAPER (2008), http://docs.flsc.ca/Common-Law-Degree-Consultation-Paper-2008.pdf.

ever, serve as a baseline for all Canadian law schools and forces a heightened level of uniformity in legal education, all under the auspices of the Federation.

III. Part 3: The Regulation of Lawyers

The Federation has also been the center of activity for a number of national initiatives that have a direct impact on the regulation of lawyers. These efforts have become the main building blocks of a much greater level of uniformity in the Canadian legal profession. The initiatives include mobility agreements, a model code of professional conduct, and national discipline standards.[60]

A. Mobility Agreements

Mobility and uniformity go hand in hand: increased mobility—whether actual or desired—creates the need for more uniformity, and increased uniformity enables greater mobility. In 2002, building upon a previous and simpler mobility agreement,[61] the National Mobility Agreement[62] was signed and implemented under the auspices of the Federation. All provincial law societies signed the agreement and, by so doing, recognized that it was "desirable to facilitate a nationwide regulatory regime for the inter-jurisdictional practice of law to promote uniform standards and procedures"[63] while still maintaining each law society's exclusive authority. The stated purpose of the agreement was to "facilitate temporary and permanent mobility of lawyers between Canadian jurisdictions."[64] The agreement achieved this by allowing lawyers licensed in one common law province to practice for up to one hundred days per year in another ("temporary mobility")[65] and by allowing lawyers in one common law province to become regular members of the law society of another with little hassle—passing a new bar examination is not required ("permanent mobility").[66] In 2006, the Territorial Mobility Agreement[67] extended permanent mobility rights to Canada's three territories.

---

[60] *National Initiatives, supra* note 11.

[61] Inter-Jurisdictional Practice Protocol, Federation of Law Societies of Can., Feb. 18, 1994, https://www.lawsociety.bc.ca/Website/media/Shared/docs/becoming /IJP-Protocol.pdf.

[62] National Mobility Agreement, *supra* note 45.

[63] *Id*. at 2.

[64] *Id.*

[65] *Id.* at cl. 7.

[66] *Id.* at cl. 32-33.

[67] Territorial Mobility Agreement, Federation of Law Societies of Can., Nov. 3, 2006, https://www.lawsociety.bc.ca/Website/media/Shared/docs/becoming/mobility-agreement_territorial.pdf. This initial Territorial Mobility Agreement was in place for five years. A 2011 agreement renewed the Territorial Mobility Agreement without a termination date. *See* Territorial Mobility Agreement, Federation of Law Societies of Can., Dec. 2011, https://flsc.ca/wp-content/uploads/2014/10/mobility3.pdf.

Though Barreau du Québec—the law society governing lawyers in Quebec—was a signatory to the 2002 National Mobility Agreement, all other signatories recognized that the particular realities of Quebec would entail a delayed and different implementation. As noted above, Quebec is Canada's only civil law jurisdiction. In 2010, the Quebec Mobility Agreement[68] brought Quebec into the mobility regime, and in 2012, an addendum to this agreement extended mobility rights to Quebec notaries.[69] These agreements did not open the doors as fully as between the common law provinces. The agreements allowed lawyers in common law jurisdictions to acquire certain restricted practice rights if they wished to practice in Quebec and vice-versa by creating a so-called "Canadian Legal Advisor" regime.[70] These restrictions only allowed transferring members to practice in areas of federal law, the law of their home jurisdiction, and public international law.[71]

The mobility agreements noted above are still in force today. In 2013, however, all Canadian law societies agreed on a new National Mobility Agreement[72] that will, when implemented, permit lawyers to transfer with ease between all provinces, including Quebec, regardless of whether they are trained in Canadian common law or civil law. Under this new mobility agreement, the Canadian Legal Advisor regime will be eliminated except regarding Quebec notaries.[73] The overarching principle of the new agreement is that lawyers can only practice in areas of the law in which they are competent. The 2013 National Mobility Agreement will come into effect only once implemented by each law society and will replace all previous mobility agreements.[74]

---

[68] Quebec Mobility Agreement, Federation of Law Societies of Can., MAR. 19, 2010, http://flsc.ca/wp-content/uploads/2014/10/mobility5.pdf.

[69] Quebec Mobility Agreement, Addendum to Extend Mobility Rights to Members of the Chambre des notaires du Québec (Chamber of Notaries of Quebec), Federation of Law Societies of Can., Mar. 15, 2012, https://flsc.ca/wp-content/uploads/2014/10/mobility6.pdf. In Quebec, there exists a distinct difference between a lawyer and a notary, the latter having generally received the same training, but specializing in matters such as wills, real estate transactions and family law. A notary cannot represent a client in contested matters. *See* Kay, *supra* note 2.

[70] *National Mobility Agreement of Legal Profession: Quebec Mobility Agreement & Addendum*, FED'N OF LAW SOC'YS OF CAN., http://flsc.ca/national-initiatives/national-mobility-of-the-legal-profession/ (last visited June 18, 2017).

[71] *Id.*

[72] National Mobility Agreement 2013, Federation of Law Societies of Can., OCT. 17, 2013, https://flsc.ca/wp-content/uploads/2014/10/mobility7.pdf. This agreement extended to Canada's three territories through an agreement signed in early 2014. Territorial Mobility Agreement 2013, Federation of Law Societies of Can., Apr. 3, 2014, http://flsc.ca/wp-content/uploads/2014/10/mobility4.pdf.

[73] *Id.* at cl. 43.

[74] *See id.* at cl. 2, 52-53.

The signing of this new National Mobility Agreement is an extremely important milestone in Canadian legal regulation. The existence of two legal regimes, common law, and civil law, in one country has long been seen as a barrier for national regulatory uniformity. By signing this new and expansive national agreement, Canadian law societies have recognized that "there are more similarities in legal training and in daily practice in Canada's two legal traditions of common and civil law, than there are differences."[75]

The impetus behind the desire for enhanced mobility within Canada is most likely a multi-faceted one. Among these facets, one could point to the declining importance of borders and barriers, the desire of lawyers, like other workers, to be free to move around the country as they please, the reality that some lawyers were already doing cross-jurisdictional work who would benefit from formal regulation, the increasing presence of national and international law firms that handle cross-border matters, and an increased—though still very limited in Canada—internationalization of the practice of law. Regardless, it is clear the mobility agreements have broken down barriers between Canada's provincial and territorial jurisdictions and have become the catalyst for other national standards initiatives undertaken by the Federation, including a model code of professional conduct and national discipline standards.

B. Model Code of Professional Conduct

A written code of professional conduct is a *sine qua non* for modern Canadian lawyer regulation. Though some critics do exist,[76] written codes have been around for such a long time that they are generally seen as a necessary feature of the profession. The existence of written codes does not, however, date back as far as the existence of law societies. The first written code of professional conduct in Canada can be traced back to the Canons of Legal Ethics, adopted as a model code in 1920 by the Canadian Bar Association.[77] The Canadian Bar Association amended and updated its model code for many decades, and it served as the basis for many codes of professional conduct in Canadian provinces and territories.[78] As time went on, a

---

[75] *New National Mobility Agreement Bridges Common Law and Civil Law Traditions*, FED'N OF LAW SOC'YS OF CAN., (Oct. 22, 2013) http://flsc.ca/new-national-mobility-agreement-bridges-common-law-and-civil-law-traditions/.

[76] *See, e.g.,* Margaret Ann Wilkinson et al., *Do Codes of Ethics Actually Shape Legal Practice?,* 45 McGILL L.J. 645, 678-80 (2000).

[77] Adam M. Dodek, *Canadian Legal Ethics: Ready for Twenty-First Century at Last,* 46 OSGOODE HALL L. J. 1, 4 (2008).

[78] MERVIN D. ABRAMOWITZ & ISIDA RANXI, PRACTICE MANAGEMENT AND RULES OF PROFESSIONAL CONDUCT 10, http://www.krmc-law.com/1Rules-of-Conduct-Paper.pdf (last visited June 18, 2017).

certain level of uniformity became apparent among the jurisdictions in light of this model code, but many differences still existed. The Canadian Bar Association is, after all, an association of Canadian lawyers and not an association of Canadian law societies. This meant that the law societies did not have a direct formal role in shaping the Canadian Bar Association's model code. Accordingly, some jurisdictions adopted a slightly amended version of the model code while others adopted more radically modified versions.

In 2009, the Federation adopted its own Model Code of Professional Conduct (Model Code)[79] to harmonize the codes of conduct across Canada. Because this was a Federation initiative, the law societies now had a direct say in the drafting of the Model Code. The purpose of the Model Code is to set out common ethical principles and expected minimum standards of conduct "so that the public can expect the same high ethical standards to apply to the legal profession everywhere in Canada."[80] The Federation treats the Model Code as "a living document that must remain contemporary and reflect changes in the law."[81] Indeed, the Model Code is permanently monitored by a Standing Committee that has not shied away from recommending changes to it as needed.[82]

The Model Code is a nearly 120-page document that covers both general and specific ethical issues that may arise in practice. It deals with the lawyer's relationship to clients,[83] the administration of justice,[84] employees,[85] the law society and other lawyers.[86] It addresses quality of service,[87] confidentiality,[88] conflicts of interest,[89] and marketing,[90] among other issues. It is meant to be a complete code of pro-

---

[79] Model of Code of Prof'l Conduct (Fed'n of Law Soc'ys of Can. 2016), http://flsc.ca/wp-content/uploads/2014/10/Model-Code-as-amended-march-2016-FINAL.pdf.

[80] *From Conference to the Nation's Capital, supra* note 9.

[81] *Consultations Begin on Amendments to Model Code of Professional Conduct*, Fed'n of Law Soc'ys of Can. (July 16, 2014), http://flsc.ca/consultations-begin-on-amendments-to-model-code-of-professional-conduct/.

[82] *See, e.g., Consultations Begin on Model Code Amendments,* Fed'n of Law Soc'ys of Can. (Feb. 2, 2017), https://flsc.ca/consultations-begin-on-model-code-amendments/.

[83] Model Code of Prof'l Conduct at c 3.

[84] *Id.* at cl 5.

[85] *Id.* at cl 6.

[86] *Id.* at cl 7.

[87] *Id.* at § 3.2.

[88] *Id.* at § 3.3.

[89] *Id.* at § 3.4.

[90] *Id.* at cl. 4.

fessional conduct, not just a backbone onto which individual law societies need to tack on other important matters.

The Model Code has now been approved and implemented, with some changes, by all law societies in Canada, except the Barreau du Quebec and the law society regulating notaries in Quebec.[91] Again, things were understandably a bit slower to occur in Quebec, but the new 2015 Quebec Code of Professional Conduct of Lawyers is generally in line with the Federation's Model Code although the presentation and format are somewhat different.[92] The Chambre des notaires du Quebec is reviewing the Model Code.[93] Implementation of the Model Code across Canada means that almost all lawyers in the country are now subject to codes of conduct that are nearly identical or that at least present very few significant differences.

C. National Discipline Standards

As noted above, the power to discipline lawyers is a fundamental power of law societies. Coming on the heels of the 2009 Model Code and the new 2013 National Mobility Agreement, a set of National Discipline Standards[94] was adopted by all law societies in 2014 for implementation in 2015. The National Discipline Standards were "established to raise the bar on how law societies carry out discipline functions, and how complaints are handled."[95] According to the Federation, they were "designed to inspire public confidence in this important aspect of law society work across Canada."[96] The standards are based on the premise that, in a world with increased lawyer mobility, consumers of legal services across Canada should be able to count on a basic level of service and accountability from the law societies that are supposed to be regulating the providers of those legal services.

The standards aim to ensure that members of the public are treated promptly, fairly, and openly by setting out both a number of specific benchmarks and a number of general principles to which law societies are to adhere. For example, the standards spell out rather specific targets on items such as the timeliness of responses to inquiries and written complaints, including a timeline to resolve or refer a com-

---

[91] *See Implementation of the Model Code*, FED'N OF LAW SOC'YS OF CAN., http://flsc.ca/resources/implementation-of-the-model-code/ (last updated Nov. 15, 2016).

[92] *See id.; see also* Code of Professional Conduct of Lawyers, C.Q.L.R. c B-1, r.3.1, (Can.), http://legisquebec.gouv.qc.ca/en/ShowDoc/cr/B-1,%20r.%203.1.

[93] *Implementation of the Model Code, supra* note 91.

[94] NAT'L DISCIPLINE STANDARDS, *supra* note 94, (FED'N OF LAW SOC'YS OF CAN. 2016), http://flsc.ca/wp-content/uploads/2014/10/DisciplineStandardsJune2016.pdf.

[95] *Federation Adopts National Standards for Discipline Process*, FED'N OF LAW SOC'YS OF CAN. (April 7, 2014), http://flsc.ca/federation-adopts-national-standards-for -discipline-process/.

[96] *Id.*

plaint.[97] The standards also touch on broader principles such as public participation[98] and transparency.[99]

But the National Discipline Standards are not as extensive as one would perhaps expect. The standards are only a few pages long and do not address many procedural and substantive issues that arise in the context of complaint and disciplinary processes. Differences in the current processes used by law societies may provide an explanation for this. But as is the case for the Model Code, the Federation established a Standing Committee on National Discipline Standards,[100] and so it may be that the standards will become more extensive over time. But even in their current form, the National Discipline Standards are yet another example of a Federation initiative that moves law societies toward greater uniformity.

IV. Part 4: Transnational Lawyering

As mentioned above, law societies have been granted a monopoly on the provision of legal services within their jurisdictions. It is law societies that decide who gets to practice law, and they have the power to seek court orders to prohibit any unauthorized practice of law and fine any individual involved.[101] The Federation's national regulatory initiatives have gone a long way toward breaking down most barriers between provinces and territories within Canada. The same, however, cannot be said regarding lawyers from other countries. Of course, it is possible for a foreign-trained lawyer to become a member of a Canadian law society. The Federation's National Committee on Accreditation[102] is the entity that "assesses the legal education credentials of individuals trained outside of Canada . . . who intend to apply for admission to a [Canadian] law society." This process will often require the applicant to complete law school courses or pass several examinations, or both.[103] Accordingly, it is meant to serve as a process of admission to a Canadian law soci-

---

[97] *See* NAT'L DISCIPLINE STANDARDS, *supra* note 94 at para. 1-3.

[98] *Id.* at para. 10-11.

[99] *Id.* at para. 12-17.

[100] *National Discipline Standards: Frequently Asked Questions*, FED'N OF LAW SOC'YS OF CAN., http://fisc.ca/wp-content/uploads/2014/10/NDSFAQpublicE.pdf (last visited June 19, 2017).

[101] *See, e.g.*, Law Society Act, R.S.O. 1990, c L.8, ss 26.1, 26.2 (Can.).

[102] Federation of Law Societies of Canada, *National Committee on Accreditation (NCA)*, FEDERATION OF LAW SOCIETIES OF CANADA (2016), http://flsc.ca/national-committee-on-accreditation-nca/.

[103] *About the NCA*, FED'N OF LAW SOC'YS OF CAN., http://flsc.ca/national-committee-on-accreditation-nca/about-the-nca/ (last visited June 19, 2017).

ety on a permanent basis. For short-term or temporary practice, however, Canada remains essentially a closed shop.

A recent case from Alberta serves as a good illustration of this. In *Lameman v Alberta*,[104] the Plaintiffs, a group of Aboriginal Canadians, claimed that the government had "infringed their treaty rights by taking up [too] much of their traditional territory." Because the Plaintiffs could not afford legal fees, certain lawyers from Tooks Chambers in the United Kingdom offered to provide services on a pro bono basis.[105] The Court was asked to allow the Tooks lawyers, who were not members of the Law Society of Alberta, to represent the Plaintiffs in the legal proceedings.[106]

The Court reviewed s. 106 of the Alberta Legal Profession Act,[107] which quite clearly prohibits individuals who are not members of the Law Society of Alberta from practicing in the province. According to the Plaintiffs, however, some flexibility was warranted under the Alberta Rules of Court.[108] These rules provide that a Court "may permit a person to assist a party before the Court in any manner and on any terms and conditions the Court considers appropriate."[109] The Plaintiffs argued that the prohibition regarding the unauthorized practice of law contained in the Legal Profession Act would not be violated because even though the Tooks lawyers would be doing the bulk of the work involved in the legal proceedings, they would be controlled and supervised by Alberta lawyers who would technically still be the lawyers on the file.[110]

In siding with the Law Society of Alberta, which had the status of intervenor in the case, the Court refused to interpret the Alberta Rules of Court in such a broad fashion.[111] The Court found that the proposed involvement of the Tooks lawyers, which was to include questioning of witnesses and advocacy before the Court, would amount to practicing law and would therefore breach the Legal Profession Act.[112] In so ruling, the Court explained that the purpose of the law is to "ensur[e], among other things, that lawyers practicing in Alberta [are] competent and proficient, adequately insured . . . and bound by the [Alberta Code of Professional Conduct]."[113]

---

[104] Lameman v Alberta, 2011 ABQB 396, 521 A.R. 99 (Can. Alta.), judgment upheld on appeal, Lameman v Alberta, 2012 ABCA 59, 348 D.L.R. 4th 45 (Can. Alta.)(Hereinafter *Lameman ABCA*).

[105] *Id.* at para. 14.

[106] *Id.* at para. 19.

[107] *See* Legal Profession Act, R.S.A. 2000, c L-8, s 106(1) (Can. Alta.).

[108] *See Lameman,* 2011 ABQB 396 at para 21.

[109] *Id.*, rule 2.23.

[110] *Lameman,* 2011 ABQB 396 at para 20.

[111] *See id.* at para. 43.

[112] *See id.* at paras. 36, 41.

[113] *Id.* at para. 37.

On appeal, the Plaintiffs' main argument was that the Tooks lawyers would not be remunerated and argued that unpaid work should not be caught by the Legal Profession Act's prohibition on legal work done by non-lawyers.[114] The Court was of the view that access to justice "is an important social value, but not the only one."[115] According to the Court, "[t]he prime aim of the Legal Profession Act . . . is to protect the public from incompetent or unethical lawyers or advocates,"[116] and the fact that the Tooks lawyers were not going to be paid by the Plaintiffs changed nothing.

Some have criticized the ruling in *Lameman* by asking whether the monopoly enjoyed by lawyers in Alberta—and, by extension, everywhere in Canada—really needs to be as extensive as it presently is. In reviewing the risks and benefits of the particular facts in *Lameman*, these critics argue that the latter outweigh the former, and that the concerns expressed by the Court are not as applicable when dealing with foreign lawyers like those from Tooks who are likely to be able to provide very competent and needed service, who are bound by codes of conduct that are similar to Alberta's, and who likely have sufficient resources to cover any professional negligence claims.[117] These critics are calling for "a more nuanced or careful approach to the provision of legal services, in which consumer and public interests are protected, but the availability of competent and helpful legal advice is not irrationally restricted."[118] But so far, such criticism has not led to any substantial reexamination of Canadian law societies' authority, nor has it affected the monopoly currently enjoyed by Canadian lawyers.

V. Conclusion

There is no question that national regulatory uniformity in the legal sphere is on the rise in Canada. In the last few years, the Federation's national coordinating function has been stronger than ever. The Federation has so far succeeded where other attempts at national regulation in other spheres have so far failed.[119] This phenomenon of uniformity in the legal regulatory context should not, however, be seen as a wholesale rejection of the pre-existing model of self-regulation or an admission of

---

[114] Lameman v. Alta, 2012 ABCA 59 at para. 15 (Can., Alta. C.A.).

[115] *Id.* at para. 21.

[116] *Id.* at para. 17.

[117] *See, e.g.,* Alice Woolley, *Unauthorized practice and access to justice*, U. of Calgary Faculty of Law (Aug. 3, 2011), http://ablawg.ca/2011/08/03/unauthorized-practice-and-access-to-justice/.

[118] *Id.*

[119] There has been an attempt, for many years, now, to create a national securities regulator in Canada to unite "provincial laws for the capital markets," so far without success. Alastair Sharp, *Canada National Securities Regulator Delayed Until 2018*, REUTERS CAN. (July 22, 2016, 2:26 PM)), http://ca.reuters.com/article/businessNews/idCAKCN102274.

failure on the part of its main actors—the law societies. In fact, the new approach can be understood as furthering the very same goals to achieve the very same advantages as before all the while enabling increased mobility for the benefit of both lawyers and the public they serve. As such, it is also a further recognition of the increasing irrelevance of borders in a country that encourages the free movement of people. Perhaps more importantly, it can be viewed as a self-imposed exercise in modernization to prevent the erosion of the self-regulation model as seen in other countries. From that perspective, the Federation's national initiatives are an attempt to be proactive and to better serve the public so that self-regulation will be preserved. The law societies may be making the wager that voluntarily accepting a bit of dilution of self-regulation now will assist in preventing an imposed radical dilution later. One could therefore view the phenomenon of national regulatory uniformity with a skeptical eye, but to the extent that it allows law societies to better fulfill their fundamental role of regulating the legal profession in the public interest, it should generally be applauded.

CHAPTER 4

THE REGULATION OF LEGAL EDUCATION AND THE LEGAL PROFESSION IN MEXICO: AN ONGOING BATTLE

By Ximena Medellín Urquiaga[1]

During the past forty years, Mexico has experienced a process of modernization and openness to external actors. It has become an enthusiastic participant in different international fora, actively promoting globalization in political, social, and economic spheres. Mexico has also updated its own national legal system in order to become more competitive and attractive to foreign investment. Structural constitutional reforms have combined with international agreements, transparency laws, and institutional building in areas such as human rights, electoral processes, and economic competition. The overall image is of a healthy and sustainable state, with a solid juridical framework, and a thriving legal community.

Despite these positive developments, Mexico is a country where inequalities still permeate all aspects of its social, political, and economic life. Inequalities also affect the legal profession, seriously endangering individual rights of access to justice, due process guarantees, and ultimately, *Estado de Derecho*.

For example, during a recent Congressional hearing on the regulation of lawyers it was argued that the quality of legal services can substantially fluctuate from one legal field to another.[2] There are also noticeable variations in opportunities to access qualified legal representation throughout different regions in the country.[3] Clients in

---

[1] Assistant Professor of Law at Centro de Investigación y Docencia Económicas (CIDE), Mexico City. Coordinator of the Law Degree Program at CIDE.

[2] Public congressional hearing on the Promotion of Quality Legal Professional Services, PDF format, http://www.senado.gob.mx/comisiones/puntos_constitucionales/docs/Audiencias/AudienciasPD_version090915.pdf (last visited October 20, 2016).

[3] *Id.*

Mexico City may have a greater choice from among a wide range of professionals. This may not be the case in other states and even less so in rural communities.[4] There can also be a sharp difference in professional fees associated with, but not necessarily correlated to, the quality of legal services. Good lawyers will normally be more expensive, leaving vast sectors of the population without adequate representation. Bearing in mind the intricate nature of the Mexican legal system, the lack of legal assistance has become a serious obstacle to access justice for most people.

Amid an ongoing debate on the regulation of lawyers in Mexico, this paper explores some relevant features of the juridical framework governing both legal education and legal practice. In particular, this paper analyzes the possible relationship between such regulation and some prevailing problems with legal services in Mexico. The paper does not suggest that regulation is the sole determining factor of the said problems; rather it argues that regulation can be an influential element. Thus, debates on social conflicts associated with the operation of the legal system ought to consider how the ways in which lawyers are regulated can perpetuate shortcomings and exacerbate such conflicts.

The paper is divided in four main sections. The first is devoted to analyzing the regulation of legal education. This section also includes a general review of the current state of law schools in Mexico. The second section is focused on regulation of the legal profession. It also explores some current debates on reform of the legal framework for regulating lawyers. The third section offers some general information about the Mexican regulation on transnational lawyering. The last section presents some general conclusions.

I. Regulation of Legal Education in Mexico

Recent academic studies have examined in detail the development of legal education in Mexico over the last forty years.[5] This paper does not attempt to duplicate those studies, but rather aims at connecting some problems associated with legal education in Mexico to its legal framework. The premise is that the rules governing

---

[4] *Id.*

[5] *See, e.g.*, Ayllón, Sergio López y Fix-Fierro, Hector, "Cambio jurídico y autonomía del derecho: un modelo de la transición jurídica en México," Estado de derecho y transicion juridical, 2002; Serna de la Garza, José María y Juarez, José Antonio Caballero, "Estado de derecho y transición jurídica," Universidad Nacional Autonoma de Mexico, 2002, p. 112; Ayllón, Sergio López y Fix-Fierro, Hector, "'¡Tan cerca, tan lejos!' Estado de derecho y cambio jurídico en México (1970-2000, UNAM, 2000); Fix Fierro, Hector, "Culturas Jurídicas Latinas de Europa y América en Tiempos de Globalización," 2003, p. 565; Lever, Lorenza Villa, "Modernización de la educación superior, alternancia política y desigualdad en México," 2013, p.81; Ayllón, Sergio López y Fix-Fierro, Hector, "Del gobierno de los abogados al imperio de las leyes; estudios sociojurídicos sobre educación y profesión jurídicas en el México contemporáneo," 2006, p. 5; Hurtado, Luis Fernando Pérez, "Content, Structure, and Growth of Mexican Legal Education," JOURNAL OF LEGAL EDUCATION, May 2010.

legal education are inadequate to assure the appropriate operation of law schools. Given the importance of legal education, guaranteeing its quality is a social imperative. Deficiencies in the training of law students will negatively influence professional practice and, in turn, may perpetuate inherent problems of the legal system.

A. General Background

One distinctive characteristic of the Mexican context is the disproportion between the number of law schools and the total population. The Centro de Estudios sobre la Enseñanza del Derecho y el Aprendizaje del Derecho (Center for Studies on Legal Education and Law Learning) has estimated that in 2013 there was one law school for every 69,861 inhabitants.[6] Such disproportion is a direct consequence of the exponential increase in law schools established in Mexico during the past forty years. According to recent studies, in 1979 there were only ninety-seven law schools and 58,000 law students. Those same studies estimate that by 2003, the number of law schools had risen to 526 and, at the same time, the number of law students was close to 200,000.[7] This trend continued over the next decade.

Although there is no official database on the exact number of law schools currently operating in Mexico, at a recent Congressional hearing, the General Secretary of the Asociación Nacional de Unversidades e Instituciones de Educacion Superior–ANUIES (National Association of Universities) affirmed that by 2014-2015 there were approximately 945 public or private institutions legally entitled to issue law degrees. He also highlighted the stunning increase in the number of law students, which by the same period amounted to over 329,000.[8] But somewhat different figures have been presented by the Center for Studies on Legal Education and Law Learning. According to their analysis, by 2013 there were over 1,608 institutions offering a law degree and/or other equivalent degrees (such as international law and international commerce).[9] The same report concluded that around 95% of law

---

[6] Las escuelas de Derecho en México, Centro de Estudios sobre la Enseñanza y el Aprendizaje del Derecho, A.C., HTML format, http://www.ceead.org.mx/art%C3%ADculos-de-investigaci%C3%B3n.html (last visited September 20, 2016).

[7] Saavedra, Camilo, "Aprender la Constitución. Un análisis sobre la enseñanza del derecho constitucional en Mexico a partir de los planes de estudio de 25 instituciones de educación superior," REVISTA DEL CENTRO DE ESTUDIOS CONSTITUCIONALES, num. 2.

[8] Public congressional hearing on the Promotion of Quality Legal Professional Services, *supra* note 2.

[9] Las escuelas de Derecho en México, *supra* note 6. For a complete list of all relevant institutions identified by the Center for Studies on Legal Education and Law Learning, *see* http://www.ceead.org.mx/base-de-datos.html (last visited November 22, 2016).

schools currently operating in Mexico are private institutions.[10] On the other hand, the Center reported less students, in comparison with ANUIES's figures.[11]

This variation in numbers may be explained by methodological divergences. In the absence of an official database, it is difficult to conclude which of these figures is more accurate. This, of course, is a problem in itself. Nonetheless, there is an undeniable conclusion: Mexico has experienced a phenomenal increase in the number of law schools. The Center for Studies on Legal Education and Law Learning estimates that in the past ten years, three law schools have been established every week throughout Mexico.[12]

Some of the problems described above intensify because of a particularly formalistic approach to legal education that still prevails in most institutions. Law students are primarily expected to learn statutory rules and some binding judicial criteria established by federal courts.[13] In general, legal training does not focus on legal skills.[14] Such drift facilitates the operation of law schools that do not have the institutional or personnel capabilities to prepare students to address complex legal problems through innovative and effective arguments. Individuals with little preparation for the role of law professors can become responsible for teaching law students, despite their own professional or academic shortcomings.[15] Although there are some ongoing debates about the need for a profound reform of legal education in Mexico, concrete

---

[10] *See* Public congressional hearing on the Promotion of Quality Legal Professional Services, *supra* note 2; Hurtado, *Content, Structure and Growth of Mexican Legal Education*, *supra* note 5, at 567.

[11] Las escuelas de Derecho en México, *supra* note 6.

[12] *Id.*

[13] A particular characteristic of the Mexican legal system is the concept of *jurisprudencia*, as an autonomous source of law, different from and additional to statutory law and judicial decisions. Once a federal court has ruled over a constitutional remedy, it can select specific paragraphs or sections of the decision that contain relevant criteria. Then, such paragraphs become of public domain after been published in *Semanario Judicial de la Federación* (Federal Judicial Weekly Report). If the same criterion is used five or more times in different decisions by the same court, it becomes binding to all lower courts. A distinction between case-law and *jurisprudencia* is that the latter focuses only on the judicial criteria established by federal judges, without referencing the relevant facts of the case. Thus, *jurisprudence* becomes another abstract and general norm, similar to statutory law. For further information about Mexican *jurisprudencia*, *see* for instance, José María Serna de la Garza, *The concept of* jurisprudencia *in Mexican law* 131 (Mexican Law Review I-2, 2009).

[14] López Ayllón and Fix-Fierro, *¡Tan cerca, tan lejos!*, *supra* note 5; Fix-Fierro, *et. al.*, *Culturas Jurídicas Latinas de Europa y América en Tiempos de Globalización*, *supra* note 5.

[15] *Id.*

initiatives are still isolated efforts by specific institutions.[16] Furthermore, there is no consensus on what such reform should mean or include. Thus, reform of legal education has not been a focal point in the current debate surrounding the legal profession. The unfortunate result is a progressive deterioration of the very foundation for the operation of any legal system: the capabilities of its own lawyers and judges.

B. Regulation of Legal Education in Mexico

The problems associated with legal education in Mexico may be at least partially located in the governing regulatory regime. As a starting point, it is important to emphasize that there is no specific national or state legislation on legal education. Instead, such matters are regulated by general norms on higher professional education.

The basic requirement to operate a law school in Mexico is incorporation to the Sistema Nacional Educativo (National Education System), as defined by the Ley General de Educación (National Education Act).[17] All public universities become part of the system immediately after they are established by law. On the other hand, in order to be incorporated to the National Educational System, private institutions must apply to the General Office for Professional Practice at the Ministry of Education for *reconocimiento de validez oficial de estudios* (official recognition of valid studies).[18] In general terms, only those institutions which are members of said system can issue valid degrees in professional occupations, including law.[19]

Formal requirements to obtain an official recognition of valid studies are fairly general and they are applicable to all forms of private education, from primary schools to professional programs. According to article 55 of the National Education Act, applicants must prove they have (i) qualified personnel; (ii) appropriate facilities which can meet health, security, and "pedagogical" needs; and (iii) curricula deemed adequate by federal or state authorities. In practice, assessment of the relevant requirements is mostly a perfunctory process, with no substantive evaluation of the institutional capabilities to train individuals in specific professional fields.

---

[16] *See, e.g.,* Magaloni, Ana Laura, Cuellos de Botella y Ventanas de Oportunidad de la Reforma a la Educación Jurídica en México de Élite; Héctor Fix-Fierro, Del Gobierno de los Abogados al Imperio de las Leyes. Estudios sociojurídicos sobre educación y profesión jurídicas en el México contemporáneo, 1a ed., Mexico, Universidad Nacional Autonoma de Mexico, 2006.

[17] Ley General de Educación [LGE] art. 10, Diario Oficial de la Federacion [DOF] 13-7-1993, últimas reformas DOF 22-03-2017 Mex.).

[18] *Id.* at art. 54.

[19] For further details on the legal framework governing creation and operation of law schools in Mexico, *see* Luis Fernando Pérez Hurtado, *Content, Structure, and Growth of Mexican Legal Education* 567 (Journal of Legal Education, May 2010).

Authorization is limited to individual programs in specific localities.[20] In other words, private institutions will have to apply for an independent official recognition of valid studies for every single program, in each campus.

Once an institution has obtained official recognition of valid studies, a non-binding periodic evaluation is left to a private association: The Consejo para la Acreditación de la Educación Superior—COPAES (Council for Accreditation of Higher Education).[21] This Council has a specific branch for law schools, known as the Consejo Nacional para la Acreditación de la Educación Superior en Derecho—CONAED (National Council for Accreditation of Higher Law Education). Accreditation by this organization is based on a self-evaluation process. Law schools must submit a work plan and complete a questionnaire designed by the Council.[22] Payment of relevant fees is also a *sine qua non* requirement. In addition to the self-evaluation questionnaire, the accreditation process before CONAED includes the participation of an external review panel. The Council will convene this panel from a predetermined pool of lawyers (not necessarily law professors), in order to assess specific aspects of the questionnaire. There is no detailed public information about the external review panel, nor about its composition or powers. Thus, it is difficult to predict how much participation or influence such a panel could have in a particular review process. From a transparency perspective, there should be enough public information to allow any person to assess the accreditation process before CONAED. Without this, there is a greater risk of manipulation and discretion on the process.

But as previously mentioned, evaluation before the Council is not legally required for the operation of a law school.[23] Currently, the Council has only certified

---

[20] Ley General de Educación, *supra* note 17.

[21] *See* COUNCIL FOR ACCREDITATION OF HIGHER EDUCATION, http://www.copaes.org/ (last visited Sept. 2016). The Council is the only private institution authorized by the Ministry of Interior to carry our evaluation process of universities and professional schools. It was created based on a recommendation of the National Association of Universities. The Ministry of Education, the National Association of Universities and other professional associations compose the Council's General Assembly, including the Mexican Bar Association. Such association is one of the most important lawyer's professional organizations in Mexico, although it is not the only one. Thus, its participation in the Council for Accreditation of Higher Education may provide a distinctive advantage, in comparison to other national or local professional associations for lawyers.

[22] *See* INSTRUMENTO DE AUTOEVALUACIÓN 2015, PDF format,http://www.conaed.org.mx/INSTRUMENTO%20DE%20AUTOEVALUACI%C3%93N%202015.pdf (last visited Sept. 2016).

[23] The accreditation process before the Council is different from evaluation before the Ministry of Education, as established in article 55 of the National Education Act. The latter is a one-time assessment, required in order to become part of the National Education System. On the other hand, evaluation by the Council is a periodic process, aiming at guaranteeing quality of education services.

sixty-one law schools out of the total universe of private and public institutions in Mexico.[24]

This general review of regulation of legal education in Mexico highlights some of its most fundamental problems. The unprecedented increase in the number of private law schools is directly related to legal requirements which are easy to meet and do not necessarily guarantee quality. Without a functional educational scheme, markets are flooded with lawyers who will replicate (and possibly aggravate) the system's characteristic inadequacies.

II. Regulation of the Legal Profession in Mexico

Lawyer regulation in Mexico is not a new phenomenon. In fact, there is a long history. In 1853, Federal Congress adopted a statute containing detailed regulation of all forms of legal practice.[25] These included judges, clerks, and lawyers. For practitioners, such as litigators, federal legislation ordered mandatory affiliation with professional associations.[26] It also established a form of professional certification by means of a rigorous examination by local or federal supreme tribunals. Despite its historic significance, the said federal statute emphasized qualifications required to practice law without addressing issues related to ongoing competence, disciplinary procedures, or accountability mechanisms.

In 1875, mandatory affiliation was terminated as a requirement for legal practice in Mexico. Nonetheless, the system continued allowing for the creation of voluntary professional associations. By 1970, there were three major national bar associations: (i) the Ilustre y Nacional Colegio de Abogados de México (1760); (ii) the Barra Mexicana, Colegio de Abogados (Mexican Bar Association) (1922); and (iii) the Asociación Nacional de Abogados de Empresas (National Association of Lawyers for Business) (1970). These national professional associations still exist today. They are complemented by an undetermined number of local organizations, created, and recognized by state law. But despite their long history, these lawyers' professional associations are widely perceived as primarily social networks, with little impact on the actual regulation of legal practice in Mexico. There is no official information on the total number of lawyers currently affiliated with national or local associations.

A. Current Regulation of Legal Practice in Mexico

Regulation of legal practice in Mexico is characterized by its fragmentation and incoherence. Different federal and local statues regulate specific aspects of the legal

---

[24] *See* INSTITUCIONES ACREDITADAS POR CONAED, HTML format, http://www.conaed. org.mx/ programas.html (last visited Oct. 2016).

[25] Ley para el arreglo de la administración de justicia, PDF format, http://bibliohistorico.juridicas.unam.mx/libros/2/999/34.pdf (last visited Sept. 2016).

[26] *Id.* at arts. 283-308.

profession.[27] At the same time, codes of ethics have been left to the realm of private organizations. Although the coexistence of multiple state and non-state regulators is not uncommon or necessarily problematic, there are conspicuous inconsistencies in how they operate. For example, crucial aspects of legal practice (such as exceptions to client-lawyer confidentiality or responsibility for negligent discharge of professional duties) are regulated with distinctively different standards in state law and private codes. This confusing scenario results in several contradictions and legal loopholes, which for all practical purposes, result in quasi-deregulated legal practice.

But there are some distinctive exceptions to this unfortunate state of affairs. Public notaries, as well as *corredores públicos* (commercial notaries), are subject to stricter regulation. These forms of legal practice entail *fe pública* (public faith) as a means of official certification of documents and legal transactions.[28] Public notaries are even empowered to intervene in family law matters, including divorces. There is, therefore, an imperative public interest in regulating the exercise of such powers. A public notary's patent can be revoked based on breach of their obligations, thereby disqualifying particular individuals from ever again engaging in this form of practice.[29]

Beyond these exceptions, legal practice in Mexico is based on a licensing scheme. The foundation of such scheme is a law degree, which as I have explained, must be issued by a state university or a private institution with official recognition of validity of studies. The relevant diploma must be registered with the Ministry of Education. In turn, the Ministry will issue a formal accreditation of individual stud-

---

[27] Commonly, discussion, commentaries and analysis on professional practice in Mexico are only based or reference to the *Professional Practice Act for Mexico City*. Although this statute was indeed adopted by the Federal Congress, it is not a federal or national law. According the Mexican Constitution, Federal Congress has been vested with powers to pass legislation applicable within Mexico City. Nonetheless, as mentioned before, such legislation is not federal in nature. That would be a misconstruction of the Mexican legal system. In fact, there are thirty local acts on professional practices, adopted by the legislators in several Mexican states. None of them refer specifically to lawyering, but still define the general framework for practicing law in the country. Consequently, a detailed analysis on the regulation of the legal profession ought to consider all these statutes, not only the *Professional Practice Act for Mexico City*.

[28] *See, e.g.,* Ley del Notariado para el Distrito Federal, arts. 42, 166, Diario Oficial de la Federación [DOF]; Ley del Notariado del Estado de Jalisco, art. 80, Diario Oficial de la Federación [DOF]; Ley del Notariado del Estado de Michoacán, art. 3, Diario Oficial de la Federación [DOF]; Ley del Notariado del Estado de Puebla, arts. 11-13, Diario Oficial de la Federación [DOF].

[29] *See, e.g.,* Ley del Notariado para el Distrito Federal, *supra* note 28, at arts. 197, 229; Ley del Notariado del Estado de Jalisco, *supra* note 28, at arts. 154-156; Ley del Notariado del Estado de Michoacán, *supra* note 28, at arts. 113, 116; Ley del Notariado del Estado de Puebla, *supra* note 28, at arts. 142, 175.

ies by means of a *cédula profesional*. In broad terms, this identification card serves as official evidence of professional training in particular fields, not limited to law. The card assigns each professional a unique identification number, which should be referenced in all documents related to professional practice, including medical prescriptions, architectural blueprints, or lawsuits.

A *cédula profesional* is valid throughout Mexico. This means that lawyers can practice law without any jurisdictional limitations, even if the relevant degree was issued by a local institution or university. Lawyers do not have to prove actual knowledge of local law before intervening in legal matters in a particular state, despite the fact that state regulation in areas such as family or criminal law can vary substantially from jurisdiction to jurisdiction.

As mentioned previously, a *cédula profesional* is an equivalent to occupational licensing that does not require affiliation to a professional association to practice law throughout Mexico. In spite of the fact that lawyers in Mexico are not obliged to be part of a professional association, several local regulations of professional practice rely on them for important purposes. Depending on the jurisdiction, such associations may be empowered to set guidelines and criteria on issues such as: professional fees, conflicts of interest, justified abandonment of legal representation, marketing and advertising, and professional secrets and privilege. In other cases, local statutes (instead, or in addition to, private codes of ethics) govern these same matters, although with different standards.

Some specific examples may shed light on the practical implications of such normative disparity. With respect to professional secrets, some state statutes establish that professionals are obligated to keep in confidence all communications with their clients, with the exception "of mandatory reports required by law."[30] But in other local legislation, the exceptions to such obligations are significantly broader.[31] In addition to state law, codes of ethics of professional associations, which also set forth lawyer-client confidentiality rules, expand its scope to cover all communications with third parties and colleagues, without requiring direct connection with a

---

[30] Ley del Ejercicio Profesional de la Ciudad de México, art. 36, Diario Oficial de la Federacion [DOF]; Ley del Ejercicio Profesional del Estado de Jalisco, art. 8 §III, Diario Oficial de la Federación [DOF].

[31] According to article 42 of the *Ley del Ejercicio Profesional del Estado de Querétaro* (Professional Practice Act for Queretaro), professionals will not be obligated to keep in confidence any information transmitted by their clients if: (i) they are expressly dispensed by the client itself; (ii) the professional sufferers a grave and unjustified attack by its client and needs such information to defend its interests; (iii) there is a judicial decision. *See* Ley del Ejercicio Profesional del Estado de Querétaro, art. 42, Diario Oficial de la Federación [DOF].

client's business.[32] Such confusion is replicated in matters such as conflicts of interest or professional fees.[33]

In sum, the current regulation of professional practice in Mexico is fragmented to such a degree that it is dysfunctional. Relevant rules can be established in specific local statutes, codes of ethics, or additional criminal, civil, or procedural legislation. As a consequence, it is not easy to determine the scope of lawyers' obligations, or even rights, which are fundamental for the legitimate discharge of professional practice.

B. Lawyers' Responsibilities and Accountability Mechanisms

In addition to the articulation of substantive norms, the comprehensive regulation of legal practice must include specific forms of liability and/or responsibility, as well as enforcement or accountability mechanisms. In Mexico, those features are also affected by the system's inconsistencies and contradictions.

Mexican law does not provide any specific means of professional liability or disciplinary procedures. Conflicts related to legal practice, such as negligence, malpractice, or wrongdoing, can instead lead to criminal responsibility or civil liability. Lawyers responsible for breaching their legal obligations may be sanctioned with imprisonment, fines, or compensatory damages, but, in general, will not be barred from the practice law. In fact, in Mexico, no form of responsibility or liability can result in permanent disqualification. Only specific crimes can result in the temporal suspension of professional practice as punishment. Thus, even lawyers who may be found criminally responsible would still be able to practice law in the future. Likewise, because membership in a professional association is not mandatory, expulsion resulting from a breach of a code of ethics would not impair future practice.

Within this general framework, it is important to underline that some of the actions punishable under Mexican criminal law include: (i) knowingly submitting

---

[32] Código de ética de la Barra Mexicana, Colegio de Abogados, arts. 10 to 12 Diario Oficial de la Federación [DOF]; Código de ética de la Asociación Nacional de Abogados de Empresas, arts. 10 to 12, Diario Oficial de la Federación [DOF]. The Code of Ethics of the Ilustre y Nacional Colegio de Abogados de México sets different standards on this same matter. As set forth in article 2 §3, professional secret covers all communications and information transmitted by the client or third parties, as long as it refers to the client's business. In other words, there is no general rule of secrecy to all third parties or colleagues, as it is established in the codes of ethics of the other national professional associations. In addition, the Code of Ethics of the Ilustre y Nacional Colegio de Abogados de México includes two different exemptions to professional secret: (i) litigation on professional fees; and (ii) voluntary confession by the client on his/her intention to commit a crime in the future. Código de ética del Ilustre y Nacional Colegio de Abogados, art. 2 §3 Diario Oficial de la Federación [DOF].

[33] Ley del Ejercicio Profesional de la Ciudad de México, *supra* note 30, at arts. 31 and 32.

false evidence into court or alleging statutes which are not in force; (ii) attempting notoriously unfounded defenses or remedies; (iii) representing opposing parties at the same time or successively; (iv) unjustified abandonment of the legal representation of a client; and (v) failing to submit all relevant evidence in criminal cases.[34]

Although criminal procedure can be considered an accountability mechanism, it has not proven to be a particularly adequate instrument to protect clients' interests. Between 1997 and 2012, less than 1,500 lawyers were prosecuted at the federal or state level for offences related to their professional practice.[35] These figures represent only a minuscule percentage of the total number of lawyers practicing law in Mexico.

In addition, it is worth noticing that criminal law in Mexico is still dominated by the notion of corporal punishment as means of public retribution. Thus, compensatory reparations for victims of a crime are commonly relegated to a secondary place in criminal procedures. Despite recent constitutional and legislative reforms aiming to strengthen the role of victims within criminal procedure, in reality, clients may not obtain adequate compensation or integral reparation, in case of criminal professional wrongdoing by their lawyers.

Parallel to criminal law, Mexican federal and state law provides a civil action in a case where one person causes damage to another, as a direct result of the intentional or negligent conduct of the former.[36] This could potentially be an additional way to enforce a lawyer's responsibilities. But the client would have the burden of proof. Furthermore, it is important to stress that Mexican law normally limits civil remedies to compensatory damages. Only in exceptional cases, not related to professional responsibility, have courts ordered punitive damages.

It must also be noted that the codes of ethics of the Mexican Bar Association and the National Association of Lawyers for Business call for lawyers to spontaneously admit their negligence, malpractice or wrongdoings, to accept their responsibility, and to proceed to compensate any damages caused to clients.[37] In addition,

---

[34] Código Penal Federal [CPF], arts. 231-233, Diario Oficial de la Federación [DOF], 14-08-1931, últimas reformas DOF 23-01-2009 (Mex.). Since criminal law in Mexico is a concurrent jurisdiction, local criminal codes may include other offences specifically directed at lawyers.

[35] Encuesta Nacional de Victimización y Percepción sobre Seguridad Pública, PDF format, http://www.beta.inegi.mx/contenidos/proyectos/enchogares/regulares/envipw/2016/doc/en vipe2016_zac.pdf (last visited Sept. 2016).

[36] *See*, Código Civil Federal [CC], art. 1910, 31-08-1928, Diario Oficial de la Federación [DOF], últimas reformas DOF 24-12-2013 (Mex.); Código Civil para el Distrito Federal, art. 1910, 26-5-1928, Diario Oficial de la Federación [DOF].

[37] Código de ética de la Barra Mexicana, Colegio de Abogados, *supra* note 32, at art. 29; Código de ética de la Asociación Nacional de Abogados de Empresas, *supra* note 32, at art. 29.

the codes of ethics of the three national associations set forth the duty of every lawyer to notify the relevant association in the case of any professional misconduct by another lawyer.[38] Disciplinary procedures are only regulated in detail by the guidelines established by the Mexican Bar Association; none of the other associations has a similar document.[39] Nonetheless, according to the statute of the said association, its Board of Honor may entertain complaints against its members, the members of other professional associations, as well as the judiciary.[40] Sanctions may vary from a simple warning, temporary suspensions from the association, or recommendation to the General Assembly for definite expulsion.[41] There are not public resolutions or statistics regarding the actual number of lawyers that have been accused of breaching the code of ethics of a professional association. As private institutions, professional associations are not bound by the Mexican transparency law and, thus, are not obligated to make such information available to the public. On the contrary, they are legally obliged to protect all private data that may include information related to disciplinary procedures.

State legislative regimes also provide some means for accountability, although there are important disparities among them. The result is a checkerboard regulatory regime. For instance, according to article 40 of Professional Practice Act for Queretaro, all professionals are obligated to pay damages resulting from their inexperience, negligence, or wrongdoing, inter alia.[42] This law does not provide specific remedies, but only refers in general terms to judicial mechanisms and decisions.[43] On the other hand, the Professional Practice Act for Jalisco refers to arbitrational procedures in the case of "client's dissatisfaction."[44] It establishes rules on specific matters such as arbitrator selection and information, which must be considered when deciding a case.[45] Alternatively, the Professional Practice Act for Mexico City calls

---

[38] Código de ética de la Barra Mexicana, Colegio de Abogados (Code of ethics of the Mexican Bar Association), article 2; Código de ética de la Asociación Nacional de Abogados de Empresas, *supra* note 32, at art. 2; Código de ética del Ilustre y Nacional Colegio de Abogados, *supra* note 32, at art. 5.9.1.

[39] Reglamento de procedimientos para el trámite de quejas ante la Junta de Honor, Diario Oficial de la Federación [DOF].

[40] Estatutos de la Barra Mexicana de Abogados, art. 35, Diario Oficial de la Federación [DOF].

[41] *Id.* at art. 43.

[42] Ley De Profesiones Del Estado de Querétaro, art. 40, 03-08-2009, últimas reformas 05-10-2011.

[43] *Id.*

[44] Ley Para El Ejercicio de las Profesiones del Estado de Jalisco, art. 14,13-08-1974, últimas reformas 20-11-2012.

for the participation of an expert witness who would have to determine whether: (i) the professional acted in accordance to "scientific principles and applicable techniques generally accepted in a given profession;" (ii) given the particular characteristics of the case and circumstances, appropriate means were used to represent the client's interests; (iii) all appropriate measures were taken to guarantee a positive outcome; (iv) the professional devoted all necessary time to the case; and (v) there were any other special circumstances which could have negatively affected discharge of duties and quality of services.[46] While at first blush this might seem promising, it must be noted that the Professional Practice Act for Mexico City also establishes that if the case is ruled against the client, she or he will have to cover not only professional emoluments and court related expenses, but also may be ordered to compensate the professional for any damages to his or her public reputation.[47] In practice, such a norm can seriously hinder clients' actions. Considering the intrinsic information asymmetry between lawyers and clients, it could be difficult for the latter to prove any wrongdoing by the former.

In July 2015, the Mexican Supreme Court of Justice [SCJN] ruled over a case involving an alleged breach of contract and the payment of excessive emoluments with respect to the legal services rendered.[48] Previously, a lower federal court had upheld that the client's free will was impaired due to information asymmetry and, thus, the contract was void.[49] The SCJN took a different approach and argued that there was a collision between the right to equal protection before the law and free development of personality.[50] After considering the relevant facts, the SCJN concluded that there was not substantive disparity between the contracting parties (*i.e.*

---

[45] *Id.* at art. 18. According to this provision, when deciding a case arbitrators must consider if the professional (including but not limited to lawyers): (i) acted with efficiency in accordance with principles, systems, and criteria generally accepted in specific professional fields; (ii) used all adequate materials, instruments, and resources, based on specific characteristics of a case; (iii) adopted all reasonable measures to ensure a positive outcome; (iv) devoted necessary time to discharge his/her obligations; (v) acted based on any agreement reach with clients; and (vi) any other relevant information.

[46] Ley Reglamentaria Del Artículo 5o. Constitucional, Relativo Al Ejercicio de las Profesiones en el Distrito Federal, art. 34 §I, Diario Oficial de la Federación [DOF] 26-05-1945, últimas reformas 19-08-2010.

[47] *Id.* at art. 35. In general terms, this article establishes that if the arbitration decision or the judgment are averse to the professional, he/she will not be entitled to charge any fees and shall also compensate the client for damages sustained. Otherwise, the customer will pay the corresponding fees, court or conventional process expenses, as well as compensation for any damage on the professional's reputation. Other similar local statutes do not provide possible compensation to the professional.

[48] Amparo Directo 6055/2014, la Primera Sala de la Suprema Corte de Justicia de la Nación.

[49] *Id.*

[50] *Id.*

the client and her lawyers) that could justify a limitation to their contractual autonomy (as part of the right to free development of their personality).[51]

The fact that the case was finally decided based on constitutional law, instead of other rules governing the professional practice of lawyers, has important implications. The standard established by the SCJN may prove difficult to replicate in other cases, and it certainly does not answer some of the most pressing questions regarding the Mexican legal framework on legal professional services.

Beside this case, it is difficult to identify other relevant judicial decisions, either by the SCJN or by other federal courts. The lack of applicable precedents and clear judicial interpretation further complicates the operation of a regulatory scheme full of legal loopholes.

C. Current Debates on Regulation of the Legal Profession in Mexico

The lack of a comprehensive regulatory regime for the legal profession has led some practitioners and scholars to advocate for a complete renovation of the juridical framework governing lawyering in Mexico.[52] The key ideas were to (re)incorporate mandatory association and develop certification mechanisms.[53] The specific proposal was twofold. It included a series of constitutional amendments, as well as a national law regulating different aspects of lawyering.[54]

According to the proposed constitutional provisions, Federal Congress would be empowered to determine the conditions required for professional practice, including mandatory association, periodic certification, or occupational licensing.[55] Those same provisions would allocate to professional associations the role of governors of professional practice.[56] In order to achieve this outcome, article 28 of the Mexican Constitution would incorporate professional associations as an explicit exception to the constitutional anti-trust clause.[57] This regulation would not be limited to lawyers, but could also apply to other professions, if the Federal Congress so decided.[58]

---

[51] *Id.*

[52] *See, e.g.*, Oscar Cruz Barney, Una Ley General de la Abogacía Mexicana, 27 HECHOS Y DERECHO 2015, https://revistas.juridicas.unam.mx/index.php/hechos-y-derechos/article/view/7244/9180.

[53] Cervantes Andrade, Raúl, "Iniciativa con Proyecto de Decreto por el que se reforman los artículos 5o , 28 y 73 en materia de Colegiación y Certificación Obligatorias," GACETA DEL SENADO, vol. LXII, num. 2SPO-86/45808, Feb. 20, 2014, p. 1, *available at* http://infosen.senado.gob.mx/sgsp/gaceta/62/2/2014-02-20-1/assets/documentos/Inic_PRI_Reforma_Constitucional.pdf.

[54] *Id.* at 1, 6.

[55] *Id.* at 10.

[56] *Id.*

[57] *Id.* at 9.

In addition to these constitutional amendments, the new regulatory framework for legal practice in Mexico would be complemented by a national (general) law, called the Ley General de la Abogacía Mexicana (Mexican Lawyering Bill) [MLB].[59] Although advocates for the new system publicly presented a Bill of the said act, it was not formally submitted for legislative discussion in Congress. Nonetheless, this Bill became the focal point of public debates on the matter. Thus, it is important to examine some of its main features.

In contrast to current regulation, the MLB established a system based on mandatory affiliation to professional associations, as well as periodic certification through non-state institutions.[60] All lawyers in private practice would have to become members of a professional association in order to practice law.[61] This requirement would apply even if they were not representing clients in court, but only providing consultancy services.[62] In contrast, lawyers in the public sector, including prosecutors and public defenders, would be excluded from affiliation and certification requirements.

The MLB also defined some of the most relevant entities of the new scheme. In this regard, bar or professional associations of lawyers were described as private entities of public interest, which by means of individual affiliation group together, in a non-transitory way, those lawyers who exercise the legal profession.[63] According to the same MLB, the goal of these associations would be the improvement, monitoring, defense, and proper exercise of the profession, as means to protect the right of access to justice of all individuals.[64] The MLB also established a maximum number of professional associations permitted at the national and state level,[65] and it set forth specific requirements which any organization would have to meet in order to be recognized as national or local professional association.[66]

---

[58] *Id.*

[59] Ley General de la Abogacía Mexicana (2015), http://renace.org.mx/renace2015/wp-content/uploads/2015/12/Ley-General-de-la-Abogac%C3%ADa-Mexicana-PROYECTO-FINAL.pdf.

[60] *Id.* at art. 3.

[61] *Id.* at art. 56.

[62] *Id.* at art. 7.

[63] *Id.* at art. 25.

[64] *Id.* at arts. 26 and 27.

[65] Ley General de la Abogacía Mexicana, *supra* note 59, art. 41, 48. According to articles 41 and 48, there could be no more than five national bar associations and the same number of local bar associations of each of the 32 federal states.

[66] *Id.* at art. 39. Essential requirements for recognition as professional association (*colegio*) include: (i) evidence of service in favor of lawyering, such as scientific publications, seminars, training courses, conferences, and other academic activities; (ii) a code of ethics; and (iii) minimum number of members.

By law, professional associations would be authorized to take all necessary actions to fulfill their mandate. Those powers would include adopting norms governing professional practice of lawyers (such as codes of ethics),[67] as well as taking actions to defend their members' interests and rights before private and public actors.[68] In other words, professional associations would control and defend lawyers at the same time.

Furthermore, professional associations would be entitled to carry out disciplinary procedures and to sanction lawyers. According to the MLB, relevant sanctions may include: (i) a private and oral warning; (ii) a written warning; (iii) a recommendation to state institutions for disqualification from legal practice for a period not exceeding two years; or (iv) an expulsion from the relevant association, with a recommendation for revocation of the patent to exercise the corresponding administrative or judicial authority.[69]

In addition to professional associations, the MLB provided for the creation of certification agencies or entities. As well as professional associations, certification entities are private institutions of public interest.[70] In order to be recognized as a certification entity, private institutions must have certification plans and instruments, adequate facilities, material, and human resources as well as "economic support" (not financial resources) in the amount determined by the relevant authorities.[71]

In general terms, private lawyers would be required to undergo an initial certification process no more than five years after their affiliation to a professional association.[72] Afterwards, they would have to renew their professional certification every five years.[73] Lawyers would not be able to be recertified if their own professional association had sanctioned them.

A third relevant actor within the proposed scheme is the Comisión Interinstitucional de Colegiación y Certificación de la Abogacía (Interinstitutional Commission for the Association and Certification of Lawyering) [CICCA]. The main mandate of

---

[67] *Id.* at art. 26 §§ I, IV-V, 27 §§I-III, 30 to 32.

[68] *Id.* at art. 26 §VI, 26 §XIV, 26 §XVIII, 27 §IV. In accordance with articles 26 and 27, lawyer's professional associations would be responsible for (i) defending the rights and interests of their members (article 26 §VI); (ii) acting as mediators or arbitrators in conflicts among lawyers and/or between them and their clients (article 26 §XIV); (iii) sanctioning their members in case of any breach of their codes of ethics (article 26 §XVIII); and (iv) informing authorities of any illegal conduct carried out by one of their members (article 27 §IV), among others.

[69] *Id.* at art. 36.

[70] *Id.* at art. 71.

[71] Ley General de la Abogacía Mexicana, *supra* note 59, art. 72.

[72] *Id.* at art. 81.

[73] *Id.* at art. 80.

the Commission is to serve as a control mechanism for the certification entities.[74] In other words, the Commission would decide whether an entity had, in fact, the capabilities to certify lawyers as the MLB requires. The decision of the Commission would have to be confirmed by the General Office for Professional Practice at the Ministry of Education.[75]

The relationships among these various institutions are quite intricate. At the center of it are the professional associations. While such institutions can also function as certification entities, they may likewise intervene in the validation processes of other organizations as certifiers.[76] As mentioned before, they are also responsible for controlling, sanctioning, and representing lawyers in all matters related to professional practice.[77] In addition, professional associations could also participate in designing and reviewing law schools' curricula.[78]

A detailed review of the MLB reveals several key points. First, it is clear that professional associations would have a prominent place in the new scheme. They would not only be able to govern legal professional services in Mexico, but also to influence other important actors in the system, including the CICCA, the certification entities, and the law schools.[79] Second, it is worth emphasizing that most of the obligations established by the MLB refer to the relationship between lawyers and their professional association. Matters related to professional duties towards clients are loosely regulated. Presumably, those provisions would have to be complemented by new codes of ethics, issued by the different professional associations. Nonetheless, bearing in mind the current state of affairs, it would have been preferable to have more detailed regulation, at least in essential issues such as professional secrecy, emoluments, and conflict of interests.

D. The Anti-Trust Commission Opinion on Mandatory Affiliation

In February 2016, the Mexican Anti-Trust Commission issued an advisory opinion on the proposed constitutional amendment. As specified by the Commission, the scope of this opinion was limited to the proposal's possible effect on the behavior of

---

[74] *Id.* at art. 7 §V.

[75] Id. at art. 10 §I.b.

[76] *Id.* at art.14. According to article 14, in order to process any applications of a private institution to function as a certifying entity, the Interinstitutional Commission on Lawyering Mandatory Association and Certification would establish a committee of experts. Professional bar associations, among other relevant actors, can propose those experts.

[77] *Id.* at art.26.

[78] *Id.* at art.26 §XIII.

[79] *Id.* at arts. 14, 26 and 75.

the market for legal services, especially with regards to economic competition.[80] Any other constitutional and legal implications, including potential restrictions to individual freedoms, were not directly or indirectly addressed in the opinion.

From the beginning, the Commission outlined some problems associated with the current regulation of professional practice in Mexico, *i.e.* the licensing model. On this basis, the Commission concluded that requirements commonly linked with such regulatory schemes tend to set artificial barriers to entry to markets for professional legal services.[81] The consequences of such barriers include reduction of supply, an anti-competitive scenario, and increases in the cost of legal services.[82] The opinion relied heavily on documents produced by third party states' governmental agencies, as well as international organizations.[83]

Building on this foundation, the Commission turned to the issue of mandatory affiliation. As would be expected, the opinion concluded that this particular regulation would create more obstacles to freedom of services, and thus, lead to even greater risks of anti-competitive behavior by relevant actors.[84] In a particularly provocative conclusion, the Commission stressed that when the regulated actors govern professional associations, they can become means to impair the practice of their competitors.[85] This concern would be even more serious if the number of professional associations were to be limited by the legal framework.[86]

The Commission concluded that in the absence of any tangible evidence of a correlation between an expected increase in quality of legal services and the proposed scheme, the identified risks were unjustified and unnecessary.[87] Therefore, the Commission recommended (i) not to continue with the constitutional amendment process, and (ii) not to adopt a system based on compulsory affiliation of lawyers.[88]

Debate about the MLB decreased significantly after the Commission issued its opinion. In fact, Congressional work on the constitutional amendment and the leg-

---

[80] Comisión Federal de Competencia Económica, Opinión OPN-012-2015 y acumulado, open letter (Feb. 3, 2016), http://www.cofece.mx:8080/cfcresoluciones/docs/Mercados%20Regulados/V9/1/2415052.pdf.

[81] *Id.*

[82] *Id.*

[83] *Id.* The Commission referred to different reports including Occupational licensing: A Framework for Policymakers (White House); Competitive Restriction in Legal Professions and Competition in Professional Services (OCDE).

[84] *Id.*

[85] *Id.*

[86] Comisión Federal de Competencia Económica, *supra* note 80.

[87] *Id.*

[88] *Id.*

islative framework has basically stopped altogether. In this regard, the opinion seems to have marked the end of the mandatory affiliation scheme, at least as it was designed in the previously described proposal. Nonetheless, given the problems also identified in this paper, it is reasonable to think that a new regulatory scheme will be up for debate sooner rather than later. There seems to be a broad consensus about the imperative to improve legal services in Mexico, as well as the shortcomings of the current regulatory regime. Thus, the question is not whether there should be a new legal regime, but what sort of normative scheme would improve legal services without disproportionately impairing freedom of professional practice and competitive behavior of relevant actors.

III. Transnational Lawyering

Transnational lawyering in Mexico is unequally regulated in different local legislations. While some local statutes explicitly forbid practice of foreign lawyers in specific states in Mexico,[89] most local legislation subjects foreign lawyers to the same licensing scheme as national lawyers.[90] In other words, a foreign lawyer may practice law in several states throughout Mexico if she or he holds a law degree that is validated, authorized, and registered by federal and/or local authorities.[91]

Relevant rules of those statutes vaguely reference international treaties concluded by Mexico, without giving further details.[92] From the context, it seems reasonable to argue that these statutes defer to any international agreement concluded by federal authorities on the matter. Likewise, the same provisions indicate that if

---

[89] *See* Ley del Ejercicio Profesional para el Estado de México, art. 15, 22-04-1957, últimas reformas 29-01-1976; *see also* Ley del Ejercicio Profesional para el Estado de Morelos. art. 18, 20-12-1967, últimas reformas 18-02-2015.

[90] *See* Ley Reglamentaria Del Artículo 50. Constitucional, Relativo Al Ejercicio de las Profesiones en el Distrito Federal, art. 15, Diario Oficial de la Federación [DOF] 26-05-1945, últimas reformas 19-08-2010.

[91] *See id.* at art. 17. According to article 17 of the said Act, if revalidation is not possible, the authority may establish a system of equivalences. In those cases, professionals (including lawyers) may be required to pass additional tests, as proof of knowledge.

[92] *See* Ley de Ejercicio de las Profesiones Para El Estado de Baja México, art. 16, 10-06-1957, últimas reformas 06-09-2002; Ley de Profesiones del Estado de Aguascalientes, art. 23, 01-01-2000, últimas reformas 20-03-2000; Ley de Profesiones del Estado de Nuevo León, art. 17, 25-07-1984, últimas reformas 22-02-2012; Ley de Profesiones Para El Estado de Guanajuato, art. 16, 16-08-1959, últimas reformas 20-12-2005; Ley Para El Ejercicio de las Profesiones del Estado do Jalisco, art. 40, 46, 13-08-1974, últimas reformas 20-11-2012; Ley Reglamentaria Del Articulo 50. Constitucional, Relativo Al Ejercicio de las Profesiones en el Distrito Federal, art. 15, Diario Oficial de la Federación [DOF] 26-05-1945, últimas reformas 19-08-2010.

there is no applicable treaty, the professional practice of foreign lawyers will be subject to rules of reciprocity.[93]

In some exceptions, such as the Professional Practice Act for Chihuahua, professional services by a foreigner are regulated in more detail. According to article 44 of this Act, in order to practice in such state, foreign lawyers must: (i) be members of a professional association in their native country; (ii) have practiced law for at least five years; (iii) have working knowledge of Spanish; and (iv) submit a recommendation letter from their professional association, attesting that the person has not been subject to any disciplinary procedures, among other requirements.[94]

In addition to state legislation, the code of ethics of the Ilustre y Nacional Colegio de Abogados de México also mentions foreign lawyers. But the relevant provisions deal with the conduct that Mexican lawyers must follow when acting in conjunction with foreign lawyers.[95] The code does not establish further requirements that the latter must meet in order to practice law in Mexico, nor does it expressly set forth obligations towards their clients.

In addition to these rules, current debates on lawyering have also addressed the issue of foreign lawyers. The MLB incorporates foreign lawyers into the new scheme of mandatory affiliation. Their professional practice in Mexico would still be subject to validation of their law degree by Mexican authorities, in accordance with international agreements or national statutes.[96] Likewise, it could be assumed that foreign lawyers would also have to join a Mexican lawyers' professional association. Without an explicit provision, it is difficult to argue that affiliation in their own native country would be enough to satisfy legal requirements in Mexico. Consequently, it is reasonable to conclude that, as it is now, in the new scheme there would not be a system of temporary licensing to practice law in Mexico. Moreover, article 26 of the MLB does mandate professional associations to keep a record of, and individual files on, all foreign lawyers practicing as "foreign legal counselors" in Mexico.[97]

---

[93] Ley de Profesiones del Estado de Nuevo León, art. 17, 25-07-1984, últimas reformas 22-02-2012; Ley Reglamentaria Del Articulo 50. Constitucional, Relativo Al Ejercicio de las Profesiones en el Distrito Federal, art. 15, Diario Oficial de la Federación [DOF] 26-05-1945, últimas reformas 19-08-2010.

[94] Ley del Ejercicio Profesiones Para el Estado de Chihuahua, art. 44, 27-12-1997, últimas reformas 04-10-2010.

[95] Código de Ética del Ilustre y Nacional Colegio de Abogados de México, art. 5 §§2, 7, 9 (1997).

[96] Ley General de la Abogacía Mexicana, art. 6 §II (2015), http://renace.org.mx/renace2015/wp-content/uploads/2015/12/Ley-General-de-la-Abogac%C3%ADa-Mexicana-PROYECTO-FINAL.pdf.

[97] *Id.* at art. 26 §VIII.

In short, according to current Mexican legislation, foreign lawyers would be able to practice law in most state jurisdictions, provided that they met the necessary requirements including those related to their immigration status. As mentioned before, there are specific exceptions to this general rule. Nonetheless, such provisions would be most likely deemed discriminatory and could be fought through constitutional remedies. In any case, it is important to stress once more that rules governing legal services by foreign lawyers in Mexico are as vague as those applicable to Mexican lawyers. Those rules provide little protection to clients, and even less to third parties that could be affected by a lawyer's wrongdoing.

IV. Conclusion

Lawyer regulation in Mexico is broader and more complex than it could appear at first glance. Nonetheless, the practical effect of this extensive normative framework seems to be exactly the opposite of what would be expected. Instead of strengthening the quality of legal education and legal services, in line with the protection of individual rights to access to justice and due process, there are persistent deficiencies in the system that seem perpetuated, at least partially, by the same rules striving for its consolidation.

Coexistence between federal and state legislation, along with private associations' codes of ethics, should not necessarily weaken the regulatory framework. But severe discrepancies among relevant provisions result in a system plagued with inconsistencies, loopholes, and contradictions. Under these conditions, it is difficult to precisely determine the scope of the rights, obligations, and responsibilities of lawyers toward their clients and the justice system at large.

There seems to be enough evidence to conclude that the problems of the Mexican legal system originate, in great part, from our legal education model. In comparison with lawyering practice, the regulation of law schools is extremely vague and highly flexible, resulting in an unprecedented spike in the number of law schools currently operating throughout Mexico. Despite its unquestionable importance, current debates about a new regulatory regime for the legal profession have almost completely excluded the issue of the governance of legal education and law schools.

The argument advanced in this paper does not attempt to undermine the importance of other contributing factors to the persistent shortcomings of the Mexican justice system. As I have mentioned from the beginning, Mexico is a country deeply marked by inequalities, informal means of justice, authoritarian political regimes, and corruption. These social, political, and economic aspects may have an even greater weight on our current problems, than inconsistent legislation on lawyering. Nonetheless, the relevance of the latter cannot be excluded altogether.

Hence, it is imperative to continue forward with a constructive and inclusive debate about an improved constitutional and legal framework for legal education and legal practice. Such debate must not only bear in mind problems associated with previous proposals, as the MLB, but should also be founded on the protection of freedoms and rights of all parties involved. Regulation must find a balance between freedom of professional practice and individual and social needs on the access to justice in Mexico. It should also consider the need to rethink the basis of legal education in Mexico. Only a complete overhaul of our regulatory framework, grounded on a profound reorientation of the role of legal services in Mexico, can add substantive value to respond to an ongoing and increasing crisis of the justice system.

CHAPTER 5

THE REGULATION OF THE TRANSNATIONAL LEGAL PROFESSION IN THE UNITED STATES

By Robert E. Lutz[1]

I. The Nature of Professional Regulation and Regulatory Methodologies[2]

---

[1] Paul E. Treusch Distinguished Professor of International Legal Studies, Southwestern Law School, rlutz@swlaw.edu. This article and the related article symposium are dedicated to the memory of Professor Steve Zamora, good friend and colleague, who inspired this and many North American transnational legal initiatives. Steve organized and served as the Executive Director of the North American Consortium of Legal Education ("NACLE"); the biennial gathering of academics from the participating law schools—on March 10-12, 2016 in Monterrey, Mexico—served as the platform for presentations from the authors of this symposium on the topic of the "Regulation of the Legal Profession." Steve's much too early and sudden death left important planned work to be done on building bridges for the legal profession among our countries, and memory of him and his steadfast commitment to these efforts will continue to inspire us.

[2] Some of the themes about professional regulation and other insights also benefitted from the author's chairmanship of and longtime active involvement in the American Bar Association's Task Force (now an ABA Standing Committee) on International Trade in Legal Services (ITIL) (2002-present), where he served as Chair for 2006-10, his chairmanship of the ABA Section of International Law (2001-02) (SIL), his chairing of the SIL Transnational Legal Practice Committee, and his participation in the La Biennale Business & Droit Rencontre Entre Acteurs de L'Entreprise et du Droit, at the Palais de la Bourse, Lyon, France (Dec. 2, 2011). An article of his on the subject was published in LA SEMAINE JURIDIQUE ENTREPRISE ET AFFAIRES (July 26, 2012; Lexis-Nexis Publishers), entitled "La conformite: Nouvelles regles et nouveaux defies pour professions juridiques internationals—Une perspective americaine" ("An Essay on the American Perspective on Lawyer Conduct and Discipline: New Norms and Challenges for the International Legal Profession"—translated from English into French by Bertrand du Marais).

A. Regulatory Methodologies

In the United States there are mixed receptions to "regulation"—whether it is directed at private commercial activity (big or small), the professions, or is designed to constrain the acts of government. When private enterprise's *laissez faire* excesses fail to account for the public interest, civil society frequently implores government to intervene on behalf of the greater good to bring equilibrium and to preserve certain public interests.   In contrast, when the clamp of governmental regulation becomes too onerous for the private sector (*via* standards-setting, licensing and compliance requirements, taxes, etc.), requests for relief ("deregulation") are often sought by affected sectors in coordination with certain public sectors which feel the government has overreached. Even the government, which maintains surveillance over its own regulatory activities, will go through various cycles of regulatory reform in order to strike the correct balance (e.g., with respect to transparency, accountability, administrative efficiency) among the goals of ensuring innovation, profitability, flexibility, freedom of action, and the public good.[3]

Thus, even though "regulation" is generally defined as "the imposition of rules by government, backed by use of penalties that are intended specifically to modify the economic behavior of individuals and firm [sic] in the private sector,"[4] the methods employed and the imposing authority may be other than "government," by delegation or simply by the desire of a business to self-regulate. In short, "regulation" can mean many things to many people, and its public acceptance can be cyclical.

II. Overview of the Regulation of the US Legal Profession

A. General

In the realm of the regulation of the professions,[5] America's lawyers may be a privileged lot, especially with respect to how their profession is regulated. Compared to the regulation of the legal profession in other countries, lawyers in the United States are, to a large extent, self-regulated. That is, they are regulated from with-

---

[3] *E.g.*, *"Over-regulated America"*, THE ECONOMIST, Feb. 18-24, 2012, at p. 9. *See also* other related articles in the same issue: *"Tangled up in green tape"* (p. 27-28); *"Of Sunstein and sunsets"* (p. 28-29); *"America is becoming a less attractive place to do business"* (p. 71); *"measuring the impact of regulation—The rule of more"* (p. 77); *"European financial regulation—Laws for all"* (p. 56).

[4] *See* "Regulation" in GLOSSARY OF INDUSTRIAL ORGANISATION ECONOMICS AND COMPETITION LAW (compiled by R.S. Khemani & D.M. Shapiro) (OECD, 1993).

[5] *See generally United States Network for Education Information,* RECOGNITION OF FOREIGN QUALIFICATIONS: PROFESSIONAL RECOGNITION, http://www.ed.gov/international/usnei/us/profrecog.doc (last visited September 10, 2016).

in the profession itself by the representative organizations of the profession.[6] US state bar associations and US state supreme courts are the principal standard-setters and enforcers on a state-by-state basis.[7] More specifically in recent years, the Conference of State Chief Judges ("CCJ"), an organization composed of sitting chief justices of state supreme courts, has focused on transnational issues involved in regulating the legal profession, attempting to guide the nation's states with respect to such issues.[8] The state supreme courts also have a principal role in governing qualification and setting standards regarding required conduct of those in the profession, as well as meting out punishment to those who may stray. While model ethical standards are developed at the national level, and mostly by the American Bar Association,[9] they are adopted and subject to implementation by the various states' legal profession, with the discipline being carried out primarily by the bar associations' disciplinary boards. Malpractice cases—where clients bring lawsuits against lawyers for failing to meet reasonable standards of providing legal services—supplement this process and can serve as an independent pathway for relief to those injured by improper lawyer conduct.[10]

Notwithstanding the state-centric (i.e., non-national) nature of this institution we call the "American Legal Profession," the pressures of globalization and the growth of technologies that make jurisdictions porous, are challenging the US' state-by-state regulatory role and imposing new pressures from beyond state borders.

B. The Relationship of Legal Education and Qualification to the Future of the Transnational Legal Profession

As presented later in this article, the challenges of technology and globalization are shaping the practice of the legal profession.[11] At the same time, legal education plays a significant role in the preparations of the lawyers who will be engaged in these challenges. The regulation of the legal educational process differs from regulation of the legal profession in terms of the regulator and subject. That is, unlike the regulation of

---

[6] *See* discussion *infra*.

[7] *See* e.g., William T. Gallagher, *Ideologies of Professionalism and the Politics of Self-Regulation in the California State Bar,* 22 PEPPERDINE L. REV. 485 (1994-1995) (illustrating California's structure).

[8] *See* CONFERENCE OF CHIEF JUSTICES, http://ccj.ncsc.org/ (last visited September 10, 2016).

[9] *See About* Us, AMERICAN BAR ASSOCIATION, CENTER FOR PROFESSIONAL RESPONSIBILITY, https://www.americanbar.org/groups/professional_responsibility/about_us.html (last visited Jan. 10, 2017).

[10] Roy Simon, *Legal Malpractice & Breach of Fiduciary Duty – Part 1,* NEW YORK LEGAL ETHICS REPORTER (Apr. 2006), http://www.newyorklegalethics.com/legal-malpractice-breach-of-fiduciary-duty-part-1/.

[11] *See* discussion *infra*.

the US legal profession—which is centered on US states—legal education is regulated in large part by an accreditation process at the national level.[12] The responsible government entity, the US Department of Education,[13] delegates accreditation responsibility to the American Bar Association's Section of Legal Education and Admission to the Bar.[14] But admission of students to accredited institutions for the Juris Doctor degree is determined in part by a nationally standardized examination, the Law School Admission Test ("LSAT") administered by the Law School Admission Council ("LSAC"), a different body.[15] The LSAT tests a student's reading comprehension, analytical and logical reasoning, and is intended to provide law schools with a uniform way to assess applicants, in addition to a student's college grade-point average ("GPA"). Thus, the front-end of the regulation of the profession—when students are preparing to become professionals—is governed at the national level by standardized testing and accreditation, but the decision as to which students enter the legal educational process (i.e., law school acceptances) is the province of the individual law school.

1. Qualification and Interstate Mobility

Although law schools are accredited nationally,[16] US state bars, frequently supervised in many states by the state's supreme court, still have control over qual-

---

[12] *See* 34 C.F.R. 4, s. 602; American Bar Association, Section of Legal Education and Admissions to the Bar, ABA Standards, https://www.americanbar.org/groups/legal_education/resources/standards.html (last visited June 9, 2017) (The ABA refers to this process as both an "approval" and accreditation process. States, usually via the state's bar association and its Supreme Court, may also impose a variety of additional requirements particularly with respect to qualifying to take the bar examination and passing it. For example, even though all states use the Multi-state Bar Examination (MBE) as part of their bar exam, states will employ quite different bar test scores to pass. *See* National Conference for Bar Examiners, Multistate Bar Examination, Jurisdictions Administering the MBE (last visited June 9, 2017). States are also known to impose additional education standards on law schools within the state. *E.g.*, the California Bar, after a study by a task force, proposed law schools should require students to take fifteen credit units of "skills" courses. *See State Bar of California, Task Force on Admissions Regulation Reform: Final Phase 1 Report,* at 15 (June 24 2013)).

[13] *See The Database of Accredited Postsecondary Institutions and Programs,* ACCREDITATION, https://ope.ed.gov/accreditation/ (last visited June 9, 2017).

[14] *See United States Network for Education Information, supra* note 5.

[15] The LSAC is composed of members from more than 200 law schools in the United States and Canada; in other words, all schools accredited by the ABA are members of LSAC. The LSAT has existed in some form since 1948, today costs $175 to take, is a half-day exam, and has six sections: four graded multiple-choice sections; an unscored experimental section; and an unscored writing section.

[16] The ABA Section on Legal Education and Admission to the Bar is delegated the authority to accredit US law schools by the US Department of Education.

ifying those who graduate from accredited law schools with respect to whether they may be licensed to practice. This is done *via* "Bar Examinations," which also contain character or moral qualification checks.[17] So, while national entities regulate the standards for accreditations, the fifty states of the United States (plus the District of Columbia), largely *via* their bar associations with support of the state's supreme court, determine whether a lawyer can successfully qualify to practice law in the state. Notwithstanding each state's control over the qualification process, efforts to make it more nationally uniform have led to the development of other examinations, namely the Uniform Bar Examination ("UBE").[18] The overall objective is to enable lawyer mobility in our fifty-plus jurisdictions; a UBE score achieved in one jurisdiction is portable because it is recognized in the other UBE jurisdictions. As of 2016, twenty-five jurisdictions have adopted the UBE.[19] Concerns about the numbers of persons entering the legal profession have circulated for years, but the issue is primarily, if at all, addressed by law schools pursuant to their admission policies and the state bars via their grading of the bar examinations. Although the standards for approval of new law schools require a showing of need, there seems to have been no apparent effort to cap the overall number of law schools and the number of law students who are annually produced.[20]

2. Interstate Practice Issues

Whether a lawyer licensed in one state can engage in interstate practice (i.e., represent his/her client in other states in the United States) without becoming a member of the other state's bar is dependent on the extent to which the other state(s)

---

[17] Only Wisconsin will license persons without a bar exam, based on their graduations from an accredited Wisconsin law school. Graduates from other ABA-accredited law schools must take a bar examination to become a member of the Wisconsin Bar.

[18] The UBE is administered by the National Conference of Bar Examiners ("NCBE"), a not-for-profit corporation that develops licensing tests for bar admission and provides character and fitness services. The website for NCBE, ncbex.org, notes that the jurisdictions adopting the UBE uniformly administer, grade and score the exam, and independently decide who may take the exam and who will be admitted to practice; determine underlying education requirements; make all character and fitness determinations; set passing scores, etc.

[19] Jurisdictions include: Alabama, Alaska, Arizona, Colorado, Connecticut, District of Columbia, Idaho, Iowa, Kansas, Massachusetts, Minnesota, Missouri, Montana, Nebraska, New Hampshire, New Jersey, New Mexico, New York, North Dakota, South Carolina, Utah, Vermont, Washington, West Virginia, and Wyoming,

[20] Currently, there are 205 ABA-accredited law schools. *See ABA-Approved Law Schools,* AMERICAN BAR ASSOCIATION SECTION OF LEGAL EDUCATION AND ADMISSION TO THE BAR, *h*ttps://www.americanbar.org/groups/legal_education/resources/aba_approved_law_schools .html (last visited June 9, 2017).

will allow such temporary interstate practice.[21] Some states have adopted the ABA Model Temporary Practice Rule[22] to facilitate such practice.[23] That rule enables a lawyer admitted in another US jurisdiction to provide temporary legal services under certain conditions. They may do so if those services:

(1) are undertaken in association with a lawyer who is admitted to practice in this jurisdiction and who actively participates in the matter;

(2) are in or reasonably related to a pending or potential proceeding before a tribunal in this or another jurisdiction, if the lawyer, or a person the lawyer is assisting, is authorized by law or order to appear in such proceeding or reasonably expects to be so authorized;

(3) are in or reasonably related to a pending or potential arbitration, mediation, or other alternative resolution proceeding in this or another jurisdiction, if the services arise out of or are reasonably related to the lawyer's practice in a jurisdiction in which the lawyer is admitted to practice and are not services for which the forum requires pro hac vice admission; or

(4) are not within paragraphs (c)(2) or (c)(3) and arise out of or are reasonably related to the lawyer's practice in a jurisdiction in which the lawyer is admitted to practice.[24]

3. Practice-ready Lawyers

What has been missing in this distribution of legal responsibility regarding legal education and qualification is that "practice" has not been integrated into the process of legal education in any comprehensive way. Students traditionally upon graduation have little or no understanding or experience about the "practice" of law.[25] Increas-

---

[21] Raymond J. Werner, *Licensed in One State, But Practicing in Another: Multijurisdictional Practice*, PROBATE & PROPERTY, 19 (Temporary practice conducted interstate or internationally is also referred to as "fly-in, fly-out" or "FIFO.").

[22] Laurel Terry, *Jurisdictions with Rules Regarding Foreign Law Practice*, THE AMERICAN BAR, (Oct. 14, 2016), http://www.americanbar.org/content/dam/aba/administrative/professional_responsibility/mjp_8_9_status_chart.authcheckdam.pdf. (Eight jurisdictions—Colorado, District of Columbia, Delaware, Florida, Georgia, New Hampshire, Pennsylvania, and Virginia—adopted this rule since it was approved by the ABA House of Delegates in 2002 after being proposed by the ABA Commission on Multijurisdictional Practice ("MJP"). In other states, such practice may be deemed "unauthorized practice of law" ("UPL") or not subject to regulatory enforcement if *de minimus*.

[23] *Id.*

[24] ABA MODEL R. OF PROF'L CONDUCT, Sec. 5.5 (c).

[25] DANA SENCHAL & THE VAULT, THE LAW SCHOOL BUZZ BOOK, 132 (2005 ed.).

ingly, however, legal education is recognizing this deficit, make advancements in teaching "skills," and expose students to practice as an integral aspect of a law school education.[26]

4. International Mobility: A Transnational Challenge

The international mobility challenge for the legal profession is what one might call "a two-way street"—it has inbound to US and outbound from the US aspects. The American Lawyer reported in 2014 that "[m]ore than 25,000 lawyers from [its list of 200 law] firms work in foreign offices in more than seventy countries."[27] From the inbound perspective, the publication named "The Bar Examiner" recently reported some startling statistics[28]: in 2013 in New York, foreign-educated applicants were almost thirty percent of those taking the bar examination, coming from 111 countries; during a ten-year span (2005 to 2015), almost 48,000 foreign-educated applicants passed the New York bar exam.[29] While many law schools have responded to the demand from foreign law students for an advanced legal education by offering Master of Laws ("LL.M") degree programs,[30] the Juris Doctor curriculum at most US law schools that could prepare students for a transnational law career is wanting.

---

[26] *See ABA Standards and Rules of Procedure for Approval of Law Schools*, ch. 3, Sec. 302-304, p. 15-18: *see also* Karen Sloan, *California's Practical-Skills Plan Alarms Out-of-State Deans*, NAT'L L. J. (2015). (Law schools are increasing their offerings of externships—some call them "internships"—most offer in-house clinical courses, and now "skills" courses.); *see also* Robert Lutz & Aliona Cara Rusnac, *The Education of Transnational Lawyers (In the United States and Abroad), in Festschrift fur Dr. Christoph Vedder—Recht and Realitat,* 511-36 (Stefan Lorenzmeier ed. 2017).

[27] *See* Drew Combs, *The Global Legal Market: By the Numbers*, THE AMERICAN LAWYER (Oct. 23, 2014).

[28] *See* Diane F. Basse, *Testing Foreign-Trained Applicants in a New York State of Mind,* THE AMERICAN BAR, (Dec. 2014) https://www.americanbar.org/content/dam/aba/uncategorized/GAO/2014dec_testingforeigntrainedapplicants.authcheckdam.pdf.

[29] *Id.*

[30] Carole Silver, *The Case of the Foreign Lawyer: Internationalizing the U.S. Legal Profession,* 25 FORDHAM INT'L L. J. 1039, 1046 (2002). Carole Silver, *Internationalizing U.S. Legal Education: A Report on the Education of Transnational Lawyers,* 14 CARDOZO J. INT'L & COMP. L. 143, 147 (2006); *see also,* Carole Silver & Mayer Freed, *Translating the U.S. LL.M Experience: The Need for a Comprehensive Examination,* 101 NW. UNIV. L.REV. 23, 23 (2006); Carole Silver, *States Side Story: Career Paths of International LL.M Students, or "I Like to Be in America,"* 80 FORDHAM L. REV. 6 (2012); Bryant Garth, *Notes Toward an Understanding of the U.S. Market in Foreign LL.M Students: From the British Empire and the Inns of Court to the U.S. LL.M,* 22 IND. J. OF GLOB. LEGAL STUD. 1 (2015).

III. Regulatory and Other Recent Changes in the United States Affecting Transnational Legal Practice

While the pressures on legal education and its responses profoundly affect the downstream regulation of the profession, legal education is but one of several analytical foci of the regulation of the US legal profession. As the comments above demonstrate, the regulation of the post-law school qualification process is also affected by academia or legal education at one end and by the practice community at the other. Thus, it is helpful to view the regulation of the legal profession as a continuum from admission to law school, education to prepare for practice, qualification by state bars, to vigilant attention to professional responsibility and protection of the public. In large part, the focus of the regulation in the United States at each of these stages is on the individual[31] and as discussed below, the primary regulator is either a national or a state entity. With the desire for single standards and pressures for uniformity, there seems to be a trend toward national norm-setting that, at a minimum, provides models for states to follow.

A. Articulation of Regulatory Objectives

Many who study the regulation of the American legal profession have encouraged the adoption of regulatory objectives,[32] especially given the array and, in some cases, disparity of state regulatory systems.[33] In February 2016, the American Bar Association's House of Delegates officially adopted a set of Model Regulatory Objectives.[34] Distinguished from the profession's core values, the objectives serve the following:

"First, the inclusion of regulatory objectives definitively sets out the purpose of lawyer regulation and its parameters. Regulatory objectives thus serve as a guide to assist those regulating the legal profession and those being regu-

---

[31] Rather than the law firm or entity providing legal services, as is frequently the case in other countries.

[32] See e.g., Laurel Terry, *Why Your Jurisdiction Should Consider Jumping on the Regulatory Objectives Bandwagon*, PROF. L. 28 (2013); *see also* Laurel S. Terry, Steve Mark & Tahlia Gordon, *Adopting Regulatory Objectives for the Legal Profession*, 80 FORDHAM L. REV. 2685 (2012).

[33] ABA Commission on the Future of Legal Services, *Report on the Future of Legal Services in the United States*, AMERICAN BAR ASSOCIATION, 39-40 (2016).

[34] *See* Commission on the Future of Legal Services, Standing Committee on Professional Discipline Criminal Justice Section, Law Practice Division, Standing Committee on Legal Aid and Indigent Defendants, Standing Committee on Client Protection, *ABA Model Regulatory Objectives for the Provision of Legal Services,* AMERICAN BAR ASSOCIATION, Resolution 105 (Feb. 2016), *available at* (https://perma.cc/A7NQ-SKKS).

lated. Second, regulatory objectives identify, for those affected by the particular regulation, the purpose of that regulation and why it is enforced. Third, regulatory objectives assist in ensuring that the function and purpose of the particular regulation is transparent. Thus, when the regulatory body administering the regulation is questioned—for example, about its interpretation of the regulation—the regulatory body can point to the regulatory objectives to demonstrate compliance with function and purpose. Fourth, regulatory objectives can help define the parameters of the regulation and of public debate about proposed regulation. Finally, regulatory objectives may help the legal profession when it is called upon to negotiate with governmental and nongovernmental entities about regulations affecting legal practice."[35]

The adopted ABA Model Regulatory Objectives for the Provision of Legal Services sets out the following points, while the Commission that developed them[36] encourages courts and bars to use them "when considering the most effective way for legal services to be delivered to the public."[37]

A. Protection of the public.
B. Advancement of the administration of justice and the rule of law.
C. Meaningful access to justice and information about the law, legal issues, and the civil and criminal justice systems.
D. Transparency regarding the nature and scope of legal services to be provided, the credentials of those who provide them, and the availability of regulatory protections.
E. Delivery of affordable and accessible legal services.
F. Efficient, competent, and ethical delivery of legal services.
G. Protection of privileged and confidential information.
H. Independence of professional judgment.
I. Accessible civil remedies for negligence and breach of other duties owed, disciplinary sanctions for misconduct, and advancement of appropriate preventive or wellness programs.
J. Diversity and inclusion among legal services providers and freedom from discrimination for those receiving legal services and in the justice system.

---

[35] *See* Terry, Mark & Gordon, *supra* note 32, at 2686.

[36] The ABA Commission on the Future of Legal Services, *supra* note 34.

[37] *Id.*, at 40 (notes that similar regulatory objectives for the legal profession have been adopted abroad in recent years in Australia, Denmark, England, India, Ireland, New Zealand, Scotland, Wales, and several Canadian provinces).

B. Inbound Regulation Initiatives

Although the typology is not perfect, one way to assess the current US regulatory system intended to foster and regulate transnational legal activity and the profession in general is to examine those initiatives that are directed at "inbound" legal activity, and then to observe significant developments regarding outbound activity that might have an impact on US legal practice in other countries.

There are five ways by which foreign lawyers might practice in the United States:

1) Full admission as licensed lawyer in a US jurisdiction;
2) License that permits only limited practice as a Foreign Legal Consultant;
3) Via a rule of court that permits temporary transactional work by foreign lawyers;
4) Via a rule of court that permits foreign lawyers to apply for *pro hac vice* admission, enabling the lawyer to appear in court before a judge; and
5) Via a rule that permits foreign lawyers to serve as in-house counsel.

Each of these approaches is described below.

1. Foreign Legal Consultants

At the heart of regulation of inbound foreign lawyers in the United States is the now iconic "foreign legal consultant" ("FLC"). Endorsed by the ABA since 1993,[38] (and adopted in similar form in many other countries[39]), the FLC rule permits lawyers from other countries to practice their home country law and "international law" while in the United States.[40] For lawyers who—for reasons of language, inadequate qualifying credentials, or other—choose not to take a bar examination to qualify as "fully-licensed," this status becomes a pathway to practicing law in a US

---

[38] See Center for Professional Responsibility, GATS/*International Agreements,* AMERICAN BAR ASSOCIATION, https://www.americanbar.org/groups/professional_responsibility/policy/gats_international_agreements.html (last visited June 9, 2017).

[39] *See e.g., The South Korea-United States Free Trade Agreement,* OFFICE OF THE UNITED STATES TRADE REPRESENTATIVE, ("KORUS FTA"), https://ustr.gov/trade-agreements/free-trade-agreements/korus-fta (provides for a phased-in FLC process for foreign lawyers seeking to practice their home country law in South Korea. (last visited Oct. 1, 2016).

[40] See Larry B. Pascal, *Making Texas More Competitive in International Law,* 77 Tex. B. J. 620, 621 (2014). (In 2006, the FLC model rule was revised and again became ABA policy upon passage by the ABA House of Delegates.)

state, albeit one that is limited in scope. It contemplates the foreign lawyer's residence in the United States, and state supreme courts are encouraged to adopt the model as a rule of court, or state legislatures to adopt it to ensure that foreign lawyers advising on their home countries' laws will not be prosecuted for "unauthorized practice of law."[41]

As of June 29, 2016, thirty-three states had adopted an FLC Rule modeled after the ABA model rule.[42] Noteworthy is the fact that some states did not go as far as the model rule in allowing FLCs to provide legal advice on local law "on the basis of advice from a person duly qualified and entitled . . . to render professional legal advice in this jurisdiction . . ." but rather limited the FLC scope of practice to the FLC's home country law and international law.[43]

2. Temporary Practice or "FIFO"

The "fly-in, fly-out" temporary practice rule, prepared by the ABA Commission on Multijurisdictional Practice ("MJP"), was adopted as ABA policy by the ABA House of Delegates in 2002 (*as amended* in 2013 pursuant to the proposal of the ABA Commission on Ethics 20/20). In 2013 and in 2015, the Conference of Chief Justices endorsed the rule noting its reasons included:

[T]he number of foreign companies with offices and operations within the United States has grown rapidly over the past decade and is expected to continue to increase . . . the proportion of the United States population with family, property, estate and business interests abroad has increased substantially over the past decade; and the number of legal transactions and disputes involving foreign law and foreign lawyers is increasing as a result of these trends.[44]

---

[41] *Resolution 2: In Support of Regulations Permitting Limited Practice by Foreign Lawyers in the United States to Address Issues Arising from Legal Market Globalization and Cross-Border Legal Practice*, CONFERENCE OF CHIEF JUSTICES, http://ccj.ncsc.org/-/media/Microsites/Files/CCJ/Resolutions/01282015-Legal-Market-Globalization.ashx (last visited June 9, 2017). *See generally* Robert E. Lutz, *Ethics and International Practice: A Guide to the Professional Responsibilities of Practitioners,* 16 FORDHAM INT'L L. J. 53, 59-61 (1992-1993).

[42] *See* Terry, *supra* note 22.

[43] *See id.* (The thirty-three jurisdictions offering an FLC status are: Alaska, Arizona, California, Colorado, Connecticut, Delaware, District of Columbia, Florida, Georgia, Hawaii, Idaho, Illinois, Indiana, Iowa, Louisiana, Massachusetts, Mississippi, Minnesota, Missouri, New Hampshire, New Jersey, New Mexico, New York, North Carolina, Ohio, Oregon, Pennsylvania, South Carolina, Texas, Utah, Virginia and Washington).

[44] *See Policy Resolutions,* CONFERENCE OF CHIEF JUSTICES, http://ccj.ncsc.org.Policy-Resolutions.aspx (last visited June 9, 2017).

The FIFO rule, now adopted by eleven jurisdictions,[45] enables foreign lawyers—who are members in good standing in their profession, in their home jurisdictions, and are subject to effective professional regulation and discipline in their home jurisdiction—to perform legal services in the US jurisdiction "on a temporary [and limited] basis" if:

- The services are performed in association with a lawyer admitted to practice in the jurisdiction and actively participates in the matter;
- The work is reasonably related to a pending or potential proceeding in a jurisdiction outside the United States in which the lawyer is authorized to appear, reasonably expects to be so authorized, or is assisting such a person;
- The services are reasonably related to a pending or potential alternative dispute resolution proceeding for which there is a nexus to the lawyer's practice in the lawyer's jurisdiction of admission; or
- The services are for a client who resides or has an office in a jurisdiction in which the lawyer is authorized to practice, the services are reasonably related to a matter that has a substantial connection to a jurisdiction in which the lawyer is authorized to practice.[46]

3. Pro Hac Vice Admission

Also, a limited practice license *pro hac vice* enables foreign lawyers to appear *at the discretion of the judge* in judicial and other adjudicative proceedings.[47] Because of the transnationality of much business today, foreign companies often desire their own counsel involved in arguing their cases in court or guiding local attorney in doing so. The *pro hac vice* Rule provides for that possibility. The Model Rule was recently modified to provide judges with guidance criteria for the exercise of their discretion.[48] In the past, this limited license was applicable only to US lawyers doing interstate work; now eighteen jurisdictions permit foreign lawyer court access via this Rule.[49]

---

[45] *See* Terry, *supra* note 22. (Colorado, Delaware, District of Columbia, Florida, Georgia, New Hampshire, New Mexico, New York, Oregon, Pennsylvania and Virginia).

[46] *Id.*

[47] Translated from the Latin, *pro hac vice* means "for this event." The term refers to the application of an out-of-state lawyer to appear in court without being licensed in the state where the trial is taking place. *Pro hac vice,* LegalDictionary.TheFreeDictionary.Com, http://legal-dictionary.thefreedictionary.com./Proacice (last visited June 9, 2017).

[48] See ABA News Archives, *Amends the ABA Model Rule on Pro Hac Vice Admission,* American Bar Association, https://www.american bar.org/news/abanewa/aba-news-archives/2013/08/amends_the_aba_model.html (last visited June 9, 2017).

4. Foreign In-House Counsel

This provision for an inbound limited practice capability of in-house counsel contains registration and scope of practice components. Both were proposed by the ABA Commission on Ethics 20/20[50] to respond to the changes that globalization and technology have brought to the legal profession. Twenty-two states have adopted versions of the scope and registration rules.[51] The Registration Rule enables foreign [licensed][52] lawyers to engage in a limited practice of law representing their employer. Registration under the model rule subjects in-counsel to Rules of Professional Conduct of the host jurisdiction and maintains jurisdiction over the registered lawyer with respect to the conduct of the lawyer to the same extent it has over lawyers admitted in the jurisdiction. A major change in the scope of practice addresses the foreign in-house counsel's ability to advise the employer about local law (i.e. of the host jurisdiction). Under the newest amendment (in 2013) to ABA Model Rules of Professional Conduct, Rule 5.5, foreign in-house may advise the corporation about local law, the law of another US jurisdiction or federal US law if "such advice shall be based upon the advice of a lawyer who is duly licensed and authorized by the jurisdiction to provide such advice."[53]

5. Other Innovations to Enhance Mobility

Pressures to accommodate the mobility of lawyers and their legal practices come hand-in-hand with the technological developments that blur boundaries between countries. However, with the territorial-based nature of lawyer regulation rooted deeply in its history and implementation in the United States, the changes come slowly and are undertaken cautiously. Nonetheless, several initiatives of recent years—regarding virtual law practice and limited specialized licensing—demon-

---

[49] *See* Terry, *supra* note 22. (Colorado, Delaware, District of Columbia, Georgia, Illinois, Maine, Mississippi, New Jersey, New Mexico, New York, Ohio, Oklahoma, Oregon, Pennsylvania, Texas, Utah (appellate courts only), Virginia, Wisconsin.

[50] *See ABA Commission on Ethics 20/20, AMERICAN BAR ASSOCIATION,* http://www.americanbar.org/groups/professional_responsibility/aba_commission_on_ethics_20_20.html (last visited June 7, 2017) (The author was a participant in the work of the Commission, which had a three and half-year life—August 2009 to February 2013.).

[51] *See supra* note 48.

[52] *See id.*

[53] MODEL RULES OF PROF'L CONDUCT, r. 5.5. (d)(1); *see also* MODEL RULE FOR REGISTRATION OF IN-HOUSE COUNSEL, B. 2. c.

strate the American legal profession's willingness to move towards greater flexibility and recognition of the need to be responsive to mobility concerns.

a. Virtual Law Office Practice (VLO)

While the regulation of the profession is state-centric and depends on a territorial-jurisdictional structure, emerging technologies and the changing nature of legal practice that largely ignores geographical boundaries pressure the regulatory structure to allow some degree of transborder physical and virtual activity. Both types of legal activity risk being the "unauthorized practice of law" (UPL) if the person performing the service is not licensed by the bar in which the activity occurs, but some temporary physical presence, recognizing the multijurisdictional nature of modern practice (MJP), is generally allowed now as qualified by the Model Rule and its commentary.[54]

VLO or "eLawyering" contrasts with MJP. It does not have to involve a physical presence where the lawyer is unlicensed, but can nevertheless raise issues of UPL. The lawyer may perform his/her services from the state of licensure; the delivery of the services, however, may occur via cyberspace to the client residing in another location where the lawyer is not licensed. If the virtual practice in the unlicensed jurisdiction is "substantial," UPL is a concern. Moreover, since we are dealing with the provision of legal services, client confidentiality safeguards are necessary and distinguishes eLawyering from just operating as a "mobile lawyer."[55]

The pace of technological development and consumer acceptance of it predict that the delivery of legal services via the Internet platform will continue to grow. Traditional law firm models and protectionist resistance can stall the legal profession's acceptance of virtual practice; yet eLawyering can affordably deliver many legal services to an ever-increasing group of consumers. "Software-powered legal services delivered over the Internet will provide the pathway for the legal profession to reinvent itself, retain its identity as a learned profession that serves society, and provide a decent living for its members."[56]

---

[54] *See* MODEL RULES OF PROF'L CONDUCT r. 5.5.

[55] Richard S. Granat & Stephanie Kimbro, *The Future of Virtual Law Practice,* THE RELEVANT LAWYER-REIMAGINING THE FUTURE OF THE LEGAL PROFESSION, 83, 87 (2015).

[56] *Id.,* at 101. *See generally* Stephanie Kimbro, *Virtual Law Practice: How to Deliver Legal Services Online* (2015); *see also* Richard Susskind, *Tomorrow's Lawyers: An Introduction into your Future* (2013).

b. Limited License Legal Technician

Much has been said about the justice gap in the United States.[57] In order to respond to consumer legal needs, a number of new, lower-cost providers have entered the legal marketplace. Such pressures, with the help of some forward-thinking futurists,[58] have spurred a reconsideration of traditional law practice and which elements of it could be routinized.[59] A major example of this in the United States is the creation of a new category of licensed legal service provider called a "limited license legal technician" (LLLT). The purpose of an LLLT is to provide services where there are unmet civil legal needs. The state of Washington established such a status in 2012.[60]

A LLLT rule could apply to any practice area for which there is unmet civil legal need, and the Washington LLLT Board, appointed to implement the rule, initially determined there were high unmet needs in: family, immigration, landlord-tenant, and elder law. Ultimately, the Board settled on family law as its first area of concentration, and developed a curriculum to qualify potential licensees, administered in collaboration with Washington law schools and the Washington community college system.[61]

The LLLT rule in Washington sent a "wake-up call" to other states that providing access to some critical legal needs can be addressed by non-lawyer professionals, properly trained and educated.

c. State Tool Kit [62]

This tool kit, designed by the Georgia State Bar's Committee on International Trade in Legal Services, demonstrates how state bars might organize and adopt rules

---

[57] *See* William C. Hubbard, *The Relevant Lawyer,* at *Foreword* (2015) ("Eighty percent of people who are poor, and many others of moderate means, do not get the civil legal assistance they need. In some states, in ninety-five percent of cases in the family courts at least one party is not represented by counsel. Almost 3.7 million people use the nation's nearly 500 court-based legal self-help centers, but many centers have to turn people away. Half of those who apply for legal aid are turned away because of lack of resources.").

[58] *See id.*

[59] *See generally* Richard Susskind, The End of Lawyers?: Rethinking the Nature of Legal Services (revised ed., 2010).

[60] *In re* Adoption of New APR 28—Limited Practice Rule for Limited License Legal Technicians, 5-6 (Wash. 2012), (No. 27500-A-105), *available at* http://www.courts.wa.gov/content/publicUpload/Press%20Releases/25700-A-1005.pdf.

[61] Stephen R. Crossland and Paula C. Littlewood, *The Washington State Limited License Legal Technician Program*, 65 S. C. L. Rev. 611, 616-17 (2013-2014).

[62] *Int'l Trade in Legal Services and Prof'l Reg.: A Framework for State Bars Based on the Georgia Experience,* American Bar Association Task Force on International Trade in Legal Services, (2014) [*hereinafter as* "State Tool Kit"].

that specifically address the ways in which foreign lawyers may appropriately performs legal services. The Georgia Committee modeled its proposal after the Georgia experience—which involved on an ongoing basis the monitoring of the impact of international developments on the legal profession from the perspective of both inbound and outbound legal services, the education of bar members on the issues and vocabulary surrounding cross-border practice, review of existing bar rules, and recommendations of appropriate rule-changes to the Georgia State Bar authorities.[63] More specifically, the Tool Kit recommends that states develop policy positions for each of the five methods by which foreign lawyers might actively practice in the jurisdiction (i.e., FLC, FIFO, *pro hac vice*, foreign in-counsel, full qualification) and provides links to the ABA's inbound foreign lawyer policies. In short, the Tool Kit provides a "roadmap" of how state legal regulatory agencies through the active engagement of the bar might organize to develop policies and rules that would facilitate transnational legal practice.

In early 2014, the Conference of State Chief Justices at its Midyear Meeting encouraged chief justices of all US states to "consider the . . . [State Tool Kit] as a worthy guide for their own state endeavors to meet the challenges of ever-changing legal markets and increasing cross-border law practices."[64]

C. Outbound Initiatives

Initiatives identified in the category of "outbound" are those that aid US lawyers to practice transnationally by easing regulatory or facilitating access to foreign bars. Some of these arrangements are designed with reciprocal treatment in mind, others are motivated by a desire to pursue international comity.

1. 2002 Directive to US Trade Representative (USTR)

In 2002, the ABA Section of International Law authored and proposed a resolution for adoption of the ABA House of Delegates regarding the rights of US lawyers seeking to practice abroad. The resolution urged the United States Trade Representative ("USTR")[65] to seek practice rights for "outbound" US lawyers that were the equivalent to the practice rights set forth in the ABA Model Rule for the Licensing and Practice of Foreign Legal Consultants (the FLC Rule). Note that US

---

[63] *Id.* at 7-8.

[64] C.C.J., Res. 11, C.C.J. Midyear Meeting (Jan. 29, 2014) (enacted).

[65] *See* OFFICE OF THE USTR, www.ustr.usgov (last visited June 7, 2017) (The USTR, in the Office of the President, is the principal negotiator of international trade agreements for the United States.).

states via other ABA policy[66] are urged to apply the same prescribed FLC rule to foreign inbound lawyers.

The 2002 Resolution remains fundamental ABA policy with respect to what it seeks from foreign jurisdictions[67] to minimally accommodate US transnational lawyers seeking to locate abroad, and articulates the ABA's basic national goals regarding foreign access to legal services provisions. It guides the US Trade Representative in its efforts to negotiate international trade deals with respect to legal services.

2. *Outsourcing of US Legal Services*

In recent years, in an effort to find less costly and more efficient methods, US practitioners have found it financially viable to outsource certain procedural/discovery pre-trial legal services.[68] After much "hand-wringing" about the role of the bar in guiding US practice as to its ethical responsibilities when US lawyers "outsource" legal work to others (in particular, in foreign jurisdictions, which is often referred to as "off-shoring"), the ABA responded with, arguably, clear policy by issuing "ABA Formal Opinion 08-451," entitled "Lawyer's Obligations When Outsourcing Legal and Non-legal Support Services."[69] That Opinion identified key ethical considerations lawyers should consider under the ABA Model Rules of Professional Conduct ("MRPC") when outsourcing domestically or internationally.[70] For business reasons, it is worth noting that providers of domestic and international outsourcing are also sensitive to ethical considerations and obligations, such as ensuring quality control, providing adequate security over personnel and information, and increasing opportunities for oversight by lawyers, law firms and clients, whose work is being outsourced.[71]

When the ABA Commission on Ethics 20/20 addressed this issue with respect to whether outsourcing raised concerns that should be reflected in the MRPC, it focused on competency, the lawyer's responsibility regarding a non-lawyer assistant's conduct, and UPL. Commentary to MR PC 1.1 was added to identify factors applicable when a lawyer is considering outsourcing work to a lawyer outside his/her firm, such as education, experience and reputation of the non-firm lawyer(s),

---

[66] *See* FLC discussion, *supra* notes 40-43.

[67] *ABA Policy on International Trade*, AM. BAR ASSN. https://www.americanbar.org/advocacy/governmental_legislative_work/priorities_policy/promoting_international rule_law/internationaltradetf/policy.html (last visited June 9, 2017).

[68] R. Lutz & E. Rosen, *The ABA and Outsourcing of Legal Services: ABA Comm'n on Ethics 20/20,* 40 ILNEWS 18 (Winter 2011).

[69] ABA Comm. On Ethics & Prof'l Responsibility, Formal Op. 08-451 (2008).

[70] *Id. e.g.*, the appropriateness of fees, competence, scope of practice, confidentiality, conflicts of interest, safeguarding client property, adequate supervision of lawyers and non-lawyers, unauthorized practice of law, and independence of professional judgment.

[71] *See* Lutz & Rosen, *supra* note 68.

the nature of the services assigned to the non-firm lawyer, and the legal and ethical environment in which the services are performed.

In the outsourcing context, non-lawyer-non-firm assistants are often engaged. Thus, commentary to MR PC 5.3 indicates that a series of factors, quite similar to those mentioned in the commentary to MR PC 1.1, are advised to determine whether the non-lawyers' activities may be reasonably expected to be compatible with the hiring lawyer's professional obligations.

Finally, vigilance is cautioned with respect to the work outsourced by US lawyers and law firms to ensure that US lawyers and law firms not run afoul of statutes and rules relating to the unauthorized practice of law. The Comment to MR PC 5.5(a) states "a lawyer may not assist a person in practicing law in violation of the rules governing professional conduct in that person's jurisdiction."[72]

3. Partnerships with Foreign Lawyers and Sharing Legal Fees with Non-lawyers

The nature of transnational lawyering that demands crossing borders physically and virtually, and the professional interactions across borders by US lawyers with lawyers and others who are not members of a US bar, demand that a variety of adjustments must be made in the typical regulatory model. To clarify the US lawyer's responsibilities in these interactions, several Formal Ethics Opinions were issued by the ABA over the last fifteen years.

For example, a 2001 Opinion[73] indicated that US lawyers were permitted to form partnerships or other entities to practice law in which foreign lawyers are partners or owners, as long as the foreign lawyers are members of a recognized legal profession in a foreign jurisdiction and the arrangement follows the law of the jurisdictions where the firm practices. The problem under the MRPC, specifically Rule 5.4, is that foreign persons of a profession not recognized as a legal profession by the foreign jurisdiction are deemed "nonlawyers," and admitting them to partnership would violate Rule 5.4 (pertaining to the professional independence of a lawyer). Accordingly, responsible lawyers in a US law firm have an ethical obligation to take reasonable steps to ensure that the foreign lawyer qualifies under this standard and that the arrangement follows the law of the jurisdictions where the firm practices. The permission granted by this opinion greatly facilitates the ability of US lawyers and firms to expand to other jurisdictions by partnering with foreign lawyers.

The expansion of multidisciplinary firms in several foreign jurisdictions imposes increasing pressure on the long-standing prohibition by the American bar regarding

---

[72] MODEL RULES OF PROF'L CONDUCT, *supra* note 54.

[73] *See* ABA Standing Committee on Ethics and Prof'l Responsibility, Formal Op. 01-423 (2001).

sharing legal fees with non-lawyers.[74] Despite these pressures, there continues to be significant resistance in the American bar to multidisciplinary practice which might include non-lawyer partnerships. A 2013 ABA Opinion[75] declared that lawyers subject to the Model Rules may work with other lawyers (or law firms) practicing in jurisdictions with rules that permit sharing legal fees with non-lawyers. In such a situation as a single billing to a client, a lawyer subject to the Model Rules may divide a legal fee with a lawyer or law firm in the other jurisdiction, even if the other lawyer or law firm might eventually distribute some portion of the fee to a non-lawyer, provided that there is no interference with the lawyer's independent professional judgment.

Related to the sharing of fees issue is the concern about "alternative business structures" (ABSs)[76] and the fear that non-lawyer ownership that might be involved may affect lawyers' independent judgment. ABSs are those business models through which legal services are delivered in ways that are currently prohibited because of the Model Rule prohibition against non-lawyer ownership, management and sharing fees. This issue will be addressed below.[77]

4. Reciprocal Disciplinary Information Exchange

Concerns about protecting the public with respect to the delivery of legal services remain high on the list of regulatory objectives for the regulation of lawyers.[78] When thinking about how to regulate the practice of foreign lawyers in one's jurisdiction, essential aspects of that regulation include the ability to verify qualifications, experience, and the professional standing of the foreign lawyer (including the status of any disciplinary proceedings involving the lawyer). They also include the obligation to communicate to the foreign regulatory body of the foreign lawyer (e.g. bar association or law society) any professional disciplinary actions by the host bar. Thus, for a host bar to feel comfortable that it has adequate enforcement tools to protect its public, it requires the ability to exchange information with foreign regulatory bodies, and possibly, to encourage reciprocal enforcement when disciplinary action is undertaken by one regulatory body or the other.

---

[74] MODEL RULES OF PROF'L CONDUCT, supra note 54, at r. 5.4.

[75] ABA Standing Committee on Ethics and Prof'l Responsibility, Formal Op. 464 (2013). *See* ABA Commission on Multidisciplinary Practices, Final Report, July 2000. (The ABA's House of Delegates rejected allowing multidisciplinary practice ("MDP") in 2000.).

[76] *See* Memorandum from ABA Commission on Ethics 20/20 Working Group on Alternative Business Structures to ABA Entities, Bar Associations, Law Schools, and Individuals AM. BAR ASSN. (Apr. 5, 2011), *available at* http://www.americanbar.org/content/dam/aba/administrative/ethics_2020/abs_issues_paper.authcheckdam.pdf.

[77] *See id.* at 4.

[78] *See id.* at *13.7*

To advance this effort, and at the request of the ABA Standing Committee on Professional Discipline and the then-ABA Task Force on International Trade in Legal Services, the ABA's House of Delegates "urge[d] the highest courts of [US] states and lawyer regulatory authorities to coordinate with their foreign regulatory counterparts and enter into voluntary arrangements to facilitate the exchange of relevant information, consistent with the jurisdictions' rules, and adopt the Guidelines for an International Regulatory Information Exchange."[79] The CCJ also adopted a resolution "in support of the proposed ABA Guidelines for an International Regulatory Information Exchange," and encouraging the ABA House of Delegates to adopt the proposed Guidelines.[80] The Guidelines are a template for an International Regulatory Information Exchange. It provides a way for state supreme courts and lawyer regulatory authorities to coordinate with their foreign regulatory counterparts and to enter voluntary arrangements to facilitate the exchange of relevant information— consistent with each jurisdiction's rules regarding the admission, licensure, and disciplinary status of its own licensed lawyers.

5. Resolving Multinational Ethical Conflicts: the Choice of Rule

Lawyers engaged in transnational practice confront a wide range of ethical issues that implicate foreign jurisdictions, as well as their own. Often a variety of ethics-related choices of law are engaged as multiple jurisdictions are also involved, and what ethical rules apply to any factually complicated legal events are difficult to ascertain. Of course, for US lawyers, a lawyer admitted to practice in a particular US jurisdiction "is subject to the disciplinary authority of this jurisdiction, regardless of where the lawyer's conduct occurs."[81] The Rule also indicates that a lawyer not admitted to the jurisdiction is subject to the disciplinary authority of the jurisdiction "if the lawyer provides or offers to provide legal services" in the jurisdiction.[82] Further, the Rule recognizes that the lawyer admitted to a jurisdiction may be subject to more than one jurisdiction, which is quite often the case in transnational law practice.

To resolve such situations, the Model Rules recognize conflicts of law rules regarding what ethical rules apply with respect to conduct in connection with mat-

---

[79] *House of Delegates: Delegate Handbook*, Am. Bar Assn. (2014-15), *available at* https://www.american bar.org/content/dam/aba/administrative/house_pf_delegates/2014 _2015_new_de;egate_handbook_final.authcheckdam.pdf.

[80] C.C.J., Res. 9, C.C.J. Annual Meeting (July 31, 2013) (enacted) (in support of the proposed ABA Guidelines for an International Regulatory Information Exchange, the resolution was proposed by the C.C.J. Task Force on Foreign Lawyers and the International Practice of Law).

[81] MODEL RULES OF PROF'L CONDUCT, r. 8.5(a) (Disciplinary Authority; Choice of Law) [hereinafter Model Rule 8.5].

[82] *Id.*

ters pending before "tribunals" (judicial entities) and other conduct (non-judicial) that might occur. Model Rule 8.5(b)(1) provides if the matter is before a foreign tribunal, the law of the tribunal's jurisdiction would usually apply.[83] In any matter not before a court (*e.g.* a transactional one), the lawyer may have to determine the jurisdiction where his/her conduct has its "predominant effect."[84] As mentioned above, this may be problematic, as there often are multiple jurisdictions involved and identifying "predominant effect" may add uncertainty to the transaction, especially where there may be conflicting rules of conduct related to conflicts of interest. To facilitate transnational transactions, the ABA Commission on Ethics 20/20 proposed a choice of rule approach to reduce the uncertainty often attached to such situations. The proposal was adopted by the ABA House of Delegates as part of the Commentary to 8.5, that "a written agreement between the lawyer and client that reasonably specifies a particular jurisdiction as [the jurisdiction of predominant effect] . . . may be considered if the agreement was obtained with the client's informed consent confirmed in the agreement."[85] Although not automatically binding on a court deciding the issue, such agreement would, according to its proponents, operate much like a choice of law clause is treated in a contract—it is enforceable by the court as a matter of contractual autonomy of the private parties.

IV. New Challenges for "Transnational" Law

The foregoing survey of regulatory approaches demonstrates efforts in the United States to facilitate the transnational provision of legal services. Legal education and qualification developments suggest greater uniformity to facilitate mobility within the profession, and the creation of new skills education that will ready graduates for practice.

Inbound regulation should seek to protect consumers of legal services and result in positive benefits for the local economy. In the case of inbound transnational practice, the consumer is frequently a sophisticated, budget and quality-conscious multinational company with bargaining power. Consumer and other public interest protections are not normally a concern. Usually, the concerns of the local bar are rooted in protectionism and the fear that there will be competition from foreign lawyers. In truth, however, most instances of inbound foreign lawyers (particularly FLCs and FIFOs) bring legal business into the local community and result in a multiplying economic effect.[86]

---

[83] *Id.*, at 8.5 (b)(1).

[84] *Id.* at (b)(2).

[85] *Id.* at cmt 5.

[86] *See* Hon. Jonathan Lippman, *Foreign Lawyers: Energizing the U.S. Practice of Law,* 22 Sw. Int'l L. J. 239, 241 (2015).

However, future developments do create new challenges. The delivery of legal services—domestically and internationally—are taking many new forms and are not necessarily by way of law firms or qualified lawyers. As mentioned, to reach persons who are not being served by the legal profession in the United States,[87] states are experimenting with specifically certified persons to deliver services more reasonably and effectively.[88] In addition, there are pressures to embrace multidisciplinary practice, which is occurring in several foreign jurisdictions, and to consider the possibility of alternative business structures ("ABS") in the form of non-lawyer ownership of law firms. And while these are areas of controversy within the profession, there are also trends to alter the regulatory approach currently in vogue, *i.e.* to regulate via law firms as well as the individual lawyer.

The regulation of outbound transnational practice takes on uniquely different challenges. First, an anti-globalism sentiment seems to be infecting initiatives to negotiate and approve multilateral trade agreements that would pave the way to foreign lawyer access.[89] The current prospects that either the TPP or the T-TIP will succeed to approval in the United States are not optimistic.[90]

Second, expanding US lawyer access to foreign jurisdictions is best achieved by some form of agreement between/among countries or bar associations. Countries need to agree to remove barriers to the trade in legal services. While many countries in the world are not subject to effective regulatory control, there is a group of countries with greater regulatory control that are willing to submit to liberalization efforts among themselves. This "group of the willing" can be used to establish a modicum of liberalized uniformity and serve as a model of how countries should regulate legal services. New initiatives, for example from the Australian Law Council that proposes a set of objectives or goals to which nations should strive with respect to transnational legal services,[91] are encouraging like-minded bars to consider agreeing to greater and more specific open access rules.

---

[87] Am. Bar Ass'n Comm'n on the Future of Legal Services, REPORT ON THE FUTURE OF LEGAL SERVICES IN THE UNITED STATES, 10-18 (2016).

[88] *See* Crossland & Littlewood, *supra* note 61.

[89] *See Trade Agreements,* USTR (2017), www.ustr.gov.https://ustr.gov/trade-agreements/free-trade-agreements (Discussions of the TransPacific Partnership Agreement (TPP) and the TransAtlantic Trade and Investment Partnership (T-TIP).

[90] *See e.g,* Richard Higgott & Richard Stubbs, *The Trans-Pacific Partnership: For, Against and Prospects,* E-INTERNATIONAL RELATIONS *Apr. 13, 2016),* http://*www.*e-ir.info/2016/04/13/the-trans-pacific-partnership-for-against-and-prospects/; *see also* Thomas Duesterberg, *Prospects for TTIP in 2015: a view from the U.S.,* ASPENIA ONLINE (Nov. 11, 2014*),* http://www.aspeninstitute.it/aspenia-online/article/prspects-ttip-2015-view-united-states.

[91] *See* Tahlia Gordon & Steve Mark, *The Australian Experiment: Out With the Old, In with the Bold* (Ch. 14), 186-196, THE RELEVANT LAWYER (2015).

Third, law firms that are permitted to expand to foreign jurisdictions need the ability to associate with local lawyers to provide legal services to their clients. What constitutes an acceptable relationship between local lawyers and foreign law firm lawyers can normally entail a wide-range of professional relationships,[92] and is dependent upon the willingness of the host country being receptive to having those services provided in part by foreign lawyers usually in concert with local ones.[93]

Professor Terry has argued that in the very new future, we will witness significant change with respect to the who, what, when, where, why and how of lawyer regulation:

> The regulatory changes elsewhere in the world to date are changes with respect to
> *who* regulates lawyers,
> *what* is regulated (individuals or firms, services, or providers),
> *when* regulation occurs,
> *where* it occurs (matching a geographic-based regulations system to a world of virtual practice),
> *why* regulation happens, and
> *how* it occurs.[94]

The transnational legal profession and its regulation have undergone significant change in the last several decades. Their educational and qualification components, the profession's legal services delivery models, and regulation of inbound access and outbound practice opportunity have all been exposed. Transnational legal practice is an important part of legal practice in the United States because of the changing demography and its role in building the rule of law in the world. State and national actors will continue to be the important stakeholders in the efforts to extinguish barriers and develop a vibrant system that promotes transnational legal practice.[95] Indeed, the future offers many opportunities and challenges for the transnational lawyer.

---

[92] *See* Int'l Bar Ass'n Int'l Trade in Legal Services Committee, *Discussion Paper: What should the Guiding Principles for ass'n between overseas and local lawyers be?*, p. 4 (Apr., 2015).

[93] *Id.*

[94] Laurel S. Terry, *Globalization and Regulation*, THE RELEVANT LAWYER, p. 157, 165, (2015)

[95] The developments recited above are the products of many efforts by ABA groups such as: the Multi-disciplinary Practice (MDP) and Multi-jurisdiction Practice Commissions (MJP), Ethics 2000, Commission of Ethics 20/20, the Commission on the Future of Legal Education, the Commission on the Future of Legal Services. All of these were formed with limited tasks and were subject to a sunset. Other groups, like the ABA Standing Committee on International Trade in Legal Services and the Working Group on Foreign Lawyers and the International Practice of Law of the Conference of Chief Justices (CCJ), are ongoing and will be prominent participants in future regulatory development. The newly formed International Conference of Legal Regulators will add international and comparative perspectives which may stimulate new ideas and approaches. While the development of model rules and approaches are developed at the national level, implementation takes place at the state level and usually depends on initiatives of the state bar through its committees.

CHAPTER 6

FREER TRADE BETWEEN THE UNITED STATES AND THE EUROPEAN UNION?

By David A. Gantz[1]

Remembering Steve Zamora

I first met Steve in the summer of 1971; I was a first-year attorney-adviser at the State Department's Office of the Legal Adviser; Steve was a rising 2L at Boalt Hall, University of California at Berkeley, standing first in his class. He became my first summer intern, at a time when he was already committed to a career in international law.

We spent much of the summer investigating the public international law implications of the Colorado River salinity problem with Mexico, with Steve doing all the research and most of the writing. The memo he wrote was a significant factor in convincing the US government and the governments of the Colorado River Basin states that the United States should seek a negotiated settlement of the dispute instead of risking otherwise certain litigation with Mexico in the International Court of Justice.

After State, Steve's and my careers developed in different directions. We did not have the opportunity to spend much time together again until I became a law professor in 1993. At that time, following up on my work at the State Department, I adopted Steve's abiding fondness and respect for Mexico, which came into its own with NAFTA. One of Steve's greatest loves and achievements was the North American

---

[1] Will Clayton Fellow in Trade and International Economics, Baker Institute for Public Policy/Center for the United States and Mexico, Rice University; Samuel M. Fegtly Professor of Law Emeritus, Rogers College of Law, the University of Arizona. Copyright© 2018, 2019, 2020, David A. Gantz.

Consortium for Legal Education (NACLE), a group of US, Mexican and Canadian law schools created to foster student exchanges and faculty interactions. After more than twenty years, some 200 students have made NACLE visits, with most of them finding a new understanding of a NAFTA partner country and forming life-long friendships. Nearly four years after Steve's death such exchanges continue. Steve and I and many other faculty members at a dozen law schools have collaborated *inter alia* on trade law, health law, energy law, environmental law, and family law projects. I like to think that these ongoing relationships have improved our ways of teaching and our ability to communicate our understanding of North American relationships to thousands of law students in the three countries; that has certainly been the case for me.

Steve was also extremely supportive of my late career switch from law practice to teaching, offering counsel and support especially during the first few years. He was a major force in helping me figure out the duties, and learning how to enjoy the pleasures, of teaching and research. He was one of the finalists for a dean search at Arizona Law in 1995, but my colleagues did not have the wisdom to choose him. A year later he was chosen as dean at Houston, where he served successfully for six years.

Steve was one of those very few who was truly both a gentleman and a scholar, a friend to everyone he met. He was also one of the finest human beings I have ever known. I was shocked by his untimely death and think of him daily, as do most of those who knew him well.

I. Introduction

President Trump's radical, off-the-cuff proposal for a Group of 7 duty-free zone probably was not carefully considered when ventured during an acrimonious G-7 meeting in June 2018 dominated by vicious personal attacks on Canadian Prime Minister Justin Trudeau and some European leaders by Trump and his economic team.[2] Given the lack of any follow-up in the ensuing months it seemed highly unlikely that the President was serious about the concept. It is equally unclear whether at the time the president or any of his economic advisers understood the full implications or the challenges of such a trade agreement among the major developed countries. It seems unlikely given the Administration's strong preference for bilateral over multilateral free trade agreements[3] that Mr. Trump had grasped that he was effectively proposing an FTA among seven nations (or even the four entities, given

---

[2] Jim Pickard & Sam Fleming, *Angry Trump Torpedoes G7's Hard Won Trade Harmony,* FINANCIAL TIMES, Jun. 10, 2018, available at https://www.ft.com/content/ba0aa2c4-6bf6-11e8-92d3-6c13e5c92914?list=intlhomepage (last visited Nov. 18, 2018).

[3] *See* Harry G. Broadman, *Trump's Misplaced Penchant for Bilateral Trade Deals,* FORBES, Jan. 31, 2018, available at https://www.forbes.com/sites/harrybroadman/2018/01/31/trumps-misplaced-penchant-for-bilateral-trade-deals/#62066e9457b9 (last visited Nov. 18, 2018) (noting Trump's "penchant for championing the negotiation of bilateral trade deals").

that any such agreement would be with the EU rather than individual EU Members of the G-7). Nor was there any indication that he or his advisers had considered the full benefits or the considerable challenges to such an arrangement, such as the requirements of non-discriminatory (MFN) treatment under GATT Article I or those of Article XXIV governing regional trade agreements.

While the Trump administration subsequently proposed legislation permitting the president to depart from MFN treatment,[4] it seems obvious that the other members of the G-7 would have insisted on meeting not only their GATT obligations but also those of the European Union. This means that any such agreement would have been among Canada, the EU as a group (on behalf of France, Germany, Italy, and at the time the United Kingdom), Japan and the United States, traditionally known as the Quad Countries. There seems to have been no consideration of sensitive imports other than autos and auto parts; it appears that steel, textiles and clothing, small trucks (where the United States imposes a 25% MFN duty[5]), and agricultural products such as dairy, grain and meat, were at the time ignored. So were services issues such as the much more recent acrimony between the United States and France over taxation of digital services, affecting primarily American high-tech enterprises,[6] and over retaliation for Airbus subsidies as authorized by the WTO.[7]

More generally, such an agreement seemed even less likely while the EU was being accused by Trump of "pursuing brutal trade policies"[8] and could well have been punished because of the US $101 billion trade deficit despite two-way trade of over $1.1 trillion annually. (There, the United States has focused on about $44 billion in auto imports from the EU and the EU's 10% tariff on imported cars.[9])

---

[4] *United States Fair and Reciprocal Tariff Act (draft),* VOLTAIRENET.ORG, Jul. 2, 2018, available at http://www.voltairenet.org/article201812.html (last visited Nov. 18, 2018).

[5] HS 8704.00 (2018).

[6] See *Importers, Wine Distributors warn USTR Against Tariffs on French Products*, WORLD TRADE ONLINE, Jan. 6, 2020, available at https://insidetrade.com/daily-news/importers-wine-distributors-warn-ustr-against-tariffs-french-products (last visited Jan. 7, 2020) (discussing retaliation for French tax on digital services).

[7] *In Airbus Case, USTR Proposed Steep Tariffs on EU Aircraft Parts, Ag Products,* WORLD TRADE ONLINE, Dec. 6. 2019, available at https://insidetrade.com/daily-news/airbus-case-ustr-proposes-steep-tariffs-eu-aircraft-parts-ag-products (last visited Jan. 7, 2020).

[8] Jim Pickard and Sam Fleming, *supra* note 2.

[9] *See* Alana Petroff, *Europe and the US Have the World's Most Important Business Ties,* CNN BUSINESS, Jul. 11, 2018, available at https://money.cnn.com/2018/07/11/news/economy/us-eu-tariffs-trade/index.html (last visited Nov. 18, 2018); Alana Petroff, *How Europe Could Fight Back if Trump Taxes Car Imports,* CNN BUSINESS, Jun. 25, 2018, available at https://money.cnn.com/2018/06/25/news/economy/europe-auto-tariffs-retaliation-trump/index.html?iid=EL (last visited Nov. 18, 2018 (both discussing overall trade and automotive trade).

Still, in a July 2018 meeting between EU Commission President Jean-Claude Juncker and President Trump, a more specific proposal emerged for a trade agreement between the United States and the EU. Subsequently, the United States completed the USMCA including Canada as well as Mexico[10] and a modest trade agreement with Japan,[11] and discussed one with the United Kingdom. The UK was not able to conclude bilateral agreements until it fully separated from the EU,[12] as of January 2020.

Earlier, the EU Commission President Juncker and Mr. Trump had agreed "to work together toward zero tariffs, zero non-tariff barriers, and zero subsidies in non-auto industrial goods. We will also work to reduce barriers and increase trade in services, chemicals, pharmaceuticals, medical products, as well as soybeans."[13] These guidelines, which of course were never implemented, in retrospect seem destined for at best limited success, given the Trump administration's overwhelming concern with trade deficits and the 10% EU auto tariffs (since autos and auto parts are a major factor in the deficit). Still, even if reducing the existing average tariffs (under 3%) in both directions, a reduction in non-tariff barriers, including customs requirements and differing standards, could produce significant benefits. Subsequent statements wisely suggested that the Trump administration was more interested in closer regulatory cooperation with the EU,[14] and less on the $180 billion trade deficit.[15]

---

[10] United States-Mexico-Canada Agreement, Nov. 30, 2018, available at https://ustr.gov/trade-agreements/free-trade-agreements/united-states-mexico-canada-agreement/agreement-between (last visited Dec. 8, 2018).

[11] US-Japan Trade Agreement, Oct. 7, 2019, available at https://ustr.gov/countries-regions/japan-korea-apec/japan/us-japan-trade-agreement-negotiations/us-japan-trade-agreement-text (last visited Jan. 7, 2019); *see also* letter from US Trade Representative Robert Lighthizer to Senator Orrin Hatch notifying Congress of the Administration's intent to initiate trade agreement negotiations with Japan, Oct. 16, 2018, available at https://ustr.gov/sites/default/files/20181017004828790-1.pdf (last visited Nov. 18, 2018) (identical letters were sent to other Senate and House leaders pursuant to the Bipartisan Congressional Trade Priorities and Accountability Act).

[12] *See* letter from US Trade Representative Robert Lighthizer to Senator Orrin Hatch notifying Congress of the Administration's intent to initiate trade agreement negotiations with the United Kingdom, Oct. 16,2018, available at https://ustr.gov/sites/default/files/2018 1017004930805-3.pdf (last visited Nov. 18, 2018).

[13] *Joint U.S.-EU Statement Following President Juncker's Visit to the White House,* EUROPEAN COMMISSION, Jul. 25, 2018, available at http://europa.eu/rapid/press-release_STATEMENT-18-4687_en.htm (last visited Oct. 27, 2018).

[14] *See* Birgit Jennen, *EU's Juncker Signals U.S. Car-Tariffs Truck May Not Last Long,* BLOOMBERG LAW, Nov. 13, 2018, available at https://www.bloomberg.com/news/articles/2018-11-12/eu-s-juncker-singals-u-s-car-tariffs-truce-may-not-last-long#xj4y7vzkg (last visited Jun. 6, 2022).

[15] James Politi, *Robert Lighthizer Says Trump "Focused" on EU Trade,* FINANCIAL TIMES, Dec.17, 2019, available at https://www.ft.com/content/3b2b24b4-20e1-11ea-b8a1-584213ee7b2b (last visited Dec. 18, 2019).

This chapter was originally written more than three years ago, during the height of the Trump administration. It is thus useful primarily for historical reasons, relating key aspects of that administration's rather sclerotic (and unsuccessful) efforts in addressing the challenges of trade with the European Union, the world's only similarly large economic unit. That being said, Mr. Trump was neither the first nor the last U.S. president to seek a more effective means of addressing trade with the European Union. President Obama pursued a wide and deep "Transatlantic Trade and Investment Partnership" (TTIP) for several years during his second administration, ultimately realizing (as did EU leadership) that the many procedural and policy gaps were simply too great to bridge, particularly at a time when significant constituencies on both sides of the Atlantic were becoming far less enthusiastic about trade and investment liberalization.[16] The Biden administration, probably wisely, adopted a more modest approach with the "Trade and Technology Council" (TTC).[17] This action followed successful efforts during the first year of the Biden administration to put the Boeing-Airbus dispute on hold for at least five years; convert Mr. Trump's section 232 "national security" tariffs to a reasonably adequate if still legally suspect tariff-rate quota; and progress toward more uniform treatment of Internet taxation. It is much too soon to know whether the Biden administration's efforts will be fruitful, but initial signals are encouraging as of May 2022.[18] Significant U.S. policy changes on the Paris accord, the future of NATO and the Iran nuclear agreement helped to make this detente possible.

The Trump era negotiations, which undoubtedly would have required months or years to finish if initiated are the focus of this article, with the caveat that the EU and United States never progressed beyond a very preliminary stage of negotiations (some could reasonably have said "never initiated"). In February 2020, some US officials were arguing that free trade negotiations with the UK should be prioritized over those with the EU, while EU officials had shied away from any actions seeming to revive the TTIP.[19] The limited prospects would have disappeared completely if the United States had imposed so-called "national security" tariffs on autos and auto parts,[20] and retaliated for Airbus subsidies or the French digital tax. Similarly,

---

[16] *See* Peter Chase, "Enhancing the Transatlantic Trade and Investment Relationship," Global Europe Program, Feb. 3, 2021, available at https://www.wilsoncenter.org/article/enhancing-transatlantic-trade-and-investment-relationship (last visited May 24, 2022).

[17] *See* "Fact Sheet: U.S.-EU Trade and Technology Council Establishes Economic and Technology Policy Initiatives," The White House, May 16, 2022, available at https://www.whitehouse.gov/briefing-room/statements-releases/2022/05/16/fact-sheet-u-s-eu-trade-and-technology-council-establishes-economic-and-technology-policies-initiatives/ (last visited May 24, 2022).

[18] Peter Chase, *supra* note16.

[19] *See Grassley: U.S. Trade Focus is on UK, "Not Worrying Much' About EU,* WORLD TRADE ONLINE, Feb. 25, 2020, available at https://insidetrade.com/daily-news/grassley-us-trade-focus-uk-%E2%80%98not-worrying-much%E2%80%99-about-eu (last visited Feb. 26, 2010).

the talks could also have failed because of other contentious issues between the EU and the United States, including but not limited to questions about the future of the WTO, the future of NATO, the withdrawal by the United States from the Iran nuclear agreement and the Paris Agreement on Climate Change. The EU and the United States also continue to trade accusations regarding each other's allegedly defective trade policies.[21] This combination of factors in retrospect made progress on a free trade agreement, or any trade agreement, extremely unlikely.

Part II provides a brief history of the unsuccessful TTIP negotiations undertaken by the Obama administration and other suggestions for a Trans-Atlantic Partnership. Part III examines the international legal options for a trade agreement between the United States and the EU; while the Trump administration was not concerned with US obligations under GATT, Article XXIV, the EU would have been. Part IV reviews the limited progress toward the EU-US agreement during the Trump administration as well as the initial positions of the parties, while Part V summarizes the challenges and potential stumbling blocks along with providing a few thoughts on the prospects of the TTC.

One of the difficulties of dealing with contemporary events is the risk (as evidenced here) that between the time of writing and the time of publication the negotiations would disappear completely. While the Trump administration insisted in November 2018 that it was negotiating with the EU from a position of "total strength," it is obvious that EU officials viewed the proposed negotiations very differently. As one EU official noted, "[O]ne thing needs to be absolutely clear: We do not feel we are in a position of weakness or inferior or we somehow have to give lots of concessions in order to make progress."[22]

II. Brief History of Prior Efforts toward Transatlantic Free Trade

The idea of free trade across the Atlantic, which would have covered trade among all G-7 Members except Japan (plus non-G-7 Member Mexico), seemed a reasonable possibility just a few years ago. The European Union, comprising twenty-seven members after the United Kingdom's withdrawal on January 31, 2020, had

---

[20] *U.S. Department of Commerce Initiates Section 232 Investigation into Auto Imports,* US DEPT. OF COMMERCE (Press Release), May 23, 2018, available at https://www.commerce.gov/news/press-releases/2018/05/us-department-commerce-initiates-section-232-investigation-auto-imports (last visited Nov. 18, 2018).

[21] *See Our Most-Read: U.S., EU Trade Barbs even as they Talk Trade,* WORLD TRADE ONLINE, Feb. 26, 2020, available at https://insidetrade.com/trade/our-most-read-us-eu-trade-trade-barbs-even-they-talk-trade (last visited Feb. 26. 2020).

[22] *See Trump: U.S. Negotiating with the EU from a Position of 'Total Strength,"* WORLD TRADE ONLINE, Nov. 1, 2018, available at https://insidetrade.com/trade/trump-us-negotiating-eu-position-%E2%80%98total-strength%E2%80%99 (last visited Nov. 1, 2018) (quoting EU Ambassador to the US David O'Sullivan).

initially established its customs union with internal free trade among the original six members in 1957, completing the customs union and internal free trade in 1973.[23] Membership reached twenty-eight with Croatia in 2013. Such regional free trade in theory will continue in a free trade area among the remaining twenty-seven EU members and the United Kingdom. It thus seemed clear even several years ago that the UK would eventually be negotiating an FTA with the United States directly rather than as part of the EU. With trade between the UK and EU remaining duty and quota free under a free trade agreement, a US-UK FTA was and is a reasonable possibility at some time in the future. However, the Biden administration for a variety of international reasons (e.g., threats by the UK government to unilaterally repudiate the special arrangements governing Northern Ireland) as well as US domestic political pressures from key Biden constituencies, has put FTA negotiations with the UK on what is best a very slow track.[24]

In April 2007, the parties to the US-UK negotiations agreed on a "framework for Advancing Transatlantic Economic Integration. Key aspects including fostering cooperation and reducing regulatory burdens and establishing (or re-establishing) a Transatlantic Economic Council to oversee the work of the Committee and re-examine at least semi-annually the objectives of the framework."[25] This accord confirms that even more than a decade ago, the EU and the United States were concerned much less about tariffs than about regulatory cooperation and non-tariff barriers caused by customs authorities and the like. It was reasonable to treat this limited agreement as a kind of precursor to the TTIP.

Canada and the EU spent almost seven years negotiating the Comprehensive Economic and Trade Agreement (CETA), which entered into provisional force in September 2017.[26] For several years, both the EU and the United States under the Obama administration made some parallel, mostly half-hearted efforts, to conclude

---

[23] *See A Timeline of the EU,* BBC NEWS, Mar. 24, 2007, available at http://news.bbc.co. uk/2/hi/europe/3583801.stm (last visited Nov. 1, 2018); *see also Joe Biden Plays Down Chances of UK-US Trade Deal, Sep. 22, 2021,* available at https://www.bbc.com/news/uk-politics-58646017 (last visited Jun. 6, 2022).

[24] *See* Trevor Hunnicutt, "Brexit Not a Factor in U.S.-UK Trade Deal Delay, U.S. official says," Reuters, Dec. 2, 2021, available at https://www.reuters.com/world/us/lack-us-uk-trade-deal-not-connected-post-brexit-concerns-us-official-2021-12-02/ (last visited May 24, 2022) (reacting to widespread reports that Northern Ireland was one of the holdups).

[25] *Framework for Advancing Transatlantic Economic Integration between the European Union and the United States of America,* Apr. 30, 2007, available at https://www.state.gov/p/eur/rls/or/130772.htm (last visited Nov. 2, 2018).

[26] Comprehensive Economic and Trade Agreement [Canada-EU], Oct. 30, 2016; provisionally in force Sep. 21, 2017, available at http://trade.ec.europa.eu/doclib/docs/2014/september/tradoc_152806.pdf (last visited Nov. 29, 2018).

the TTIP,[27] although neither the Trump administration nor the EU Commission made any perceptible effort to restart the negotiations.

Some observers, including the author, have pointed out that having three separate FTAs with the NAFTA countries would wreak havoc among other provisions with rules of origin. This is because in many product lines, such as autos and auto parts, an auto "manufactured" in the United States, Canada or Mexico has a substantial content from the other two NAFTA Parties,[28] and might not meet the rules of origin in each of three bilateral trade agreements. A prominent Canadian legal scholar, Armand de Mestral, also strongly urged the United States, Canada, Mexico, and the EU, following up on CETA, to combine their efforts toward a single transatlantic trade agreement.[29] Now that the United States-Mexico-Canada Agreement has been concluded,[30] none of the four jurisdictions seems to have much interest. With the generally successful efforts by the EU and Mexico to modernize their twenty-five-year-old FTA,[31] which process is still pending as of mid-2022, it seems more probable that should the United States and the EU ever be successful in concluding a trade agreement, it will operate in parallel with CETA and the revised Mexico-EU trade agreement.

In most respects, the TTIP was a much more ambitious undertaking than the trade agreement that was contemplated by the Trump administration. Recognizing that most non-agricultural tariffs between the United States and the EU (with autos at 10% entering the EU and small trucks at 25% entering the United States among the most important exceptions) are less than 3%,[32] the Commission and Obama administration were focused on standards, regulatory coherence, services including

---

[27] *See* European Commission, *The Transatlantic Trade Investment Partnership,* 2016, available at http://ec.europa.eu/trade/policy/in-focus/ttip/ (last visited Nov. 29, 2018) (showing EU negotiating texts last updated in July 2016).

[28] *See* David A. Gantz and Laura Nielsen, *TTIP and the Post-Bali World* Order, INTERNATIONAL ECONOMIC LAW AND GOVERNANCE: ESSAYS IN HONOUR OF MITSUO MATSUSHITA, ch. 22, (Julien Chaisse and Tsai-yu Lin, eds.) (Oxford; Oxford University Press, 2016).

[29] Armand de Mestral, *We Need a Trade Pact for All North Atlantic Countries,* CENTER FOR INT'L GOVERNANCE INNOVATION, Feb. 16, 2017, available at https://www.cigionline.org/articles/we-need-trade-pact-all-north-atlantic-countries (last visited Oct. 26, 2018). He suggests that such an agreement among largely complementary economies would also make the regions more competitive against the rising economic power of China.

[30] United States-Mexico-Canada Trade Agreement, *supra* note 10.

[31] *See* European Commission, *EU-Mexico Trade Agreement, Jul. 16, 2019,* available at https://ec.europa.eu/trade/policy/in-focus/eu-mexico-trade-agreement/ (last visited Dec. 18, 2019).

[32] *See Tariff Rate, Applied, Simple Mean, All Products (%)-Country Ranking*, INDEX MUNDI, 2016, available at https://www.indexmundi.com/facts/indicators/TM.TAX.MRCH.SM.AR.ZS/rankings (last visited Nov. 29, 2018) (showing 1.92% for the EU and 2.79% for the United States).

financial services, and a broader objective of setting a standard for international trade that could affect other regional trade agreements as well as the WTO.[33] The challenges were daunting, including but limited to extensive stakeholder opposition to reducing high barriers to agricultural imports, and resistance in regulatory agencies on both sides of the Atlantic toward achieving common regulatory standards, or even equivalence where warranted, and the effort was largely dormant for some months before Mr. Trump became president, although the negotiations were not formally terminated until he took office.[34] Perhaps some of the TTIP discussions will ultimately be carried over to the current Trade and Technology Council deliberations.

III. Legal Options: WTO Requirements for Free Trade Agreements

It is by no means evident that a trade agreement as envisioned by the Trump administration would have been consistent with GATT/WTO rules, particularly Article XXIV governing customs unions and free trade agreements. While this may not have been important to the Trump administration, where policies suggested a desire to withdraw from the WTO[35] and the Appellate Body is no longer functioning because of the United States' refusal to appoint judges,[36] it presumably would have been a significant factor for the EU, which appears dedicated to maintaining the WTO as a viable organization.

Article XXIV of the GATT permits parties to free trade agreements to depart from GATT Article I MFN tariff obligations provided that the Members meet a few conditions:

A. "The duties and other restrictive regulations of commerce . . . are eliminated on substantially all the trade between the constituent territories in products originating in such territories."[37] This means that not all tariffs must go to

---

[33] *See, e.g.,* David A Gantz, *A Transatlantic Trade and Investment Partnership?*, in LIBERALIZING INTERNATIONAL TRADE AFTER DOHA 247-55 (Cambridge University Press, 2013).

[34] For a discussion of the various negotiating rounds, *see* EU Commission, *The Transatlantic Trade and Investment Partnership: Making Trade Work for You,* available at http://ec.europa.eu/trade/policy/in-focus/ttip/ (last visited Nov. 2, 2018).

[35] *See* Renae Reints, *Secretary of Commerce Says It's 'a Little Premature' to Discuss a U.S. Withdrawal from the WTO,* Jul. 2, 2018, FORTUNE, available at http://fortune.com/2018/07/02/wilbur-ross-wto-withdrawal/ (last visited Nov. 29, 2018) (quoting Commerce Secretary Wilbur Ross).

[36] *See* Jonathan Josephs, *WTO Chief: "Months" Needed to Fix Disputes Body,* BBC NEWS, Dec. 10, 2019, available at https://www.bbc.com/news/business-50736344 (last visited Dec. 18, 2019).

[37] GATT, art. XXIV, para. 8(b).

zero, but the FTA must have substantial sectoral coverage, probably including at least some trade in agriculture.

B. The liberalization must take place within a reasonable period of time, usually ten years.[38]

C. "The duties and other regulations of commerce maintained in each of the constituent territories . . . shall not be higher or more restrictive than the corresponding duties and other regulations of commerce existing in the same constituent territories prior to the formation of the free-trade area."[39]

D. RTAs under negotiation must be notified to the WTO and the WTO Committee on Regional Trade Agreements.[40]

Regional trade agreements on services are governed by similar exceptions in the General Agreement on Trade in Services, Article V, which provides in pertinent part:

1.This Agreement shall not prevent any of its Members from being a party to or entering into an agreement liberalizing trade in services between or among the parties to such an agreement, provided that such an agreement:
(a) has substantial sectoral coverage, and
(b) provides for the absence or elimination of substantially all discrimination, in the sense of Article XVII, between or among the parties, in the sectors covered under subparagraph (a), through: (i) elimination of existing discriminatory measures, and/or (ii) prohibition of new or more discriminatory measures. . . . [41]

Regional trade agreements have proliferated in the past several decades for a variety of reasons. As of September 2019, 302 RTAs were in force and the WTO had received a total of 481 notifications.[42] The reasons for their popularity include dissatisfaction with the lack of progress in multilateral trade negotiations in the Doha Round, essentially dormant since 2009; a belief that it is easier to negotiate trade liberalization among two, three, or even a dozen countries than among the 164 Members of the WTO; the desire to exclude some countries (e.g. China) from duty-free

---

[38] GATT, art. XXIV, para. 5(I); Understanding on the Interpretation of Article XXIV of the General Agreement on Tariffs and Trade 1994, Apr. 15, 1994, para. 3.

[39] GATT, art. XXIV, para. 5(b).

[40] Transparency Mechanism for Regional Trade Agreements, Dec. 14, 2006, WT/L/671 (Dec. 18, 2006), paras. 3, 18.

[41] GATS, art. V(1), Annex 1(b) to the WTO Agreement, Apr. 15, 1993.

[42] *See* WTO Secretariat, *Regional Trade Agreements*, available at https://www.wto.org/english/tratop_e/region_e (last visited Oct. 2, 2019).). Notifications for goods and for services, often addressed in the same agreement, are counted separately.

tariff treatment; and the desire to cover modern issues so far not included in WTO negotiations such as e-commerce, supply chain management, broader regulatory cooperation and small and medium sized enterprises (SMEs), among others.[43] Also, the oversight of such agreements provided by the WTO's Committee on Regional Trade Agreements has been hampered by a lack of clarity in the WTO rules, despite a continuing effort to consider means of improving the transparency mechanism.[44]

The United States-EU agreement as proposed would not appear to have raised questions as to whether trade restrictions would be eliminated within a reasonable period of time, or because of the notice requirements. However, the "substantially all trade" requirement—which is not defined in GATT or supplemental documents— would likely have proven to be a significant stumbling block if the agreement were to exclude both trade in agriculture and trade in autos and auto parts as proposed by the Trump administration. Arguably, excluding agriculture is not an insuperable problem; some other regional trade agreements, such as the United States-Korea FTA, barely covered agricultural trade at all.[45] However, automotive trade constitutes a significant portion of total trade between the EU and the United States. In 2017, the EU exported €37.4 billion worth of passenger cars to the United States and the United States exported €6.2 billion to the EU.[46] Even with auto parts included the auto trade is probably less than 10% of total bilateral goods trade of $686 billion,[47] meaning that there is at least a reasonable prospect that the agreement would pass GATT muster even if both agriculture and autos were excluded. (This is different for the GATT-questionable United States-Japan Trade Agreement, which covers only US agricultural exports to Japan and certain machinery exports to the United States, representing about $55 billion in total trade but excluding trade in autos and auto parts, the latter of which represented more than a third of US imports from Japan.[48])

---

[43] See David A. Gantz, LIBERALIZING INTERNATIONAL TRADE AFTER DOHA 191-196 (Cambridge; Cambridge University Press, 2013, 2014) (discussing the pros and cons of regional trade agreements).

[44] *WTO, WTO and Free Trade Agreements,* AUSTRALIAN GOVERNMENT DEPARTMENT OF FOREIGN AFFAIRS AND TRADE, 2018, available at https://dfat.gov.au/trade/organisations/wto/Pages/the-world-trade-organization-wto-free-trade-agreements.aspx (last visited Nov. 29, 2018).

[45] US-Korea Free Trade Agreement, Jun. 30, 2007 (entered into force Mar. 15, 2012), available at https://ustr.gov/trade-agreements/free-trade-agreements/korus-fta/final-text (last visited Jan. 20, 2019).

[46] *See EU-US Automotive Trade: Facts and Figures,* EUROPEAN AUTO MANUFACTURERS ASSN., Jul. 2018, available at https://www.acea.be/uploads/publications/EU-U.S._automobile_trade-facts_figures.pdf (last visited Nov. 2, 2018).

[47] USTR, European Union Trade, 2017, available at https://ustr.gov/countries-regions/europe-middle-east/europe/european-union (last visited Nov. 2, 2018).

While historically the risks of a formal WTO challenge to the legality of an EU-US regional trade agreement are low, an agreement between the world's two largest economic partners is likely to receive unusually strong scrutiny at the WTO, if and when it is completed. Similarly, if the agreement were to be considered GATT-non-compliant, while a waiver could be sought it seems unlikely that the WTO Membership would be receptive, and in any event substantial compensation could be required by any member who asserted that its benefits under the system were being nullified or impaired.[49]

Should a US-EU Agreement have covered little more than tariffs and limited non-tariff barriers in the regulatory cooperation area (a non-compliant FTA under GATT Article XXIV), GATT/WTO rules would not have prevented the parties from deciding to eliminate all manufactured goods tariffs except those on autos and auto parts. However, the reductions in MFN tariffs to zero for trade between the United States and the EU would automatically apply to imports from all other WTO members under most-favored nation treatment,[50] including of course China and India. Ample precedent exists for such actions in the Uruguay Round of GATT negotiations, where the industrialized countries agreed as part of their tariff commitments under the Uruguay Round to reduce tariffs to zero on construction equipment, agricultural equipment, medical equipment, steel, beer, distilled spirits, pharmaceuticals, paper, toys, and furniture.[51]

Those reductions benefitted all WTO members, including for example, China, which did not enter the WTO until six years later. However, the idea of reducing many tariffs for China would have been an anathema for the Trump administration (as it would be today for the Biden administration). It seems to me inconceivable that the any US president in the foreseeable future would agree to eliminate all manufactured goods tariffs for imports from other major world traders such as China, Brazil, India, and Indonesia among others without receiving significant tariff benefits in return. I thus conclude that this approach would not have been politically or economically feasible except perhaps in a few specific sectors.

---

[48] *See* Congressional Research Service, *U.S.-Japan Trade Agreement Negotiations,* Oct. 3, 2019, available at file:///C:/Users/DAVID/AppData/Local/Temp/IF11120.pdf (last visited Jan. 7, 2019) (showing US imports from Japan in 2018 of $179.1 billion of which $56 billion were motor vehicles and parts).

[49] *See Understanding in Respect of Waivers of Obligations under the General Agreement on Tariffs and Trade 1994,* 1994, available at https://www.wto.org/english/docs_e/legal_e/11-25_e.htm (last visited Nov. 2, 2018).

[50] GATT, art. I.

[51] *See* EU Commission, *Balance Sheet of Seven Years of [Uruguay Round] Negotiations,* (1993), sec. 3.2, available at http://europa.eu/rapid/press-release_MEMO-94-24_en.htm (last visited Jul. 23, 2018).

Alternatively, if the EU and the United States were to focus exclusively on regulatory cooperation and non-tariff issues, as appears to be the case with the Trade and Technology Council, no issues under GATT Article XXIV are likely to arise. Coverage of services that meets the requirements of GATS, Article V as quoted above, would also be feasible, and avoid the complications of a full free trade agreement on goods. Of course, the question of WTO legality is for now mooted as of December 2019, when the WTO's Appellate Body no longer had sufficient judges to hear new appeals.[52]

IV. No Serious US-EU FTA Negotiations

The negotiations never really began, and the few preparations made earlier never progressed. On October 16, 2018, then US Trade Representative Robert Lighthizer formally notified Congress under the Trade Promotion Authority legislation of the Administration's intent to negotiate a trade agreement between the United States and the European Union.[53] This meant that under Trade Promotion Authority provisions then in force the United States could formally have initiated negotiations as of January 14, 2019.[54] In the letter to Congress the Administration provided little indication of the possible intended content of an agreement: "Our aim in negotiations with the EU is to address both tariff and non-tariff barriers and to achieve fairer, more balanced trade in a manner consistent with the objectives that Congress has set out in section 102 of the Trade Priorities and Accountability Act."[55]

Considerably more detail was provided in United States "Specific Negotiating Objectives" in January 2019 by the US Trade Representative.[56] Major features of the generally ambitious objectives, some borrowed from the United States-Mexico-

---

[52] Shawn Donnan and Bryce Baschuk, *Trump's Bid to Dismantle Global Trading System Poised for a Win,* BLOOMBERG, Jul. 30, 2019, available at https://www.bloomberg.com/news/articles/2019-07-30/trump-s-bid-to-dismantle-global-trading-system-poised-for-a-win (last visited Sep. 17, 2019).

[53] Letter from Robert Lighthizer to Democratic Leader Charles Schumer, Oct. 16, 2018, available at https://ustr.gov/sites/default/files/20181017004903138_2.pdf (last visited Oct. 27, 2018), citing Section 105(a)(1)(A) of the Bipartisan Congressional Priorities and Accountability Act (TPA). The other Congressional and Senate leadership received identical letters.

[54] *Id.*

[55] Letter from US Trade Representative Robert Lighthizer to Speaker of the House Paul Ryan, Oct. 16, 2018, available at file:///F:/DOCSV/Misc%20docs%202018/EU%20us%20notification%20letter%2010-18-18.pdf (last visited Nov. 17, 2018). Identical letters were sent to other House and Senate leaders.

[56] USTR, *Summary of Specific Negotiating Objectives," supra* note 23, Jan. 2016, available at https://ustr.gov/sites/default/files/01.11.2019_Summary_of_U.S.-EU_Negotiating_Objectives.pdf (last visited Jun. 6, 2022).

Canada Agreement (USMCA),[57] were as follows (with notes in brackets as appropriate):

- Securing duty-free market access for US industrial goods exports, including textiles and apparel, with disciplines to address non-tariff barriers that restrict US exports [without repeating the earlier US position seeking exclusion of autos];
- Securing commitments "with respect to greater regulatory compatibility" and reduce "burdens associated with unnecessary differences in regulation" [a major objective of the TTIP was regulatory coherence, the same concept that wisely remains included in the upcoming negotiations];
- Securing "comprehensive market access for US agricultural goods in the EU by reducing or eliminating tariffs" [strongly opposed by the EU as discussed elsewhere in this article];
- Efforts to limit US access to third-country agricultural export markets through sanitary and phytosanitary measures that are not based on ascertainable risk [e.g., based on GMO content or growth hormones];
- Providing for streamlined and expedited customs treatment for express delivery shipments, along with simplified customs procedures for low value goods and reciprocal *de minimis* levels [US levels are probably the highest in the world at $800 but Canada and Mexico in the USMCA refused to go above about $150[58]];
- Requiring the application of decisions on technical barriers to trade made by the WTO's TBT Committee;
- Facilitating market access and greater compatibility between US and EU regulations through improved regulatory practices;
- Reducing discrimination against foreign services suppliers, restrictions on the number of suppliers in the market and eliminate local present requirement, in all service sectors, with the usual US exception for maritime services;
- Obtaining EU commitments to refrain from imposing restrictions on cross-border data flows or localization [sure to be a contentious issue given widely different EU and US approaches to issues such as data privacy[59]];

---

[57] United States-Mexico-Canada-Trade Agreement, Nov. 30, 2019, available at https://ustr.gov/trade-agreements/free-trade-agreements/united-states-mexico-canada-agreement/agreement-between (last visited Feb. 26, 2020).

[58] USMCA, *supra* note 10, art. 7.8.1(f).

[59] *See* European Commission, *A New era for Data Protection in the EU,* May 2018, available at https://ec.europa.eu/commission/sites/beta-political/files/data-protection-factsheet-changes_en.pdf (last visited Jan. 20, 2019) (discussing the data protection reforms including inter alia provision for fines of up to €20 million for violations; no comparable legislation exists in the United States).

- Securing a commitment to refrain from imposing customs duties on digital products such as software, music, videos, and e-books [endorsed generally by the WTO but without binding obligations];
- Seeking rules to reduce or eliminate investment barriers to US investment in the EU [with no mention of investor-state-dispute settlement];
- Promoting high levels of intellectual property protection and prevent the improper utilization of geographical indications to undermine market access on the basis of geographical indications requirements that do not protect common generic terms [reflecting EU efforts in other trade agreement to protect such names as Chardonnay, Gouda, and Feta as geographical indications, in conflict with US policies];
- Establishing or affirming "basic rules for procedural fairness on competition law enforcement" and avoiding extra-territorial remedies except where there is an appropriate nexus to the Party's territory [recognizing that harmonization of substantive anti-trust laws is virtually impossible];
- Incorporating International Labor Organization core standards, improve various aspects of procedures and ensure that labor issues are subject to the same dispute settlement mechanisms as for trade disputes [all essential elements if any US trade agreement is to be approved by Congress];
- Providing for the establishment of "strong and enforceable environmental obligations" again subject to the general dispute settlement mechanisms and *inter alia* address illegal fishing and prevent harmful fisheries subsidies [preserving each Party's ability to enact and enforce its own environmental laws, and with no mention of climate change];
- Preserving "the ability of the United States to enforce rigorously its trade laws" including antidumping, countervailing duty and safeguard laws with new efforts to address evasion [as in virtually all US regional trade agreements];
- Ensuring reciprocity in government procurement opportunities for US goods and services in the EU and its Member states, but preserve the right of American states not to participate; and
- Incorporating State-to-state dispute settlement that is transparent but addresses situations where "a panel has clearly erred in its assessment of the facts and obligations that apply" [a repeat of efforts in USMCA to make the mechanism essentially voluntary, ultimately rejected by Mexico and Canada];
- Including termination provisions that can be exercised "under appropriate circumstances" [reflecting efforts by the United States in USMCA to establish a five-year Sunset clause, ultimately raised to sixteen years];
- Incorporating various prohibitions against direct or indirect boycotts of Israel; and

• Ensuring that the EU and Member states "avoid manipulating exchange rates in order to prevent effective balance of payments adjustment or to gain an unfair comparative advantage" [again similar to USMCA].

In November 2018, at the request of then US Trade Representative Lighthizer, the US International Trade Commission commenced a study of "the Probable Economic Effect of Providing Duty-Free Treatment for Currently Dutiable Imports" under a United States-EU trade agreement.[60] That study like other work of the USITC delayed by the partial US government shut-down that began December 21 and has resulted in the furlough of hundreds of thousands of government workers, including all or most of the USITC staff as "non-essential."[61] It does not appear to be publicly available although it was supposed to be released on April 23, 2019.[62]

On the EU side, a negotiating mandate for the talks would have required approval by the Council and EU Parliament. Draft proposals were published in January 2019 but do not appear to have been approved given the difference in views as to whether agricultural trade liberalization is to be discussed.[63] (Agriculture is explicitly excluded from the draft EU mandate.)

The initial proposed scope of the agreement was wisely narrower than the stalled TTIP negotiations. However, potential disagreements over the exclusion of autos (in doubt for the United States despite the negotiating objectives) and agriculture (the latter of which was said to be a non-starter for the EU), appeared to have been largely driven by a desire on the part of the EU to avoid a trade war on automobiles, given the then ongoing section 232 "national security" investigation (abandoned by the Biden administration) which ultimately could have resulted in 20% to 25% tariffs on autos and auto parts imported into the United States for most or all

---

[60] US Int'l Trade Commission, *U.S.-EU Trade Agreement: Advice on the Probable Economic Effect of Providing Duty-Free Treatment for Currently Dutiable Imports; Institution of Investigation and Scheduling of Hearing*, 83 Fed. Reg. 59418, Nov. 23, 2018, available at https://www.gpo.gov/fdsys/pkg/FR-2018-11-23/pdf/2018-25677.pdf (last visited Nov. 28, 2018).

[61] *See* Nicole Ogrysko, *Agencies to Send Second Furlough Notices if Government Shutdown hits 30-day Mark*, FEDERAL NEWS NETWORK, Jan. 18, 2019, available at https://federalnewsnetwork.com/government-shutdown/2019/01/agencies-to-send-second-furlough-notices-if-government-shutdown-hits-30-day-mark/ (last visited Jan. 19, 2019) (noting that as of January 20 the thirtieth day will be reached).

[62] *See* USITC, *U.S.-EU Trade Agreement: Advice on the Probable Economic Effect of Providing Duty-Free Treatment for Currently Dutiable Imports*, 84 Fed. Reg. 4536 (Feb. 15, 2019) (postponing the release date to April 23).

[63] EU Commission, *EU-U.S. Trade Talks: European Commission Presents Draft Negotiating Mandates*, Jan. 18, 2019, available at https://europa.eu/rapid/press-release_IP-19-502_en.htm (last visited Sep. 17, 2019).

sources.[64] With the Trump administration's fixation on tariff peaks, such as the 10% EU duties on autos and on bilateral trade deficits, it is forever uncertain as to whether automotive trade would be excluded, but it is worth keeping in mind that the US MFN tariff on small trucks is 25%,[65] a high tariff which protects the most profitable aspect of the US "Big Three" producers.[66] For the EU, given the Trump administration focus on auto tariffs for US exports to the EU, it is difficult to understand why either Party would want to proceed if autos are excluded.

As of April 2020, negotiations had not progressed, and they were abandoned subsequently. EU and US officials had widely differing views, at least in public, about the nature of the trans-Atlantic relationship, with some US officials such as the US ambassador to the EU touting a strong partnership between the EU and the Trump administration. At the same time, the EU agricultural commissioner saw the EU as at best a reluctant partner given what many believed were very short-sighted trade policies espoused by the Trump administration.[67] The French suggested that the United States wasn't really interested in a trade deal to reduce non-auto tariffs to zero, particularly given the US interest in opening the EU agricultural markets; the EU was offering zero tariffs on industrial goods but apparently little else.[68] The EU membership more generally then and now would prefer to exclude trade in agricultural products entirely but is probably open to discussing autos according to the draft blueprint unveiled in mid-January 2019 by the EU Commission,[69] a position on agriculture that is likely to be strongly opposed by US agricultural interests suffering

[64] *See U.S. Department of Commerce Initiates Section 232 Investigation into Auto Import,* *supra note [12].*; Andrew Ganz, *Trump Threatens 25-Percent Tariff on Foreign Cars,* THE CAR CONNECTION, Nov. 29, 2018, available at https://www.thecarconnection.com/news/1120190_trump-threatens-25-percent-tariff-on-imported-cars (last visited Nov. 29, 2018).

[65] Harmonized Tariff Schedule of the United States (2018), HS 8705.22.50 (GVW under 5 metric tons), available at file:///C:/Users/DAVID/Downloads/Chapter%2087%20(1).pdf (last visited Nov. 29, 2018).

[66] *See, e.g.,* Matthew Rocco, *Why the Ford F-150 is a Profit Machine,* FOX BUSINESS, May 9, 2018, available at https://www.foxbusiness.com/markets/why-the-ford-f-150-is-a-profit-machine (last visited Jan. 21, 2018)(indicating that the F-Series trucks "account for most of Ford's profits").

[67] *U.S., EU Officials Paint Contrasting Pictures of Trans-Atlantic Relationship,* WORLD TRADE ON LINE, Sep. 7, 2018, available at https://insidetrade.com/daily-news/us-eu-officials-paint-contrasting-pictures-trans-atlantic-relationship (last visited Nov. 1, 2018) (citing US Ambassador to the EU Gordon Sondland and EU Agricultural Commissioner Phil Hogan).

[68] *French Ambassador: EU Not Convinced that U.S. in Interested in a Trade Deal,* WORLD TRADE ONLINE, Sep. 10, 2018, available at https://insidetrade.com/daily-news/french-ambassador-eu-not-convinced-us-interested-trade-deal (last visited Nov. 1, 2918).

[69] Philip Blenkinsop, *EU open to discussing cars, not farming in U.S. trade talks,* REUTERS BUSINESS NEWS, Jan. 18, 2019, available at https://www.reuters.com/article/us-usa-trade-eu/eu-open-to-discussing-cars-not-farming-in-us-trade-talks-idUSKCN1PC13B (last visited Jan. 18, 2019).

from a decline in soybean and other sales to China.[70] This differing approach was reflected *inter alia* in meetings of the EU-US working group that took place in October 2018 and earlier. One may speculate that some in the Trump administration were fully prepared to say to the EU negotiators, "If you want to cover autos and avoid any future 'national security' tariffs on US auto imports, agriculture must be part of the negotiations."

V. The Challenges

If these negotiations had ever moved forward, many challenges and questions would have remained:

A. President Trump in his public tweets had often focused on a few tariff *peaks*, with emphasis on the 10% EU tariff on automobile imports, as he did with highly restrictive limits, equivalent to a tariff of about 275%, on milk solids imports into Canada, resolved in part by the USMCA.[71] Such peaks exist in every country, as with the 25% US tariff on small trucks imported into the United States, which the United States has no interest in eliminating.[72] This approach in theory probably makes sense since the trade-weighted tariffs for manufactured goods among the G-7 are in almost all cases four percent or less. Also, the main problem with world trade among developed countries, as recognized in TTIP and CPTPP,[73] is regulatory coherence and cooperation to facilitate bilateral and multilateral trade, which now appears to be one of the key US negotiating objectives as noted earlier. Fortunately, neither side appeared interested in including investor-state dispute settlement in the negotiations, presumably because of opposition by some EU Members and their citizens.[74]

---

[70] *Id. See also U.S. Agricultural Exports up from a Year Ago, But Chinese Tariffs Dim Soybean Prospects*, FARM POLICY NEWS, Nov. 7, 2018, available at https://farmpolicynews.illinois. edu/2018/11/u-s-agricultural-exports-up-from-a-year-ago-but-chinese-tariffs-dim-soybean-prospects/ (last visited Jan. 18, 2019) (discussing the effect of trade tensions on soybean exports to China).

[71] USMCA, Annex 3-B, sec. C (Dairy Pricing and Imports).

[72] *Trump: U.S. Negotiating with the EU from a position of 'Total Strength,'* WORLD TRADE ONLINE, Nov. 10, 2018, available at https://insidetrade.com/trade/trump-us-negotiating-eu-position-%E2%80%98total-strength%E2%80%99 (last visited Jun. 6, 2022).

[73] Comprehensive and Progressive Transpacific Partnership, Mar. 8, 2018, available at vhttp://international.gc.ca/trade-commerce/trade-agreements-accords-commerciaux/agr-acc/cptpp-ptpgp/text-texte/cptpp-ptpgp.aspx?lang=eng (last visited Dec. 7, 2018).

[74] *See* USTR, *United States-European Union Negotiating Objectives, supra* note 48, at 7 (which makes no mention of investment arbitration).

B. Evidence is lacking that eliminating tariffs and quotas would have reduced the US trade deficit, another major Trump administration objective, except perhaps if auto imports from Germany and other EU countries had been reduced by 20-25% "national security" tariffs on autos. This would almost certainly have resulted in retaliation by the EU against imports from the United States and the termination of any prospect of a bilateral trade agreement. Experience with the 2020 Phase One agreement with China confirms this conclusion: continuation of 7% or 25 % tariffs on over $350 billion worth of US imports from China has not reduced the US trade deficit with China.[75]

C. The negotiating objectives provided extensive coverages of services, including telecommunications and financial services' market opening, a major opportunity to deal with what constitutes 75%-80% of both economies. However, given the difficulties in the TTIP negotiations this would have very difficult to achieve even if they had been a major focus of the negotiations, despite the enormous US services trade surplus (about $250 billion globally and $55 billion with the EU alone).[76] The same is of course true if any broader effort on services were made within the framework of the Trade and Technology Council under Biden.

D. The legal question of whether a regional trade agreement, excluding autos and automotive parts as well as agriculture, would pass muster under the GATT with the "substantially all trade" requirement for free trade agreements is unresolved. Any completed agreement would likely have been challenged at the WTO by any WTO Members who believed they would have been adversely affected, particularly Brazil, China, and India, as noted in Part III, above. Still, with the Appellate Body non-functional,[77] the Dispute Settlement Body could not have imposed sanctions in any proceeding in which the losing Party requested its appeal to the Appellate Body.[78]

---

[75] In 2021, the US trade deficit with China, despite the penalty tariffs, was $355,308,700 according to US census data.

[76] *See* Mark J. Perry, *America Has Large and Growing Trade Surpluses for Services,* Jun. 21, 2016, AMERICAN ENTERPRISE INSTITUTE, available at http://www.aei.org/publication/america-has-large-and-growing-trade-surpluses-for-services-q-do-those-result-from-our-unfair-trade-practices/ (last visited Nov. 2, 2018).

[77] As of December 11, 2019, only one Appellate Body member remained in place, under a system that requires three members to adjudicate appeals. *See* WTO, *Appellate Body Members, 2019,* available at https://www.wto.org/english/tratop_e/dispu_e/ab_members_descrp_e.htm (last visited Jan. 7, 2019).

[78] The WTO's Dispute Settlement Body makes the resolution of an appeal where one is requested a condition precedent to further steps such as the imposition of sanctions for non-compliance. *See* DSU, art. 17.1 ("The Appellate Body shall hear appeals from panel cases.")

E. The prospect of a successful negotiation under Trump was always threatened by non-trade issues, such as widespread dislike of the President in the EU, including in many EU governments; resentment of the United States' withdrawal from the Iran nuclear agreement and the re-imposition of sanctions that have dashed hopes of continuing EU trade with Iran; US policies that appeared to be designed to emasculate if not destroy entirely the World Trade Organization; US repudiation of the Paris Agreement on Climate Change;[79] US "national security" tariffs imposed on steel and aluminum on European exporters and other allies as noted earlier;[80] US policies designed to roll-back auto emission standards and encourage the use of coal in the United States and abroad;[81] and the movement of some EU nations closer to US adversaries such as Russia and China. For example, French President Emmanuel Macron has stated, "From the French side, I do not agree with signing broad trade agreements with countries that do not respect the Paris Agreement" (referring to a proposed agreement with Mercosur).[82] While none of these might have torpedoed the negotiations individually, taken together would have reduced the willingness of some of the Members of the EU to offer the compromises that would have been necessary if an agreement were to be concluded.

All of these considerations either doomed the negotiations to failure or made it highly unlikely that they would have succeeded even if pursued in good faith by both the United States and the EU. The Trump administration achieved some success by completing the USMCA with two much smaller economies that are overwhelmingly dependent on the United States as their major export market,[83] and the "Phase One" agreement designed in part to moderate the trade war with China which after

---

[79] *See* US Dept. of State, *Communication Regarding Intent to Withdraw from the Paris Agreement,* Aug. 4, 2017, available at https://www.state.gov/r/pa/prs/ps/2017/08/273050.htm (last visited Nov. 30, 2018) (indicating "U.S. intent to withdraw from the Paris Agreement as soon as it is eligible to do so") [approximately three years].

[80] *See* US Customs and Border Security, *Section 232 Tariffs on Aluminum and Steel (Update),* Oct. 24, 2018, available at https://www.cbp.gov/trade/programs-administration/entry-summary/232-tariffs-aluminum-and-steel (last visited Dec. 8, 2018).

[81] *See, e.g.,* Devin Henry, *Trump Signs Bill Undoing Obama Coal Mining Rule,* THE HILL, Feb. 16, 2017, available at https://thehill.com/policy/energy-environment/319938-trump-signs-bill-undoing-obama-coal-mining-rule (last visited Nov. 30, 2018).

[82] Andres Schipani, *Macron Warns EU-Mercosur Deal Hangs on Bolsonaro,* FINANCIAL TIMES, Nov. 29, 2018, available at https://www.ft.com/content/da19561c-f41f-11e8-9623-d7f9881e729f (last visited Nov. 30, 2018).

[83] Seventy-four percent of Canada's exports and of Mexico's exports are destined for the United States, OBSERVATORY OF ECONOMIC COMPLEXITY (Canada), available at https://atlas.media.mit.edu/en/profile/country/can/ (last visited Jan. 20, 2019); (Mexico), available at https://atlas.media.mit.edu/en/profile/country/mex/ (last visited Jan. 20, 2019).

two years seems to have done little to reduce the US trade deficit or cause China to change its anti-competitive policies.[84] A Trump administration trade agreement with the EU—an economy of roughly equal size which sends only about 14 percent of its total exports to the United States[85] and is much more difficult to bully than smaller trading partners—would have failed. One can hope that President Biden's more modest Trade and Technology Council will fare better.

Abbreviations

Brexit	Process of United Kingdom withdrawal from the EU
CETA	Comprehensive Economic and Trade Agreement (EU and Canada)
CPTPP	Comprehensive and Progressive TPP (TPP members less the United States)
EU	European Union
FTA	Free Trade Agreement
GATT	General Agreement on Tariffs and Trade
G-7	(Canada, France, Germany, Italy, Japan, the United Kingdom, and the United States)
GMO	Genetically modified organisms
MFN	Most Favored Nation Treatment
NAFTA	North American Free Trade Agreement
SME	Small and Medium-Sized Enterprises
TBT	Technical Barriers to Trade agreement (WTO)
TPA	Trade Promotion Authority
TTIP	Transatlantic Trade and Investment Partnership
TPP	Transpacific Partnership (Australia, Brunei, Canada, Chile, Japan, Malaysia, Mexico, New Zealand, Peru, Singapore, the United States and Vietnam)
TTC	US-EU Trade and Technology Council
UK	United Kingdom
USITC	US International Trade Commission
USMCA	United States-Mexico-Canada Agreement ("NAFTA 2.0")
USTR	Office of the US Trade Representative
WTO	World Trade Organization

---

[84] *See, e.g., Trade Deal Buys Xi Time before Next U.S.-China Battle,* BLOOMBERG NEWS, Dec. 16, 2019, available at https://www.bloomberg.com/news/articles/2019-12-16/trump-trade-deal-buys-xi-time-before-next-u-s-china-battle (last visited Dec. 18, 2019).

[85] European Commission data, available at https://atlas.media.mit.edu/en/profile/country/mex/ (last visited Jan. 20, 2019).

CHAPTER 7

STATE-TO-STATE DISPUTE SETTLEMENT UNDER THE USMCA: BETTER THAN NAFTA?

By J. Anthony VanDuzer[1]

Introduction

After thirteen months of negotiation, the United States, Mexico, and Canada agreed to the United States-Mexico-Canada Agreement (USMCA) on September 30, 2018, signing the final text on November 30, 2018.[2] The USMCA replaces the North American Free Trade Agreement (NAFTA),[3] the treaty that had governed continental trade since January 1, 1994. The new agreement contains a few significant alterations to NAFTA provisions, such as the phasing out of investor-state dispute settle-

---

[1] Professor of Hyman Soloway Chair in Business and Trade Law, Common Law Section, Faculty of Law, University of Ottawa (vanduzer@uottawa.ca).

[2] The agreement had to be ratified by each country in accordance with their domestic procedures and implemented into domestic law. Mexico ratified the treaty on June 19, 2019 (Amanda Connolly, "With the House of Commons adjourned for the summer, here's where things stand with NAFTA" Global News, 20 June 2019, online: https://globalnews.ca/news/5411239/new-nafta-ratification-summer-2019/ accessed 16 September 2019). The US House of Representatives approved the agreement with an amending protocol on December 19, 2019 and Senate approval was received on January 16, 2020. President Trump completed the US ratification process on January 29, 2020, signing the agreement into law (Public Law No. 116–113)). Canadian implementing legislation came into force on March 13, 2020 (*An Act to Implement the Agreement between Canada, the United States and the United States of Mexico*, S.C. 2020, c. 1) and Canadian ratification was announced on April 3, 2020 (Statement of the Deputy Prime Minister on Canada's ratification of the new NAFTA, April 3, 2020).

[3] Done December 17, 1992, reprinted in 32 I.L.M. 670 (1993) [NAFTA].

ment between Canada and the US and stricter rules of origin for automobiles. As well, some up-dating was done, such as adding a chapter on digital trade. But the rules for state-to-state dispute settlement in NAFTA Chapter 20 were brought forward in Chapter 31 of the USMCA largely unchanged.

On December 10, 2019, however, the USMCA parties agreed to a protocol of amendment (the 2019 Protocol). The agreement now provides better protection for labor rights and the environment and eliminates some of the enhanced protection for pharmaceutical patents previously agreed to in 2018.[4] Significantly, the state-to-state dispute settlement process was also changed. The key improvement was to make it more difficult for one state party to block the formation of state-to-state dispute settlement panels, which, as discussed below, had sometimes frustrated the state-to-state dispute settlement process under NAFTA.

From one point of view, even maintaining the *status quo* in state-to-state dispute settlement would have been considered a victory for the international rule of law compared to what might have been negotiated. The American government had proposed to weaken the process by rendering decisions by adjudicative panels hearing state-to-state disputes merely advisory.[5] On the other hand, failing to address the endemic failings of NAFTA Chapter 20 would have been a lost opportunity. NAFTA Chapter 20 had become so dysfunctional that its panel process had not been used since the third case was initiated in 1998.[6] With the WTO Appellate Body com-

---

[4] Protocol of Amendment to the Agreement between Canada, the United States and the United Mexican States, done December 10, 2019 [2019 Protocol].

[5] In its revised negotiating objectives released in November 2017, the USTR added the following goal: "provide mechanisms for ensuring that the Parties retain control of disputes and can address situations when a panel has clearly erred in its assessment of the facts or the obligations that apply" (USTR, *Summary of Objectives for the NAFTA Renegotiation* (November 2017)). *See also* Josh Wingrove and Eric Martin, "U.S. Proposes Gutting NAFTA Legal Dispute Tribunals," Bloomberg Markets, October 14, 2017.

[6] *In the Matter of Cross-Border Trucking Services* (USA-Mex-98-2008-01), Final Report of the Panel, February 6, 2001 [*Cross-Border Trucking*]. The other cases were *Tariffs Applied by Canada to Certain U.S.-Origin Agricultural Products* (Can-US-95-2008-01), Final Report of the Panel, December 2, 1996 [*Agricultural Products from US*]; *U.S. Safeguard Action Taken on Broomcorn Brooms from Mexico*, USA-97-2008-01, Final Report of the Panel, November 1, 1998 [*Brooms from Mexico*]. All decisions can be found on the USMCA Secretariat Website, online: <https://can-mex-usa-sec.org/secretariat/report-rapport-reporte.aspx?lang=eng> (accessed May 25, 2022). A fourth case was commenced in 1998, *Cross-Border Bus Services* (USA-98-2008-02), though no panel decision was ever made public (Rafael Leal-Arcas, "Comparative Analysis of NAFTA's Chapter 20 and the WTO's Dispute Settlement Understanding," (2011) Queen Mary University of London, School of Law Research Paper No. 94/2011 [Leal-Arcas, 2011]. One other case used the Chapter 20 process: "In the Matter of British Columbia's June 1, 1998, Stumpage Reduction" though it was under the Softwood Lumber Agreement, May 29, 1996, 35 I.L.M. 1195 (David Gantz, Addressing Dispute Resolution Institutions in a NAFTA Renegotiation, (2018) Mexico Center, Rice University's Baker

pletely ceasing to function in December 2019,[7] failing to ensure that the US, Canada, and Mexico have a robust system to address issues related to their trade relationship would be especially troubling.

The reason the NAFTA parties failed to make improvements in the 2018 USMCA was not because it is difficult to make state-to-state dispute settlement more effective. There is a deep academic literature discussing how dispute settlement systems may be made to work as well as some real-world examples of treaties with state-to-state procedures that address some of the technical problems with NAFTA Chapter 20.[8]

Rather, the problem has been that North American states, particularly the United States, have been unwilling to be subject to a dispute settlement system that would lead to enforceable decisions by independent adjudicators regarding their compliance with the rules they agreed to. In NAFTA Chapter 20, compliance is contemplated as the "normal" outcome when a party is found to have acted contrary to its obligations and retaliation in the form of suspension of concessions is permitted if no resolution can be agreed. But, ultimately, NAFTA Chapter 20 decisions rely on the goodwill of the state found not to be in compliance to change its regime.[9] Nev-

---

Institute for Public Policy at 17) [Gantz, Institutions 2018]. Apparently, the case settled (David Gantz, "Assessing the impact of WTO and regional dispute resolution mechanisms on the world trading system," in, ESTABLISHING JUDICIAL AUTHORITY IN INTERNATIONAL ECONOMIC LAW, Joanna Jemielniak, Laura Nielsen and Henrik Palmer Olsen, eds (Cambridge: Cambridge University Press, 2016, at 49).

[7] The US has blocked appointments to the Appellate Body as part of a strategy to force WTO members to negotiate new rules that address concerns regarding the Appellate Body's practice and decisions. When the terms of the last two members ended on December 10, 2019, the Appellate Body ceased to be able to function. See Tetyana Paysova, Gary Hufbauer & Jeffrey Schott, "The Dispute Settlement Crisis in the World Trade Organization: Causes and Cures," (2018) Peterson Institute for International Economics Policy Brief 18-5.

[8] *E.g.*, David Gantz, "Government to Government Dispute Resolution under NAFTA Chapter 20: A Commentary on the Process," 11 AM. REV. INT'L ARB. 481 (2000) [Gantz, 2000]; Frank J. Garcia, "Decision Making and Dispute Resolution in the Free Trade Area of the Americas: An Essay on Governance," 18 MICH. J. INT'L L. 357 (1997), at 379; Patrick Specht, "The Dispute Settlement Systems of WTO and NAFTA—Analysis and Comparison" 27 GA. J. INT'L & COMP. L. 57 (1998), at 122; Carrin Anne Arnett, "The Mexican Trucking Dispute: A Bottleneck to Free Trade: A Tough (Road) Test on the NAFTA Dispute Settlement Mechanism," (2002-03) 25 HOUS. J. INT' L. 561; Gary Clyde Hufbauer, Jeffrey J. Schott, Paul L.E. Grieco, Yee Wong, NAFTA REVISITED: ACHIEVEMENTS AND CHALLENGES (Washington: Peterson Institute, 2005) at 215. Regarding how problems have been addressed in other recent treaties, *see* the discussion in Simon Lester, Inu Manak & Andrej Arpas, "Access to Trade Justice: Fixing NAFTA's Flawed State-to-State Dispute Settlement Process," WORLD TRADE REV. 1 (2018)[Lester, Manak & Arpas].

[9] *Cross-Border Trucking*, *supra* note 6, was decided in 2001 but no resolution of the non-compliance has been agreed to.

ertheless, panel decisions on compliance and recommendations regarding how compliance can be achieved can play a role in facilitating compliance. Unfortunately, the utility of the dispute settlement process in this regard is further watered down in the USMCA.

Practice under NAFTA Chapter 20 had shown that it did not guarantee that a state with a complaint about another state's non-compliance would be able to make its case before a panel and obtain an authoritative decision regarding its concerns. Since 1998, by refusing to appoint panelists, the US has stymied Mexico's attempts to have a Chapter 20 panel adjudicate its claim that the US has breached its NAFTA obligation to provide access to the US market for Mexican sugar.[10] Unless a state with a concern about another state's non-compliance can force that other state into an adjudicative process, the system has little value. This problem was not effectively addressed in the USMCA signed in 2018. The 2019 Protocol, however, makes significant improvements to the rules ensuring, in almost all cases, that a panel can be put in place. The protocol was adopted largely to respond to concerns in the US House of Representatives that threatened to stall or even preclude approval of the USMCA. But, at least in relation to this aspect of the dispute settlement process, it has delivered an improvement that Canada and Mexico had not been able to secure in the original negotiation.[11]

This paper describes the state-to-state dispute settlement system under Chapter 31 of the USMCA, highlighting both its similarities to and differences from NAFTA Chapter 20, and identifying the persisting problems. It then briefly assesses the likely effectiveness of the USMCA procedure. In short, a few of the changes made in the USMCA, like those addressing the panel appointment problem, may improve its effectiveness compared to NAFTA, while others may further discourage its use.

USMCA Chapter 31 on State-to-State Dispute Settlement

The NAFTA rules on state-to-state dispute settlement were being negotiated at the same time as the WTO Dispute Settlement Understanding (DSU)[12] and the

---

[10] This is discussed in *Cargill v United Mexican States*, ICSID Case No ARB(AF)/05/02, Award (September 18, 2009), at paras 85-100.

[11] David Gantz and Sergio Puig, "The Scorecard of the USMCA Protocol of Amendment" EJIL:Talk (December 23, 2019), online: <https://www.ejiltalk.org/the-scorecard-of-the-usmca-protocol-of-amendment/> (accessed January 2, 2020) [Gantz & Puig].

[12] Dispute Settlement Understanding forming Annex 2 to the Marrakesh Agreement establishing the World Trade Organization, done April 15, 1994, reprinted in 33 I.L.M. 81 (1994) [DSU].

NAFTA parties had access to the draft DSU text.[13] Nevertheless, Chapter 20 largely imported the features of the dispute settlement procedure in Chapter 18 of the Canada-United States Free Trade Agreement.[14] Canada, the US and Mexico have continued to follow the same approach to state-to-state dispute settlement in the USMCA that they did in NAFTA. Chapter 31 of the USMCA adopts the structure and, in many places, the text of NAFTA Chapter 20. The following section describes the essential features of the Chapter 31 process as compared to NAFTA Chapter 20.

Scope of Chapter 31

Like NAFTA Chapter 20, USMCA Chapter 31 begins with a general commitment of the party states to seek agreement on issues regarding the interpretation or application of the agreement and to cooperate and consult to achieve a mutually satisfactory resolution of any matter that might affect the treaty's operation.[15] The formal dispute settlement process is available to deal with disputes among USMCA parties "regarding the interpretation and application of" the agreement or whenever a party state believes that an actual or proposed measure[16] of another USMCA state is or would be inconsistent with that state's obligations under the USMCA. Unlike the NAFTA side deals on labor and the environment, the obligations in the USMCA's labor and environment chapters can be subject to dispute settlement so long as certain preliminary steps to resolve the dispute prescribed in those chapters

---

[13] David Gantz, "The United States and Dispute Settlement under the North American Free Trade Agreement: Ambivalence, Frustration and Occasional Defiance," in THE SWORD AND THE SCALES: THE UNITED STATES AND INTERNATIONAL COURTS AND TRIBUNALS, Cesare Romano, ed. (Cambridge: Cambridge University Press, 2009) 356 [Gantz, 2009]; Gantz, 2000, *supra* note 8, at 488.

[14] Canada-United States Free Trade Agreement (December 22, 1987 and January 2, 1988), 27 I.L.M. 281 (1988) [Canada-US FTA]. *See* Gantz, 2000, *supra* note 8, at 488; Sidney Picker, "NAFTA Chapter Twenty—Reflections on Party-to-Party Dispute Resolution," 14 ARIZ. J. INT'L & COMP. L. 465 (1997), at 466 [Picker, Reflections 1997]. North American Free Trade Implementation Act, Statement of Administrative Action, reprinted in James R. Holbein & Donald J. Musch, NORTH AMERICAN FREE TRADE AGREEMENTS, Booklet 8, at 190 (New York: Oxford University Press, 1994)[US Statement of Administrative Action]. Among the most significant changes was the elimination of the option for the Free Trade Commission to refer the dispute to "binding arbitration," as an alternative to the panel process. *See* Canada-US FTA, art. 1806. Chapter 18 was the model followed even though the dispute settlement system under the Canada-US FTA had been criticized (*e.g.*, Joint Working Group on Dispute Settlement of the American Bar Association, Canadian Bar Association and the Barra Mexicana, cited in Picker Reflections 1997, *Id.*, at 475) and the US, which lost every case under the Canada-US FTA, was unhappy with the procedure (Gantz, 2009, *Id*, at 29).

[15] USMCA art. 31.1. NAFTA art. 2003 is virtually identical.

[16] The DSU does not permit complaints based on proposed measures.

have been exhausted.[17] No recourse to dispute settlement is available for some of the new chapters, such as Chapter 25 on small and medium sized enterprises (art. 25.7) and Chapter 26 on competitiveness (art. 26.3). The new chapters on digital trade (Chapter 19) and State-Owned Enterprises (Chapter 22), however, are subject to dispute settlement.[18] Matters covered under the NAFTA's Chapter 19, which provides for the establishment of bi-national panels to review the decisions of national administrative agencies in anti-dumping and countervailing duty cases were excluded from dispute resolution under NAFTA Chapter 20, but the corresponding chapter in the USMCA is subject to dispute settlement, undoubtedly reflecting long-standing US concerns about the operation of the NAFTA bi-national panel review process.[19]

Like NAFTA, state-to-state dispute settlement under the USMCA is also available where a party is concerned that a measure of another party nullifies or impairs the benefit that the first party reasonably expected to receive under the agreement, even if the measure is not a violation of the treaty.[20] These so-called "non-violation" complaints can be made only in relation to the USMCA provisions dealing with trade in goods in Chapters 2-7, sanitary and phyto-sanitary measures in Chapter 9, government procurement in Chapter 13, cross-border trade in services in Chapter 15,

---

[17] USMCA, arts. 23.17(11) (labor), 24.32 (environment). The 2019 Protocol, *supra* note 3, provides for a rapid response mechanisms to address the denial of the right of free association or collective bargaining Annex 31-A (United-States-Mexico Facility-Specific Rapid Response Labor Mechanism) and Annex 31-B (Canada-Mexico Facility-Specific Rapid Response Mechanism). This is a major innovation for dispute settlement related to labor rights but is beyond the scope of this paper.

[18] The obligations regarding effective enforcement of laws combatting corruption in Chapter 27 are not subject to dispute settlement (art. 27.6(4)). Chapter 28 on good regulatory practices is also excluded from dispute settlement (art. 28.20). Chapter 29 on publication and administration is subject to dispute settlement but only in relation to a "sustained and recurring course of action or inaction inconsistent" with the chapter (art. 29.15). Obligations under Chapter 33 on macro-economic policy and exchange rate matters is subject to dispute settlement only in relation to alleged breaches of its transparency or reporting requirements in a recurring and persistent manner (art. 33.8). Like NAFTA, inconsistency with USMCA related to tax conventions can only be addressed with the agreement of the relevant national tax authorities (art. 32.3). As under NAFTA, the dispute settlement process operates somewhat differently in relation to financial services (USMCA art. 17.23).

[19] USMCA Chapter 10. The broad scope of the NAFTA exclusion in art. 2004 was confirmed in an investor-state dispute under NAFTA Chapter 11 in *Canfor Corporation v United States of America and Terminal Forest Products Ltd. v. United States of America*, Decision on Preliminary Question, June 6, 2006. NAFTA also requires that disputes regarding certain environmental treaties and standards measures be dealt with under Chapter 20 at the request of a party. There is no equivalent provision in the USMCA.

[20] USMCA art. 31.2(1)(c).

and intellectual property in Chapter 20.[21] The scope for non-violation complaints is a bit broader than NAFTA Chapter 20 which did not permit such complaints regarding government procurement.[22]

Following NAFTA Chapter 20, the USMCA prohibits the party states from providing civil rights of action under their domestic laws that would allow private parties to sue a USMCA party in their domestic courts claiming that some action of that party is inconsistent with its treaty obligations.[23]

USMCA Chapter 31 also follows NAFTA Chapter 20 in establishing a scheme to govern disputes that arise under both the WTO rules and the USMCA. Such disputes can arise frequently because there are substantial overlaps in the substantive coverage of the two agreements. Indeed, as in NAFTA, the USMCA directly incorporates some WTO obligations.[24] USMCA provisions, however, cover a much

---

[21] NAFTA art. 2004 and Annex 2004. The non-violation jurisdiction of the NAFTA is drawn from a similarly worded provision in the GATT (Cherie Taylor "Dispute Resolution as a Catalyst for Economic Integration and an Agent for Deepening Integration: NAFTA and MERCOSUR?" 17 Nw. J. INT'L L. & BUS. 850 (1997), at 883). Nevertheless, complaints based on "the existence of any other situation" which are permitted under GATT, art. XXIII.1(c), cannot be brought under NAFTA Chapter 20 or the USMCA. One Canada-US FTA panel report, *Puerto Rico Regulations on the Import, Distribution and Sale of UHT Milk from Quebec*, USA-93-1807-01, considered as an alternative claim whether US action to prohibit the sale of Canadian UHT milk in Puerto Rico nullified or impaired Canadian benefits without violating the NAFTA and the Panel found nullification and impairment.

[22] Non-violation complaints cannot be made in relation to the following obligations: Recognition of the Mexican State's Direct, Inalienable, and Imprescriptible Ownership of Hydrocarbons (Chapter 8); Technical Barriers to Trade (Chapter 11); Trade Remedies (Chapter 10); Investment (Chapter 14); Temporary Entry (Chapter 15); Financial Services (Chapter 16); Telecommunications (Chapter 18), Competition Policy (Chapter 21); State-owned Enterprises (Chapter 22); Small and Medium-sized Enterprises (Chapter 25); Competitiveness (Chapter 26); Anti-corruption (Chapter 27); Good Regulatory Practices (Chapter 28), Publication and Administration (Chapter 29); Administrative and Institutional Provisions (Chapter 30); Dispute Settlement (Chapter 31); Exceptions and General Provisions (Chapter 32), Macroeconomic Policies and Exchange Rate Matters (Chapter 33); and Final Provisions (Chapter 34). By comparison, under NAFTA Chapter 20 non-violation complaints could be made in relation to Technical Barriers to Trade (Chapter 9) but not Investment (Chapter 11), Procurement (Chapter 10), Telecommunications (Chapter 13), Financial Services (Chapter 14), Competition Policy (Chapter 15), Temporary Entry (Chapter 16), Publication, Notification and Administration of Laws (Chapter 18), Review of Dispute Settlement in Antidumping/Countervailing Duty Matters (Chapter 19), Exceptions (Chapter 21), or Final Provisions (Chapter 22).

[23] USMCA art. 31.21 following NAFTA art. 2021.

[24] *E.g.*, the GATT national treatment obligation is incorporated in USMCA art. 2.3. *See* J. Johnson, THE NORTH AMERICAN FREE TRADE AGREEMENT: A COMPREHENSIVE GUIDE (Toronto: Canada Law Book, 1994), at 488 for a summary of GATT obligations incorporated in NAFTA and parallel obligations in the two agreements.

broader range of economic activity and, as noted, contain a few distinctive provisions. Disputes under provisions unique to the USMCA can only be brought under the USMCA.[25] At the same time, the WTO covers some matters that are not addressed in USMCA, including standards for national regimes in the critically important areas of anti-dumping, subsidies and countervailing measures.[26] Where there is overlap, states can choose where to bring their claims, as under the NAFTA.[27] Once a dispute settlement proceeding has been initiated under either USMCA or the WTO, however, proceedings cannot be initiated under the other forum in relation to the same subject matter.

Consultations

Like the NAFTA Chapter 20 process, consultations are the first step in dispute settlement under the USMCA. Consultations are commenced by a formal written request from the complaining state to the other parties through their national sections of the Secretariat,[28] a body established under the treaty.[29] The parties are obliged to make every attempt to resolve the matter in a mutually satisfactory way.[30] If the third USMCA party state is not directly involved in the dispute it may nevertheless partic-

---

[25] *E.g.*, the WTO does not include provisions equivalent to USMCA provisions on the review of trade remedies determinations (Chapter 10), Investment (Chapter 14), Temporary Entry (Chapter 15), Competition Policy (Chapter 21), State-owned Enterprises (Chapter 22), Small and Medium-sized Enterprises (Chapter 25), Competitiveness (Chapter 26), Anti-corruption (Chapter 27), Good Regulatory Practices (Chapter 28), Publication and Administration (Chapter 29), Macroeconomic Policies and Exchange Rate Matters (Chapter 33), nor, of course, would WTO dispute resolution be available for specific tariff reduction commitments unique to USMCA. WTO dispute settlement under the DSU applies to state measures that are inconsistent with an obligation under one of the covered agreements or otherwise cause nullification or impairment of any benefit another state party could reasonably expect to accrue to it under the obligation. Only NAFTA Chapter 20 and the USMCA allow dispute resolution to be initiated in relation to proposed measures (NAFTA art. 2004; USMCA art. 31.2(1)(b)). Interpretive issues may be addressed under the Marrakesh Agreement establishing the World Trade Organization, done April 15, 1994, reprinted in (1994) 33 I.L.M. 81, art. IX.2.

[26] As well, because the USMCA affirms the parties' WTO obligations (art. 1.2), it may be that the parties can resort to USCMA dispute settlement for any WTO obligation. Gantz suggested that this would result from the same obligation in NAFTA (art. 103.1)(Gantz, Institutions 2018, *supra* note 6, at 49).

[27] In NAFTA, Chapter 20 dispute resolution is required in particular cases. *See* Johnson *supra* note 23, at 488 for a summary of these exceptions in NAFTA, arts. 2005(3) and (4). There is no equivalent in the USMCA.

[28] USMCA art. 31.4 following NAFTA art. 2006(2).

[29] USMCA art. 30.6. NAFTA art. 2002 creates the similar NAFTA Secretariat.

[30] USMCA art. 31.1 following NAFTA art. 2003(5).

ipate in the consultations if it considers that it has a "substantial interest" in the dispute.[31] Pursuant to Article 31.4(6) of USMCA, the parties have three responsibilities during the consultation phase: (1) to provide the other parties with sufficient information to enable a full examination of how the measure or proposed measure might affect the operation or application of the USMCA; (2) to treat information designated as confidential on the same basis as the party providing it; and (3) to avoid a resolution that adversely affects the interests of any other party under the treaty.[32]

While the parties have used consultations under NAFTA Chapter 20 on at least eight occasions not including the three cases in which panels were established,[33] there is no public record, official or unofficial, of the number of consultations. Often the country initiating consultations has publicly disclosed that it has done so. There are, however, varying estimates of the number of cases that have been the subject of consultations and the other preliminary stages of Chapter 20. There is little evidence, however, that consultations under Chapter 20 have helped the NAFTA states to resolve their disputes.[34]

---

[31] USMCA art. 31.4(4) following NAFTA art. 2006(3). The DSU provision regarding third party participation is very similar, though a "substantial trade interest" is required (DSU art. 4.11). The meaning of this provision was considered in *European Communities – Regime for the Importation, Sale and Distribution of Bananas (Complaint by Ecuador, Guatemala, Honduras, Mexico and the United States)*, AB-1997-3 (Appellate Body Report)(September 9, 1997).

[32] NAFTA art. 2006(5) is almost identical.

[33] Mcrory lists 8 consultations to 2003 (Patrick Mcrory, "Chapters 19 and 20 of NAFTA: An Overview and Analysis of NAFTA Dispute Settlement," in THE FIRST DECADE OF NAFTA: THE FUTURE OF FREE TRADE IN NORTH AMERICA, Kevin Kennedy, ed (Ardsley, NY: Transnational, 2004), at 491-2. Gantz lists 11 consultations between 1994 and 2001 (*Gantz*, 2000, *supra* note 8, at 519-521) with only 3 resolved at the consultation stage. In 2000, Alvarez said there had been 14 disputes under NAFTA Chapter 20 in addition to the three cases in which panels were established (Guillermo Aguilar Alvarez, "The Mexican View on the Operation of NAFTA for the Resolution of Canada-U.S.-Mexico Disputes," CAN.-U.S. L. J. 219 (2000), at 222 (6 settled and 2 suspended at the consultation stage, 2 settled, 2 suspended and 2 unsettled at the Commission stage). An earlier study by the Economic Commission for Latin America and the Caribbean found that there had been 11 in the first 3 years of NAFTA (to December 31, 1997) though the study did not identify the cases (ECLAC, *NAFTA Implementation in Canada: The First Three Years*, online: <http://www.eclac.org/publicaciones/xml/8/9098/nafta-cn.html> (accessed December 18, 2018). López, cites 8 as of December 1996 that reached the consultation phase with 1 resolved at that stage, 5 advancing to the Commission and one (*Brooms from Mexico, supra* note 6) advancing to a panel (David Lopez, "Dispute Resolution Under NAFTA: Lessons from the Early Experience" 32 TEX INT'L L. J. 163 (1997) [Lopez], at 168-9). Hufbauer, Schott, Grieco & Wong, *supra* note 8, identified only 8 cases between 1994 and 2004 (at 245).

[34] Gantz, 2000, *supra* note 8, at 520-1.

Under the USMCA, the parties may decide at any time to undertake alternative dispute resolution procedures, such as mediation.[35] There is no equivalent provision in NAFTA, though the parties could always have agreed to proceed in this way. There is no evidence that they ever did so.

Role of Free Trade Commission Abolished

Under NAFTA, if consultations failed to resolve the dispute within 30 days of the delivery of the request for consultations, the next step was that any of the consulting states could request a meeting of the Free Trade Commission, a body established under NAFTA and composed of the trade ministers of each of the NAFTA countries or their designates.[36] Unless its members agreed otherwise, the Free Trade Commission had to meet within ten days and "endeavor to resolve the dispute."[37] The Commission could seek to assist the parties to reach a mutually satisfactory solution by calling on technical advisors, establishing working groups or expert groups, using good offices, conciliation, mediation or other dispute resolution procedures or making recommendations.[38]

The mandatory involvement by the Free Trade Commission was a feature of the NAFTA process that distinguished it from WTO dispute settlement where a panel may be immediately requested if consultations fail.[39] Although the parties in WTO disputes may agree on good offices, conciliation or mediation and such assistance may be offered by the WTO Director-General,[40] these procedures have been seldom used in WTO practice.[41]

The USMCA provides for the establishment of a Free Trade Commission with the same characteristics as the NAFTA Free Trade Commission and the 2018 USMCA contemplated a virtually identical role for the Commission in dispute set-

---

[35] USMCA arts. 31.5(6)-(9).

[36] The Free Trade Commission is established under USMCA art. 30.1. The time period that must elapse before a panel may be requested may vary from 45 days if a third party has participated in the consultations to 15 days if the dispute relates to perishable goods. The parties may also agree to a longer period of time (USMCA art 31.5(1)). NAFTA is identical (art. 2007(1)).

[37] NAFTA art. 2007(4).

[38] NAFTA art. 2007(5).

[39] DSU art. 6. The minimum period of consultations under the DSU is 60 days.

[40] DSU art. 5.

[41] Joost Pauwelyn, "The Limits of Litigation: "Americanization" and Negotiation in the Settlement of WTO Disputes," 19 OHIO ST. J. DISP. RESOL. 121 (2003), at 137; Robert MacDougall, "Making Trade Dispute Settlement More Accessible and Inclusive" (2017) CIGI, online: <https://www.cigionline.org/articles/making-trade-dispute-settlement-more-accessible-and-inclusive> (accessed October 29, 2018).

tlement.[42] The 2019 Protocol, however, eliminates the Commission's involvement entirely. This may have been done because the NAFTA Free Trade Commission had not played a significant role in the resolution of disputes.[43] As a practical matter, the trade ministers are likely to have been involved in the disputes from the outset in any case.

Establishment of a Panel

The arrangements for the establishment of a panel under the USMCA follow NAFTA in most respects. Where consultations have failed to resolve the dispute within seventy-five days from the date of the request for consultations (or any other period agreed by the parties), any USMCA party involved in the consultations may request the establishment of a panel to hear the dispute by filing a written notice with the other party's section of the Secretariat.[44] If the third USMCA state was not involved in the consultations, it can join as a complaining party if it considers that it has a "substantial interest" in the dispute.[45] Alternatively, on delivery of a written notice to the disputing parties and to the Secretariat, the third state is entitled to attend all hearings, to make written and oral submissions to the panel and to receive written submissions of the disputing parties.[46] Once a request for a panel has been made, the panel is established.[47]

Like NAFTA, the USMCA provides standard terms of reference for panels. The language follows WTO DSU Article 7.1, mandating panels to ". . . examine, in light of the relevant provisions of the Agreement, the matter referred to in the request for the establishment of a panel under Article 31.6 (Establishment of a Panel)."[48] If a complaining party bases its claim on nullification or impairment, then the terms of reference must specify that. If either party wants the panel to make findings as to the degree of adverse trade effects, that must be included in the terms of reference as well.[49]

---

[42] The Free Trade Commission is established under USMCA art. 30.1 and its role in dispute settlement was set out in arts. 31.5(1)-(5).

[43] Gantz concluded that the FTC has not played much of a role in resolving disputes (Gantz, 2000, *supra* note 8, at 524).

[44] USMCA art. 31.6(1). Under NAFTA, a request for a panel can be filed 30 days after the Commission had been convened if the matter is not resolved (NAFTA art. 2008(1)).

[45] USMCA art. 31.6. *See* identical provision in NAFTA art. 2008(3).

[46] USMCA art. 31.14.

[47] USMCA art. 31.6(4).

[48] USMCA art. 31.7(1). DSU art. 7.1 goes on to say "to make such findings as will assist the DSB in making the recommendations or in giving the rulings as provided in that/those agreements." Under the USMCA, the parties can agree not to use these terms of reference.

Panel Roster and Composition

As under NAFTA, USMCA dispute settlement panels consist of 5 members, though the 2019 Protocol permits the parties to agree on there being only 3 members. Panelist are "normally" to be appointed from a roster of up to thirty individuals.[50] Roster members are appointed for at least three years and may be reappointed.[51]

The roster is to be composed of individuals who

- possess "expertise or experience in international law, international trade, other matters covered by this Agreement, or the resolution of disputes arising under international trade agreements,"[52]
- are selected on the basis of "objectivity, reliability, and sound judgment,"
- are independent of all three USMCA countries, and
- comply with a code of conduct established by the Commission.[53]

The code of conduct was established by the Commission effective July 1, 2020.[54]

In addition to these requirements, the USMCA requires panelists in disputes arising under Chapter 23 (Labor), Chapter 24 (Environment) or Chapter 27 (Anti-Corruption) to possess relevant expertise in these areas.

Under NAFTA Chapter 20, the appointment of roster members has been a critical problem. NAFTA provides that the roster is to be established by consensus of the three state parties. Such a consensus proved difficult to achieve. While there is very little information in the public domain, David Gantz, a leading NAFTA commentator and former state department official, has said that at some point in the 1990s the parties "informally agreed on a roster of approximately five persons per party, but it was never adopted formally."[55] In late 2004, the Canadian government passed an order-in-council appointing 10 Canadian roster members for a three-year

---

[49] USMCA arts. 31.7(2) and (3). *See* similar provision in NAFTA arts. 2012(3), (4), and (5).

[50] USMCA art. 31.9(3). *See* similar provision in NAFTA art. 2011(3).

[51] USMCA art. 31.8(1). *See* similar provision in NAFTA art. 2009(1).

[52] *See* similar provision in NAFTA art. 2009(2)(a). This is slightly different from the Canada-US FTA requirement that panelists have expertise in the particular matter under consideration (Canada-US FTA, art. 18). Under the DSU, panels must be composed of "well-qualified governmental and/or non-governmental individuals" who "should be selected with a view to ensuring the independence of the members, a sufficiently diverse background and a wide spectrum of experience" (art. 8).

[53] USMCA art. 31.8(2).

[54] The code of conduct is available on the USMCA Secretariat website, online: <https://can-mex-usa-sec.org/secretariat/agreement-accord-acuerdo/usmca-aceum-tmec/code-code-codigo.aspx?lang=eng> (accessed May 25, 2022) [USMCA Code of Conduct].

[55] Gantz, Institutions 2018, *supra* note 6, at 16; Gantz, 2000, *supra* note 8, at 492 (n 56).

term beginning in 2006 and ending in December 2009 to take effect on the date the appointments were approved by the Free Trade Commission.[56] According to one Canadian government official, the Canadian appointees were approved by the Free Trade Commission along with roster members from the US and Mexico to put in place a full thirty-person roster for a term that ended December 31, 2009.[57] The 2006 appointment of a full roster was recently confirmed by Lester, Manak & Arpas based on their conversations with officials at the NAFTA Secretariat. There is no evidence, however, that a roster was put in place following the expiry of the roster appointed in 2006. As discussed below, the absence of a roster has fundamentally undermined the effectiveness of NAFTA Chapter 20.

Little was done in the 2018 USMCA to address the challenge of requiring the agreement of all three parties on a roster. NAFTA's consensus approach was retained. The 2018 USMCA only added a provision intended to prevent the roster, once established, from being diminished or eliminated by the expiry of members' terms with no replacements appointed. Roster members were to stay in place until replaced.

The 2019 Protocol, however, addresses head on the problems experienced with the NAFTA roster. While the parties must "endeavour to achieve consensus on the appointments" to the roster, each party is to designate ten roster members and, if there is no consensus within one month of the entry into force of the USMCA, the roster is composed of the designated individuals. Where an existing roster member is unable or unwilling to continue, the party that designated that member shall designate a replacement. If there is no consensus on that individual joining the roster within a month of the designation, the individual is added to the roster. Under this regime, a recalcitrant party cannot block the establishment of at least a partial roster composed of designates of the other two parties. The roster would only fail if no party designated anyone. A full 30-person roster was put in place prior to the USCMA coming into force.[58]

Appointment of Panelists

The appointment process for panelists under the USMCA is almost identical to that under NAFTA. In the usual case, where there are only two disputing parties, the

---

[56] Order-in-Council 2004-1484 (Vol. 138, Can. Gazette Part 1, No. 51, December 18, 2004).

[57] Email from official in Canada's Department of Foreign Affairs and International Trade dated November 19, 2008, on file with the author. In the Fall of 2018, the Canadian government was engaged in a process to identify Canadian nominees for the NAFTA Chapter 20 roster. *See* online: <https://www.international.gc.ca/gac-amc/appointments-nominations/appointments-nominations-IT_CA-CI_NC.aspx?lang=eng> (accessed December 16, 2018).

[58] The roster is available on the USMCA Secretariat website, online: <https://can-mex-usa-sec.org/secretariat/dispute-differends-controversias/members-membres-miembros.aspx?lang=eng> (accessed May 25, 2022).

parties must first try to agree on a panel chair. If there is no agreement within fifteen days of the delivery of the request for a panel, a disputing party chosen by lot can choose the chair who cannot be a citizen of that party.[59] This default appointment process was never used under NAFTA.[60] In the three cases under NAFTA, the parties agreed on a chair who was not a national of a NAFTA party state. Because the default procedure was never used, there is some uncertainty regarding how it is to operate. The 2019 Protocol provides the useful clarification that if the responding party "refuses to participate in or fails to appear for the choosing by lot procedure, the complaining Party shall select an individual from the roster who is not a citizen of that Party" and then notify the responding party.[61] This clarification is designed to ensure that the responding party cannot prevent the appointment of a panel chair.

The process for appointment of the other panel members follows the distinctive reverse selection approach in NAFTA.[62] Each disputing party selects two panelists who are nationals of the *other* NAFTA party.[63] If no selection is made by a party within fifteen days, the panelists not appointed are to be selected by lot from the roster members who are citizens of the other party.[64] As with the chair selection process, the 2019 Protocol stipulates that where the responding party refuses to participate in or fails to appear for the choosing by lot procedure, the complaining party can appoint the remaining panel members, in this case by selecting two individuals from the roster who are its citizens.[65] Again, this provision is designed to ensure that the responding party cannot frustrate the appointment of a panel.

---

[59] USMCA art. 31.9(1)(b). NAFTA art. 2011(1)(b), is the same.

[60] Under the Canada-US FTA, the chair was chosen last by the Commission and, in default of a decision of the Commission, by the 4 panelists already appointed (art. 1807(3)). This meant less control of the process by the states (Picker, Reflections 1997, *supra* note 14, at 470-1).

[61] USMCA art. 31.9(1)(c).

[62] NAFTA art. 2011(1)(c). This reverse selection process was not used under the Canada-US FTA. According to Gantz, this approach was suggested by Guillermo Aguilar, one of the principal Mexican NAFTA negotiators. Apparently, he thought that it would ensure that governments would choose only truly independent and objective individuals (Gantz, 2009, *supra* note 13, at 25).

[63] USMCA art. 31.9(1)(c).

[64] USMCA art. 31.9(1). Cases under NAFTA and Canada-US FTA Chapter 18 have not split on national lines. Where all three USMCA parties are involved in the dispute, the process operates somewhat differently as under NAFTA (art. 2011(2)). *See* USMCA art. 31.9(2).

[65] USMCA art. 31.9(1)(d) actually provides that this procedure applies whenever *any party* refuses to participate in or fails to appear for the choosing by lot procedure. In practice, it is not likely that the complaining party will fail to appoint panelists to hear a dispute it has initiated.

Panelists are "normally" to be chosen by parties from the roster. Any disputing party may exercise a preemptory challenge against any individual not on the roster who is proposed as a panelist by another party within fifteen days after the panelist has been proposed.[66]

In NAFTA Chapter 20 disputes, the inability of the parties to agree on a roster meant that panelists were selected in other ways in practice. Though the parties have followed the reverse selection process in the first instance, preemptory challenges have been frequently exercised.[67] In the absence of a roster, there is no limit on the use of such challenges. In the three cases under NAFTA where a panel was established substantial delay in appointing panelists occurred partly as a consequence of preemptory challenges.[68] Panel selection in two of the NAFTA cases took six months while in the third it took 16 and a half months.[69] In at least one case, the failure by a party to choose panelists actually prevented a panel from being established.[70] Without a roster, there is no way to give effect to the choosing by lot process where a party fails to appoint panelists. As noted above, there has been a long ongoing dispute between Mexico and the US regarding access to the US market for Mexican sugar.[71] Since 1998, by refusing to appoint panelists the US has frustrated Mexico's

---

[66] USMCA art. 31.9(3). *See* the similar provision in NAFTA art. 2011(3). A caveat was introduced into the USMCA rules in the November 30, 2018 text. A pre-emptory challenge to a non-roster choice is not available if "no qualified and available individual on the roster possesses the necessary specialized expertise." In such a case, the disputing party can only "raise concerns that the panelist does not meet the requirements for qualification to the roster."

[67] Debra Steger, "Dispute Settlement under the North American Free Trade Agreement," in J. Lacarte and J. Granados eds., Intergovernmental Trade Dispute Settlement: Multilateral and Regional Approaches (London: Cameron May, 2004) citing interviews with Canadian and US government officials.

[68] Steger, *Id.*

[69] Gantz, 2000, *supra* note 8, at 501. For example, in *Agricultural Products from the US*, *supra* note 6, four panelists were selected by early October 1995 with the US panelist selected by Canada and the Canadian panelists selected by the US. The parties experienced substantial difficulty in agreeing upon a fifth panelist, the chair. Canada and the United States finally agreed on a chair, English jurist Eli Lauterpacht, in January 1996 (Lopez, *supra* note 33, at 172).

[70] Steger, *supra* note 67.

[71] *Supra* note 10. In a WTO case brought by the US to challenge measures taken by Mexico in response, Mexico asked first the panel and then the Appellate Body to decline to exercise WTO jurisdiction because the matter was "inextricably linked to a broader dispute" which only a NAFTA Chapter 20 panel could properly decide. The Appellate Body rejected this argument, deciding that a WTO panel could not refuse to exercise jurisdiction once it was established that the panel had jurisdiction (*Mexico - Tax Measures on Soft Drinks and Other Beverages*, Appellate Body Report, WT/DS308/AB/R, adopted March 24, 2006, paras. 10, 40, 57.

attempts to have a Chapter 20 panel adjudicate its claim that the US has breached its NAFTA obligation to provide access to the US market for Mexican sugar.[72]

The amendments to the state-to-state dispute settlement process in the 2019 Protocol are intended to remove the impediments to establishing a panel caused by a recalcitrant party. The new rules provide that the failure of a party to designate panelists to the roster does not prevent the establishment of a panel and the Rules of Procedure established by the Free Trade Commission address how to compose a panel in that situation.[73]

With respect to the chair, if the disputing parties cannot agree on a chair, the disputing party chosen by lot is entitled to choose one. If one party refuses to participate in this procedure, the other party can select the chair from the roster. The only limitation is that the chair must not be a citizen of the selecting party. In most real-world scenarios, this process should allow a party that seeks to establish a panel to adjudicate a dispute to choose a chair, despite the refusal of the other party to agree or participate.[74]

With the reverse selection process for the appointment of the remaining panelists, a complaining party must appoint panelists who are citizens of the other disputing party. Here it is possible to imagine a scenario where the establishment of the panel could be frustrated. Unless an appointment is from the roster, the other disputing party has the right to prevent the proposed person from becoming a panel member by a preemptory challenge. If the other disputing party has not appointed any of its citizens to the roster (and none of the other parties have either), then the complaining party will have to appoint someone who is not on the roster and risk a preemptory challenge.[75] The estab-

---

[72] In a subsequent dispute, Mexico insisted that the dispute regarding its tuna exports to the US be dealt with at the WTO despite US preference for NAFTA Chapter 20 (Gantz, Institutions 2018, *supra* note 6, at 19). See Appellate Body Report, *United States-Measures Concerning the Importation, Marketing and Sale of Tuna and Tuna Products,* WT/DS381/AB/R, adopted June 13, 2012.

[73] USMCA art. 31.8(1), Rules of Procedure, art. 17. The Rules of Procedure are available on the USMCA Secretariat website, online: <https://can-mex-usa-sec.org/secretariat/agreement-accord-acuerdo/usmca-aceum-tmec/rules-regles-reglas/chapter-chapitre-capitulo_31.aspx?lang=eng#art10> (accessed May 25, 2022) [Chapter 31 Rules of Procedure].

[74] *E.g.*, if Canada wanted to establish a panel in a dispute with the US, Canada and the US could not agree on a chair and the US refused to participate in the choosing by lot procedure, Canada could choose a non-Canadian as the panel chair from the roster. This would only fail if there were no non-Canadian roster members because (i) the parties had agreed on a roster composed only of Canadians or (ii) the parties had not agreed on a roster and either no party has designated any roster members or the only roster members designated by the US, Canada and Mexico are Canadians. Of course, none of these situations is likely. The Chapter 31 Rules of Procedure, *supra* note 73, create a process for the selection of a chair in the event a party has failed to designate its individuals to the roster and, as a result, this process cannot be followed (art. 17).

[75] *E.g.*, where the US had not designated any members of roster and neither Canada nor Mexico had designated any US citizen as a roster member if Canada wanted to establish a panel in a dispute with the US, there would be no US citizens on the panel it could appoint. If Canada appointed a US citizen who was not on the roster, the US could use a preemptory challenge to defeat the establishment of the panel.

lishment of the panel would not be guaranteed. In accordance with the 2019 Protocol, the Rules of Procedure provide a mechanism to allow for the appointment of a panel where a party has failed to designate individuals to the roster or participate in the panel selection process, but they do not address the situation where there is no person on the roster who is a citizen of the party in default or the availability of preemptory challenges for off-roster appointments. If preemptory challenges are possible in such a situation, the establishment of the panel could be frustrated.[76]

So long as a roster is in place that has citizens of all three countries as members, however, this problem would not arise. This is true even if the party complained against refused to choose its members of the panel. In this case, the new rules provide that the complaining party can choose by lot from its citizens on the roster. If the party complained against refused to participate in the choosing by lot process, the complaining party can simply select two of its citizens from the roster and the panel would be established.[76]

Once appointed, panelists must comply with a code of conduct to be adopted by the parties.[77] Panelists can be removed where the parties determine that the person has violated the code of conduct.[78] As noted, a code of conduct was adopted by the Free Trade Commission prior to the USMCA coming into force.[79] It is mainly directed at ensuring the avoidance of conflicts of interest.

Panel Proceedings

Once the panel is in place, proceedings are to be conducted in accordance with Rules of Procedure to be established by the Free Trade Commission.[80] USMCA article 31.11(1) prescribes the essential features of the proceedings to be addressed in the rules.

- Disputing parties have the right to at least one hearing before the panel.
- Each party has the opportunity to make initial written submissions, as well as rebuttal submissions, and to make its case at an oral hearing.

---

[76] USMCA arts. 31.11, 30.2. Chapter 31, Rules of Procedure, *supra* note 73, art. 17. *See also* the NAFTA Model Rules of Procedure for Chapter 20 (online: <http://www.nafta-sec-alena.org/DefaultSite/index_e.aspx?DetailID=237>) (accessed October 22, 2018) [Model Chapter 20 Rules].

[77] USMCA art. 31.8(2)(d).

[78] USMCA art. 31.9(4). *See* identical provision in NAFTA art. 2011(4). Article 31.10 addresses what to do when a panelist needs to be replaced because they resign, were removed, or are unable to serve. There is no equivalent provision in NAFTA Chapter 20.

[79] USMCA Code of Conduct, *supra* note 54.

[80] USMCA, arts. 31.11, 30.2. NAFTA has the same requirement (art. 2012). *See* Model Chapter 20 Rules, *supra* note 76.

- Any hearing shall be open to the public and held in the national capital of the responding party unless the disputing parties agree otherwise.
- The parties' submissions, any written versions of oral communications with the panel, the panel's deliberations and the panel's initial report are to be made public as soon as possible, subject to the protection of confidential information.
- The panel must consider any request from a non-governmental entity located in the territory of a disputing party to provide written views regarding the dispute that may assist the panel in evaluating the submissions and arguments of the disputing parties.[81]

The default requirement that hearings and documents will be accessible to the public is in sharp contrast to the approach taken initially under NAFTA Chapter 20 where every aspect of the process and all documents were treated as confidential.[82] Limited openness was introduced in a subsequent exchange of letters.[83] Each party was permitted, though not obliged, to disclose their own pleadings and the submissions of other parties subject to the redaction of confidential information. Hearing transcripts could be made public by a party fifteen days after the final panel report was made public.

For the most part, NAFTA Chapter 20 proceedings were concluded behind closed doors, though the US made its submissions available in *Cross-Border Trucking*.[84] As well, there were some breaches of confidentiality in NAFTA Chapter 20 cases. In the first Chapter 20 panel proceeding the names of the panelists as well as the interim report of the panel were leaked to the media. The interim reports in the other two cases were also leaked.[85]

---

[81] USMCA art. 30.11. The Rules of Procedure for Chapter 31 (Dispute Settlement) set out detailed requirements for public disclosure of requests for consultations, written submissions, hearing transcripts, and final reports (art. 19) as well as the submission of written views by non-governmental entities (art. 20) (Chapter 31 Rules of Procedure, *supra* note 73.)

[82] NAFTA art. 2012(1); Model Chapter 20 Rules, *supra* note 76, Rule 35.

[83] Supplementary Procedures to Rule 35 on the Availability of Information in exchange of letters dated July 13, 1995.

[84] Gantz, 2000, *supra* note 8, at 508.

[85] The interim report in the first case was published in "Confidential Interim NAFTA Panel Decision on U.S.-Canada Dairy/Poultry Dispute," *Inside NAFTA*, July 24, 1996 at 20. The public disclosure of the interim report in *Brooms from Mexico*, *supra* note 5 is described in Sidney Picker, "The NAFTA Chapter 20 Dispute Resolution Process: A View from the Inside," CAN.-U.S. L. J. 525 (1997), at 469; and Picker, Reflections 1997, *supra* note 14, at 527-8. *See* Gantz, 2000, *supra* note 8, at 508-9 regarding the leak of the initial report in *Cross-Border Trucking*, *supra* note 6.

It is not surprising Canada, the US and Mexico have agreed to more transparent proceedings in the USMCA. In 2004, Canada, the US and Mexico committed to having NAFTA Chapter 20 hearings open to the public.[86] Of course, no such hearings were held because there were no new cases subsequent to this commitment. Apparently, Mexico's position in the USMCA negotiations was that greater transparency was the main improvement needed in the state-to-state dispute settlement process.[87] The USMCA transparency requirements are consistent with a broad trend toward greater transparency in international trade and investment agreements.[88]

The possibility of non-party participation through written submissions was not contemplated under NAFTA Chapter 20 and has not occurred in practice though it has become accepted in investor-state disputes under Chapter 11 and other trade and investment treaties.[89] The real prospect for such participation and its effectiveness will depend on the requirements for information about the dispute to be made public and the rules governing such participation which are set out in the USMCA Rules of Procedure.

The rules provide that a party making a request for consultations or the establishment of a panel make a copy public within seven days of its delivery.[90] With knowledge of a request for a panel, a non-party could consider whether to make a submission if a panel is established. The window for non-parties to make their submissions following the establishment of a panel is narrow. Non-parties must seek leave to make a submission within 20 days of the appointment of the last panelist. The disputing state parties have 14 days to make public the establishment of a panel, possibly leaving only six days for a non-disputing party to draft and file its application. Applications for leave must set out the non-party's nationality, membership, sources of financing, the nature of its activities, and its relationship with any state party as well as the issues of fact or law that it will address and how its submissions will assist the panel by "bringing a perspective, particular knowledge, or insight that is different from that of any of the participating Parties."[91] If leave is granted, submissions are

---

[86] NAFTA Free Trade Commission Joint Statement, San Antonio, Texas, July 16, 2004. The statement indicates that the ministers asked officials to develop rules to govern such proceedings. No such rules have ever been made public.

[87] Gantz, Institutions 2018, *supra* note 6, at 19.

[88] Iza Lejárraga and Ben Shepherd, "Quantitative Evidence on Transparency in Regional Trade Agreements", OECD Trade Policy Papers, No. 153 (Paris: OECD Publishing, 2013), online: <http://dx.doi.org/10.1787/5k450q9v2mg5-en> (accessed December 18, 2018).

[89] J Anthony VanDuzer, "Enhancing the Procedural Legitimacy of Investor-State Arbitration Through Transparency and *Amicus Curiae* Participation," 52 McGill L.J. 681 (2007); Ljiljana Biukovic, "Transparency Norms, the WTO System and FTAs: The Case of CETA," 39 Leg. Issues Econ. Integration 93 (2012).

[90] Chapter 31 Rules of Procedure, *supra* note 73, art. 19.

[91] *Id.* at art. 20.2. If leave is granted, submissions are limited to 10 pages.

limited to 10 pages.[92] The state parties have an opportunity to respond to the submission and the panel is not obliged to address the submission in its submission.[93] These requirements are similar to those for non-party participation in investor-state arbitration. Those rules have been criticized as failing to provide effective participation rights.[94]

The 2019 Protocol also introduced one other meaningful change: requirements regarding evidence to be implemented in the Rules of Procedure.[95] These include the right to submit testimony in various forms, as well as the right for each party and the panel to test testimony submitted. Anonymous testimony may be submitted in "appropriate circumstances." A panel has the authority to request evidence and take any failure to comply with such a request into account in its decision.

Other aspects of the USMCA process follow the approach in NAFTA Chapter 20. A panel may seek information and advice of any person, either on its own initiative or on the request of a party,[96] but the parties must agree to the panel seeking such information or advice and be given an opportunity to comment on it. The similar process under NAFTA was not used, although apparently it was requested by a party in one case.[97] Also, a party that is not a disputing party may, on notice to the others, attend all hearings and make written and oral submissions.[98] The identical right in NAFTA Chapter 20 was exercised in two of the three panel proceedings.[99]

Similar to NAFTA Chapter 20 and the WTO dispute settlement process,[100] a panel must provide its initial report within 150 days of the selection of the last panelist appointed.[101] The initial report must be based on an objective assessment of the

---

[92] *Id.* at art. 20.7.

[93] *Id.* at arts. 20.8, 20.9.

[94] *See e.g.,* Nicolette Butler, "Non-Disputing Party Participation in ICSID Disputes: Faux Amici?" 66 NETHERLANDS INT'L L. REV. 143 (2019).

[95] USCMA art. 31.11(2).

[96] USMCA art. 31.15.

[97] NAFTA arts. 2014, 2015. *Cross-border Trucking, supra* note 6, at para. 200.

[98] USMCA art. 31.14. See the substantially similar provision in NAFTA art. 2013. The USMCA imposes a new requirement for the third state to give notice of its intention to participate within 10 days of the delivery of the request for the establishment of the panel.

[99] Gantz, 2000, *supra* note 8, at 496.

[100] NAFTA art. 2016(2); DSU art. 15.

[101] USMCA art. 31.17(1). The deadline may be extended by the panel for a maximum of 30 days in exceptional circumstances (art. 31.17(2)). NAFTA requires panel reports to be provided within just 90 days (art. 2016(2)). Under Chapter 20 the report must contain the panel's determination of whether the measure at issue is inconsistent with NAFTA or causes nullification or impairment as well as the descriptive elements of the report. In fact, the requirement for initial reports followed by country comments in the WTO is based on this NAFTA practice (Steger, *supra* note 67). The procedures work somewhat differently in that

matter before it and set out the panel's findings of fact, its conclusions regarding whether (i) the measure in dispute is inconsistent with the USMCA, (ii) a party has otherwise failed to carry out its obligations in the agreement, (iii) the measure is causing nullification and impairment, and any other determination requested in the terms of reference. Reasons must be provided for the panel's findings, conclusions, and determinations.[102] Recommendations for resolving the dispute are to be made only if the parties have jointly requested them. Under NAFTA Chapter 20, recommendations were to be provided unless the parties agreed otherwise.[103] The USMCA provides that the findings, conclusions, determinations, and recommendations of the panel shall not "add to or diminish the rights and obligations of the parties" under the USMCA.[104] This provision has no counterpart in NAFTA and reflects long-standing US concerns regarding the WTO Appellate Body's decisions.[105]

Within 15 days after receipt of the initial report, the parties may submit their written comments. The panel's final report must be submitted to the parties within 30 days following delivery of the initial report after considering any comments.[106] Panels are to take decisions by consensus, but if no consensus can be reached, then by majority vote. Separate opinions may be included in the report though the author is not to be identified.[107] All three NAFTA Chapter 20 reports were unanimous. Like NAFTA Chapter 20, a USMCA panel is specifically required to base its report on the relevant provisions of the agreement, the parties' submissions, and arguments of the parties as well any expert information or opinions provided.[108]

The final report must be made available to the public within 15 days after it has been presented to the parties, subject to the redaction of any confidential information.[109] Under NAFTA, the Free Trade Commission could decide not to publish a report, though all NAFTA Chapter 20 reports were published.[110]

NAFTA panels can make whatever revisions they choose in preparing the final report. At the WTO, if there are no comments, the interim report becomes the final report.

[102] USMCA art. 31.13(1).

[103] NAFTA art. 2016(2)(c).

[104] USMCA art. 31.13(8).

[105] Lester, Manak & Arpas, *supra* note 8.

[106] USMCA art. 31.1(4).

[107] NAFTA art. 2016 (3) and 2017(2).

[108] USMCA art. 31.3(8). *See* the similar provision in NAFTA art. 2016(1).

[109] USMCA art. 31.13(2) provides that reports must be published unless the Free Trade Commission decides otherwise.

[110] NAFTA art. 2017(4). If a NAFTA state is participating, not as a disputing party, but as a third party, it is not entitled to receive the final report except through its membership on the Free Trade Commission (NAFTA art. 2016(2), (4)).

The timelines set out in NAFTA Chapter 20, if complied with, would result in a final panel decision within approximately eight months (240 days) of the initial request for consultations. In practice however, this timeline was never met due to delays at each stage in the process. The consultation period has extended beyond the stipulated 30 days. As discussed above, a more significant source of delay has been the appointment of panelists. The other time periods set in NAFTA Chapter 20 have been described as unreasonably short and have been routinely exceeded. No panel has completed its work within the minimum time specified. In the three NAFTA cases, the time from a request for consultations to the panel decision has been highly variable ranging from 17 months[111] to more than five years.[112]

Under the USMCA, the time period for the initial panel report has been extended from ninety days to a more reasonable 150 days, but the timelines in the USMCA are otherwise mostly unchanged. While some variation is permitted, the USMCA contemplates that from consultations to the publication of the final panel report, the process will take almost 10 months (295 days).

Compliance with Panel Report

Once a final report has been delivered to the parties, if it contains findings that a measure is inconsistent with a party's treaty obligations, a party has otherwise failed to carry out its obligations, or a measure is causing nullification and impairment, the parties "shall endeavor to agree on a resolution of the dispute."[113] As an alternative to eliminating any non-conformity or nullification or impairment, the parties may resolve the dispute through the payment of mutually acceptable compensation, or in some other way.[114] The preference for compliance embedded in NAFTA Chapter 20 has been removed. Under NAFTA art. 2018(1), the resolution "normally" should conform to the panel's conclusions and recommendations,

---

[111] *Brooms from Mexico, supra* note 6. *Agricultural Products from the US, supra* note 6 was resolved in 660 days (Lopez, *supra* note 33, at 205).

[112] *Cross-Border Trucking, supra* note 6, beginning from the initial request for consultations on December 21, 1995. This case is still not resolved. Mcrory notes that decisions under the Canada-US FTA were issued much more quickly. All were produced their reports within 4-9 months of the appointment of the panel (Mcrory *supra* note 33). Panelists were appointed from a roster and the time varied from 3 days to 2.5 months (Gantz, 2000, *supra* note 8, at 502-3). Picker suggests that another source of delays caused by the absence of a roster is the need to do an extensive assessment of whether prospective panelists have a conflict of interest due to an association with one of the governments (Picker, Reflections, *supra* note 14, at 472). A roster would in effect provide a list of pre-cleared candidates. *See* similarly Gantz, 2000, *Id*, at 502-3, 524, 526.

[113] USMCA art. 31.18.

[114] US Statement of Administrative Action, *supra* note 14, states that they are not binding (at 195).

including, "wherever possible," not implementing or removing any measure that is not in compliance with NAFTA or causing nullification and impairment.[115] The USMCA also diminishes the role of the panel by providing that it is not to make any recommendation regarding the resolution of a party's non-compliance unless the parties jointly ask it to.[116] Under NAFTA Chapter 20, a panel could make any such recommendation it determines is appropriate.[117]

As in NAFTA Chapter 20, if there has been no mutual agreement on a resolution of a USMCA dispute within thirty days, the complaining party may suspend trade concessions that are equivalent in effect to the non-conformity or nullification and impairment until the parties can agree on a resolution of the dispute.[118] A process is provided by which a disputing party can ask for a review of any suspension of concessions that it thinks is "manifestly excessive" or a determination that it has eliminated any non-conformity or any nullification or impairment found by the panel.[119] Under the USMCA, the original panel is to be reconvened to consider these matters. If it considers the retaliation to be manifestly excessive, the panel is to provide its views as to the level of benefits it considers to be of equivalent effect. The process under NAFTA was slightly different. The Commission was required to establish a new panel to determine whether the level of benefits suspended was manifestly excessive. There was no process to seek a determination that a party had brought its regime into compliance.

While the almost immediate right to retaliate without prior approval or qualification in USMCA may seem like a powerful weapon to induce compliance compared to the very drawn-out compliance process in the WTO, it did not prove to be so in practice under NAFTA, though admittedly the data is admittedly very scanty. In one of the two NAFTA cases where non-compliance was found, retaliation was not used. *Broomcorn Brooms* was resolved through implementation in nine months.[120] In fact, there was no need for the complaining party, Mexico, to retaliate against the US because Mexico had already imposed new tariffs in response to the US safeguard action that was the subject of its Chapter 20 complaint, which it was entitled to do under NAFTA.[121] In *Cross-Border Trucking*, Mexico finally decided to

---

[115] NAFTA art. 2018(1) is the same.

[116] USMCA art. 31.13(1)(c).

[117] NAFTA art. 2016(2)(c).

[118] USMCA art. 31.19(1). NAFTA art. 2019(1) is the same. As under the WTO, the sectors chosen for the suspension of benefits should be the same as those that have been affected by the measure that is inconsistent with the agreement or causing nullification and impairment unless that is not practicable.

[119] USMCA art. 31.19(3). NAFTA art. 2018 is the same.

[120] *Brooms from Mexico*, *supra* note 6, and *Cross-Border Trucking*, *supra* note 6.

[121] NAFTA art. 802.6.

retaliate in 2009, eight years after the panel decision.[122] The dispute, however, remains unresolved. As a practical matter, 30 days is never likely to be a sufficient time period for implementation even where a party is highly motivated to comply. As well, states that have been successful in their claim are likely to refrain from acting so long as the other state is, in good faith, seeking to comply.[123]

Assessment

State-to-state dispute settlement under the USMCA largely follows the structure and features of NAFTA Chapter 20. One crucial difference is that the new agreement demonstrates a greater commitment to transparency and contemplates the participation by NGOs and other third parties. Significantly, the problem of parties blocking panel appointment has been addressed. But on the other key problem of the NAFTA process, the limited role of authoritative adjudication by panels in facilitating compliance, little has been done.

Indeed, the USMCA waters down the role of panel decisions regarding a state's compliance with its obligations compared to NAFTA Chapter 20. Where a party has been found not to be in compliance, NAFTA's preference for a resolution that involves that party bringing its regime into compliance has been removed. As well, under the USMCA, a panel is no longer to provide recommendations regarding how non-compliance should be resolved unless requested by both parties. As noted, under NAFTA, a panel was entitled to provide such recommendations unless the parties agreed otherwise.

In some ways, however, these changes in the USMCA regarding compliance represent a relatively small shift from the NAFTA regime. Ultimately, NAFTA relied on the agreement of the parties to resolve disputes. A panel decision was never more than what David Gantz has called a "strong recommendation."[124] Even where a violation of NAFTA was found, there was no unequivocal obligation on the party in violation to bring its regime into compliance. Solutions other than compliance, including compensation, were expressly permitted, as they are under the USMCA.

---

[122] Mexico imposed more than $2.4 billion in trade sanctions on US imports in 2009 (Diario Oficial (Mexico), March 18, 2009), cited in Leal-Arcas, 2011, *supra* note 6, at 16.

[123] Rafael Leal-Arcas, "Choice of Jurisdiction in International Trade Disputes: Going Regional or Global," 16 MINN. J. INT'L L. 1, (2007), at 29-30.

[124] Gantz, 2000, *supra* note 8, at 487. The failure of the process to produce a binding decision was described as a "major flaw" by Canada's Standing Senate Committee on Foreign Affairs (Uncertain Access: The Consequences of US Security and Trade Actions for Canadian Trade Policy (Volume 1), Report of the Standing Senate Committee on Foreign Affairs, The Honourable Peter Stollery, Chair, The Honourable Consiglio Di Nino, Deputy Chair, Fourth Report June 2003 [Uncertain Access] (online:< http://www.parl.gc.ca/37/2/parlbus/commbus/senate/Com-e/fore-e/rep-e/rep04jun03part1-e.htm> (accessed December 15, 2018).

In any case, an authoritative adjudication regarding compliance backed up by strong measures to ensure compliance will not be the most desirable process in all cases. Where disputes are particularly sensitive politically, the party complained against may not want to risk an adjudication that its regime is non-compliant. Equally, in a case that is particularly sensitive for a state complained against, the state making the complaint may decide not to escalate the dispute beyond confidential consultations. David López suggests, for example, that the Canadian and Mexican governments decided not to pursue their concerns about compliance with NAFTA regarding the US Helms-Burton legislation beyond the consultations stage in the interests of not arousing hostility to NAFTA in the US.[125] As well, where disputes touch on issues that are sensitive politically, even a robust dispute settlement process like the WTO's is unlikely to lead to compliance.[126]

For disputes that do not raise significant political sensitivities, however, an authoritative adjudication regarding compliance, combined with recommendations regarding how a defaulting state can bring its regime into compliance and a treaty preference for a resolution that involves compliance could play a more vital role in negotiations between the parties to resolve the matter. If a dispute involves US measures, the inherent inequality in bargaining power between Canada and Mexico on the one hand and the United States on the other means that having to negotiate for a mutually agreed solution may be especially difficult.[127] In this context, a panel's recommendations regarding compliance might inspire and encourage, in a modest way, an agreed resolution that leads to compliance. By eliminating NAFTA's preference for compliance as the most appropriate way to resolve disputes and reducing the prospect for panels to make recommendations regarding how this could be done, the USMCA undermines the already weak role played by panel adjudication in NAFTA Chapter 20.

The benefits of the panel process, whatever they may be, will not be realized if a state cannot require the establishment of a panel after consultations have failed to yield a resolution. With the 2019 Protocol changes, the USMCA does largely address the frustrating problems with panel appointments that arose under NAFTA Chapter

---

[125] López, *supra* note 33, at 201. Mcrory reaches the same conclusion. Mcrory also suggests that by resorting to NAFTA Canada and Mexico would retain control over the case. At the WTO, the European Union or another member could have forced a panel proceeding (Mcrory, *supra* note 33, at 487-8). Gantz suggests some other reasons that the parties might have chosen NAFTA Chapter 20 over the WTO (David Gantz, "Dispute Settlement under the NAFTA and the WTO: Choice of Forum Opportunities and Risks for the NAFTA Parties" 14 AMERICAN U. INT'L. L. R. 1026 (1999) [Gantz, Choice], at 1093-4).

[126] Leal-Arcas, 2011, *supra* note 6, at 13-15.

[127] Canada's Standing Senate Committee on Foreign Affairs described the Chapter 20 process as follows. "By the very nature of the process, the final decision on the dispute remains in the hands of the parties and is susceptible to diplomacy and power politics." Uncertain Access, *supra* note 124.

20. No party can prevent the appointment of a roster. The other parties can designate roster members on their own where no consensus among the parties can be reached. Once a roster is in place, the terms of members will not expire unless a replacement is appointed.[128] So long as the roster includes members who are not citizens of the complaining party, it will be possible to appoint a chair who is a roster member and immune from preemptory challenges. Equally, if a party refuses to appoint panelists in a dispute against it, the other party can appoint them from the roster. Only where a party complained against had failed to designate any of its citizens as roster members (and no other party had done so either), would the establishment of a panel not be guaranteed. In this situation, the complaining party could not appoint citizens of the party complained against from the roster as contemplated in the USMCA because there would not be any and any off-roster appointment could be defeated by a preemptory challenge by the party complained against. As noted, this gap seems not to be addressed in the Rules of Procedure.

It is a bit curious that the parties did not fix the panel appointment problem in NAFTA in a more straightforward way. As Lester, Manak & Arpas suggest, there are at least two ways to ensure that panels are established despite one party's refusal to cooperate: (i) give an independent appointing authority the power to appoint a panel member from the roster if a party delays making an appointment beyond the stipulated time and (ii) eliminate or limit preemptory challenges for off-roster choices.[129]

Of course, because all three USCMA parties have agreed on the appointment of a roster the problem of establishing panels should be resolved. It remains to be seen, however, to what extent, in practice, complaining parties will use the tools in the USMCA to push ahead with a dispute where the party complained against clearly does not want to go to a panel.

So far, these tools have not been needed. In the roughly one and a half years since the USMCA came into force, all USMCA parties have shown a strong commitment to the panel process and it has worked effectively, even on politically sensitive issues, like Canadian restrictions on dairy imports imposed as part of its highly protective supply management program. While a full discussion of the cases to date is far beyond the scope of this chapter, it is useful to make a few points about the three cases that have already been initiated, two of which have been completed. In the first case, Canada–Dairy TRQ Allocation Measures, the US successfully challenged Canada's allocation to Canadian processors of between 85 and 100% of its

---

[128] It is possible for a roster member to be removed for violating the Code of Conduct if the parties agree (USMCA art. 31.9(4)).

[129] Lester, Manak & Arpas, *supra* note 8, at 15-6. They also suggest (i) making roster member terms indefinite so that there can never be a lapse in the roster, and (ii) some further specification regarding how a panelist is to be chosen "by lot."

quota for reduced tariff rates on various dairy products as contrary to the USMCA.[130] In the second case, US–Crystalline Silicon Photovoltaic Cells Safeguard Measure, Canada successfully challenged a US safeguard action on the basis that Canadian products should have been excluded.[131] The third case, United States–USMCA Automotive Rules of Origin is by far the most economically significant. It is a complaint by Mexico, joined by Canada, regarding the US application of the automotive rules of origin in the USMCA. The request for a panel was made on January 6, 2022 and a five-person panel is in place.[132]

The first two cases took advantage of the new USMCA option of having a panel of three rather than five members. This may account, in part, for their relatively expeditious completion. While the tight USMCA timelines were not fully met overall, the final report in Canada-Dairy was submitted just over six months after the request for a panel, bettering the USMCA requirement. Similarly, in US—Chrystalline Silicon Photo—Voltaic Cells, the final report was submitted less than six months after the panel was requested. Transparency requirements were largely observed and in Canada-Dairy, the International Cheese Council of Canada, a not-for-profit association of small and medium-sized Canadian cheese importers and their foreign (including US) suppliers, obtained leave to submit its written views to the panel on the negative effects on its members and the Canadian economy of Canada's quota allocation. It is not clear to what extent the submission was effective. The panel did not refer to the submission in its decision. Early indications are that compliance may be forthcoming in both cases.[133] The parties' willingness to resort to

---

[130] Secretariat file no. CDA-USA-2021-31-01.

[131] Secretariat file no. USA-CDA-2021-31-01.

[132] Secretariat file no. USA-MEX-2022-31-01.

[133] On April 22, 2022, Canada posted proposed changes to its TRQ allocation in response to the USMCA ruling: Canada, "Public Consultations: CUSMA Dairy Tariff Rate Quotas (TRQs) Panel Report Implementation—Proposed Allocation and Administration Policy Changes," online: https://www.international.gc.ca/trade-commerce/consultations/TRQ-CT/cusma_dairy_changes-produits_laitiers_aceum_changements.aspx?lang=eng (accessed May 25, 2022). The US government, however, has expressed its dissatisfaction with these proposals and has initiated consultations (International Dairy Foods Association, "IDFA Applauds U.S. Government's Renewed Call for Consultations with Canada on Dairy Tariff Rate Quotas, Urges USG to Remain Vigilant," online: <https://www.idfa.org/news/idfa-applauds-u-s-governments-renewed-call-for-consultations-with-canada-on-dairy-tariff-rate-quotas-urges-usg-to-remain-vigilant> (accessed May 25, 2022). On February 4, 2022, President Biden authorized the US Trade Representative to negotiate with Canada and Mexico to exclude the application of the safeguard to Canadian and Mexican goods (Proclamation 10339 of February 4, 2022, To Continue Facilitating Positive Adjustment to Competition From Imports of Certain Crystalline Silicon Photovoltaic Cells (Whether or Not Partially or Fully Assembled Into Other Products), online: <https://www.federalregister.gov/documents/2022/02/09/2022-02906/to-continue-facilitating-positive-adjustment-to-competition-from-imports-of-certain-crystalline> (accessed May 25, 2022).

USCMA state-to-state dispute settlement and work diligently within its rules to complete cases in a timely way represents a stark shift from the experience under NAFTA.

Conclusion

The changes that have been made in the USMCA, especially the improvements to the panel appointment process, improve the effectiveness of state-to-state dispute settlement procedure in North America. The enhanced transparency and non-disputing party participation requirements for the panel process in the USMCA are welcome improvements that will enhance the democratic legitimacy of the state-to-state process as they have in investor-state arbitration. One could imagine that having to deal with disputes in a much more public way and the prospect of third-party participation could deter states from using the panel process at least in some cases. In other cases, of course, a more public process might be considered a strategic advantage by a state with a grievance.

At the same time, however, the USMCA further diminishes the role of authoritative, independent adjudication of a state's compliance with its obligations. Even if a panel is established and finds non-compliance, the USMCA does not prioritize the resolution of the dispute by the defaulting state bringing its regime into compliance. Panels' ability to facilitate the resolution of a dispute by making recommendations regarding how to address any non-compliance depends on both parties agreeing to ask the panel to provide such recommendations.

Despite, this shift, the three cases to date suggest a much stronger engagement by the USMCA parties in state-to-state dispute settlement compared to the rarely used NAFTA Chapter 20 and its utility where the parties are committed to making it work. Undoubtedly, if the WTO process can be salvaged in some form, the three countries will continue to prefer to use that forum. The advantages of being able to make common cause with other states and a much more fully developed compliance process are significant advantages of going to the WTO. In that case, USMCA dispute settlement may be used primarily in relation to those commitments that do not have counterparts in the WTO agreements, as in the three cases to date. As well, the future of the USMCA state-to-state process may turn significantly on what happens in *US-USMCA Automotive Rules of Origin*, but the limited experience to date provides grounds for cautious optimism that state-to-state dispute settlement under the USMCA will provide a useful tool for the US, Mexico and Canada to manage their relationship.

CHAPTER 8

PROFESSOR STEPHEN ZAMORA'S INTEREST IN MEXICO'S EFFORTS TO REFORM ITS ENERGY INDUSTRY[1]

By James W. Skelton, Jr.[2]

Introduction

Professor Steve Zamora was dedicated to improving the relationship and understanding between the U.S. and Mexico in several ways: a social and personal basis; an institutional standpoint; an intellectual perspective; and a legal viewpoint. Over

---

[1] Portions of a prior version of this article were published under the title of "Mexico's Energy Industry Reform Movement: Is it Sustainable?" in Vol. 1, No. 1, International Newsletter of the International Law Section of the State Bar of Texas 20 (September 18, 2018), http://files. constantcontact.com/cf349dd3701/b45c3ac1-4ba9-4f88-b822-ef13de029bf2.pdf; and in the IBA Oil and Gas Law Committee Newsletter (September 6, 2018) www.ibanet.0rg?Article/New/Detail.aspx?ArticleUid=B495C5A9-84ED-4867-949A.

[2] Mr. Skelton has practiced law for 46 years, specializing in international and domestic energy transactions, which has taken him to 35 countries around the world. He began his legal career in private practice, worked for Conoco for 28 years, and then returned to private practice as a sole practitioner and an international legal consultant. He served as an Adjunct Professor of Law at the University of Houston Law Center from 2008 to 2016, teaching the course in Energy Law: Doing Business in Emerging Markets, and coauthored the textbook for the course. He holds a B.S. in Economics from Arizona State University, a J.D. from South Texas College of Law Houston and an LL.M. in International Legal Studies from New York University. He served as Chairman of the Advisory Board of the *Houston Journal of International Law* from 1999 to 2010 and has been a member of the Advisory Board since 1980. He has published 26 articles for legal periodicals and books, a textbook, an anthology, and a memoir.

the many years that I knew him and was fortunate enough to call him a friend, I learned that Steve was also interested in a host of public and private international law issues, including the field of oil and gas transactions.

Steve always made time to follow those other interests in a meaningful way too. I will never forget the time I was one of five participants in a Conference on "Investing in Russia Under the Law on Production Sharing Agreements: Eliminating the Conflicts and Other Obstacles" in April 1998.[3] The presentation was sponsored by the *Houston Journal of International Law* and was held at the University of Houston Hilton Hotel. When I was introduced by the moderator, Professor William Streng, I took my place at the podium and looked out at the audience just as Steve took his seat near the middle of the large room and waved to me. I was so pleasantly surprised by the fact that, despite his pressing duties as the Dean of the Law Center, Steve had taken the time to attend the conference that day. I knew he had a lot of other things to do, but he apparently wanted to learn more about the Russian PSA Law. I was even more amazed when he quietly stood up and left the meeting room after I finished my presentation. I was stunned and felt honored when I realized Steve had only allotted a certain amount of time and he had chosen to listen to my presentation.

This was just one of many examples of the way in which Steve maintained his friendships and pursued his other academic interests while meeting all the responsibilities that came with occupying the Office of the Dean from 1995 to 2000. He was indeed an extraordinary man who had such a strong academic and legal background that he was able to teach a wide variety of courses at the Law Center, including International Business Transactions, International Trade, NAFTA, Contracts, International Banking Law, Mexican Law, and Conflicts of Law.[4]

Mexico's Efforts to Reform its Petroleum Law

Steve delivered many significant accomplishments during his tenure as a Professor and the Dean at the University of Houston Law Center, one of the most important of which was the establishment of the Center for U.S. and Mexican Law. The Center was the first such research center in any American law school devoted to the independent study of Mexican law and legal aspects of relations between the United States and Mexico. After he retired from teaching in 2014, he continued as the Director of the Center for U.S. and Mexican Law.[5]

---

[3] Conference on *Investing in Russia Under the Law on Production Sharing Agreements: Eliminating the Conflicts and Other Obstacles*, 20 Hous. J. Int'l L. 518 (1998).

[4] James W. Skelton, Jr., *In Memory of Professor Stephen T. Zamora*, 39 Hous. J. Int'l L. 2 (2017).

[5] *Id.* at 3.

It was around this time that Steve joined Tony Payan and José Ramón Cossío Díaz to write and publish a book about Mexican Energy Reform and the Rule of Law.[6] This book covers several topics related to the then recent attempt to reform the energy industry in Mexico, some of which Steve and I had discussed during our frequent conversations at the Law Center. What follows is a review of some of the problem areas and workable solutions that we had anticipated would become critical to the success of such a radical transition from an exclusive to an inclusive oil and gas industry in Mexico.

During much of my career, I was convinced that Pemex would continue to dominate the Mexican oil and gas industry due to the Mexican Constitution's prohibition of the participation of private investors in the industry. On December 20, 2013, however, a decree of President Enrique Peña Nieto was published in the Mexican Official Gazette, which amended Articles 25, 27 and 28 of the Constitution, allowing such private investment in the energy industry.[7] In August 2014, the Constitutional amendments were approved by the Congress through implementing legislation, which opened the door to the creation of an entirely new kind of oil and gas industry in Mexico.[8] The legislation included the passage of nine new laws and the amendment of twelve existing laws to improve the way in which the energy industry was regulated. By so doing, the government hoped it would attract foreign and domestic private investment to its sluggish economy.

Much has been written about the reform movement, one of the most interesting of which was a law review article authored by Fernando Cano-Lasa.[9] Therein, Mr. Cano-Lasa specifically described the concepts behind the old system and the new reform system.[10] According to Mr. Cano-Lasa, under the reform concept, "the Mexican State reassumes its position in the center as the owner of the reserves. For the first time in years Pemex is not at the core of the industry, but is instead seen as one additional actor. The regulators have now grown teeth and have full authority to rule over private parties and governmental entities. Private investment is now permitted, one way or another, in all sectors of the map: upstream, midstream, and downstream."[11]

---

[6] Tony Payan, Stephen Zamora & Jose Ramon Cossío Díaz, *State of Energy Waste and Reform in Mexico*, (Tirant lo Blanch Treaties ed., Mexico City 2016).

[7] Decree by which various provisions of the Political Constitution of the United Mexican States are amended and added, in the Matter of Energy, Official Gazette of the Federation DOF 12-20-2013 (Mex.).

[8] Income Law on Hydrocarbons, DOF 11-8-2014 (Mex.).

[9] Fernando Cano-Lasa, *Mexico Energy Reform: Dispute Resolution for Operators Facing Administrative Rescission of Their Exploration and Production Agreements*, 39 Hous. J. Int'l L. 5 (2017).

[10] *Id.* at 7-9.

The upstream sector is the most important of the three, and it may well hold the most upside potential for the government, Pemex, and private investors, both foreign and domestic. There are several practical challenges contained in the details of the reform legislation, as well as some major social problems, all of which could prove to be such serious obstacles that private investors would not be willing to participate.

Several factors worked against the effectiveness of the reforms right from the beginning. For example, the free fall of oil prices in the latter half of 2014 served to make everyone wonder whether the reforms could overcome the negative effect of the over-supply of oil throughout the world, especially in North America. On June 20, 2014, the price of a barrel of West Texas Intermediate (WTI) crude oil reached its peak at $107.26,[12] and no one could have predicted that it would decrease to $43.46 per barrel by March 17, 2015.[13] This represented an incredible and unimaginable plunge of 59.5%.

Some of the problems that Steve foresaw were linked to the rule of law and were highlighted in December 2016 in a paper entitled "Security, the Rule of Law and Energy Reform in Mexico," which was written by the Mexico Center at Rice University's Baker Institute for Public Policy.[14] The paper refers to three issues that are related to the rule of law, as follows: "the capacity of the Mexican state to protect energy projects from the onslaught of organized crime; the capability to offer guarantees against the web of corruption that currently envelopes the country; and the ability to prevent and deal with social conflicts related to natural resource allocation, such as land and water."[15] Of these three, organized crime and corruption appeared to be the most troubling and most difficult to address. Despite the government's gallant efforts to provide more security to fight organized crime throughout the country, the authors of the paper concluded that such activities have actually "increased the level of violence, further evidenced the weakness of the state and angered civil society,"[16] which is exactly the opposite of what one would have expected. This apparent incongruity, coupled with the fact that "there is no agreement among the political parties on what type of anti-corruption system must be put in place,"[17] could

---

[11] *Id.* at 8-9.

[12] Ryan Holywell & Colin Eaton, *Falling oil prices lower the boom*, SAN ANTONIO EXPRESS-NEWS, February 2, 2015, at 4, www.expressnews.com/business/eagle-ford-energy/article/Falling-oil-prices-lower-the -boom.html.

[13] R. Meyers, *Surge of shale begins to slacken, government reports*, HOU. CHRON., March 18, 2015, at D1.

[14] Jeff Falk, *Three Rule of Law Issues Threaten Mexico's Energy Reform: Experts*, RICE UNIV. BAKER INST., December 6, 2016, at 1. https://phys.org/news/2016-12-rule-of-law-issues-threaten-mexico-energy.html.

[15] *Id.* at 2.

[16] *Id.*

lead one to the conclusion that the energy reforms would not become implemented until considerable progress is made in these areas of organized crime and corruption.

Of course, the challenges to the implementation of the reforms are not limited to the rule of law issues described above. Indeed, there are a variety of practical problems that are directly related to oil and gas field operations, some of which have been described as including, "a lack of security, field mismanagement, corruption, water shortages for shale, infrastructure dearth, and pipeline bunkering (theft) just to name a few."[18] The question that Steve posed to me more than once was whether the positive attributes of the Mexican petroleum industry could remain strong enough to attract investment regardless of the apparent obstacles. As one who has had a lot of experience advising oil company executives regarding potential impediments to investment, I told him that it is remarkable how many investors are willing to take on more than the normal amount of risk if they believe the prospective rewards are sufficiently substantial.

The Forbes article quoted in the preceding paragraph went as far as to declare that the reforms were "perhaps the most comprehensive and complex energy rule changes in any nation, at any time; lifting strict state control over the oil/gas and electricity sectors, hoping for much more foreign investment."[19] For me, however, the shadow of Pemex still hung over the entire industry, which made me wonder whether Pemex could actually be relegated to the level of just another participant in the industry rather than the monopolistic leader. Forbes' view was "Although change won't be easy, the good news is that the Mexican government has lowered its over-reliance on Pemex, with the company now accounting for 20% of the federal budget, down from 40% a few years ago."[20] Nevertheless, it has proven to be extremely difficult for Pemex to change its deep-seated corporate culture of monopolistic thinking, planning, and operating.

In addition, a passage in a recent University of Texas Energy Institute paper asserted, "When you have an institution like Pemex that for 75 years has been a state monopoly, it is inherently corrupt in the way that it does business."[21] Moreover, the

---

[17] *Id.*

[18] Jude Clemente, *Mexico's Emerging Oil Opportunities Are Great*, FORBES, June 18, 2017, at 4. https://www.forbes.com/sites/judeclemente/2017/06/18/mexicos-emerging-oil-opportunities-are-great/#7144c8546aa3

[19] *Id.* at 2.

[20] *Id.* at 3.

[21] Lorne Matalon, *Mexico's Energy Reform and Pemex: Both Face Challenges as U.S. Energy Sector Watches*, UNIV. TEX. ENERGY INST., February 21, 2017, at 1. http://energy.utexas.edu/2017/02/24/mexicos-energy-reform-and-pemex-both-face-challenges-as-u-s-energy-sector-watches.

issue of pipeline bunkering (theft) mentioned above was highlighted in the same paper, claiming, "Some Pemex workers are almost certainly working with organized crime to steal oil. Pemex says the current gasoline shortage in Mexico, one that is sparking continuing outrage, is in part caused by oil theft. Pemex admits corruption is an issue."[22] Assuming these statements are accurate, they constitute a troublesome insight into the current state of the corporate culture of Pemex and single out what may be the most crucial obstacle to the success of anticorruption efforts.

Some commentators were even more bullish and consider this extraordinary and historic attempt to reform the energy industry as creating "an unprecedented opportunity for oil companies looking to tap into Mexico's huge energy potential."[23] One CEO, Steve Hanson of International Frontier Resources, went so far as to declare that "In short it is the largest energy opportunity in the world today—and the door has just been opened."[24] Such a positive approach was as encouraging as it was surprising considering the continuing low oil price scenario and the lists of potential problems discussed in two of the preceding paragraphs.

The ongoing worldwide low oil price dilemma was, however, less of a problem for Mexico than other oil producing countries. For example, "Development costs in Mexico's oil business averaged around $23 per barrel in 2017, and nearly 60% of Mexico's output came from areas that cost around $10-$20 per barrel to develop."[25] Although this is an impressive statistic, it is probable that the calculation of such comparatively low development costs was based more on onshore operations than the more costly offshore operations. Nonetheless, this was a positive element in the overall due diligence equation, which could have tipped the scale in favor of committing to an onshore upstream investment in some cases.

Mexico's lack of refining capacity is a critical infrastructure shortcoming that has recently been addressed by Mexico's populist president, Andreas Manuel López Obrador, who is determined to do whatever it takes to help Mexico achieve energy self-sufficiency. The President single handedly took what began in March 2019 as an invitation to four international companies and consortia to tender bids to build a refinery and turned it into a gift that was presented to Pemex and the Energy Ministry two months later.[26] It has been reported that López Obrador's government has

---

[22] *Id.* at 4.

[23] James Stafford, *Why Mexico's Oil Reform Is a Huge Opportunity for Investors*, OIL PRICE, November 21, 2016, at 1. http://oilprice.com/Energy/Energy-General/Why-Mexico's-Oil - Reform-Is-A-Huge-Opportunity-For-Investors.html.

[24] *Id.* at 2.

[25] Clemente, *supra* note 18, at 5.

[26] Elisabeth Malkin, *An $8 billion refinery? Mexican president says, yes we can*, N.Y. TIMES, May 5, 2019, at 1. https://www.nytimes.com/2019/05/09/world/americas/mexico-refinery-pemex.html.

"provided a $5 billion relief package to Pemex to help boost sagging domestic production and begun building a $14 billion refinery in Tabasco, his home state, in southeastern Mexico."[27] Subsequently, López Obrador claimed that the actual cost of the refinery would not exceed $8 billion,[28] but the latest estimate is $12.5 billion, which exceeds that by more than half.[29] This prediction was made despite the fact that the three companies that tendered bids in the initial stage of the project "offered bids that estimated construction costs at $10 to $20 billion."[30] It's likely that the deficiency in Mexico's refining capacity infrastructure could be mitigated to some degree by López Obrador's new refinery policy, but it is not clear how much it would help move the energy industry closer to the creation of a self-sufficient national petroleum industry.

The Auction Process

Five rounds of auctions were scheduled to take place between 2014 and 2019 to jump start the reform movement and award available acreage to Pemex and private investors. These auctions of rights to explore and develop oil fields were viewed as one of the most crucial elements in the reform movement. The results of the initial rounds of auctions were mixed through 2018. A brief review of those auctions is set forth below.

In the first round, there was no outside participation because it was reserved for Pemex, which was permitted to "retain areas in which it already produced, and it was awarded 83% of proven and probable reserves in the first round, 'Round Zero.' Pemex was given 21% of prospective reserves, 67% of what it had requested."[31] The majority of the Round Zero reserves were in shallow water. Even Pemex's CEO José Antonio González Anaya admitted that Pemex did not have the resources or the technology (or expertise) to undertake petroleum operations in deep water areas without partners.[32]

Five separate tenders were scheduled for Round One of the auction process, the first of which took place in December 2014 and included 14 blocks of reserves in shal-

---

[27] Emily Pickrell, *Mexican leader's focus on oil leaves a blind spot: natural gas*, Hou. Chron., December 8, 2019, at B1.

[28] Malkin, *supra* note 26.

[29] George Baker, *After domestic setbacks, Mexico's president seeking an international role*, Texas Inc, May 16, 2002, at B12.

[30] Malkin, *supra* note 26, at 2.

[31] R. Vietor & H. Sheldahl-Thomason, *Mexico's Energy Reform*, Harv. Bus. School, January 23, 2017, at 8. https://sites.hks.harvard.edu/hepg/Papers/2017/MexicanEnergyReform-Draft1.23.pdf.

[32] *Id.*

low water in the Southern Gulf area.[33] Only two bids were successful, which reflected both the low oil price environment at the time and the tough bid terms that were required by the Mexican government.[34] It was readily apparent that a relaxing of some of the auction terms would be needed in order to attract more bidders to the tenders.

The second tender occurred on September 30, 2015, was conducted under slightly different auction terms, and, consequently, was more successful. This time three out of the five shallow water blocks were granted to different bidders under production sharing contracts, one of the three new types of agreements permitted by the government.[35] Even though the price of oil had decreased to less than half the amount it was "when the government started planning for these auctions,"[36] there was a counter-balancing element at work. That is, the main thing working in Mexico's favor this time was "the fact that the government is offering proven reserves, areas that have already been discovered."[37] Simply stated, the elimination of exploration risk made these projects much more attractive than the shallow water blocks had been in the first tender.

In contrast, the third tender of Round One took place in December 2015, was focused on the licensing of small onshore fields, and resulted in the award of all twenty-five licenses, eighteen of which were won by Mexican entities.[38]

The fourth tender of Round One took place in December 2016 and was "considered the most lucrative one" because it "offered tenders for 10 deep water reserves off the coast of Mexico."[39] Eight of the ten blocks offered received bids and were awarded to several big-time majors like ExxonMobil, Total, BP and CNOOC. In addition, Pemex offered a partnership in the development of the deep-water Trion Block, which was won by BHP Billiton's bid of $624 million, and which included a commitment to invest $1.2 billion in the project.[40] With these results, it became apparent that the major oil companies were far more interested in the deep-water opportunities than the other projects that had been offered. In fact, one newspaper went so far as to claim,

---

[33] *Id.* at 9.

[34] *Id.*

[35] *Id.* at 7. The other new types were profit sharing agreements and licenses (service contracts continued to be permitted by the government).

[36] Nick Cunningham, *Second Oil Auction Goes Much Better for Mexico*, OIL PRICE, October 1, 2015, at 2. http://oilprice.com/Energy/Crude-Oil/Second-Oil-Auction-Goes-Much-Better-For-Mexico.html.

[37] *Id.*

[38] Vietor & Sheldahl-Thomason, *supra* note 30, at 9.

[39] *Id.*

[40] Amy Stillman & Adam Williams, *Mexico Oil Auction Succeeds in Drawing World's Biggest Drillers*, BLOOMBERG NEWS, December 5, 2016, at 1. https://www.bloomberg.com/news/articles/2016-12-05/bhp-billiton-named-as-pemex-s-first-deep-water-oil-partner.

"The sale was validation of Mexico's decision to open its former government-monopoly energy business to foreign investment and expertise."[41]

The first tender of Round Two took place in June 2017 and involved shallow water blocks that were located far from the deep-water blocks offered in December 2016. Nevertheless, the results were far above expectations because "Mexico awarded 10 of the 15 blocks that were offered."[42] The most notable winners were Eni, Lukoil, Total and Shell, which marked Shell's first upstream investment in Mexico.[43] After two and a half years of auction activity, many majors were willing to invest in Mexico despite the depressed oil price and some of the other risks enumerated above.

Unfortunately, the election of López Obrador brought the auction process to a screeching halt just a few days after he took office in December 2018, when he announced that the oil exploration and production auctions would be suspended for three years.[44] During a news conference, however, he claimed contracts that were awarded during the prior administration's energy reform process were considered safe—"as long as they were productive."[45] He went even further, saying, "We're going to have a three-year truce so that there is investment. We do not want investment titles that are only used for speculation. We want them to produce and we need them to—production is falling."[46] As discussed in the section below, this so-called truce may have been unilaterally terminated by virtue of a speech that was given by López Obrador in September, which could result in a permanent cancellation of the auction process.

Interference in the Reforms by President Andrés Manuel López Obrador

The election of López Obrador, a former mayor of Mexico City, as the President of Mexico came as no surprise to most of the citizens of Mexico due to his widespread popularity and the overwhelming desire for change among those citizens.

Prior to the election, López Obrador sharply criticized international oil companies and threatened "to cut off Mexican oil imports and freeze new foreign invest-

---

[41] Elisabeth Malkin & Clifford Krauss, *Oil and Gas Industry Leaders Eagerly Take Stakes in Mexican offshore Fields*, N.Y. Times, December 5, 2016, at 1. https://www.nytimes.com/2016/12/05/business/erergy-environment/oil-and-gas-industry-takes-stakes-in-Mexican-offshore-fields.html.

[42] Nick Cunningham, *Oil Majors Snatch Up Mexican Oil Blocks*, Oil Price, June 20, 2017, at 1. http://oilprice.com/Energy/Crude-Oil/Oil-Majors-Snatch-Up-Mexican-Oil-Blocks.html.

[43] *Id.* at 2.

[44] Jude Webber, *Mexico's López Obrador suspends oil auctions for 3 years*, Fin. times, December 5, 2018, at 1. https://www.ft.com/content/6cec89fa-f899-11e8-af46-2022a0b02a6c.

[45] *Id.*

[46] *Id.*

ment in Mexico's oil and gas fields."[47] On the eve of the election, however, he
". . . softened his tone, raising questions about how far the populist leader is willing
to go on his promise to shake up the country's energy sector—again—and rollback
market reforms that essentially ended 75 years of state control of oil, gas and fuel
production."[48]Although he has promised to respect the market economy,[49] he also
". . . promised to review dozens of outstanding oil and gas exploration contracts for
corruption, potentially delaying hundreds of billions of dollars in foreign investment."[50] If some corrupt practices are uncovered during the process of reviewing
those contracts, López Obrador will have another reason to attempt to terminate the
reform movement. López Obrador has made it quite clear that he wants Pemex to
reclaim its role as the dominant player in the Mexican energy industry. As mentioned
above, he has already provided funds for Pemex to build a new refinery to reduce
dependence on foreign gasoline, which may have a significant impact on U.S. refin-
ers that have been shipping more than half of U.S. gasoline exports to Mexico, mostly from the Texas Gulf Coast.[51] The problem is that Pemex's refineries have historically operated at two thirds of capacity, and in 2016 the level of refined products
dropped to its lowest point since 1995 even though domestic sales were at record
highs.[52] In addition, "Mexico has been forced to export its own crude to the U.S.
Gulf area, have it refined, and then import it again as gasoline. The U.S. has 2.5
times more people than Mexico, but it has 25 times more refineries."[53] It is obvious,
therefore, that Mexico's shortage of refining capacity is an anomaly that must be
addressed to make progress toward building a more efficient and self-sufficient
national petroleum industry.

In addition, there has been a major increase in the number and duration of shortages of gasoline around the country since López Obrador's election, resulting directly from his attempt to prevent gasoline theft from pipelines, which reportedly costs
Pemex approximately $3.5 billion per year.[54] In order to counter the problem of theft

---

[47] James Osborne, *As Mexican president Obrador softens his tone, U.S. oil sector crosses fin-
gers*, Hou. Chron., June 29, 2018, at A1.

[48] *Id.*

[49] Azam Ahmed & Ernesto Londono, *Mexico Delivers Another Defeat to the Status Quo in
Latin America*, N.Y. Times, July 2, 2018, at A7. https://www.nytimes.com/2018/07/02/
world/americas/mexico-latin-america-elections.html.

[50] M. Shear & A. Swanson, *President-Elect of Mexico and Trump Have a Chat*, N.Y. Times,
July 3, 2018, at A7.

[51] Osborne, *supra* note 46, at A20.

[52] Clemente, *supra* note, 18 at 5.

[53] *Id.* at 5-6.

[54] Amy Stillman, *Mexicans running on fumes in gas shortage*, Hou. Chron., January 13, 2019,
at B2.

from gasoline pipelines, the President instituted a program of shutting down pipelines and substituting tanker trucks to transport gasoline across the country.[55] As mentioned above, the theft of fuel has become an endemic problem in Mexico, and employees of Pemex are said to be involved in this criminal practice. It will be difficult to rein in the fuel thieves, known as *"huachicoleros,"* as demonstrated in the paragraph below.

In January 2019, just three weeks after President López Obrador began a campaign against fuel theft gangs, the question of oil theft literally blew up and dominated the headlines due to a tragic gasoline pipeline explosion in Tlahuelilpan, a town north of Mexico City.[56] The "carnival atmosphere" ensued when "a man rammed a piece of rebar into a patch and gasoline shot 20 feet into the air, like water from a geyser."[57] A crowd of more than 600 people armed with plastic jugs gathered, and "Giddy adults soaked in gasoline filled jugs and passed them to runners. Families and friends formed human chains and guard posts to stockpile containers with fuel."[58] That is when the gasoline caught fire and a fireball "engulfed those scooping up gasoline," resulting in the death of eighty-five people, the hospitalization of fifty-eight, and dozens more were listed as missing.[59] This horrific disaster was quite an embarrassment to the López Obrador administration and could be interpreted as evidence of the high level of frustration that exists among the citizens of Mexico. It may also represent the volatile situation that exists among the government, its citizens, and the energy industry.

Although López Abrador spent a year and a half of his presidency promising to preserve the "reforms that opened Mexico's energy markets to competition and foreign investment,"[60] in July 2020, he "dropped any pretense of wanting to maintain the market reforms, speaking openly for the first time about the possibility of repealing the energy laws by amending the Constitution—again."[61] He clearly intends to return Pemex and the Comision Federal de Electricidad (CFE) to their strategic development roles and to maintain control of Mexico's natural resources.[62]

More recently, López Obrador told the Reforma newspaper, "We need to rescue Pemex (and other state energy companies). If that is not possible under the current

---

[55] *Id.*

[56] Mark Stevenson, *Mexico explosion site popular with gas thieves*, HOU. CHRON., January 21, 2019, at A15.

[57] *Id.*

[58] *Id.*

[59] *Id.*

[60] Emily Pickrell, *With midterms looming, leader sees chance to repeal reforms*, HOU. CHRON., September 20, 2020, at B1.

[61] *Id.* at B6.

[62] *Id.*

legal framework, I will send, if necessary, an initiative to reform the Constitution."[63] He has been constructing bureaucratic roadblocks that have been described as follows: "Essentially it's been a slow-rolling expropriation done through Mexico's regulatory bodies, and that's making it increasingly difficult to do business in the country."[64] For instance, in July 2020, the "government ordered Talos Energy to work with Pemex in developing Zama, a massive oil field in the Gulf of Mexico, which the Houston firm had discovered three years earlier."[65] Talos thought it had exclusive rights to carry out such development operations, but it has been ordered by the Energy Ministry to merge that discovery "with the overlapping Uchukil field owned by Pemex."[66] This action proved that foreign investors would be forced to conduct joint operations with Pemex.

In order to amend the constitution, however, López Obrador must gain the approval of two-thirds of both the Chamber of Deputies and the Senate, as well as seventeen of the thirty-two states (where his Morena party and allied parties hold majorities), which would have required a huge win in the elections that took place in June 2021, but it failed to achieve the two-thirds majority in the Chamber of Deputies.[67] Nevertheless, it is clear that the reform movement will be eliminated, and Mexico will return to its old, monopolistic practices.

Conclusion

I believe Steve Zamora would have been pleased with the initial progress of the reform movement in the Mexican petroleum industry. Even though it appeared to get off to a slow start, it gained momentum by virtue of the success of the more recent auctions. The rapid escalation of accomplishments in the auction process set a positive tone for future tenders, which briefly made believers of those who doubted the reforms would succeed.

Based on the most recent developments discussed in the section above, however, I think Steve would have been disappointed with what has transpired since López Obrador took office four years ago. It appears that both current and potential investors are watching and waiting with trepidation to see what López Obrador's government does next. Ultimately, there is no doubt that he will continue to attempt to put an end to the reform movement by amending the constitution. Thus, the

---

[63] James Osborne, *In Mexico, U.S. energy firms facing a slow "expropriation,"* Hou. Chron., December 15, 2020, at A9.

[64] *Id.*

[65] *Id.*

[66] Max de Haldevang & Amy Stillman, *Playing hardball in Mexico makes investment tougher*, Hou. Chron., December 27, 2020, at B4.

[67] Baker, *supra* note 29, at B12.

reforms in the Mexican energy industry may soon be reduced to an historical footnote.

If it were not for the election of López Obrador, his suspension of the auctions, and his interference with the reforms, Steve would probably have predicted even more positive improvements in the process and the petroleum industry as a whole, and I would have agreed. Regrettably, the reform movement in the Mexican petroleum industry has been stopped in its tracks and may be eliminated while Pemex regains its prominent position in the driver's seat with López Obrador riding shotgun.

CHAPTER 9

EXPANDING MARINE SCIENCE COOPERATION BETWEEN MEXICO, CUBA, AND THE UNITED STATES IN THE GULF OF MEXICO THROUGH ENERGY PRODUCTION ACTIVITIES AND ENVIRONMENTAL MANDATES

By Richard J. McLaughlin[1]

I. Introduction

The late Stephen T. Zamora, as an eminent scholar of the legal system in Mexico and founding director of the Center for U.S. and Mexican Law at the University of Houston Law Center, was an enthusiastic supporter of any project that improved the interaction between attorneys and regulators from the two nations. After Steve read a couple of articles that I had written about the international legal implications of the United States and Mexico sharing hydrocarbons in an offshore area beyond national jurisdiction in the Gulf of Mexico (GOM) called the Western Gap, he contacted me and asked if I would like to expand on that research with colleagues affiliated with his center. This offer led to a productive and enjoyable collaborative experience first with Dr. Miriam Grunstein and later with Dr. Guillermo Garcia Sanchez. In addition to producing a couple of legal articles on the topic of transboundary energy management, Steve, Guillermo, and I organized and hosted the *Symposium on Improving Cooperation for a Sustainable Gulf of Mexico After the 2014 Mexican Energy Reform*, that brought together leading attorneys, energy regulators, and academics from the two nations to discuss methods of enhancing sustainable

---

[1] Endowed Chair and Professor of Coastal and Marine Policy and Law, Harte Research Institute for Gulf of Mexico Studies, Texas A&M University-Corpus Christi.

management of hydrocarbon resources in the GOM.[2] One theme that was consistently highlighted during the symposium was the importance of collecting adequate scientific information to support regulatory and management responsibilities. Moreover, an emphasis was placed on improving cooperation between scientists from the two nations (as well as from Cuba), as a necessary precondition to effectively engage in sustainable management of oil and gas activities in a large marine ecosystem such as the GOM. This article describes current international efforts to collaborate on marine science in the GOM Region and encourages additional cooperation to meet regulatory mandates associated with growing hydrocarbon activities.

International cooperation within the marine science and government regulatory communities of the United States, Mexico, and Cuba in the GOM Region is accelerating. Counterintuitively, events relating to offshore energy development are encouraging the nations surrounding the GOM to work more closely together to assess, predict and manage the marine environment. There are several reasons why cooperation is increasing: First, new discoveries of hydrocarbon resources in the remote deep-water areas of the Gulf, closer to the three nations' maritime boundaries, create incentives to manage the resources and protect the oceanic environment collaboratively rather than separately.[3] Second, in 2014, Mexico reformed its energy laws to allow foreign offshore energy producers to operate in Mexican waters for the first time in seven decades spurring international business and governmental collaboration.[4] Third, the massive environmental impacts caused by the Deepwater Horizon oil spill in 2010 have proved the need for coordinated scientific baseline information and transboundary response strategies and have provided research funding.[5] These, and related events on a smaller scale, are encouraging the three nations to cooperate in identifying and addressing the priority marine science research issues fundamental to effectively managing the GOM. This information is of value to the governmental agencies charged with regulating and managing resources in their respective 200 nautical mile exclusive economic zones and in ocean areas beyond national jurisdiction.[6] Each nation recognizes that the only way to manage the GOM

---

[2] Proceedings and a transcript of oral presentations from the symposium are published in 9:2 SEA GRANT L. & POL'Y J. (2018). Available at http://nsglc.olemiss.edu/sglpj/archive/vol9.2/index.html.

[3] *See infra* notes 16-21 and accompanying text.

[4] *See infra* note 19 and accompanying text.

[5] As a result of the Deepwater Horizon oil spill, BP was required to pay $20.8 billion in criminal and civil penalties to the US government. It also paid $500 million prior to the court settlement for a ten year research initiative known as the Gulf of Mexico Research Initiative. A relatively small portion of the more than $21 billion dollars paid by BP is dedicated to marine scientific activities and an even smaller portion to international collaborative science activities. For a summary of how the BP funding has been spent *see*: http://www.noaa.gov/explainers/deepwater-horizon-oil-spill-settlements-where-money-went.

effectively, as one large marine ecosystem, is to balance each nation's sovereign rights with collaborative management principles knowing that environmental damage to one portion of the Gulf can have international consequences.

The environmental health and economic productivity of the GOM is immensely important to the three nations that surround it. More than fifty-five million people live in the GOM's coastal belt and are dependent on its abundant resources and economic benefits.[7] Several key economic sectors such as recreational and commercial fishing, tourism, marine transportation, vessel construction, the petrochemical industry, and offshore energy production are concentrated in the GOM Region. It is also extremely valuable in terms of biological productivity with more than 15,000 identified marine species.[8] These living marine resources are in a diverse set of marine habitats including tropical and temperate ecosystems, shallow inshore waters with varying salinity regimes, soft bottoms, rocky bottoms, and reef communities. Large portions of the GOM fall within the deep ocean and sustain unique and highly productive chemosynthetic communities as well as globally important nursery areas for fish species such as blue fin tuna and other ecologically beneficial attributes.[9] Unfortunately, natural and anthropogenic stresses such as overfishing, climate change, degraded water quality, potential oil and chemical spills, and loss of critical habitats and connectivity are compromising the economic and environmental well-being of the region.

In the GOM, as in other areas of the world, coastal and ocean areas have traditionally been managed and governed at specific, isolated levels with limited cooperation or collaboration across, local, state, tribal, federal, or international boundaries.[10] Cultural, historical, and political tensions between nations in the GOM

---

[6] For a discussion of coastal nation international legal rights and obligations in these ocean juridical zones, *see* Richard McLaughlin and Katya Wowk, *Managing Areas Beyond National Jurisdiction in the Gulf of Mexico: Current and Developing Legal Authority and Future Challenges*, 9 SEA GRANT L & POL'Y J. 16-40 (2018).

[7] C. Susan, M. A. Navarrete & N. Barajas, *The Gulf of Mexico Large Marine Ecosystem: Background and Strategic Action Program Implementation*, in McKinney, et al., *infra* note 28.

[8] Felder, DL, Camp DK (editors). 2009. Gulf of Mexico origin, waters, and biota: volume 1 biodiversity. College Station (TX): Texas A&M University Press at Table 3, p. 5.

[9] Richard J. McLaughlin, *Establishing Transboundary Marine Energy Security and Environmental Cooperation Areas as a Method of Resolving Longstanding Political Disagreements and Improving Transboundary Resource Management in the Gulf of Mexico*, Issues in Legal Scholarship, Frontier Issues in Ocean Law (2008): Article 1. University of California at Berkeley Electronic Press. http://www.bepress.com/ils/iss11/art1 at 3.

[10] B. Cicin-Sain, and S. Belfiore 05): *Linking marine protected areas to integrated coastal and ocean management: A review of theory and practice.* 48 Ocean & Coastal Management 847 (2005). While all three nations aspire to achieve truly integrated coastal management, none are currently close to reaching that goal.

Region make coordinating environmental assessment and management strategies especially difficult. For example, long-standing Constitutional constraints in Mexico that prohibited foreign interests from owning any natural resources within Mexican territory prevented U.S. companies from partnering with Mexican counterparts until very recently.[11] These historical legal constraints, coupled with a whole host of additional political disagreements over immigration, trade, drug enforcement, border security (including which nation should pay for a proposed border wall) and other bilateral issues make it exceedingly difficult to manage transboundary resources in the GOM cooperatively.[12]

Political tensions between the United States and Cuba create even more profound barriers to cooperation. After nearly sixty years of antagonistic relations, the Obama administration's efforts in 2014 to improve political conditions have led to increased scientific and government-to-government communication.[13] The recent rollback of many of these measures by President Trump and the continued enforcement of the trade embargo between the two nations have slowed down, but not stopped, growing efforts in bilateral collaboration on marine science.[14]

II. Energy Production in the GOM Is Stimulating Greater International Marine Science Cooperation[15]

Despite these historical impediments, the three nations are moving forward by viewing the GOM as one large marine ecosystem. An essential feature of governing offshore energy development is obtaining scientific information needed to effectively assess, predict, and manage potential impacts from hydrocarbon exploration and production activities. There are strong reasons for U.S., Mexican, and Cuban scientists to work towards maximizing cooperative efforts in marine environmental research and data collection. Increased production is likely in the GOM during the

---

[11] Mexican Constitution, Title. I, Art. 27. In 2013, Art. 27 was amended to allow foreign investment, see *infra* note 19 and accompanying text.

[12] McLaughlin, R., *supra* note 9.

[13] *See, U.S. Cuba Joint Statement on Environmental Cooperation*, available at https://cu.usembassy.gov/november-24-2015-u-s-cuba-joint-statement-environmental-cooperation/.

[14] From Cuba's perspective see, *Can Ocean Science Bring Cuba and the United States Together?* THE CONVERSATION, June 5, 2017, available at http://theconversation.com/can-ocean-science-bring-cuba-and-the-united-states-together-75369.

[15] Portions of Section II and III have been adapted from Richard J. McLaughlin, *Improving Cooperation in U.S./Mexican Marine Science to Better Manage Offshore Hydrocarbon Activities in the Gulf of Mexico*, in McKinney, et al., *infra* note 28.

next five to ten years.[16] In fact, there is nowhere in the world where targeted scientific information is more crucial than in the GOM. With more than 3500 existing offshore structures and 33,000 miles of pipelines, the GOM is one of the world's most important and intensively developed offshore production areas.[17] Mexico and the United States have exploited hydrocarbons in their respective portions of the GOM for decades. Unlike earlier production, which was primarily in shallow nearshore areas, technological advances have pushed current production further out onto the deeper continental shelf to the point that of the more than 567 million barrels of oil produced in the U.S. GOM in 2009, eighty percent took place in depths of 1000 feet or deeper.[18] We have far less scientific knowledge about the deeper and more remote areas of the GOM than the shallower areas closer to shore.

Accelerating this trend toward deep-water production is Mexico's recent decision to reform its energy industry. On December 5, 2016, Mexico completed its first deep-water hydrocarbon auction in the GOM. This ended a seventy-five year monopoly held by state-owned *Petróleos Mexicanos*, or Pemex, and opened Mexico's offshore areas, with their huge hydrocarbon potential, to foreign investment. By all measures, the auction was phenomenally successful with international oil giants such as France's Total, the China National Offshore Oil Corporation, and Exxon Mobil and Chevron of the United States winning bids on exploratory blocks estimated to contain as much as eleven billion barrels of oil and natural gas.[19]

The rapidly increasing exploration activities in Mexico, especially in areas near the U.S.-Mexico maritime boundary, coupled with a ramping up of offshore production activity proposed by the Trump Administration in U.S. waters make it imperative that the two nations begin to work more closely together to manage hydrocarbon resource development in the GOM.[20] Despite setbacks in its exploration activities, Cuba also continues to seek to attract foreign investment to develop its offshore hydrocarbon potential.[21] Collaboration in collecting, analyzing, and

---

[16] The Trump Administration's Department of Interior has released an ambitious plan to open much of the nation's continental shelf to offshore exploration, including expanded areas in the GOM after 2022. *See* https://www.doi.gov/pressreleases/secretary-zinke-announces-plan-unleashing-americas-offshore-oil-and-gas-potential.

[17] Mark J. Kaiser, *The Louisiana Artificial Reef Program,* 30 MARINE POL'Y 605, 605 (2006) (existing structures and pipeline data).

[18] Rebecca K. Richards, Deepwater Mobile Oil Rigs in the Exclusive Economic Zone and the Uncertainty of Coastal State Jurisdiction, 10 J. INT'L BUS. & L. 387-401 (2011).

[19] E. Malkin and C. Krauss, *Oil and Gas Leaders Eagerly take Stakes in Mexican Offshore Fields,* N.Y. TIMES, December 5, 2016. Available at: https://www.nytimes.com/2016/12/05/business/energy-environment/oil-and-gas-industry-takes-stakes-in-mexican-offshore-fields.html?mcubz=0&_r=0.

[20] Implementing an America-First Offshore Energy Strategy, E.O. 13795, April 28, 2017, 82 FR 20815.

storing marine scientific information is essential to support each of the government's responsibilities in carrying out their regulatory and management duties.

Several bilateral cooperative agreements between the United States and Mexico have already been negotiated to manage oil and gas development more effectively in the GOM. For example, the *MEXUS Agreement* controls how the two nations respond to transboundary oil spills.[22] Of even greater scope and importance, the *2012 Agreement on the Exploitation of Transboundary Hydrocarbon Resources in the Gulf of Mexico* creates a legal framework that allows the two nations to jointly exploit the shared oil and gas resources that straddle the maritime boundary and promotes the creation of common environmental standards.[23] In 2016, the U.S. Bureau of Safety and Environmental Enforcement (BSEE) and Mexico's National Agency for Industrial Safety and Environmental Protection of the Hydrocarbons Sector (ASEA) signed a MOU specifying various cooperative measures related to the implementation of regulations for companies that develop offshore hydrocarbons, stating that priority should be given to the safety of people and environmental protection in both Mexico and the United States.[24] Public/private sector bilateral efforts are even taking place such as that between the American Petroleum Institute (API), which represents the U.S. oil and gas industry, and Mexico's oil and gas regulatory agency ASEA, to assure that ASEA will be able to include API recommended environmental and safety standards and practices into its own regulations.[25] Periodic technical meetings between U.S. and Mexican offshore energy regulators are also occurring to improve information sharing and collaborative management opportunities.[26]

---

[21] David Ferris and Nathanial Gronewold, *The U.S. Opportunity in Cuba,* E&E NEWS, April 10, 2015, available at https://www.eenews.net/stories/1060016531.

[22] US Coast Guard, "Mexus Plan, The Joint Contingency Plan Between the United Mexican States and the United States of America Regarding Pollution of the Marine Environment by Discharges of Hydrocarbons and Other Hazardous Substances," February 25, 2000 (revised August 3, 2017). *See* http://mariners.coastguard.dodlive.mil/2017/08/03/832017-coast-guard-mexican-navy-sign-joint-pollution-response-contingency-plan/.

[23] Agreement Concerning Transboundary Hydrocarbon Reservoirs in the Gulf of Mexico, Feb. 20, 2012, available at http://www.state.gov/documents/organization/185467.pdf. *See also*, Guillermo J. Garcia Sanchez & Richard J. McLaughlin, *The 2012 Agreement on the Exploitation of Transboundary Hydrocarbon Resources in the Gul of Mexico: Confirmation of the Rule or Emergence of a New Practice?*, 37 HOUS. J. INT'L L 681 (2015).

[24] A copy of the MOU is available at https://www.bsee.gov/sites/bsee.gov/files/mou_-_2016 bsee-asea.pdf.

[25] https://www.api.org/news-policy-and-issues/news/2016/06/13/api-partnership-with-asea-demonstrates-l.

[26] Personal communication with Dr. Rodney Cluck, Chief Division of Environmental Sciences, BOEM, April 11, 2018.

Bilateral agreements such as these, which seek to promote more efficient and environmentally safe methods of managing oil exploration and production, are extremely important as Mexico continues to open its offshore areas to development in the future. Cuba and the United States have also completed eleven non-binding agreements since restoring diplomatic relations in 2015. These include: agreements dealing with environmental cooperation; coordinating management of marine protected areas; and oil spill response strategies; among others.[27] Successful implementation of all these international agreements depends on having a strong understanding of the state of marine and coastal science in both the Southern and Northern portions of the GOM. In this regard, it is important that the marine scientific information that is collected in each nation's respective ocean waters is properly identified, cataloged, and shared.

An important effort to accomplish this goal recently took place in Houston, Texas at the Gulf of Mexico Workshop on International Research (GOMWIR).[28] This workshop, which was supported, by the U.S. Department of Interior's Bureau of Ocean Energy Management (BOEM), the National Academy of Sciences Gulf of Mexico Research Program, and the Harte Research Institute for Gulf of Mexico Studies at Texas A&M University-Corpus Christi, brought together 165 scientists and governmental officials to improve cooperative science among the three GOM nations. GOMWIR was structured to address four objectives:

1. To assess existing research, identify gaps, and detail institutional capabilities, particularly in the southern Gulf of Mexico through an inventory-type process.
2. To bring together leading scientists and institutions with international experience to assess the state of research in and about the Gulf, identifying and prioritizing research needs.
3. To generate a proceedings document that summarizes both the preworkshop inventory and workshop outputs to identify existing data and information, assess gaps, prioritize research needs and examine institutional capabilities.
4. To establish an international network of scientists, research-oriented organizations, and institutions to facilitate collaborative efforts in addressing priority international research needs for the southern GOM.[29]

---

[27] Discussed at https://2009-2017.state.gov/r/pa/prs/ps/2016/12/264968.html.

[28] McKinney LD, Besonen M, Withers K (editors) (Harte Research Institute for Gulf of Mexico Studies, Corpus Christi, Texas). 2019. Proceedings: The Gulf of Mexico Workshop on International Research, March 29–30, 2017, Houston, Texas. New Orleans (LA): U.S. Department of the Interior, Bureau of Ocean Energy Management. OCS Study BOEM 2019-045. Agreement No.: M16AC00026.

[29] *Id.* at 17.

GOMWIR showcases the type of collaborative marine science initiatives that should be implemented and expanded in coming years. These activities should include marine scientific cruises such as an unprecedented effort by several Mexican institutions, begun in 2015, to engage with international collaborators to establish an oceanographic observation network of physical, geochemical, and ecological processes in the GOM.[30] The ultimate goal of this set of cruises is to respond to the challenges and needs associated with the exploration and exploitation of hydrocarbons in deep waters of the GOM, using an interdisciplinary approach and implementing cutting-edge technologies identified by PEMEX's Exploration and Production Unit.[31]

Cuba and the United States are also engaging in collaborative cruises such as the recent project between Cuba's National Center of Seismological Investigation and the U.S. Geological Survey.[32] The purpose of this cruise is to study a zone of seismological activity off the western coast of Cuba, which commonly produces small and moderate earthquakes.[33] Cuban and U.S. marine biologists are also collaborating in a series of cruises intended to characterize the extent of deep-water coral reefs in Cuba and to compare the health and connectivity (physical, genetic, and ecological) among the reef systems in Cuba and the United States.[34]

Long-standing marine science initiatives such as the Trinational Initiative founded in 2007 with the goal of establishing a framework of collaboration for ongoing joint scientific research and to develop a regional plan of action for the GOM and Western Caribbean should be supported and made a priority.[35] Similarly, the United Nations funded Transboundary Diagnostic Analysis of the Gulf of Mexico Large Marine Ecosystem (TDA) also promotes international scientific collaboration.[36] The TDA determined the baseline for transboundary priority issues in the Gulf region and served as the basis for the Strategic Action Program (SAP), in which the U.S. and Mexican governments established shared legal and institutional actions to address priority transboundary problems in the GOM.[37] In the current phase of the project (2016-2021), science agencies from the two nations will collaborate to implement the activities outlined in the SAP.[38]

---

[30] GOMWIR Proceedings at 75-77. *Supra* note 28.

[31] *Id.*

[32] *See*, https://www.telesurtv.net/english/news/Seismologists-Geologists-From-US-Cuba-Cooperate-on-Research-20180605-0025.html.

[33] *Id.*

[34] *See* https://oceanexplorer.noaa.gov/explorations/17cuba-reefs/welcome.html.

[35] *See* http://www.trinationalinitiative.org/about.html.

[36] M. A. Navarrete & C. Susan, *The Gulf of Mexico Large Marine Ecosystem: Background and Strategic Action Program Implementation*, in McKinney, et al., *supra* note 28.

[37] *Id.* at 17-18.

III. Marine Science Must Align with Legislative Environmental Mandates

These existing collaborative initiatives and the GOMWIR process are beginning to lay a foundation to determine where gaps exist in this scientific knowledge and how best to prioritize future collaborative research efforts. However, additional efforts need to be made to better align the region's science needs with specific legislative mandates within each nation's territory. Agencies are required to address certain scientific questions prior to providing governmental approval to conduct hydrocarbon exploration or production. In the absence of this scientific information, leases and permits will be delayed or not granted. For example, BOEM, tasked with managing development of U.S. offshore resources, has an Environmental Studies Program that supports its offshore leasing requirements. This program's mandate derives from provisions of the National Environmental Policy Act (NEPA)[39] and the Outer Continental Shelf Lands Act (OCSLA).[40] OCSLA Section 20 establishes three primary goals:

1. To establish the information needed for assessment and management of environmental impacts on the human, marine, and coastal environments of the OCS and the potentially affected coastal areas;
2. To predict impacts on the marine biota which may result from chronic, low-level pollution or large spills associated with OCS production, from drilling fluids and cuttings discharges, pipeline emplacement, or onshore facilities; and
3. To monitor human, marine, and coastal environments to provide time series and data trend information for identification of significant changes in the quality and productivity of these environments, and to identify the causes of these changes.[41]

Information from this program also meets additional legislative mandates to protect the marine environment such as those in the Endangered Species Act,[42] the Marine Mammal Protection Act,[43] the Clean Air Act,[44] the Magnuson-Stevens Fishery Conservation and Management Act,[45] Historic Preservation Act,[46] and other

---

[38] *Id.*

[39] 2 U.S.C. §§ 4332 et seq.

[40] 43 U.S.C. §§ 1331 et seq.

[41] 43 U.S.C. § 1346.

[42] 16 U.S.C. §§ 1531 et seq.

[43] 16 U.S.C. §§ 1361 et seq.

[44] 42 U.S.C. §§7401 et seq.

[45] 16 U.S.C. §§ 1801 et seq.

federal statutes. Without adequate scientific information, BOEM would not be capable of conducting environmental reviews, including NEPA analyses, and producing compliance documents required from a whole host of applicable environmental statutes.

Mexico has similar legislative mandates and priorities. One of the greatest challenges posed by the rapid pace of Mexico's energy reforms is developing a fully functioning regulatory regime to deal with potential environmental impacts of its growing offshore hydrocarbon activities. ASEA has been authorized to establish regulations regarding the conditions and actions that will be taken for any environmental damage that occurs. Article 3 of the Internal Regulations of ASEA establishes that the executive director of the agency will have the authority to "coordinate the studies of economic assessment of environmental externalities and risks associated with the facilities, activities, and operations of the sector based on a methodology which takes best international practices into account."[47]

ASEA does not currently have the expertise or effective capacity to regulate and monitor all the exploration and production projects that may be developed in Mexican waters. Consequently, the agency plans to require all lessees to employ "best international practices," which will then be reviewed and approved by ASEA officials.[48] It is currently unclear exactly how this process will be implemented. However, regardless of whether the so-called best practices come from countries such as the United States, United Kingdom, Norway or elsewhere, there will be a strong need for a broad spectrum of scientific research and monitoring capabilities to address these regulatory requirements.

Cuba's offshore hydrocarbon exploration and production activities have not reached the stage to warrant development of detailed environmental regulations. Instead, it manages its offshore areas through a series of legal and policy instruments developed by ministries with jurisdiction over different economic sectors and activities.[49] As it moves forward in seeking to promote exploration of its offshore hydrocarbon resources, marine science will be given prominence in any regulatory program because of Cuba's national commitment to education and scientific development.[50]

---

[46] 54 U.S.C. §§ 300101 et seq.

[47] Luis Serra, The Rule of Law and Mexico's Energy Reform: The Environmental Challenges of the Energy Reform, James A. Baker III Institute for Public Policy (2017) at 18.

[48] Nick Snow, *Watching Government: Mexico's ASEA Moves Ahead*, OIL AND GAS JOURNAL, Oct. 10, 2016, available at https://www.ogj.com/articles/print/volume-114/issue-10a/general-interest/watching-government-mexico-s-asea-moves-ahead.html.

[49] *See* José L Gerhartz-Muro, et al., *An Evaluation of the Framework for National Marine Environmental Policies in Cuba*, BULL MAR SCI. 94(0):000–000. 2018 https://doi.org/1 0.5343/.

In light of the rapidly evolving regulatory regime in Mexico and the potential transboundary impacts associated with increased offshore oil and gas activity in the GOM in the next decade, it is important for scientists and regulators from the three nations to engage in a process of coordinating their activities. These efforts should include prioritizing research needs; conducting joint, or at least coordinated cruises; and finding methods to expand upon the GOMWIR process to effectively share and analyze collected scientific data in the future.

III. Conclusion

If the three nations fail to cooperate fully, effective regulatory and management efforts of hydrocarbon activities will not occur or will suffer from redundancy and duplication of effort. A better understanding of the environmental assessment and regulatory requirements in Mexico and Cuba should also be promoted so that scientists from industry, government, academic, and NGOs can begin to plan for collection and monitoring activities and prioritize the type of information that would best meet the region's needs. Funding sources for priority research needs as well as support for training future scientists from the three nations should be located and encouraged.

Trinational meetings and projects between scientists are occurring with greater frequency and focus.[51] Moreover, government officials from the three nations are beginning to find opportunities to share regulatory capabilities and concerns. Future efforts need to bring together the scientific needs of mission-driven agencies, such Mexico's ASEA, and the U.S.' BOEM and BSEE with the expertise of working marine scientists from all three nations. A significant amount of funded science in the GOM in coming years will address the need of complying with each nation's regulatory and environmental permitting mandates. Bringing together the nations' regulatory and science communities to determine the best path forward to accomplish this important task as effectively and inexpensively as possible should be a high priority.

---

[50] *Id.* at 11.

[51] *See supra* notes 28-38 and accompanying text.

CHAPTER 10

PROFESSOR STEPHEN ZAMORA'S CONTRIBUTIONS TO LEGAL EDUCATION AND TRANSNATIONAL LAW

By Susan L. Karamanian[1]

I. Introduction

During Professor Stephen Zamora's life as a lawyer and teacher from 1972 to 2016, the law in the United States and the role of a lawyer and law professor changed dramatically. A relatively insular U.S. legal system opened up, defined by free trade and the relative ease in the movement of people across borders.[2] Open borders brought the prospects of welfare enhancement.[3] Economics would not be the exclusive measure of the latter. The development and expansion of relationships, whether State to State, individuals or legal persons to foreign States, or a business in one State to a business in another State, became paramount. A premium would be on

[1] Dean, College of Law, Hamad Bin Khalifa University, Doha, Qatar. I am grateful to Kathleen Vanden Heuvel, Director, Law Library, Berkeley Law, who kindly secured information about Berkeley Law courses and professors when Professor Zamora was a student there. I am also grateful to Professor Lois Parkinson Zamora of the University of Houston (Professor Zamora's beloved wife); Professor David Gantz, Samuel M. Fegtly Professor of Law, University of Arizona, James E. Rogers College of Law; and Professor James W. Skelton, Jr., the University of Houston Law Center, who reviewed an earlier version of this paper.

[2] See David Gantz, *Introduction to U.S. Free Trade Agreements*, 5 BRIT. J. AM. LEG. STUD. 299, 302-13 (2016).

[3] David M. Gould, Graeme L. Woodbridge, and Roy J. Ruffin, *The Theory and Practice of Free Trade*, Ec. Rev., Fourth Quarter 1993, available at https://www.dallasfed.org/~/media/documents/research/er/1993/er9304a.pdf.

improving the understanding between and among individuals, corporations and governments that operate across borders, as well as those affected by such activity.[4]

Professor Zamora was at the forefront of transnational law.[5] He had the remarkable ability to work seamlessly between public and private aspects of the law. To a certain extent, given his legal education, he was destined to play this pivotal role. His work, however, went well beyond contributions to doctrine and principles by way of academic scholarship, in which he had an outstanding record.[6] In my judgment, Professor Zamora's contributions to promoting human capacity in transnational law, perhaps not fully appreciated except by those who worked closely with him, will be his most lasting influence.

As the post-World War II liberal economic order comes under intense questioning, it is only appropriate to reflect on someone who was devoted to transnational law, yet who recognized its limits. Professor Zamora was instrumental in strengthening ties between people across borders, as he appreciated the value of mutual understanding derived from social interaction.

Thus, this essay's focus will be on two of Professor Zamora's major initiatives that promoted understanding, both technically and socially. The first is the North American Consortium on Legal Education (NACLE), a consortium of law schools in Canada, Mexico, and the United States, which he founded. The second is the Academy of American and International Law (Academy), a five-week summer program for non-U.S. lawyers sponsored by the Center for American and International Law (CAIL) in Plano, Texas.[7] Professor Zamora was a regular Academy instructor.

---

[4] In his final State of the Union, President Ronald Reagan described the promise of free trade throughout the Americas as follows: "Our goal must be a day when the free flow of trade, from the tip of Tierra del Fuego to the Arctic Circle, unites the people of the Western Hemisphere in a bond of mutually beneficial exchange." Ronald Reagan, *Address before a Joint Session of Congress on the State of the Union - January 25, 1988*, 1988 Pub. Paper 84, 88 (1988).

[5] "Transnational law" is "all law which regulates actions or events that transcend national frontiers . . . [including] [b]oth public and private international law . . . [plus] other rules which do not wholly fit into such standard categories." Philip C. Jessup, TRANSNATIONAL LAW 2 (1956).

[6] *See, e.g.*, Stephen Zamora, et al., MEXCIAN LAW (Oxford University Press 2005); *infra* notes 27 and 30 (identifying some of Professor Zamora's journal articles).

[7] I was fortunate to have worked with Professor Zamora on both NACLE and the Academy. A third program that he developed later in his life, the Center for U.S. and Mexican Law (US-Mex. Law Center) at the University of Houston Law Center, further illustrates his comparative law focus with a practical bent. The U.S.-Mex. Law Center is "devoted to the independent, critical study of Mexican law and legal aspects of U.S.-Mexico relations." Mission Statement of U.S.-Mex. Law Center, available at https://www.law.uh.edu/mexican-law/MissionStatement.asp.

In reflecting on these developments and examining them from today's moment of marked U.S. reentrenchment, one can better understand and appreciate the work and dedication of Professor Zamora. In important respects, Professor Zamora fostered and shaped the glory years of international and comparative law for the United States, particularly regarding U.S.-Mexico relations.

II. Professor Zamora and Transnational Law

A native of California, Professor Zamora graduated from Stanford University in 1966 with a B.A. degree in political science.[8] After two years in the Peace Corps in Colombia, he returned to the United States and attended the University of California at Berkeley Law, where he graduated first in his class in 1972.[9]

The United States of 1972 was in turmoil. The country was attempting to extricate itself from what was then its longest foreign war, Vietnam. Berkeley had been the seat of anti-war protests.[10] A month after Professor Zamora's graduation from law school, news of a break-in at the Democratic Party Headquarters at the Watergate in Washington, D.C. began to surface.[11] That episode would imperil the presidency of Richard M. Nixon.[12]

Yet, not all was doom and gloom on the international front. In fact, 1972 was the beginning of a thaw in global tensions between the United States and two other major world powers, the People's Republic of China, and the Soviet Union. In February of 1972, President Nixon took his path-breaking trip to China and met with Mao Zedong, Chair of the Communist Party of China.[13] The opening of U.S.-China relations would lead to one of the most important international economic and political developments in Professor Zamora's life.

At or near the time of Professor Zamora's law school graduation, President Nixon visited Moscow, the first U.S. President to have done so, and met with the General Secretary of the Central Committee of the Communist Party of the Soviet Union, Leonid Brezhnev.[14] The upshot was the signing of the Anti-Ballistic Missile Treaty (ABM Treaty) and the Strategic Arms Limitations Talks Agreement (SALT I).[15] The former limited anti-ballistic missile systems;[16] the latter limited strategic

---

[8] Resume of Stephen Zamora 2, available at http://www.law.uh.edu/faculty/SZamora/resume.pdf.

[9] *Id.*

[10] *See* Tom Dalzell, THE BATTLE FOR PEOPLE'S PARK, BERKELEY 1969 (2019).

[11] Carl Bernstein & Bob Woodward, ALL THE PRESIDENT'S MEN (1974).

[12] Bob Woodward & Carl Bernstein, THE FINAL DAYS (1976).

[13] Margaret MacMillan, NIXON AND MAO: THE WEEK THAT CHANGED THE WORLD (2006).

[14] The Moscow Summit, NY TIMES, Sec. E, p. 12 (May 28, 1972).

[15] Raymond L. Garthoff, "SALT I: An Evaluation," WORLD POLITICS 1, 6 (1978).

ballistic missile launchers and imposed other restrictions on the number of nuclear submarines.[17]

Berkeley Law (then known as Boalt Hall)[18] in the late 1960s/early 1970s had a diverse faculty teaching in international and comparative law, with many of them steeped in the civil law tradition. The faculty included luminaries educated in Europe, such as the international lawyer Stefan Riesenfeld, conflict of laws scholars Albert Ehrenzweig and Herbert L. Bernstein, Roman law expert David Daube, and contracts law expert, Friedrich "Fritz" Kessler.[19] Joining them were the comparative legal scholar, Richard M. Buxbaum, international lawyer Frank Newman, the legal historian who was the leading U.S. expert on Canadian law, Thomas G. Barnes, and Canon Law scholar John Noonan.[20]

The curriculum reflected the breadth and depth of the Berkeley faculty. As one of the nation's top law schools, Berkeley Law joined peer institutions by offering courses in international law, conflict of laws, and comparative law. Yet its curriculum expanded well beyond core courses in these subjects. Professor Ehrenzweig taught "Comparative Jurisprudence," which offered a comparative perspective of the world's major legal systems from a theoretical perspective.[21] A second creative and unique course offered by Professor Ehrenzweig was "International Conflict of Laws," described as comparing the approach of U.S. conflict of laws to other countries.[22] In the international law area, Professor Riesenfeld taught "International and Maritime Law," while Professor Newman taught "International Human Rights" and "International Organizations."[23] Professor Richard Buxbaum taught "International Tax and Business Problems" and "International Business Transactions."[24]

Professor Zamora's experience in the Peace Corps in Colombia gave him an understanding of a society and culture outside of the United States and presumably a glimpse into the Colombian legal system. Although I have not confirmed the class-

---

[16] Alan Platt, "The Anti-Ballistic Missile Treaty" in Michael Krepon & Dan Caldwell (eds.) THE POLITICS OF ARMS CONTROL TREATY RATIFICATION 229 (1991).

[17] Garthoff, *supra* note 15, at 8-10.

[18] The name "Boalt" was removed from UC Berkeley School of Law in 2018. "UC Berkeley Removes Racist John Boalt's Name from Law School," BERKELEY NEWS (Jan. 30, 2020), available at https://news.berkeley.edu/2020/01/30/boalt-hall-denamed/.

[19] Email from Kathleen Vanden Heuvel, Director of Berkeley Law Library, to author (Dec. 30, 2018). On file with author.

[20] *Id.*

[21] Email from Kathleen Vanden Heuvel, Director of Berkeley Law Library, to author (June 2, 2020). On file with author.

[22] *Id.*

[23] *Id.*

[24] *Id.*

es that Professor Zamora took at Berkeley Law, I have conferred with his wife, Professor Lois Parkinson Zamora, a professor of comparative literature at the University of Houston. She indicated that Professors Buxbaum and Riesenfeld had a profound effect on Professor Zamora.[25] Professor Buxbaum, in particular, encouraged Professor Zamora to apply for a Danforth Fellowship, which enabled Professor Zamora to attend the University Consortium for World Order Studies in Geneva, Switzerland.[26] In Geneva, he researched maritime law and produced two publications related to international shipping.[27]

This snapshot of Berkeley Law of the late 1960s/early 1970s describes the intellectual environment during Professor Zamora's formative years in the law. He was an active law student, as evidenced by serving as Chief Articles and Book Review Editor of the *California Law Review*.[28] The strong international and comparative law tradition at Berkeley Law during this period surely had a profound influence on him. In fact, after graduating and finishing his postgraduate fellowship in Geneva, Professor Zamora worked as an associate attorney at the law firm of Cleary, Gottlieb, Steen & Hamilton in Washington, D.C. from 1974 to 1976 and in the Legal Department of the World Bank from 1976 to 1978.[29] Perhaps reflecting his work during these formative years, Professor Zamora's early publications dealt with international financial issues, particularly exchange controls with a focus on Mexico.[30]

As Professor Zamora left the practice of law and joined the University of Houston Law Center, he brought his expertise in international business and finance into the classroom. He would go on to teach courses such as international business transactions, international trade law, and international banking.[31]

---

[25] Email from Professor Lois Zamora to author (Dec. 13, 2018). On file with author.

[26] *Id.*

[27] Stephen Zamora, *Carrier Liability for Damage or Loss to Cargo in International Transport,* 23 AM. J. COMP. L. 391 (1975); Stephen Zamora, *UNCTAD III: The Question of Shipping,* 7 J. WORLD TRADE L. 91 (1973).

[28] Zamora Resume, *supra* note 8, at 2.

[29] *Id.*

[30] *See, e.g.*, Stephen Zamora, *Recognition of Foreign Exchange Controls in International Creditors' Rights Cases: The State of the Art,* 21 INT'L LAW. 1055 (1987); Stephen Zamora, *Mexico and the Global Financial Market: Capital Flight as a Factor in National Economic Policymaking,* 18 CAL.W.J. INT'L L. 35 (1987); Stephen Zamora, *Mexican Exchange Controls: A Case Study in the Application of IMF Rules,* 7 HOUS. J. INT'L L. 103 (1984); Stephen Zamora, "Peso-Dollar Economics and the Imposition of Foreign Exchange Controls in Mexico," 32 AM. J. COMP. L. 99 (1985); and Stephen Zamora, *Regulating Foreign Bank Operations in Texas,* 19 HOUS. L. REV. 427 (1982).

[31] Zamora Resume, *supra* note 8, at 1.

III. Dedication to Transnational Law

Professor Zamora understood that learning required extensive, meaningful personal interaction, and this was particularly true when the subject matter was of a comparative nature. Two of his activities, to which he dedicated substantial time and energy, NACLE and the Academy of CAIL, confirm this fact.

a. NACLE

i. Background.

In 1992, the United States, Canada and Mexico signed the North American Free Trade Agreement (NAFTA).[32] The sweeping trade agreement ushered in an era of openness among the three North American economic powerhouses, largely defined by the flow of goods, service and people across the relevant borders.[33] With the agreement came enormous optimism as open markets meant enhanced consumer welfare, whether through lower production costs or easier access to a wider range of goods.

For Professor Zamora, who had expertise in the laws of two of the NAFTA partners, the United States and Mexico, the emergence of NAFTA was the natural progression of his professional focus. He quickly understood that NAFTA's vision of trade and investment liberalization would require more than the passage of a trade agreement and revision of domestic legislation. In short, it would require a cadre of legal professionals skilled with an understanding of relevant national and international law and able to work across boundaries to fulfill mutually beneficial objectives. With NAFTA, came the birth of the North American Consortium of Legal Education (NACLE) in 1999, which was the brainchild of Professor Zamora. Also leading the establishment of NACLE was Professor David A. Gantz, the Samuel M. Fegtly Professor of Law the University of Arizona, James E. Rogers College of Law. Professor Gantz shared Professor Zamora's knowledge of and interest in trade and investment law. Fluent in Spanish like Professor Zamora, he practiced law in Washington, D.C., before joining the legal academy.[34]

The premise of NACLE is the need for law students and professors from each of the NAFTA countries to understand the laws of the other NAFTA countries as

---

[32] North American Free Trade Agreement, Can.-Mex.-US, Dec. 17, 1992, 32 I.L.M. 289 (1993).

[33] For Professor Zamora's views on NAFTA, *see* Stephen Zamora, *Rethinking North America: Why NAFTA's Laissez Faire Approach to Integration Is Flawed, and What to Do About It,* 53 VILLANOVAL L. REV. 631 (2011); Stephen Zamora, *A Proposed North American Regional Development Fund: The Next Phase of North American Integration Under NAFTA,* 40 LOYOLA U. CHICAGO L. J. 93 (2008).

[34] Professor Gantz had also worked in the Office of the Legal Adviser, US Department of State. *See* Professor Gantz's biography at https://law.arizona.edu/david-gantz.

well as relevant international legal principles. NACLE sought "to promote cross-border legal exchanges among members" of the consortium.[35]

Yet, NACLE was more than a way to impart traditional learning. The development and nurturing of inter-personal relationships was critical. Accordingly, Professor Zamora understood the need for a "consortium" as opposed to a series of bilateral or multilateral agreements with a single purpose, such as student exchanges. NACLE envisioned a sustained relationship among law schools from each of the NAFTA states. The nine founding NACLE schools, with at least one in the capital of each NAFTA state, are as follows:

Canada: Dalhousie University Faculty of Law, McGill University Faculty of Law, and the University of Ottawa Faculty of Law
Mexico: Instituto Tecnológico y de Estudios Superiories de Monterrey (ITESM), Universidad Nacional Autonoma de Mexico, Facultad de Derecho and Instituto de Investigaciones Jurídicas (UNAM), and Universidad Panamericana, Facultad de Derecho
United States: University of Houston Law Center, University of Arizona, James E. Rogers College of Law, and George Washington University Law School

The schools reflect the common law and civil law and collectively teach law in three languages: English, French, and Spanish.[36]

The NACLE institutions came together under a Memorandum of Understanding (MOU). Further, the founding institutions entered into an Operating Agreement to address financial aspects of the relationship. The MOU was amended in 2012 to add the University of British Columbia Faculty of Law from Canada, Centro de Investigación y Docencia Económicas (CIDE) from Mexico, and the Southwestern Law School and Suffolk University Law School from the United States. The schools also amended the Operating Agreement.[37]

ii. Curriculum Development

Professor Zamora succeeded in securing a $350,000, four-year grant from the U.S. Fund for Improvement of Post-Secondary Education (FIPSE) from the U.S.

---

[35] Revised Memorandum of Understanding for the North American Consortium on Legal Education 2 (Aug. 27, 2012), available at http://www.law.uh.edu/nacle/About/NACLE-MOU-Updated.pdf.

[36] Barbara Atwood, Graciela Jasa Silveira, Nicole LaViolette & J. Thomas Oldham, *Crossing Borders in the Classroom: A Comparative Law Experiment in Family Law,* 55 J. Leg. Educ. 542, 543 (2005).

[37] Two other US law schools, Berkeley Law and Fordham Law School, were NACLE members at various times.

Department of Education.[38] The FIPSE grant funded NACLE "curriculum development workshops," which enabled a regular series of workshops among the NACLE schools over the course of a decade.[39] The workshops, typically held at one of the NACLE schools, focused on topics relevant to course offerings, such as family law, environmental law, labor rights, energy, trade law, and investment law.

These themes would later translate into course materials. For example, an area of collaboration that emerged from a NACLE workshop in 2001 was cross-border family law among the NAFTA States. Professors from a few of the NACLE schools subsequently prepared an experiential module on family law for use in any law school.[40] They were later joined by a professor from the Faculty of Law of the University of Sonora University in Mexico (a non-NACLE school).

The family law module was designed "to enable students to converse across nationalities and cultures."[41] More specifically, the faculty team stated:

> Our goal was to create a cross-border and comparative law module that could enrich the content of an existing course in family law or conflict of laws, or could be offered as a freestanding independent study project. We identified several objectives for the teaching module. We wanted a project that would allow students from each jurisdiction to interact with each other. This would require us to use new teaching technologies, such as video conferencing, websites, and electronic bulletin boards. In addition, we needed to select family law issues that could highlight legal differences in each jurisdiction, and at the same time could be transformed into actual court orders to be exchanged between the students. Students would therefore be called upon to research not only family law, but also questions relating to conflict of laws.[42]

The module had two components: (1) research phase involving a question of substantive law; and (2) enforcement of a foreign court order.[43] It was implemented in various NACLE schools yet not as a stand-alone course.[44]

The NACLE workshops continued after FIPSE funding ended. They became one of the defining features of NACLE as faculty from the NACLE schools as well as local and international experts gathered to discuss and analyze specific issues related to NAFTA.

---

[38] Jeffrey Atik & Anton Subbot, *International Legal Education,* 36 INT'L L. 715, 718 (2002).

[39] *Id.*

[40] Barbara Atwood, et al., *supra* note 36, at 543.

[41] *Id.*

[42] *Id.* at 544.

[43] *Id.* at 545.

[44] *Id.* at 555.

iii. Student Paper Competitions

The workshops also involved the active engagement of students, specifically through a paper competition dealing with a theme related to the focus of the workshop. The paper competitions, again the brainchild of Professor Zamora, enabled each institution to nominate a student to attend the workshop and present his or her paper before a panel of judges.

iv. Faculty-Student Collaboration with CEC

Further, the workshops enabled planning for and reporting of other NACLE-related activities. In this regard, a significant contribution of NACLE was the development of substantive issues relating to NAFTA. For example, in 2011, NACLE established the Comparative Environment Law Research Project, in which students and faculty from various NACLE schools teamed up with the NAFTA Commission on Environmental Cooperation (CEC) to conduct joint research on environmental issues.[45] NACLE students would later have internship opportunities at the CEC.[46]

In 2014, UBC Law in Vancouver hosted a NACLE workshop titled "Re-Energizing North America: Pipelines and Policy."[47] In addition to hosting panels on topics related to the workshop theme, students and faculty held a separate session on research projects they had undertaken under a partnership between NACLE and the CEC.[48] In the session, students from two NACLE schools, GW Law and Suffolk Law, presented findings regarding environmental assessment for hydraulic fracturing in the NAFTA States.[49] Focus was on getting feedback for a later presentation to the CEC "regarding the coordination and harmonization of environmental assess-

---

[45] NACLE students and faculty met with the CEC in Montreal, Canada on June 14-15, 2011 to "plan the 2011-2013 comparative law research agenda that will focus on NAAEC Article 14 & 15." *See* "Meeting of the North American Consortium on Legal Education (NACLE) Comparative Environmental Law Research Project," Commission for Environmental Cooperation, available at http://www.cec.org/news-and-outreach/events/meeting-north-american-consortium-legal-education-nacle-comparative-environment-law-research-project.

[46] *See* "CEC Provides Summer Legal Internship Opportunities to Two International Law Students" (Dec. 20, 2016), available at http://www.cec.org/news-and-outreach/press-releases/cec-provides-summer-legal-internship-opportunities-two-international-law-students.

[47] "Re-Energizing North America: Pipelines and Policy," NACLE Workshop Program (Mar. 14-15, 2014), program previously available on May 29, 2020 (but now removed) at http://www.allard.ubc.ca/sites/www.allard.ubc.ca/files/uploads/ncbl/events/2013%20-2014/ubc_nacle_workshop_agenda.pdf.

[48] *Id.*

[49] *Id.*

ment laws" in the NAFTA States.[50] Further, at the workshop, Suffolk Law students presented research results on environmental law and international trade.[51]

v. Student Exchanges

Student exchanges were another defining feature of NACLE. Each NACLE school that offered courses agreed to accept a limited number of students within the consortium for a semester. The exchange students would not be charged tuition under the principle of reciprocity among all the NACLE schools.

A popular destination for students from Canada and Mexico was the George Washington University Law School. Among the exchange students who attended GW Law were a student from McGill University who later clerked for a justice on the Supreme Court of Canada and a student from Universidad Panamericana who later clerked for the Chief Justice of Mexico.

vi. Faculty Interaction

Another critical aspect of NACLE was the opportunity for faculty interaction. In this regard, Professor David Gantz spent a semester at GW Law as a visiting professor, where he taught international trade law. He also participated in a number of other non-NACLE sponsored events at GW Law. Professor Gabriel Cavazos Villanueva from Monterrey Tech would frequently visit the NACLE schools, including to deliver a lecture on the future of NAFTA at the University of Houston.[52] After Professor Zamora's death, Professor Cavazos assumed the responsibility of Interim Director of NACLE.

b. CAIL: Academy of American and International Law

The second principal activity of Professor Zamora was his near 20-year dedication to the Academy of American and International Law of CAIL. The Academy is a five-week summer program on U.S., international and comparative law, designed for lawyers from around the world. It is held each May-June in Plano, Texas.

In 1947, Dean Robert G. Storey of Southern Methodist University School of Law established CAIL as the Southwestern Legal Foundation. A former member of the U.S. prosecution team at Nuremberg under Justice Robert H. Jackson, Dean Storey returned from Europe with the conviction that "strengthening relations between lawyers would contribute to the creation of a fabric of world peace."[53] Key

---

[50] *Id.*

[51] *Id.*

[52] "Trade Expert Questions Future of NAFTA at UHLC Lecture" (Feb. 8, 2017), available at https://www.law.uh.edu/news/spring2017/0208NAFTA.asp.

[53] Charles R. Norberg, *Legal Exchange: Necessity and Opportunity,* IX INTERNATIONAL EDUCATION AND CULTURAL EXCHANGE 28, 28 (1974).

to fulfilling his vision was "person-to-person contacts between leaders of the legal profession" to promote "mutual understanding of difficult questions of fact and in defining legal arrangements to solve a problem."[54] Devoted to the promotion of the rule of law and the legal profession, Dean Storey was President of the American Bar Association, the Texas Bar Association, and the Inter-American Bar Association.[55]

Consistent with Dean Storey's desire to promote continuing legal education, he helped launch the Academy in 1964. Each summer since, except in 2020 and 2021, a group of lawyers from around the world has come to north Texas for an intensive educational experience.[56] Academy graduates include legal luminaries, such as the former Prime Minister of Peru, Hon. Martha Beatriz Merino, President of the United Nations General Assembly and Foreign Minister of Uruguay, Hon. Didier Opertti, Chief Justice of the Philippines, Hon. Marcelo B. Fernan, and President of the U.N. International Criminal Tribunal for the former Yugoslavia, Hon. Antonio Cassese.[57]

Subjects taught in the Academy include an Introduction to the U.S. Legal System (taught by me), International Taxation (taught by Professor Charles Gustafson of Georgetown University Law Center), Legal Writing (taught by Editor-in-Chief of Black's Law Dictionary Bryan Garner), and Corporate Law (taught by Stanley Siegel of New York University School of Law).

Professor Zamora was one of the regular Academy lecturers. Each summer, he devoted two days to teach international litigation and conflict of laws. Two features distinguished his Academy tenure: (1) the enthusiasm he brought into the classroom; and (2) his overwhelming dedication to the students. According to CAIL President (retired) Mark Smith, who was also Academy Dean, "when Professor Zamora entered a classroom, he embraced his students. He cared about them as lawyers and as people."[58]

Mr. Smith's observations about Professor Zamora's devotion to the Academy students are consistent with mine. On a number of occasions, I would arrive at the Academy faculty-student hotel late in the evening, after having flown in from Washington, D.C. I would invariably find Professor Zamora leading evening discussions around the pool. In other words, after a full day of teaching, he managed to find the time and energy to stay up with the students and share life stories. Invariably, he

---

[54] *Id.*

[55] A.J. Thomas, Jr., *In Memoriam: Dean Robert Gerald Storey,* 35 SW. L. J. 553, 555 (1981).

[56] For many years, the Academy had its home at SMU Law in Dallas, Texas. In the 1990s, CAIL moved its headquarters to Plano, Texas, where it has a spacious, state-of-the-art learning center, and the Academy moved with it. Due to COVID-19, the 2020 Academy and 2021 Academy were cancelled.

[57] CAIL, Storey Award, available at https://www.cailaw.org/Southwestern-Institute-for-International-and-Comparative-Law/About-Us/storey-award.html.

[58] Email from CAIL President Mark Smith to author (May 23, 2020). On file with author.

would invite me to join in the conversation. I would politely accept yet manage only 30 minutes before needing to get my rest.

IV. Conclusion

This account of the contributions of Professor Zamora to transnational law demonstrates the breadth of his engagement, whether in the United States or beyond, and his lifetime dedication to teaching and building understanding. It does not remotely begin to convey, however, the human qualities that enabled him to guide and inspire his students and professional colleagues. Professor Zamora was a careful listener whose wise counsel and optimism enabled him to motivate others. He also had the ability to implement his vision, an enviable quality particularly given constant change and the inevitable administrative and financial hurdles. Finally, he was generous in terms of expressing gratitude to all of those who joined him on his journey. We can all hope to have some of these qualities as we manage the pressing problems of today's world.

CHAPTER 11

CLANDESTINE TAPPING AND ENVIRONMENTAL LIABILITY IN MEXICO

By Josefina Cortés Campos[1]

Introduction

Six years after the implementation of the energy reform, the future for the sector still remains uncertain. In general, the objective and the results obtained from having generated highly contested markets appear to have been postponed or dissolved in time. In contrast with such lack of definition, certain energy industry sectors show signs of over-regulation and reveal the absence of a common regulatory vision among the relevant authorities.

Let us look at some figures that partly serve to illustrate the aforementioned scenario. The 2013 constitutional energy reform required the issuance of nine new legal dispositions, as well as the modification of twelve preexisting laws. This generated a multiplying effect in terms of regulatory changes. For example, there are at least eighty-three regulatory texts and 318 requirements in the hydrocarbons industry,[2] all processed by numerous government agencies and a few institutional coordination bodies.

It is true that the qualitative argument does not suffice to evaluate a regulatory system negatively because the multiplicity of dispositions could be explained by the

---

[1] Professor and researcher in the Department of Law, Tec de Monterrey. Doctor in Law at Universidad Carlos III, Madrid, Spain.

[2] See Orellana M. A. (2018), *GPS Energía. Sector Hidrocarburos en México*. México, Ed. Tirant Lo Blanch.

need to regulate a sector comprehensively and systematically. In the case of the energy industry, for instance, the multiplicity of dispositions could well be the result of the complexity of the different value chains themselves, the diversity of its participants, and the objectives established by the latest constitutional reform (competitiveness, social equity, productivity, and sustainability, among others).

In this essay, I refer to a regulatory segment in which the aforementioned condition is not fulfilled; that is, the environmental liability system in cases of hydrocarbons spillage caused by clandestine tapping. It is a regulatory domain in which the diversity and multiplicity of regulations, as well as the absence of a common regulatory vision, jeopardize compliance with constitutional mandates, such as the right to a healthy environment and establishing environmental liability as a guiding principle to be observed by state productive enterprises.

I. Hydrocarbons Spillage from Clandestine Tapping and Protection of the Environment as a Constitutional Mandate

Through the years, fuel theft or so-called "clandestine tapping" has become a difficult challenge for the government to confront. It is a generalized illegal activity, which has uncovered complex corruption networks involving not only public and

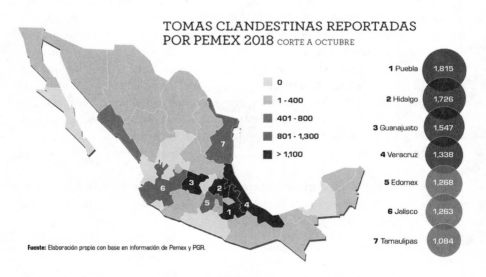

https://www.mexicoevalua.org/huachicol-desabasto-justicia-3/

private actors but also numerous communities throughout the country. The graph above illustrates the magnitude of the problem at hand:[3]

In the most recent report by Pemex (2018), 12,581 clandestine taps were documented in twenty-five out of thirty-two states in the federation.

The scenario described opens the door to various perspectives for analysis, as might be the economic effects derived from these actions, along with the environmental impact and the way in which Mexican legislation has sought to tackle the problem. Let us look at the second aspect.

The right to a healthy environment is expressly recognized and guaranteed under the Mexican Constitution in Article 4, fifth paragraph, where it is stated that ". . . all persons have the right to a healthy environment that ensures their development and well-being. The State guarantees the respect for such right. Under the law, environmental damage and deterioration generates a liability for those responsible who provoke it."

The right to a healthy environment, as established by Mexico's Supreme Court, refers to a right that is often unclear in terms of the interests it covers. It may not be divided or appropriated by any given party. This is so because the collective suffers severely as a result of any negative externalities generated by any detriment to the environment. Moreover, the right in question involves considerations such as solidarity with future generations whose survival depends on the environmental legacy left by us as a society.[4]

In light of the regulatory contents with which the constituent has safeguarded the right to a healthy environment, it is possible to identify three regulatory principles or pillars: conservation and restoration; control; and lastly that relating to liability and sanctioning resulting from environmental damage. The constitutional text establishes certain guidelines for this, as follows: environmental damage and deterioration are causes of liability, and liability is attributable to any party that generates environmental damage or deterioration. In other words, there must be a causal link between action or omission by a party and the damage generated, and it is the responsibility of the legislators to determine the environmental damage and deterioration liability system that is to be applied.

It is important to point out that in the case of parties that may potentially be held environmentally liable, the Mexican constitutional regulation makes no distinction between the public or private status of the party responsible for causing the damage. Under article 25, it thus establishes that the public, social, and private sectors must be guided by a criterion of sustainability. More specifically, with state productive

---

[3] Source: Mexico evaluates. Consultation: https://www.mexicoevalua.org/2019/01/09/huachi-col-desabasto-justicia/

[4] *See* amparo under review 1890/2009.

enterprises such as Pemex, the Constitution establishes that these must be regulated by Congress from an environmental liability perspective.[5]

II. Legislative Convergence and Divergence, a Possible and Desirable Harmonization

Taking into consideration the contents and constitutional basis mentioned in the section above, reference is made to the way in which legislators have built a liability regime for cases in which a hydrocarbons spillage occurs as a result of clandestine tapping.

Let us begin by indicating that there is no single regulating body that is applicable for purposes of environmental liability (there are three laws that regulate these matters: The General Law of Ecological Balance and Environmental Protection, The General Law for the Prevention and Integral Management of Waste, and The General Environmental Liability Law. Neither is there a specific hydrocarbons sector regulation establishing the consequences, in terms of environmental liability, derived from a hydrocarbons spillage resulting from fuel theft.

These affirmations are the result of considering that the Hydrocarbons Law, sectorial regulation, does not contain a proprietary or detailed environmental liability regime. The above may be corroborated by, for example, considering that article 47, section 9, establishes that assigns and contractors are responsible for hydrocarbons spillages and related damages that may result in terms of the applicable legal dispositions. Article 130, on the other hand, indicates that assigns, contractors, authorized parties, and licensees shall undertake the environmental or ecological balance damage prevention and compensation actions caused by their activities, and are required to cover the costs inherent to such repair whenever they are declared responsible by the competent authorities *in terms of the applicable dispositions.*

It is worth noting that environmental pollution or damage under the Mexican legal system may lead to distinct types of liability — such as civil, penal, and administrative.[6] Referring specifically to the manner in which environmental pollution or damage is treated for administrative purposes, it is worth bearing in mind that the action that results in the environmental damage brings on various regulatory consequences. The authorities are thus required to establish control and vigilance measures, security measures, and sanctions,[7] while the party obliged is required to conform to "licit conduct."

---

[5] *See* transitory article 20 of the energy reforms decree published in the Official Gazette dated December 20, 2013.

[6] *See* article 203 of the General Ecological Balance and Environmental Protection Law.

[7] *See* article 1 of the General Integral Waste Prevention and Management Law, section 8.

It is precisely in the administrative sphere of environmental liability that Mexican legislators are considered to have over-regulated the sector, having overlooked the harmonization of various related legal dispositions already in place. This not only promotes legal uncertainty for industry participants but also places the right to a healthy environment in a position of fragility or simple vulnerability.

As a matter of fact, in recent years, the lack of legislative harmonization has been accompanied by sentences marked by a refusal to analyze the complexity of the environmental pollution legal system in place, instead opting to favorably justify, for example, Pemex's hydrocarbons spillages resulting from clandestine tapping.

Some of the more notable considerations generated at the judicial seat are the following: Pemex, as a public company is not liable to pay environmental compensation as gasoline is not considered a dangerous material. For hazardous waste to be deemed to exist it is indispensable for its proprietor to have dumped it. Because public funds are available to finance environmental redressing, the exemption from environmental liability argument is valid. No environmental damage can be said to exist whenever the conduct in question is the result of a premeditated action by a third party. To blame Pemex for environmental damage, whenever such damage is caused by clandestine tapping of ducts, would be tantamount to transferring the responsibility of the State in the domain of public safety.

It is my opinion that such considerations are the result of a partial analysis of the legal system, which could potentially have the effect of debilitating the environmental liability system in Mexico because it does little to generate adequate incentives aimed at ensuring that industry participants contribute to the halting of fuel theft in Mexico. For this reason, it is necessary to put forward an interpretation other than that proposed by the judiciary.

In the following pages, regulatory arguments will be suggested, thus allowing for an analysis of instances of environmental pollution derived from a hydrocarbon spillage caused by clandestine tapping, as viewed from a strict liability perspective. This will allow for remediation to be guaranteed in the majority of polluted sites so as to reduce pollutants to a level that is safe for health and the environment.

III. Urgency Measures and Remediation as a Rule

Let us begin by stating that the interpretation we propose involves distinguishing between urgency and compensation measures as opposed to other measures implemented by administrative authorities and which must become due conduct for industry participants.

Firstly, in the case of urgency and compensation measures, it is important to consider that they operate under the public interest burden regime, aimed at guaranteeing the human right to a healthy environment in the face of the risk created. No justification can be argued here.[8] With regard to the remaining measures and due conducts,[9] such as the requirement to pay costs associated to the integral management of waste, damage and repair, or compensation,[10] payment of damages, or the payment of an economic sanction, these scenarios may be construed to open up the possibility to an exemption from cases of acts of God or Force Majeure. Additionally, agreements aimed at commuting and/or reducing the sanction due to anticipated compliance or its equivalent may also be reached.[11]

The proposed distinction is based on the legal texts set forth below.

a. General Integral Waste Prevention and Management Law (Waste Law)

In its first article, the Waste Law establishes that it is a regulatory law that forms part of the legal constitutional dispositions referring to the protection of the environment in the prevention and comprehensive management of resources in the country. Its object is to guarantee all persons the right to a healthy environment, promote sustainable development by preventing the generation, valorization, and comprehensive management of hazardous waste, or of solid urban waste, and waste requiring special handling. It is also aimed at preventing the pollution of sites and to carry out their remediation.

With regard to the environmental liability regime, the Waste Law, in chapter 5, in accordance with the constitutional mandate, presents the following regulatory components: (a.) establishment of a general environmental liability principle; (b.) establishment of the existence of a causal link as a requirement for assignment; and (c.) although reference is made to fortuitous events or Force Majeure, such a scenario does not represent an exemption from liability in relation to urgency measures or compensation. Let us analyze such components in greater detail.

The Waste Law indicates, under articles 2 and 42, in relation to the environmental liability principle, that any party that generates waste is not only responsible for its management and final disposition but is also required to pay the related costs and compensation for damages, if applicable.

In conformity with article 5 of the Waste Law, waste means all materials or products for which the proprietor or holder is responsible for dumping in solid or semisolid state, or in liquid or gas form and that are contained in receptacles or deposits, or materials that are likely to be revalued or must be subjected to treatment

---

[8] *See* article 3 of the General Integral Waste Prevention and Management Law, section 3.

[9] *See* article 2 of the General Integral Waste Prevention and Management Law.

[10] *See* articles 15 and 17 of the Environmental Liability Law.

[11] *See* article 111 of the General Integral Waste Prevention and Management Law, as well as articles 168 and 173 of General Ecological Balance and Environmental Protection Law.

or final disposal in conformity with the Waste Law and related applicable provisions. This condition is applicable to hydrocarbons spillages (gasoline).[12]

With regard to the causal link, the provisions above establish, in article 68, that whoever is responsible for the pollution of a site is required to pay damages, regardless of whether such site has been polluted, or whether the damage has occurred directly or indirectly.

The Waste Law makes specific reference to fortuitous events or Force Majeure. However, it is important to indicate that, in terms of the Waste Law and its related Regulations, a fortuitous event or Force Majeure is not construed as a relief from environmental liability. Even in such cases, the general rule requires the imposition of emergency and remediation measures. This may be corroborated by considering that the Waste Law, in article 72, establishes that whenever pollution is attributable to a fortuitous event or Force Majeure, the authorities are required to impose the necessary emergency measures in face of such contingency so as not to endanger health or the environment.

Similarly, articles 129 and 130 of the Regulations to the Waste Law indicate that whenever spillages, seeping, discharge, or dumping of hazardous waste occurs in quantities exceeding a cubic meter, the party responsible for the hazardous material or the generator of the pollution, as the case may be, along with the company rendering the related service, must implement immediate measures to contain such material or waste, duly notifying of such spillage, implementing the necessary measures, and initiating the work of describing the polluted site, as well as undertaking the required remediation actions.

The remediation measures of polluted sites, in accordance with article 3, section 28, of the Waste Law, consist of a series of measures to which polluted sites must be subjected in order to eliminate or decrease pollutants to a level that is safe for health and the environment or to prevent their dispersion into the environment without modifying them.

The parties required to undertake remediation are, in accordance with article 69, those responsible for activities relating to the generation and handling of hazardous materials and waste that have caused pollution, together with the proprietors or holders of private property. Also, the holders of areas held under license whose soils are polluted will be held jointly liable for undertaking remediation actions, regardless of whether such proceedings are also leveled against the party responsible for the pollution.

In terms of article 77 of the dispositions analyzed, all actions to remediate, repair, and compensate for damages to the environment shall be carried out in conformity with that indicated under the Regulations to the Waste Law and in accordance with that established under the Environmental Liability Law. Thus, article 78 of the aforementioned dispositions establishes that the Ministry of the Environment, in

---

[12] *See also* article 151 y 152 Bis of the General Ecological Balance Law.

coordination with the Ministry of Health, shall issue Official Mexican Standards describing the polluted sites and shall evaluate the risks for the environment and health derived from such pollution in order to determine the remediation actions required based on such risk.

With regard to the legal nature of the remediation measures, in terms of the Waste Law, such measures should take the form of sanctions. This is corroborated by articles 71, last paragraph, and 112, which expressly refer to remediation as one of the administrative sanctions that may be applied by the competent authority against those responsible for polluting a site.

To impose the aforementioned sanctions, the application of the General Ecological Balance and Environmental Protection Law shall be applicable.

b. The General Environmental Liability Law (Environmental Liability Law)

To complete the environmental liability regime analysis derived from hydrocarbons spillage it is necessary to refer to article 68 of the Waste Law, second paragraph: "Any individual or corporate entity which, directly or indirectly, pollutes a site, or generates damage or affectation to the environment as a result of the generation, handling, release, discharge, seeping, or incorporation of material or waste that is hazardous to the environment, shall be held liable and must make the respective restitution or compensation in conformity with that established under the Environmental Liability Law."

In accordance with article 1, the purpose of the Environmental Liability Law is to regulate environmental liability derived from damages caused to the environment, as well as to regulate the restitution and compensation of such damages whenever required by legal proceedings, or alternative conflict resolution methods, administrative proceedings, and those governing the perpetration of illicit acts against the environment and environmental management.

As in the case of the Waste Law, the Environmental Liability Law, under article 10, establishes the general liability principle based on the existence of a causal link, and also stipulates that any individual or corporate entity, which, through its action or omission, directly or indirectly causes damage to the environment, shall be held liable and will be required to compensate for the damage. Whenever this is not possible, it will be required to provide environmental compensation.

Under article 2, section 3 of the Environmental Liability Law, environmental damage is defined as the loss, change, deterioration, detriment, affectation, or adverse and measurable modification of the habitat, ecosystems, and natural resource elements, or their chemical, physical, or biological conditions, or related interaction relations, as well as of the environmental services that they provide. However, in accordance with that established under article 6 of the same legal dispositions, not all environmental damage is considered adverse and is not construed as grounds for liability, either because it has been previously recognized before the administrative authorities and has been contained or because the permissible pollution levels have not been exceeded.

With regard to the applicable type of liability in the event of environmental pollution or damage, the legislators have declared that liability for environmental damage caused in determined scenarios must be considered to have occurred as a result of negligence (in the terms of the Environmental Liability Law "subjective liability"), which means it is strict liability.

Article 11 of the Environmental Liability Law establishes subjective liability to be derived from illegal acts or omissions whose consequence is the requirement to pay an economic sanction. Environmental liability is construed as being "objective" or strict whenever the damage to the environment is derived directly or indirectly from any related action or omission involving hazardous materials or waste, or from the scenarios and conducts contemplated under article 1913 of the Federal Civil Code, which establishes the following: Whenever a person uses mechanisms, instruments, apparatus, or hazardous substances which are essentially dangerous due to their velocity or their explosive or inflammable nature, or as a result of the power of the electric of the current they employ, or for other reasons, such person is required to answer for the damage caused even if no illegal action may be imputed, unless the party accused can demonstrate that such damage is attributable to the inexcusable guilt or negligence of the victim.

On the subject of exemption from liability, article 24 establishes that no liability can be deemed to exist whenever environmental damages are caused exclusively by a fortuitous event or Force Majeure. Also, for purposes of exemption, the Environmental Liability Law, in article 2, sections 4 and 7, refers to so-called indirect damages and defines them as all damages, which, as part of a causal chain, do not represent an immediate effect of the act or omission imputed against a person. In terms of the aforementioned precept, section 6, no indirect damages can be said to exist whenever, between the time of the conduct imputed and the results attributed, a premeditated third-party action takes place that is completely determinant of the damages. Such relief shall not be applicable whenever the third-party acts in representation of or for the benefit of the party deemed responsible. In other words, in the case of premeditated third-party actions that are absolutely determinant of damages, no liability for direct damages can be deemed to exist.

It is important to indicate that the Environmental Liability Law, under article 13, uses a concept that is broader than remediation, as is compensation. This concept/genre allows us to see the breadth and variety of conducts that may be construed as environmental damages (restoration, reestablishment, treatment) among which remediation is included.

As in the Waste Law (article 70), the Environmental Liability Law, in article 13, establishes that proprietors and holders who are affected by the environmental damage compensation actions undertaken by third parties shall be entitled to repeat with regard to the person that results responsible for the damages caused.

Finally, the Environmental Liability Law establishes that, under articles 18 and 45, the Federal Executive, through the Ministry of the Environment and Natural Resources shall, for reasons of urgency or importance, have the subsidiary power to compensate for environmental damages caused by third parties through the Fund established under the law.

c. Necessary harmonization

With regard to the regulatory framework that we have been analyzing, it is important to observe the apparent regulatory contradiction between the Waste Law and the Environmental Responsibility Law in terms of the exemption from liability relief derived from fortuitous events or Force Majeure. Although the Waste Law clearly establishes that, in the case of fortuitous events or Force Majeure, urgency measures may be applied along with the determination of compensation liability, the Environmental Liability Law establishes that no liability whatsoever can be deemed to exist whenever the environmental damages are caused exclusively by a fortuitous event or Force Majeure. Moreover, as contemplated under the same legal provisions, in cases of third-party premeditated actions that are absolutely determinant of damage, no indirect damages liability shall be deemed to exist.

This regulatory condition is resolved by means of a harmonic and inclusive interpretation and by considering, especially, that the relation that arises between the aforementioned dispositions is the result of supposed supplementary legislation.

Thus, as expostulated by the Supreme Court of Justice, the supplementary application of a law with respect to another is valid in order to comprise an omission in the law or when seeking to interpret its provisions and to ensure that they are integrated into other provisions or general principles contained in other laws. More specifically, this supplementary action shall be valid whenever the law to be supplemented does not contemplate the institution or the legal questions to be applied in a supplementary manner or, even if it does, it fails to develop them or does so deficiently.[13]

The application of the aforementioned legal criterion clearly shows that the exemptions from liability contemplated under the Environmental Liability Law are not applicable in the event of urgency or compensation measures. Otherwise, the preferential legislation on the subject, which is the Waste Law, would have some of its contents and principles overlooked, specifically those relating to the determina-

---

[13] The information to locate the aforementioned jurisprudence is the following Tenth Period. Registration: 2003161. Instance: Second Chamber. Type of Thesis: Jurisprudence. Source: Official Gazette Book 18, March 2013, Volume 2. Subject (s): Constitutional. Thesis: 2a./J. 34/2013 (10a.). Page: 1065.

tion that the administrative authorities may impose the necessary emergency measures to confront the contingency even in cases of pollution derived from fortuitous events or Force Majeure. This is the case in order to avoid endangering health or the environment (articles 2, 3, and 72), which is not otherwise possible in regulatory terms under a regime of a supplementary nature.

The determination of the legislators in the sense that exemptions for fortuitous events or Force Majeure are not applicable in the case of urgency or compensation measures, is also congruent with comparative law. In this respect, specialized doctrine explains the following:[14]

Fortuitous events or Force Majeure are institutions with a limited application domain, particularly in cases of objective or strict liability. Thus, in the case of grave risks, it is common for fortuitous events or Force Majeure not to operate as exemptions of liability given that the interest of the legislators is precisely to ensure that whoever carries out the activity assumes any associated risk. Under this criterion, the greater the intensity of the risk created by the respective activity, the less tolerance there will be in face of the Force Majeure excuse.

In the same sense, whenever damages are caused while carrying out an activity subject to objective or strict liability, the victim will usually not be entitled to argue that third party negligence causally intervened in its occurrence, which does not, however, impede legal proceedings from being instituted against such third-party.

Based on the legal analysis proposed and on the accompanying considerations, it is viable to affirm that any pollution or environmental damages caused by hydrocarbons spillages, even in the case of clandestine tapping, shall result in the application of urgency or remediation measures. All this regardless of the fact that the remaining legal conducts derived from environmental damages, such as compensation or payment of damages, payment of economic sanctions, must be considered case by case. Exemption due to fortuitous events or Force Majeure, as well as exemption due to premeditated actions relating to indirect damages must invariably be proved by the party making the allegation.

Final Consideration

Certain amparo courts in Mexico have maintained in various sentences handed down that, as opposed to what happens in the case of contractual and extra-contractual civil liability damages caused, environmental damages cannot be studied exclusively from an economic and individualistic perspective, but, rather, require a consideration to be made in the sense that the environment represents a human right of a diffused nature and that successive impact has been made on environmental

---

[14] Cfr. Barros Bourie Enrique (2006), *Tratado de Responsabilidad Extracontractual*, Chile, Editorial Jurídica de Chile, pp. 477-478.

balance in the present day. This makes it indispensable to guarantee remediation of the environment at all costs. As a public interest burden, no distinction should be made between whether the party responsible inscribes its conduct in public or private intersubjective relations or whether the damage is generated as a consequence of a premeditated act or not.[15]

Although it is true to say that the environmental liability regime is subject to the legislator's configurative freedom, it is also true to say that the public power in its different facets (executive, legislative, and judiciary) must be bound to safeguard the constitutional principles and mandates, such as the protection of a healthy environment.

It is in light of such considerations that the legal interpretation proposed in this essay is what best serves the constitutional structure to protect the right to a healthy environment. It can also serve to generate a part of the regulatory strategy to bring fuel theft to a halt in Mexico.

Bibliography

Barros Bourie Enrique (2006), Tratado de Responsabilidad Extracontractual, Chile, Editorial Jurídica de Chile, pp. 477- 478.

Orellana M A. (2018), *GPS Energía. Sector Hidrocarburos en México*, México, Ed. Tirant Lo Blanch.

Roauix, P. (2016), Génesis de los artículos 27 y 123 de la Constitución Política de 1917, Secretaría de Cultura, México, Instituto Nacional de Estudios Históricos de las Revoluciones de México.

Digital Hemeroraphic Resources

Cortés Campos, J. (2019), *Reformas Estructurales y Calidad Regulatoria*, México, VLex- El Economista: https://www.eleconomista.com.mx/gestion/Reformas-Estructurales-y-Calidad-Regulatoria-20181025-0076.html.

Mexico evaluates. Consultation: https://www.mexicoevalua.org/2019/01/09/huachi-col-desabasto-justicia/.

Legal Texts

Environmental Liability Law

General Ecological Balance and Environmental Protection Law

General Integral Waste Prevention and Management Law

Political Constitution of Mexico

---

[15] *See* Semanario Judicial de la Federación, Novena Época, Tribunales Colegiados de Circuito, Tesis Aislada I.4o.A.810 A (9a.), Libro XI, Agosto de 2012, Tomo 2, Materia Administrativa, Número de Registro: 159999.

CHAPTER 12

STEVE ZAMORA AND LEGAL EDUCATION IN MEXICO

By Luis Fernando Pérez Hurtado[1]

Introduction

Stephen Zamora was a great connector of ideas and of people who would influence the quality of legal education in Mexico. His energy, optimism, good humor, and love for this country, combined with his intelligence, technical knowledge, network of contacts, experience, and initiatives, made him a great ally for various projects. To me, he was a mentor, a leader, an ally, and a friend to whom I owe much of what we do at the *Centro de Estudios sobre la Enseñanza y el Aprendizaje del Derecho, A.C.*, CEEAD (Center for the Teaching and Learning of Law Studies).

In this article I will share some examples of initiatives and projects in which Steve was involved; they reflect his commitment to the teaching of Law in Mexico and his initiative when facing new challenges. I will rely on various documents that we developed, emails we exchanged, and experiences shared.

Beginnings

My first encounter took place in 2006, during my doctoral studies at Stanford Law School. Back then, I spent a lot of time and effort searching for data on legal education and the professional practice of Law in Mexico. This information was

---

[1] General Director, *Centro de Estudios sobre la Enseñanza y el Aprendizaje del Derecho*, A.C., CEEAD (Center for the Teaching and Learning of Law Studies).

scarce. But one of the few publications on the subject that I managed to find was the book *Mexican Law*,[2] of which Steve was co-author.

I contacted him to introduce myself and asked him if he had more information on the subject or if he planned to update what had already been published. He immediately replied, at that moment he had no further information, yet he would soon be working on the new edition of the aforementioned book.

Upon completion of my doctoral studies in 2008, I returned to Mexico to found the CEEAD, an independent, non-profit institution dedicated to the research, development, implementation, and evaluation of initiatives to transform legal education and the professional practice of law.[3] From this space, we seek to contribute to the consolidation of the Rule of Law, democracy and social justice in Mexico, through the training of legal professionals with technical competence, ethics and commitment to their environment.

Steve was one of the first people I contacted to talk about this initiative and to invite him to join the project. After several emails exchanging ideas on the subject, we met for the first time on June 25, 2009, during one of those summers Steve spent with Lois at their San Ángel home in Mexico City.

Right from that first meeting, I knew that Steve would be someone important in my professional development and in strengthening CEEAD. We spent two hours sharing ideas, contacts, projects, concerns, and dreams. That summer, I did a research stay at the University of Ottawa and he put me in touch with his friends from the School of Law. He also told me about NACLE, one of Steve's projects that most filled him with pride and enthusiasm.

NACLE

The North American Consortium on Legal Education (NACLE) is a group of 12 law schools in the United States, Canada, and Mexico to promote the understanding of the legal systems of the countries of North America, as well as to strengthen the capacities of each member to offer education and quality legal research, according to the needs of the region.[4] It was created in 1998 and Steve was its managing director for many years.

During our first meeting, Steve invited me to lecture at the NACLE 2009 annual meeting, which was held in Mexico City during the month of October. Below, I

---

[2] Stephen Zamora et al., MEXICAN LAW (2005).

[3] For more information, see www.ceead.org.mx.

[4] For more information, see www.law.uh.edu/mexican-law/NACLE.asp.

transcribe my participation in said event in English, as it was presented on that occasion.[5]

Good morning, everyone. Thank you for inviting me to the 2009 NACLE conference. I am especially happy for sharing some ideas with dear colleagues and friends.

During my talk I would like to highlight some general characteristics of Mexican legal education, not on its content but on its structure.

Let me begin with some data about our legal education system:

a) *The basic law degree—called Licenciatura en Derecho or LED—is not a graduate program, as it is in the United States and most of Canada, but an undergraduate degree preceded by a high school degree.*

b) *There are approximately 1,100 law schools, with 245,000 law students. By 2003, the Licenciatura en Derecho was the bachelor degree with the highest enrollment in the country with 11% of the total enrollment.*

c) *In most law programs, the curriculum is rigid. This means law students at each level have assigned courses, professors, and schedules without the possibility of making choices regarding these matters. In every law program, students take between 40 and 70 mandatory courses during their studies.*

d) *Over 90% of law professors combine teaching with professional practice, and most of the law programs do not have full-time faculty. In general, law schools function only as centers for the transmission of knowledge, not as research institutions.*

During the 1997 academic year, there were 170,210 law students distributed among 364 law schools. Ten years later, the number of law students increased to approximately 240,000 distributed among 930 institutions. This represents a 41% increase in enrollment with a corresponding 156% increase in law schools offering a law program. This is as if, during these ten years, every week a new law school opened its doors to 134 new law students.

I want to focus in the following three questions:

1. Who authorizes and supervises these new law schools?

2. What are the characteristics of these new law schools?

3. What caused such growth?

To define who authorizes and supervises new law schools, first, we have to understand how the license to practice law is obtained.

---

[5] 2009 NACLE Presentation, in Mexico City, on October 2, 2009. Information from my J.S.D. Thesis: The Next Generation of Mexican Lawyers: A Study of Mexico's System of Legal Education and Its Law Students (May 2008).

At first glance, the process that allows lawyers to practice law seems to be straightforward. After graduating from high school, a student enrolls in the Licenciatura en Derecho in a law school that is part of the National Education System. There, the student passes the courses, meets the institution's graduation requirements, and obtains the degree diploma. The student then registers the diploma at the General Office of Professions, which is an office of the federal government, and finally obtains the license, known as cédula profesional. This license will allow that individual to practice as a lawyer throughout the country and without any further requirements.

The key element here is the way in which each law school enters the National Education System, because this defines which institution will supervise the new law school, and in certain way, the requirements that those students shall meet in order to obtain their license. It is very interesting that neither the legal profession, nor the judicial branch have formal and direct participation on this process.

Only the law schools that are part of the National Education System are authorized to award law diplomas. Public law schools enter this System at the time of their creation. Whereas private universities require either (i) a recognition of official validity of studies, known as RVOE, or (ii) incorporation to a public university in order to be part of the system. The RVOE that is required for private universities is the explicit agreement of the federal or state governments, in which they recognize the validity of the academic program offered by a private institution, in a specific location, and with qualified faculty. The Incorporation is the authorization awarded to a private university by a public university to use its curriculum, system, and methods, with the public institution remaining in charge of the academic and administrative supervision of the private institution.

To give you an idea of the complexity of the system, the 1,006 licenciaturas en derecho in private law schools during the 2006 academic year obtained their RVOE or Incorporation from 36 different sources. Each source has its own criteria for approving law programs and for supervising them.

The way in which each law school enters the National Education System determines the degree of academic and administrative "freedom" or "flexibility" such law school will have. All public universities and most private universities decide on the content of their curriculum, as well as the requirements their graduates must fulfill in order to obtain the law diploma and consequently their license to practice law.

The common requirements to obtain a law diploma are the following: (i) to attend and pass all law curriculum courses; (ii) to complete mandatory pro bono service, usually between 200 and 400 hours of service; and (iii) to fulfill the graduation requirements stated in the internal rules of the institution.

Each institution determines its graduation requirements in their internal rules. This is important because, once the law school awards the degree, obtaining the license for professional practice requires only an administrative process, which con-

sists of registering the law diploma with the appropriate authorities. To a certain extent, the difference between a law graduate who cannot practice as a lawyer and one who is allowed to is the fulfillment of the university requirements to obtain the law diploma.

In other countries—the United States and Canada, for instance—the local bar association or the judicial branch determines the requirements a law graduate must fulfill in order to practice. Generally, in these countries, the requirement is to pass a standardized exam once they have obtained their law degree. However, in Mexico, the law schools are the ones that determine the requirements their own law graduates must complete in order to be able to practice law.

These graduation requirements are generally called "options for degree conferral," or opciones de titulación. The traditional option for degree conferral was to write a professional thesis, which must be defended before an evaluation committee. However, nowadays, there is a wide variety of options for degree conferral, so the thesis option is less and less used. Three options have become important in both public and private universities. The first is called "automatic degree conferral" or "option zero," where the only requirement is to have passed all the courses and completed the pro bono service. The second option is a standardized exam administered by the National Center for Higher Education Evaluation, known as "CENEVAL." The third option for degree conferral is "professional experience," which means that the law graduate has worked at least five years in law-related matters.

As already mentioned, once the graduate obtains the law diploma, obtaining the professional license is a simple administrative procedure, which consists of registering the diploma at the General Office of Professions. The federal government, through this office, is the authority in charge of the registration of all diplomas awarded by public and private institutions. It is the only authority allowed to issue professional licenses, which are valid throughout the country.

It is important to mention that, even if the lawyer's profession requires a license to practice law, this license is necessary only when working with judiciary authorities and in administrative disputes when acting as an agent, employer or adviser, except when acting as an agent in labor, agrarian or cooperative law matters. Therefore, those who do not have a license to practice law cannot present themselves as lawyers, and act in the situations noted above, but they may give legal advice and express their opinion in legal matters without incurring in unauthorized practice of law.

There are also two relatively new mechanisms to assure academic quality in law programs: the diagnostic assessment and the accreditation of academic programs. However, these mechanisms are voluntary procedures for the law schools, and until now their main effects are "public recognition" of the program's quality and access of public universities to additional government funding.

Once we described who authorizes and supervises the law schools, let us explore the characteristics of the new law schools. The larger increase in the number of law schools has occurred (a) in private education, especially in small universities and in those that belong to a system of institutions; (b) in regions that used to offer fewer educational opportunities; and (c) in locations outside major cities.

The increase of law programs in private institutions has been impressive. During the decade from the 1997 academic year to 2007, their enrollment increased 97% and the number of universities offering the law degree rose 177%. In contrast, the increase in public institutions was moderate. In the same period, their law enrollment grew only 8% and the number of universities offering the law degree increased 61%. Since 2004, private institutions have enrolled more law students than their public counterparts.

One major reason for the growth of private universities is that public universities have been unable to satisfy the large demand for higher education. Public education massification during the nineteen-seventies affected educational quality and the institutions' ability to properly perform their functions; consequently, they limited enrollment. Another reason for this growth is the ability of private institutions to adapt to demand in certain ways. Most of these institutions offer law degrees in less time, have eliminated the thesis requirement to obtain the professional diploma, offer attractive class shifts for working students, have study plans mostly focused on the practice of law, and some of them offer specialized programs. In addition, as we will see later, a large number of these institutions are located in areas that offered few or no opportunities to pursue a higher education degree, so they are more and more accessible to a large number of individuals.

One major characteristic of most of the private institutions created during the last decade is their small enrollment. At present, more than half of the law programs in private institutions have fewer than one hundred students. In contrast, during the 1997 academic year, 42% of the programs had fewer than one hundred students. That year, most law programs had between 101 and 250 students.

Another characteristic of private institutions created during the last decade is that they are members of a system or group of private institutions. In the 1997 academic year, there were 31 systems of private institutions with 115 law schools, which means that 38% of the private institutions were part of a system. In the 2006 academic year, the numbers grew to 103 systems of private institutions with 457 law schools, which means that 57% of the private institutions were part of a system. The fact that most private institutions belong to a system clearly indicates that, to a certain extent, expansion of higher education has been generated by institutions or groups with experience in higher education and institutional administration and operation expertise. Most of these systems are operated by companies, families or religious groups.

The larger increase in the amount of law schools has occurred in regions with fewer educational opportunities. In general, the lower the enrollment rate, the larger the growth. Regions with relatively greater increases were Central and Southern Mexico. It is interesting to note that in the poorest states within these regions, enrollment decreased. The reduction may be caused because few individuals have economic means to afford private education, which are the ones that offer most of the new higher education programs, and also offer fewer opportunities for their graduates to participate in the job market.

The larger increase in the number of law schools has also occurred in locations outside major cities, like state capitals and urban areas with a population with over 500,000 people. From the 1997 academic year to 2007, enrollment in major cities barely exceeded the rate of general population growth, while enrollment outside these cities doubled.

To summarize, the amount of law schools has experienced rapid growth during the last decades. The relatively larger increase during the last ten years is associated to private institutions with small enrollments; they are part of a system of private institutions; they are located in Central and Southern Mexico; and they are outside the major cities.

What caused such increase of law schools? The main causes might be, first, the general expansion of availability of higher education in Mexico as a response to the growing demand. Second, the ease with which a new law program may be created, including the low investment required. And third, the diversity of reasons that students have to study law.

The first cause might be the increase in higher education enrollment in general. Higher education enrollment has almost tripled during the last two-and-one-half decades, going from 731,147 students in 1980 to 2,150,146 in 2006. During the last decade, enrollment increase has surpassed the average of the Organization for Economic Cooperation and Development (OECD) member countries. This growth will continue. Higher education enrollment rate in Mexico is still less than the average rate for Latin America. And if we compare Mexico's rate with the OECD countries, the difference is even larger. Interest in enrolling in a higher education program is related to easy access to those programs, combined with the general perception that, with higher educational degrees, higher positions and salaries will come.

The second cause of legal education growth might be the ease with which a Licenciatura en Derecho can be opened. As I already explained, the procedure to obtain proper authorization is not complicated because there are multiple options for obtaining the RVOE or Incorporation. Additionally, one of the government's goals in education policy is to increase access to higher education. Also, economic investment for obtaining the RVOE or Incorporation is rather low since they refer mainly to the contents and structure of the curriculum, the safety of the facilities, and having a faculty with bachelor's degrees.

The third cause of legal education growth might be the diversity of reasons for studying law. Based on a questionnaire answered by almost 22,000 law students throughout the country, we observed that the law degree is very attractive to students for a combination of reasons. Professionally, it offers a broad range of areas and locations for professional practice. At the personal level, it represents an appropriate income, access to certain social networks, as well as prestige. Socially, it offers the opportunity to expand democracy, social justice, and common good.

To finish my participation, I would like to leave some questions for discussion either during this panel or for later.

1. What are the differences among law schools regarding what they teach and how they do it?
2. How could the increase in the number of law schools affect the quality of Mexican legal education and legal practice?
3. What are the advantages and disadvantages of Mexico's system of legal education?

Thank you very much for your attention.

After NACLE, we continued with several initiatives together. During the summer of 2010, we hosted Zach Lee at CEEAD, who was Steve's student at the University of Houston and the first participant in our research summer program. Zach participated in several of our research projects and published an article on the justice reform system in Mexico in the *Houston Journal of International Law*. I also invited Steve to join CEEAD's Advisory Board, along with other people who had supported CEEAD in its first projects, such as José Ramón Cossío, Martín Böhmer, Héctor Fix-Fierro, Lawrence M. Friedman, Bryant G. Garth, Ana Laura Magaloni, Rogelio Pérez-Perdomo and Sylvia Schmelkes.

In July 2011, he sent me an email to tell me about his next big initiative, the Center for U.S. and Mexican Law at the University of Houston Law Center.

Center for U.S. and Mexican Law

The Center's initial strategic plan was developed by Steve himself, which I transcribe as I first received it by email.[6]

The University of Houston proposes to create the Center for U.S.–Mexican Law and Policy as an academic and professional program based at the University of Houston Law Center. As a research center, the Center will conduct independent research on issues related to its core mission of increasing the understanding of U.S.

---

[6] E-mail from Stephen Zamora, on July 6, 2011, author's archives.

and Mexican laws and legal institutions and improving bilateral relations between the United States and Mexico. As a center for bilateral professional cooperation and education, the Center will work with partner institutions and professional groups to enhance cross-border understanding.

As its mission statement, the Center for U.S.-Mexican Law and Policy at the University of Houston Law Center is dedicated to increasing the understanding of Mexican law and legal institutions in the United States; to increasing the understanding in Mexico of U.S. laws and legal institutions; and to the promotion of a solid foundation of U.S.–Mexican relations, by enhancing cooperation between individuals and institutions in the United States and Mexico. The Center's principal goals are:

- *to improve understanding in the United States of Mexican laws and legal institutions, and to improve understanding in Mexico of U.S. laws and legal institutions;*
- *to study the development of Mexican laws and legal structures, with the goal of providing independent, objective analysis of the development of Mexican legal institutions;*
- *to undertake independent research and educational programs to further the development of laws and policies that will improve U.S.–Mexico relations;*
- *to promote cross-border education of law students, lawyers and judges from Mexico and the United States;*
- *to take advantage of Houston's position as an important bridge between U.S. and Mexican citizens and institutions.*

From the beginning, I considered the Center to be a great initiative for various reasons. First, it was necessary to have an institution that focused on the legal challenges of the Mexico-U.S. relationship, and the University of Houston was one of the indicated spaces. Second, he appointed Ignacio Pinto-León, as its first assistant, not only a great lawyer, but also a great person and a great friend, as we were roommates when we studied Law at the Universidad Panamericana in Mexico City. Third, Steve invited me to participate as a member of the Board of Directors, along with very prominent people from both Mexico and the United States. Its wide network of collaborators and its convening power was reflected both in the formation of the Board and in many of the activities it carried out.

On June 1, 2012, the Center's inaugural event and the first meeting of the Board of Directors were held. From then on, the Center became a great ally of CEEAD and the space to start new projects with Steve.

One of the first projects that CEEAD launched in conjunction with the Center for U.S. and Mexican Law was on cross-border legal services between Mexico and the United States, entitled Provision of Cross-Border Legal Services between the and Mexico: Assessing Trade in Legal Services, Governance of Lawyers, and Legal Education. The initial justification and description of the project was developed jointly between both institutions, in English. I transcribe it below as it was first presented at the Advisory Council meeting.[7]

Movement of people and trade of goods and services between Mexico and the United States has a significant impact. In 2010, 12 million American citizens visited México. To date 738,103 American citizens live in Mexico, with the latter country being the main destination abroad for Americans. On the other hand, 13.4 million Mexicans traveled to the United States during the previous year and currently more than 12 million of them live there, representing approximately one third of all migrants to that country. On the economic side of the equation, more than 393 billion dollars in merchandise are traded bilaterally each year, and 35 billion more in services, generating a total of 103 billion in foreign direct investment.

There has been a considerable increase on the need for legal services that allow compliance with applicable regulation and gives predictability to clients. This increase is a natural consequence of the intricate relationship between the two countries and their legal systems. Naturally, lawyers seek to know the legal system, best practices and legal market of Mexico and the United States to satisfy their clients' needs. As an example of this new reality, more and more Mexican lawyers seek Master of Laws (LL.M.) degrees in law schools in the United States, and an augmenting number of American law firms open shop in Mexico or pursue strategic alliances with Mexican law firms.

Despite this constant and continuous exchange of legal services between Mexico and the United States, little is known in one country over the regulation of the practice of law in the other, and on the limitations applicable to the professional practice of a foreign–licensed attorney, and the sanctions for ethical shortcomings in the provision of their legal services. It is urgent to analyze the regulation, reach and limitations of cross–border legal services, to allow for an adequate environment for the professional practice of lawyers in both countries.

The goal of this research program is to be developed in phases that allow analyzing different forms in which lawyers deliver cross-border legal services between Mexico and the United States, as well as its regulation, reach and limitations.

Some of the issues to be analyzed are:

- *What are the requirements to get licensed to practice law on each country?*
- *What is the scope or reach of this licensing on regards to cases related to the law of the other country?*

---

[7] Provision of Cross-Border Legal Services between the U.S. and Mexico: Assessing Trade in Legal Services, Governance of Lawyers and Legal Education, distributed at the Center for U.S. and Mexican Law Advisory Board Meeting on June 1, 2012, author's archives.

- *Which law regulates conditions and limits on cross-border legal services?*
- *What does the North American Free Trade Agreement (NAFTA) and the General Agreement on Trade and Services (GATS) of the World Trade Organization (WTO) say on the issue?*
- *How does the foreign legal consultant (FLC) figure of the NAFTA work on each country?*

Phase One of this research program will analyze the status of the cross-border legal practice between Mexico and the United States. The specific goals of this first stage will be the following:

- *Defining what constitutes cross-border legal services (CBLS) between Mexico and the United States*
- *Examining the regulatory framework for the practice of law in Mexico and the United States*
- *Analyzing the reach and limitations of the practice of law by Mexican-licensed attorneys in the United States, and by American-licensed lawyers in Mexico*

Subsequent phases of the Program include:

- *Identifying challenges faced by lawyers and clients in the provision of Mexico-U.S. cross-border legal services and to find possible solutions that promote effectiveness and ethical delivery of such services.*
- *Analyzing the content and effectiveness of academic programs in law schools of Mexico and the United States in producing lawyers ready to provide transnational professional services in the actual reality.*
- *Delivering proposals that improve regulation of cross-border legal services in both countries.*

This project went on for several years, including other researchers who were taking the lead and achieving initial results, such as Oscar Cruz Barney, Robert Lutz, Manuel Gómez, Rogelio Pérez-Perdomo and Alberto Abad Suárez.

CEEAD Congress on Legal Education

In July 2010, Steve wrote an email to me saying he had a meeting with Héctor Fix-Fierro. They talked about the importance of CEEAD and the UNAM Institute for Legal Research co-sponsoring a congress on legal education. In his words: ". . . There are many law schools, including very good schools that are satisfied with conditions that, I believe, do not demonstrate a level of professional education that a sophisticated and developed country like Mexico should enjoy. I know the issue is going to be a sensitive one—there are many, including lawyers, who support the status quo. I picture the congress to be organized and sponsored by two main entities—the Institute, and CEEAD—but perhaps some other institutions could collaborate. I think the University of Houston, through my Leonard Rosenberg Chair, could contribute to the event as well. In my point of view, the congress would be critical, with the intervention of well-prepared and conscious people in their criticism."[8]

We were already thinking about this initiative and his advice was very pertinent, so it "fell on fertile ground." Therefore, the first edition of the CEEAD Congress on Legal Education was held from April 27 to 30, 2016 in the city of Monterrey. Its goal has been to provide a space for collaboration, discussion and reflection for professors, postgraduate students, researchers, and university managers interested in improving legal education. Since that first edition, the Congress has been co-organized with the UNAM Institute for Legal Research and other universities such as CIDE, ITAM, Tecnológico de Monterrey, Universidad Autónoma de Nuevo León, Universidad de Monterrey, Facultad Libre de Monterrey Law, the U-ERRE and the Universidad Metropolitana de Monterrey.

In its first edition, the University of Houston Law Center was one of the sponsors of the Congress. Steve participated every day and collaborated as moderator and expert at some of the tables. As always, his attendance enriched the discussions and strengthened his relationships with law schools. One hundred seventy-two professors and researchers from forty-two law schools in nineteen Mexican states participated in the Congress, in addition to experts from Argentina, Brazil, Chile, Colombia, Costa Rica, Ecuador, Spain, the United States, France and Peru.

At the end of the event, he sent me a series of comments to improve the event and expand its scope and impact. In the mail, Steve told me the following:[9]

Observation No. 1: As you know, the AALS (Association of American Law Schools) has more than one hundred sections, substantive and administrative, that deal with most of the substance of the AALS annual meeting, in which you have participated. I recommend that you consider the possibility—perhaps for the third, if not the second, Congress—of establishing sections to organize the Congress program. I like the "democratic" initiative that this implies.

Observation No. 2: I liked the panels that I was able to attend, but I had to leave some early—especially the panel on the quality of legal education in Mexico. One thing is to debate about legal education models and another one is to focus on the lack of resources universities dedicate to their law schools. I mentioned this several times. The lack of resources seems so obvious to me, but I did not hear any comments on this. Universities are not going to dedicate more funds to law schools without

---

[8] E-mail from Stephen Zamora, on July 30, 2010, author's archives.

[9] E-mail from Stephen Zamora, on May 12, 2016, author's archives.

something external happening: whether it is mandatory bar registration of law grad-uates after rigorous examination; or much stricter accreditation standards.

Observation / Proposal No. 3: A project should be started to support the publi-cation of an excellent course text, including faculty from three or four Mexican legal schools. If I am not mistaken, the different law schools (CIDE, ITAM, UNAM) have their texts, but I have the impression that they are "intramural" texts, although all law schools give the same basic courses. It would be worth trying to publish an updated "super text" with new concepts that could be used in various schools. As you know, in the U.S. "casebooks" are published by private publishers and this hap-pens in Mexico too. But perhaps a very good basic text could be produced, combin-ing efforts. Such a project would be an extension of what takes place in the Congress of Legal Education.

These were very good suggestions that we have been analyzing in different edi-tions. I hope we can make progress on these issues in the near future.

Farewell

Curiously, the book *Mexican Law* was the way by which I met Steve and the last project we talked about. On June 27, 2016, he wrote me an email telling me that he was working with José Roldán Xopa, Leonel Pereznieto Castro, Héctor Fix-Fierro on a new edition of the book. He invited me to participate as a co-author by review-ing the chapter on Legal Education and Legal Profession. Of course, I accepted. I was pleased to be able to support the update of a book that was important in the beginning of my research and also to work on a project with Steve. On July 5, 2016 I received the last email from Steve with deliverable dates.

Since Steve's passing on July 8, 2016, some of his initiatives have kept their momentum. That year, the interim management of NACLE was taken by Gabriel Cavazos, from the Tecnológico de Monterrey. The Center for U.S. and Mexican Law also continued thanks to the support of the law school Dean, Leonard M. Baynes, as well as its former director, Alfonso López de la Osa Escribano. Other projects such as the one related to cross-border professional practice and the updating of the *Mex-ican Law* book are still on hold. I hope they can move forward and achieve their objectives, as they are great projects.

Within the framework of the 2018 CEEAD Congress on Legal Education, the organizing institutions launched the "Engrane" Awards in order to recognize ideas and people who are transforming the teaching of law. The awards are called "Engrane" because they distinguish efforts of students, teachers, researchers, man-agers, and professionals who move to action and impact; connect ideas and projects; collaborate in improvement initiatives; and they are key pieces in the transformation of law education.

The recognized categories are: Best Bachelor Thesis, Best Postgraduate Thesis, Best Research Article, Best Innovative Teaching Practice, and Trajectory Recognition. The call for papers and proposals is open for several months and a qualifying jury was appointed consisting of managers and representatives from the organizing universities of the Congress.

That year, the jury decided to award only to the category of Career Recognition, which seeks to recognize a person who, from the academic, governmental, labor, or civil society sector, has distinguished herself or himself for her/his contributions in promoting and transforming legal education. In that first edition, the prize was awarded postmortem to Stephen Zamora.

Steve's unexpected passing left us with a huge emptiness. We lost a great ally, a charismatic leader, and a dear friend. I hope that through our work to transform the teaching of Law in Mexico we can honor his memory and his legacy.

CHAPTER 12

STEVE ZAMORA Y LA EDUCACIÓN JURÍDICA EN MÉXICO
(SPANISH AND ENGLISH-LANGUAGE VERSION)

Luis Fernando Pérez Hurtado[1]

Introducción

Stephen Zamora fue un gran impulsor y conector de ideas y personas que buscamos incidir en la calidad de la educación jurídica en México. Su energía, optimismo, buen humor y amor por este país, combinado con su inteligencia, conocimientos técnicos, red de contactos, experiencia e iniciativas, lo convirtieron en un gran aliado de diversos proyectos e iniciativas. Para mí fue un mentor, un impuso, un aliado, un amigo al que le debo mucho de lo que hacemos ahora desde el CEEAD.

En este artículo compartiré algunos ejemplos de iniciativas y proyectos en los que Steve estuvo involucrado; en ellos se refleja su compromiso con la enseñanza del Derecho en México y su iniciativa frente a nuevos retos. Me basaré en diversos documentos que desarrollamos, correos electrónicos que intercambiamos y experiencias que vivimos juntos.

Inicios

Los primeros contactos con Steve se dieron en 2006 durante mis estudios de doctorado en la Universidad de Stanford. En esos años dediqué mucho tiempo y esfuerzo a buscar datos sobre la educación jurídica y el ejercicio profesional del

---

[1] Director general del Centro de Estudios sobre la Enseñanza y el Aprendizaje del Derecho, A.C. (CEEAD).

Derecho en México. Esta información era realmente escasa. Una de las pocas publicaciones al respecto que logré encontrar fue el libro Mexican Law[2], del cual Steve fue coautor.

Lo contacté para presentarme y preguntarle si tenía más datos sobre el tema o si pensaba actualizar los que ya estaban publicados. Inmediatamente me respondió, diciéndome que por el momento no contaba con más información, pero que pronto estaría trabajando en la nueva edición del citado libro.

Al concluir mis estudios de doctorado en 2008, regresé a México a fundar el Centro de Estudios sobre la Enseñanza y el Aprendizaje del Derecho, A.C. El CEEAD es una institución independiente, sin fines de lucro, dedicada a la investigación, desarrollo, implementación y evaluación de iniciativas para transformar la educación jurídica y el ejercicio profesional del Derecho.[3] Desde este espacio buscamos contribuir a la consolidación del Estado de Derecho, la democracia y justicia social en México, a través de la formación de profesionales del Derecho con competencia técnica, ética y compromiso con su entorno.

Una de las primeras personas a quien contacté para comunicarle acerca de esta iniciativa y sumarlo al proyecto fue a Steve. Después de varios correos intercambiando ideas sobre el tema, nos reunimos por primera vez el 25 de junio de 2009, durante esos veranos que Steve pasaba con Lois en su casa de San Ángel en la Ciudad de México.

Desde esa primera reunión supe que Steve sería alguien muy importante en mi desarrollo profesional y en el fortalecimiento del CEEAD. Fueron dos horas de compartir ideas, contactos, proyectos, inquietudes y sueños. Ese verano yo estaría haciendo una estancia de investigación en la Universidad de Ottawa y me puso en contacto con sus amigos de la escuela de Derecho. También me platicó de NACLE, uno de los proyectos de Steve que más lo llenaban de orgullo y entusiasmo.

NACLE

El North American Consortium on Legal Education (NACLE) es un consorcio entre 12 escuelas de Derecho de Estados Unidos, Canadá y México para promover la comprensión de los sistemas jurídicos de los países de Norteamérica, así como fortalecer las capacidades de cada integrante para ofrecer educación e investigación jurídica de calidad y acorde a las necesidades de la región.[4] Fue creada en 1998 y Steve fue su director administrativo durante muchos años.

Durante nuestra primera reunión, Steve me invitó a impartir una conferencia en la reunión anual de NACLE 2009, la cual se llevó a cabo en la Ciudad de México

---

[2] Stephen Zamora et al., Mexican Law (2005).

[3] Para más información, ver www.ceead.org.mx.

[4] Para más información, ver www.law.uh.edu/mexican-law/NACLE.asp.

durante el mes de octubre. A continuación, transcribo mi participación en dicho evento en idioma inglés, tal y como se presentó en esa ocasión.[5]

Good morning everyone. Thank you for inviting me to the 2009 NACLE conference. I am especially happy for sharing some ideas with dear colleagues and friends.

During my talk I would like to highlight some general characteristics of Mexican legal education, not on its content but on its structure.

Let me begin with some data about our legal education system:

a) *The basic law degree—called Licenciatura en Derecho or LED—is not a graduate program, as it is in the United States and most of Canada, but an undergraduate degree preceded by a high school degree.*

b) *There are approximately 1,100 law schools, with 245,000 law students. By 2003, the Licenciatura en Derecho was the bachelor's degree with the highest enrollment in the country with 11% of the total enrollment.*

c) *In most law programs, the curriculum is rigid. This means law students at each level have assigned courses, professors, and schedules without the possibility of making choices regarding these matters. In every law program, students take between 40 and 70 mandatory courses during their studies.*

d) *Over 90% of law professors combine teaching with professional practice, and most of the law programs do not have full-time faculty. In general, law schools function only as centers for the transmission of knowledge, not as research institutions.*

During the 1997 academic year, there were 170,210 law students distributed among 364 law schools. Ten years later, the number of law students increased to approximately 240,000 distributed among 930 institutions. This represents a 41% increase in enrollment with a corresponding 156% increase in law schools offering a law program. This is as if, during these ten years, every week a new law school opened its doors to 134 new law students.

I want to focus in the following three questions:

1. *Who authorizes and supervises these new law schools?*
2. *What are the characteristics of this new law schools?*
3. *What caused such growth?*

---

[5] Presentación, NACLE Conference 2009 en Ciudad de México, octubre 2, 2009. Información tomada de mi tesis de doctorado The Next Generation of Mexican Lawyers: A Study of Mexico's System of Legal Education and Its Law Students (mayo 2008).

To define who authorizes and supervises new law schools, first, we have to understand how the license to practice law is obtained.

At first glance, the process that allows lawyers to practice law seems to be straightforward. After graduating from high school, a student enrolls in the Licenciatura en Derecho in a law school that is part of the National Education System. There, the student passes the courses, meets the institution's graduation requirements, and obtains the degree diploma. The student then registers the diploma at the General Office of Professions, which is an office of the federal government, and finally obtains the license, known as cédula profesional. This license will allow that individual to practice as a lawyer throughout the country and without any further requirements.

The key element here is the way in which each law school enters the National Education System, because this defines which institution will supervise the new law school, and in certain way, the requirements that those students shall meet in order to obtain their license. It is very interesting that neither the legal profession, nor the judicial branch have formal and direct participation on this process.

Only the law schools that are part of the National Education System are authorized to award law diplomas. Public law schools enter this System at the time of their creation. Whereas, private universities require either (i) a recognition of official validity of studies, known as RVOE, or (ii) incorporation to a public university in order to be part of the system. The RVOE that is required for private universities is the explicit agreement of the federal or state governments, in which they recognize the validity of the academic program offered by a private institution, in a specific location, and with qualified faculty. The Incorporation is the authorization awarded to a private university by a public university to use its curriculum, system, and methods, with the public institution remaining in charge of the academic and administrative supervision of the private institution.

To give you an idea of the complexity of the system, the 1,006 licenciaturas en derecho in private law schools during the 2006 academic year obtained their RVOE or Incorporation from 36 different sources. Each source has its own criteria for approving law programs and for supervising them.

The way in which each law school enters the National Education System determines the degree of academic and administrative "freedom" or "flexibility" such law school will have. All public universities and most private universities decide on the content of their curriculum, as well as the requirements their graduates must fulfill in order to obtain the law diploma and consequently their license to practice law.

The common requirements to obtain a law diploma are the following: (i) to attend and pass all law curriculum course; (ii) to complete mandatory pro bono service; usually between 200 and 400 hours of service; and (iii) to fulfill the graduation requirements stated in the internal rules of the institution.

Each institution determines its graduation requirements in their internal rules. This is important because, once the law school awards the degree, obtaining the license for professional practice requires only an administrative process, which consists of registering the law diploma with the appropriate authorities. To a certain extent, the difference between a law graduate who cannot practice as a lawyer and one who is allowed to, is the fulfillment of the university requirements to obtain the law diploma.

In other countries—the United States and Canada, for instance—the local bar association or the judicial branch determines the requirements a law graduate must fulfill in order to practice. Generally, in these countries, the requirement is to pass a standardized exam once they have obtained their law degree. However, in Mexico, the law schools are the ones that determine the requirements their own law graduates must complete in order to be able to practice law.

These graduation requirements are generally called "options for degree conferral", or opciones de titulación. The traditional option for degree conferral was to write a professional thesis, which must be defended before an evaluation committee. However, nowadays, there is a wide variety of options for degree conferral, so the thesis option is less and less used. Three options have become important in both public and private universities. The first is called "automatic degree conferral" or "option zero", where the only requirement is to have passed all the courses and completed the pro bono service. The second option is a standardized exam administered by the National Center for Higher Education Evaluation, known as "CENEVAL." The third option for degree conferral is "professional experience", which means that the law graduate has worked at least five years in law-related matters.

As already mentioned, once the graduate obtains the law diploma, obtaining the professional license is a simple administrative procedure, which consists of registering the diploma at the General Office of Professions. The federal government, through this office, is the authority in charge of the registration of all diplomas awarded by public and private institutions. It is the only authority allowed to issue professional licenses, which are valid throughout the country.

It is important to mention that, even if the lawyer's profession requires a license to practice law, this license is necessary only when working with judiciary authorities and in administrative disputes when acting as an agent, employer or adviser, except when acting as an agent in labor, agrarian or cooperative law matters. Therefore, those who do not have a license to practice law cannot present themselves as lawyers, and act in the situations noted above, but they may give legal advice and express their opinion in legal matters without incurring in unauthorized practice of law.

There are also two relatively new mechanisms to assure academic quality in law programs: the diagnostic assessment and the accreditation of academic programs.

However, these mechanisms are voluntary procedures for the law schools, and until now their main effects are "public recognition" of the program's quality and access of public universities to additional government funding.

Once we described who authorizes and supervises the law schools, let us explore the characteristics of the new law schools. The larger increase in the number of law schools has occurred (a) in private education, especially in small universities and in those that belong to a system of institutions; (b) in regions that used to offer fewer educational opportunities; and (c) in locations outside major cities.

The increase of law programs in private institutions has been impressive. During the decade from the 1997 academic year to 2007, their enrollment increased 97% and the number of universities offering the law degree rose 177%. In contrast, the increase in public institutions was moderate. In the same period, their law enrollment grew only 8% and the number of universities offering the law degree increased 61%. Since 2004, private institutions have enrolled more law students than their public counterparts.

One major reason for the growth of private universities is that public universities have been unable to satisfy the large demand for higher education. Public education massification during the nineteen-seventies affected educational quality and the institutions' ability to properly perform their functions; consequently, they limited enrollment. Another reason for this growth is the ability of private institutions to adapt to demand in certain ways. Most of these institutions offer law degrees in less time, have eliminated the thesis requirement to obtain the professional diploma, offer attractive class shifts for working students, have study plans mostly focused on the practice of law, and some of them offer specialized programs. In addition, as we will see later, a large number of these institutions are located in areas that offered few or no opportunities to pursue a higher education degree, so they are more and more accessible to a large number of individuals.

One major characteristic of most of the private institutions created during the last decade is their small enrollment. At present, more than half of the law programs in private institutions have fewer than 100 students. In contrast, during the 1997 academic year, 42% of the programs had fewer than 100 students. That year, most law programs had between 101 and 250 students.

Another characteristic of private institutions created during the last decade is that they are members of a system or group of private institutions. In the 1997 academic year, there were 31 systems of private institutions with 115 law schools, which means that 38% of the private institutions were part of a system. In the 2006 academic year, the numbers grew to 103 systems of private institutions with 457 law schools, which means that 57% of the private institutions were part of a system. The fact that most private institutions belong to a system clearly indicates that, to a certain extent, expansion of higher education has been generated by institutions or groups with experience in higher education and institutional administration and operation expertise. Most of these systems are operated by companies, families or religious groups.

The larger increase in the amount of law schools has occurred in regions with fewer educational opportunities. In general, at lower enrollment rate, the larger the growth. Regions with relatively greater increases were Central and Southern Mexico. It is interesting to note that in the poorest states within these regions, enrollment decreased. The reduction may be caused because few individuals have economic means to afford private education, which are the ones that offer most of the new higher education programs, and also offer fewer opportunities for their graduates to participate in the job market.

The larger increase in the number of law schools has also occurred also in locations outside major cities, like state capitals and urban areas with a population with over 500,000 people. From the 1997 academic year to 2007, enrollment in major cities barely exceeded the rate of general population growth, while enrollment outside these cities doubled.

To summarize, the amount of law schools has experienced rapid growth during the last decades. The relatively larger increase during the last ten years is associated to private institutions with small enrollments; they are part of a system of private institutions; they are located in Central and Southern Mexico; and they are outside the major cities.

What caused such increase of law schools? The main causes might be, first, the general expansion of availability of higher education in Mexico as a response to the growing demand. Second, the ease with which a new law program may be created, including the low investment required. And third, the diversity of reasons that students have to study law.

The first cause might be the increase in higher education enrollment in general. Higher education enrollment has almost tripled during the last two-and-one-half decades, going from 731,147 students in 1980 to 2,150,146 in 2006. During the last decade, enrollment increase has surpassed the average of the Organization for Economic Cooperation and Development (OECD) member countries. This growth will continue. Higher education enrollment rate in Mexico is still less than the average rate for Latin America. And if we compare Mexico's rate with the OECD countries, the difference is even larger. Interest in enrolling in a higher education program is related to easy access to those programs, combined with the general perception that, with higher educational degrees, higher positions and salaries will come.

The second cause of legal education growth might be the ease with which a Licenciatura en Derecho can be opened. As I already explained, the procedure to obtain proper authorization is not complicated because there are multiple options for obtaining the RVOE or Incorporation. Additionally, one of the government's goal in education policy is to increase access to higher education. Also, economic investment for obtaining the RVOE or Incorporation are rather low, since they refer main-

ly to the contents and structure of the curriculum, the safety of the facilities, and having a faculty with bachelor's degrees.

The third cause of legal education growth might be the diversity of reasons for studying law. Based on a questionnaire answered by almost 22,000 law students throughout the country, we observed that the law degree is very attractive to students for a combination of reasons. Professionally, it offers a broad range of areas and locations for professional practice. At the personal level, it represents an appropriate income, access to certain social networks, as well as prestige. Socially, it offers the opportunity to expand democracy, social justice, and common good.

To finish my participation, I would like to leave some questions for discussion either during this panel or for later.

1. *What are the differences among law schools regarding what they teach and how they do it?*
2. *How could the increase in the number of law schools affect the quality of Mexican legal education and legal practice?*
3. *What are the advantages and disadvantages of Mexico's system of legal education?*

Thank you very much for your attention.

Después de NACLE continuamos con varias iniciativas en conjunto. Durante el verano de 2010 recibimos en el CEEAD a Zach Lee, estudiante de Steve en la Universidad de Houston y primer participante de nuestro programa de verano de estancias de investigación. Zach estuvo participando en varios de nuestros proyectos de investigación y publicó un artículo en el Houston Journal of International Law sobre la reforma al sistema de justicia en México. También invité a Steve a sumarse al Consejo Consultivo del CEEAD, junto con otras personas que habían apoyado al CEEAD en sus primeros proyectos, como José Ramón Cossío, Martín Böhmer, Héctor Fix-Fierro, Lawrence M. Friedman, Bryant G. Garth, Ana Laura Magaloni, Rogelio Pérez-Perdomo y Sylvia Schmelkes.

En julio de 2011 me envió un correo para contarme sobre su siguiente gran iniciativa, el Center for U.S. and Mexican Law de la Universidad de Houston.

Center for U.S. and Mexican Law

El plan estratégico inicial del Centro lo elaboró el propio Steve, el cual transcribo tal y como lo recibí por primera vez por correo electrónico:[6]

The University of Houston proposes to create the Center for U.S.–Mexican Law and Policy as an academic and professional program based at the University of

---

[6] Correo electrónico de Stephen Zamora, de fecha 6 de julio de 2011, en archivo del autor.

Houston Law Center. As a research center, the Center will conduct independent research on issues related to its core mission of increasing the understanding of U.S. and Mexican laws and legal institutions, and improving bilateral relations between the United States and Mexico. As a center for bilateral professional cooperation and education, the Center will work with partner institutions and professional groups to enhance cross-border understanding.

As its mission statement, the Center for U.S.-Mexican Law and Policy at the University of Houston Law Center is dedicated to increasing the understanding of Mexican law and legal institutions in the United States; to increasing the understanding in Mexico of U.S. laws and legal institutions; and to the promotion of a solid foundation of U.S.–Mexican relations, by enhancing cooperation between individuals and institutions in the United States and Mexico. The Center's principle goals are:

- *to improve understanding in the United States of Mexican laws and legal institutions, and to improve understanding in Mexico of U.S. laws and legal institutions;*
- *to study the development of Mexican laws and legal structures, with the goal of providing independent, objective analysis of the development of Mexican legal institutions;*
- *to undertake independent research and educational programs to further the development of laws and policies that will improve U.S.-Mexico relations;*
- *to promote cross-border education of law students, lawyers and judges from Mexico and the United States;*
- *to take advantage of Houston's position as an important bridge between U.S. and Mexican citizens and institutions.*

Desde un inicio consideré que el Centro era una gran iniciativa por varios motivos. Primero, era necesario contar con una institución que se enfocara a los retos jurídicos de la relación México-Estados Unidos y la Universidad de Houston era uno de los espacios indicados. Segundo, como primer director asistente nombró a Ignacio Pinto-León, no solamente un gran abogado, sino también una gran persona y un gran amigo, pues fuimos *roommates* cuando cursamos la licenciatura en Derecho en la Universidad Panamericana en Ciudad de México. Tercero, Steve me invitó a participar como miembro del Consejo Directivo, junto con personas muy destacadas tanto de México como de Estados Unidos. Su amplia red de colaboradores y su poder de convocatoria se vio reflejado tanto en la conformación del Consejo, como en muchas de las actividades que realizó.

El 1 de junio de 2012 se realizó el evento inaugural del Centro y la primera reunión del Consejo Directivo. A partir de ese momento, el Centro se convirtió en un gran aliado del CEEAD y el espacio para iniciar nuevos proyectos con Steve.

Uno de los primeros proyectos que lanzamos entre el Center for U.S. and Mexican Law y el CEEAD fue sobre servicios jurídicos transfronterizos entre México y Estados Unidos, titulado Provision of Cross-Border Legal Services between the U.S. and Mexico: Assessing Trade in Legal Services, Governance of Lawyers and Legal Education. La justificación y descripción inicial del proyecto fue desarrollada en conjunto entre ambas instituciones, en idioma inglés. La transcribo a continuación tal y como se presentó por primera vez en la reunión del Consejo asesor.[7]

Movement of people and trade of goods and services between Mexico and the United States are impactful. In 2010, 12 million American citizens visited México. To date 738,103 American citizens live in Mexico, with the latter country being the main destination abroad for Americans. On the other hand, 13.4 million Mexicans traveled to the United States during the previous year and currently more than 12 million of them live there, representing approximately one third of all migrants to that country. On the economic side of the equation, more than $393 billion dollars in merchandise are traded bilaterally each year, and $35 billion more in services, generating a total of $103 billion in foreign direct investment.

There has been a considerable increase on the need for legal services that allow compliance with applicable regulation and gives predictability to clients. This increase is a natural consequence of the intricate relationship between the 2 countries and their legal systems. Naturally, lawyers seek to know the legal system, best practices and legal market of Mexico and the United States to satisfy their clients' needs. As an example of this new reality, more and more Mexican lawyers seek Master of Laws (LL.M.) degrees in law schools in the United States, and an augmenting number of American law firms open shop in Mexico or pursue strategic alliances with Mexican law firms.

Despite this constant and continuous exchange of legal services between Mexico and the United States, little is known in one country over the regulation of the practice of law in the other, and on the limitations applicable to the professional practice of a foreign–licensed attorney, and the sanctions for ethical shortcomings in the provision of their legal services. It is urgent to analyze the regulation, reach and limitations of cross–border legal services, to allow for an adequate environment for the professional practice of lawyers in both countries.

The goal of this research program is to be developed in phases that allow analyzing different forms in which lawyers deliver cross–border legal services between Mexico and the United States, as well as its regulation, reach and limitations.

---

[7] Provision of Cross-Border Legal Services between the U.S. and Mexico: Assessing Trade in Legal Services, Governance of Lawyers and Legal Education, distribuido en la reunión del Consejo Asesor del Center for U.S. and Mexican Law de fecha 1 de junio de 2012, en archivo del autor.

Some of the issues to be analyzed are:

- *What are the requirements to get licensed to practice law on each country?*
- *What is the scope or reach of this licensing on regards to cases related to the law of the other country?*
- *Which law regulates conditions and limits on cross–border legal services?*
- *What does the North American Free Trade Agreement (NAFTA) and the General Agreement on Trade and Services (GATS) of the World Trade Organization (WTO) say on the issue?*
- *How does the foreign legal consultant (FLC) figure of the NAFTA works on each country?*

Phase One of this research program will analyze the status of the cross–border legal practice between Mexico and the United States. The specific goals of this first stage will be the following:

- *Defining what constitutes cross–border legal services (CBLS) between Mexico and the United States*
- *Examining the regulatory framework for the practice of law in Mexico and the United States*
- *Analyzing the reach and limitations of the practice of law by Mexican–licensed attorneys in the United States, and by American–licensed lawyers in Mexico*

Subsequent phases of the Program include:

- *Identifying challenges faced by lawyers and clients in the provision of Mexico-U.S. cross–border legal services and to find possible solutions that promote effectiveness and ethical delivery of such services.*
- *Analyzing the content and effectiveness of academic programs in law schools of Mexico and the United States in producing lawyers ready to provide transnational professional services in the actual reality.*
- *Delivering proposals that improve regulation of cross–border legal services in both countries.*

Este proyecto continuó durante varios años, incluyendo a otros investigadores que fueron tomando el liderazgo y logrando los primeros resultados, como Oscar Cruz Barney, Robert Lutz, Manuel Gómez, Rogelio Pérez-Perdomo y Alberto Abad Suárez.

Congreso CEEAD sobre Educación Jurídica

En julio de 2010, Steve me escribió un correo comentándome que tuvo una reunión con Héctor Fix-Fierro y platicaron sobre la importancia de que el CEEAD y el Instituto de Investigaciones Jurídicas de la UNAM copatrocinen un congreso sobre educación jurídica. En sus palabras: " . . . creo que hay muchas escuelas de Derecho, inclusive escuelas muy buenas, que se sienten satisfechos con condiciones que, creo yo, no demuestran un nivel de educación profesional del que debe gozar un país sofisticado y desarrollado como México. Sé que el tema va a ser sensible —hay muchos, inclusive abogados, que apoyan el estatus quo. Pienso que el congreso sería organizado y patrocinado por dos entidades principales —el Instituto, y CEEAD— pero tal vez algunas otras instituciones podrían colaborar. Creo que la Universidad de Houston, a través de mi cátedra de Leonard Rosenberg, podría contribuir al evento también. En mi punto de vista, el congreso sería crítico, con la intervención de personas bien preparadas y concientes [sic] en sus críticas".[8]

Ya estábamos pensando en esa iniciativa y sus consejos fueron muy atinados, por lo que "cayeron en tierra fértil". Así, la primera edición del Congreso CEEAD sobre Educación Jurídica se llevó a cabo del 27 al 30 de abril de 2016 en la ciudad de Monterrey. Su objetivo ha sido facilitar un espacio de colaboración, discusión y reflexión para profesores, estudiantes de posgrado, investigadores y directivos universitarios interesados en mejorar la educación jurídica. Desde esa primera edición, el Congreso ha sido coorganizado con el Instituto de Investigaciones Jurídicas de la UNAM y otras universidades como el CIDE, el ITAM, el Tecnológico de Monterrey, la Universidad Autónoma de Nuevo León, la Universidad de Monterrey, la Facultad Libre de Derecho de Monterrey, la U-ERRE y la Universidad Metropolitana de Monterrey.

En su primera edición, el Law Center de la Universidad de Houston fue uno de los patrocinadores del Congreso. Steve participó durante todos los días y colaboró como moderador y experto en algunas de las mesas. Como siempre, su asistencia enriqueció las discusiones y fortaleció sus relaciones con las escuelas de Derecho. En el Congreso participaron 172 profesores e investigadores de 42 escuelas de Derecho en 19 entidades federativas de México, además de expertos de Argentina, Brasil, Chile, Colombia, Costa Rica, Ecuador, España, Estados Unidos, Francia y Perú.

Al finalizar el evento, me envió una serie de comentarios para mejorar el evento y ampliar su alcance e impacto. En el correo, Steve me comentó lo siguiente.[9]

Observación No. 1: como sabes, la AALS (Association of American Law Schools) tiene más de 100 secciones, sustantivas y administrativas, que se ocupan de la mayor parte de lo sustantivo de la reunión anual de AALS, en que has participado.

---

[8] Correo de Stephen Zamora de fecha 30 de julio de 2010, en archivo del autor.
[9] Correo de Stephen Zamora de fecha 12 de mayo de 2016, en archivo del autor.

Recomiendo que consideras la posibilidad —tal vez para el tercer Congreso, si no el segundo— de establecer secciones para organizar el programa del Congreso. Me gusta la iniciativa "democrática" que esto implica.

Observación No. 2: Me gustaron los paneles que pude escuchar, pero tuve que salir antes de algunos —especialmente el panel sobre calidad de la educación jurídica en México. Una cosa es debatir modelos de educación jurídica, otra enfocarse a la falta de recursos dedicados a las facultades de derecho por sus universidades. Mencioné esto varias veces. La falta de recursos me parece tan obvio, pero no escuché comentarios sobre esto. Las universidades no van a dedicar más fondos a las facultades de derecho sin que suceda algo externo: sea colegiación obligatoria de egresados, después de un examen riguroso; o sea normas de acreditación mucho más estrictas.

Observación/Propuesta No. 3: Se debe iniciar un proyecto para apoyar la publicación de un excelente texto de curso, utilizando académicos de 3 ó 4 escuelas jurídicas mexicanas. Si no me equivoco, las distintas facultades (CIDE, ITAM, UNAM) tienen sus textos, pero tengo la impresión de que son textos "intramurales", aunque todas las facultades dan los mismos cursos básicos. Valdría la pena tratar de publicar un "súper texto," al día y con nuevos conceptos, que se podría utilizar en varias escuelas. Como sabes, en EUA los "casebooks" son publicados por editoriales privadas y esto sucede en México también. Pero tal vez podría producirse un texto básico, de muy buen nivel, combinando esfuerzos. Tal proyecto sería una extensión de lo que están haciendo con el Congreso de Educación Jurídica.

Estas fueron muy buenas sugerencias que hemos estado analizando en diferentes ediciones. Espero que en un futuro podamos avanzar en estos temas.

Despedida

Curiosamente el libro Mexican Law fue el medio por el que conocí a Steve y el último proyecto del que platicamos. El 27 de junio de 2016 me escribió un correo donde me comenta que José Roldán Xopa, Leonel Pereznieto Castro, Héctor Fix-Fierro y él estaban trabajando en una nueva edición del libro. Me invitó a participar como co-autor revisando el capítulo sobre Legal Education and Legal Profession. Desde luego que acepté. Me dio mucho gusto poder apoyar en la actualización de un libro que fue importante en los inicios de mis investigaciones y también trabajar en un proyecto con Steve. El 5 de julio de 2016 fue el último correo que recibí de Steve con las fechas del entregable.

Desde el fallecimiento de Steve el 8 de julio de 2016, algunas de sus iniciativas mantuvieron su impulso. Ese año la dirección interina de NACLE la tomó Gabriel Cavazos, del Tecnológico de Monterrey. También el Center for U.S. and Mexican Law continuó gracias al apoyo del decano de la escuela de Derecho, Leonard M. Baynes, así como de su antiguo director, Alfonso López de la Osa Escribano. Otros proyectos como el relacionado al ejercicio profesional transfronterizo y la actualización del libro de Mexican Law continúan en pausa. Espero que puedan avanzar y lograr sus fines, pues son grandes proyectos.

Dentro del marco del Congreso CEEAD 2018 sobre Educación Jurídica, las instituciones organizadoras lanzamos los Premios Engrane con el fin de reconocer las ideas y las personas que están transformando la enseñanza del derecho. Los premios se denominan "Engrane" porque distinguen esfuerzos de estudiantes, profesores, investigadores, directivos y profesionistas que mueven a la acción y al impacto; conectan ideas y proyectos; colaboran en iniciativas de mejora; y son piezas clave en la transformación de la enseñanza del derecho.

Las categorías que se reconocen son mejor tesis de licenciatura, mejor tesis de posgrado, mejor artículo de investigación, mejor práctica docente innovadora y reconocimiento a la trayectoria. La convocatoria para recibir trabajos y propuestas estuvo abierta durante varios meses y se nombró un jurado calificador integrado por directivos y representantes de las universidades organizadoras del Congreso.

El jurado resolvió otorgar ese año el premio solamente a la categoría de Reconocimiento a la trayectoria. Esta categoría busca reconocer a una persona que, desde el sector académico, gubernamental, laboral, o desde la sociedad civil, se haya distinguido por sus contribuciones en la promoción y transformación de la educación jurídica. En esa primera edición, el premio se otorgó *post mortem* a Stephen Zamora.

La inesperada partida de Steve nos dejó un gran vacío. Perdimos a un gran aliado, un carismático líder y un querido amigo. Espero que a través de nuestro trabajo por transformar la enseñanza del Derecho en México podamos honrar su memoria y su legado.

CHAPTER 13

SOURCES OF JUDICIAL INDEPENDENCE: AN INTEGRATED APPROACH FOR THE COMPARATIVE STUDY OF STATE ADMINISTRATIVE COURTS IN MEXICO[1]

By Amalia Mena-Mora[2]

Introduction

Since the 1990s, constitutional reforms,[3] alternation of power at the federal level, variation in congressional majorities, and the strengthening of electoral insti-

---

[1] This analysis derives from the second and fourth chapters of the author's Ph.D. dissertation with some minor additions.

[2] Amalia Mena-Mora passed away on December 15, 2019 at the age of 43 in Houston, Texas. She was born in Mexico City, Mexico on December 19, 1975 to Alberto Mena-Hernandez and Amalia Mora-Navarro. Amalia was married to Diego Galer for twenty years, and is survived by him, her son, Ari, her daughter, Nurit, her mother, Amalia, and her sisters, Ana and Silvia.

Amalia served as a Senior Research Associate at Galer Law Firm and an Affiliate Scholar at the Center for U.S. and Mexican Law at the University of Houston Law Center. She earned a Ph.D. in Political Science from The University of Houston, and taught courses on American Government, Comparative Political Behavior, and International Business at Rice University and The University of Houston.

[3] The constitutional reforms of 1994 played an important role strengthening judicial independence in Mexico. They limited the participation of the executive in justices' appointments, modified their service periods to protect them from incumbent presidents, increased the scope of judicial review through constitutional actions (*acciones de inconstitucionalidad*), and enhanced the constitutional control powers of the Supreme Court through constitutional controversies (*controversias constitucionales*) (Domingo 2000, Magaloni 2003).

tutions have transformed Mexico into an emergent democracy. At the subnational level, legislatures began to challenge the power of the governors. Such a change has been crucial to judicial independence because governors often appoint judges with the approval of the state legislature. While in some states the legislatures appoint and confirm judges, other states have the judiciary in charge of this task. Another change that has diminished the power of the governor over the state judicial branch has to do with increasing the tenure of judges. It is unclear, however, whether new reforms or long-standing constraints have facilitated or impeded state judicial independence. Therefore, the question of this study is why some Mexican state courts are more independent than others.

The purpose of this analysis is to examine key factors that influence judges' decision-making in subnational arenas. I extend extant arguments about judicial independence at the federal level to the subnational level. I argue that both individual and contextual variables affect judicial autonomy. The individual traits of judges, specifically length of service in the state court, influence judicial independence. More specifically, judges' longer terms of service increase judicial independence. In addition, I also expect that contextual variables such as political competition (divided government and turnover of the governor's party), life tenure, and methods of appointment that do not involve the participation of the state executive at the subnational level also enhance judicial autonomy.

This chapter surveys prior studies on the factors that have an impact on judicial independence, advances the hypotheses, and tests quantitatively four hypotheses. It proposes an integrated approach that considers both structural and individual explanatory variables to better understand judicial autonomy in Mexican state courts. The analysis is organized as follows. The first section presents a justification of the integrated approach to analyze state judiciaries in Mexico. The second section examines prior studies that have evaluated judicial independence and the separation of powers approach. It also surveys studies that have incorporated structural and individual explanatory variables into their research and tested in several countries including Mexico. Examples of such variables include political competition, life tenure, and method by which judges are selected, among other individual variables related to judges' attributes. The third section presents five main hypotheses derived from extant judicial theories. The fourth section describes the characteristics of the state administrative courts in Mexico based on the variables examined in the literature review. The last section tests four hypotheses using data of six Mexican states from the 2006-2008 period.

An Integrated Approach

The study of federal and local judiciaries in the United States and several countries in Latin America has been carried out mostly through two different levels of analysis. One strand of research has focused its investigation on the effect of variables measured at an aggregate-level. In these studies, the unit of analysis tends to be grouped observations (courts). Abundant studies have examined judicial issues by concentrating their attention on aggregated evidence from one or several courts (Benesh and Reddick 2002, Beer 2006, Brace and Hall 2001, Bill Chávez, Ferejohn, and Weingast 2011, Cameron, Segal and Songer 2000, Cooter and Ginsburg 1996, Eskridge 1991a, 1991b, Feld and Voigt 2003, 2004, Fierro and García 2010, García and Tello 2010, Gibson and Caldeira 2003, Hansford and Spriggs II 2006, Magaloni 2003, 2008, Gely and Spiller 1990, Johnson 1987, Moreno, Crisp and Shugart 2003, McNollgast 1995, 2006, Ríos-Figueroa and Taylor 2006, Ríos-Figueroa 2007, Rodríguez-Raga 2011, Shapiro 1981, Staton 2006). The other strand of judicial research has emphasized individual level variables. Instead of estimating outcomes from evidence aggregated at the court level, the observations these studies use tend to come from subjects, in this case, individual judges (Epstein, Hoekstra, Segal and Spaeth 1998, Martin and Quinn 2002, Tiede, Carp and Manning 2010).

Despite the usefulness of these studies, they are not free from criticism. Aggregate analyses may lead to ecological fallacy, where relationships observed in groups are assumed to occur in individuals. In contrast, studies focused on individuals may lead to atomistic fallacy, where inferences about groups are incorrectly made from this type of data (Luke 2004). More recently, increasing attention has been devoted to a combined approach in the analysis of the judiciaries. The theoretical and methodological deficiencies appear to be greatly diminished by integrating the aggregate and individual perspectives (Bartels 2009, Boyd, Epstein and Martin 2010, Brace and Hall 1995, 2000, Carroll and Tiede 2011, Ferejohn 1999, Gates 1991, Hall and Bonneau 2008, Hettinger, Stefanie, and Martinek 2004, Iaryczower, Spiller, and Tommasi 2002, Schanzenbach and Tiller 2007, 2008, Songer, Humphries Ginn and Sarver 2003, Tiede 2006, Ulmer and Johnson 2004, VonDoepp 2006).

Similar to these recent works, this chapter proposes to examine state administrative courts in Mexico by utilizing an integrated approach that permeates both theory and methods. The point is not only to know how judges' characteristics influence judges' decisions, but also how the institutional and political contexts impact these decisions.

Literature Review

This section briefly reviews the concept of judicial independence and the separation of powers approach. It surveys prior aggregate and individual-level studies that have used political fragmentation, career stability, and method of appointment to explain judicial independence. This section also reviews individual variables related to judges' attributes and background such as seniority, judges' appointment, tenure, party affiliation, age, gender, and professional and academic experience.

Judicial Independence: Concepts and Approaches

Numerous studies have defined judicial independence by considering notions such as impartiality, neutrality, and the freedom of the judges or the courts to express their own judgment when arbitrating interbranch disputes and safeguarding rights (Gibson, Caldeira and Baird 1998, Lane 1985, Shapiro 1981, and Shetreet 1985). However, more recent research recognizes that judicial independence is conditional and depends on a variety of political factors (Domingo 2000, Feld, and Voigt 2003, Ferejohn 1999, Ferejohn, Rosenbluth, and Shipan 2007, Helmke 2002, Ramseyer and Rasmusen 2001, Leiras, Giraudy, and Tunon 2009, McNollgast 1995, 2006, and Ríos-Figueroa and Staton 2008). In this regard, Tiede's (2006) work offers a precise concept of judicial independence. She defines judicial independence in two steps. First, she analyzes "the judiciary's independence from the executive branch [. . .]" and highlights that her concept considers independence from the executive instead of the legislature in as much as courts can never be entirely independent from the legislative branch, which is the prominent body that makes the laws interpreted by the judges and provides them with a budget. Second, once the level of independence from the executive is determined, Tiede then focuses on the discretion of individual judges. Similar to Tiede's work and other analyses (i.e., Leiras et al. 2009, and Kapiszewski and Taylor 2008), I consider judicial independence of state administrative judges from the state executive branch.

The approach I follow in this study is based on the strategic/separation of powers model, which assumes that justices are sophisticated individuals who, in order to achieve their goals, make decisions based not only on their own preferences, but also on the preferences of others. The three main ideas of the strategic account are: justices' actions are intended to achieve their purposes; justices are strategic; and institutional rules constrain justices' interactions (Epstein and Knight 1998). A variety of studies have analyzed, at the national level, judges' preferences as a function of the behavior of other relevant actors such as the executive and the legislators. For instance, Bill Chavez, Ferejohn, and Weingast (2009), Gely and Spiller (1990), Iaryczower, Spiller, and Tomassi (2002), and McNollgast (2006) explain judicial independence in the United States and Argentina based on a strategic/separation of powers model.

One of the most influential scholars of the judicial independence literature within the separation of powers approach is Ferejohn (1999), who discusses independent judges in dependent judiciaries. Ferejohn's explanation of the structure of institutional protections for judges and legal processes within the federal government sheds light on the understanding of how to approach the study of judicial independence. Specifically, Ferejohn´s seminal article elucidates on the two levels he proposes to understand judicial independence: the internal or normative level, and the external or institutional level. The first level examines the idea of a judge making decisions as a human being free from the potential punishment or reward from another person. The institutional level encompasses the idea of independence of courts or the judicial institution as a whole from other branches such as the executive branch or Congress. Political interventions in the judicial branch are contingent on high levels of coordination among politicians from the other branches to overcome the constitutional checks and balances (i.e., two-thirds of the vote in the Senate is necessary for judicial impeachment).

Contextual Sources of Judicial Independence: Political Fragmentation, Executive Turnover, Career Stability, and Selection Method

The literature on national and state judicial studies suggests that partisan composition of Congress and political institutions (i.e., career stability and judges' selection method) play a crucial role in the way judges make their decisions.

Previous studies of U.S., Latin American and Mexican courts have been concerned with the effect of political fragmentation on judicial independence. An important finding of this literature is that political divisions tend to provide judges with greater discretion, which increases the probability that judges will constrain the executive and protect individual rights (Eskridge 1991a, 1991b, Segal 1997, Gely and Spiller 1990, Iaryczower et al. 2002, Bill Chávez 2004, Ríos-Figueroa 2007). A coordination problem between the executive and the legislature under divided government is associated with an empowered judiciary, which can defect against the government. Therefore, the judiciary will be weaker or stronger contingent on the power of the other two branches.

The strategic interactions among the different government branches also have been shown to affect judicial independence. Literature focused on the United States has argued that in periods of divided government judicial independence should be enhanced because one of the chambers or the executive will tend to veto legislation which would overturn decisions of the Supreme Court[4] (Ferejohn, Rosenbluth and Shipan 2007, McNollgast 2006, and Whittington 2003). Similar hypotheses have been tested using data from U.S. state judiciaries (Brace, Hall, and Langer 1999). Others have also considered whether judicial independence is related to the original civil or common law system of the court (Berkowitz and Clay 2006). Recently, Garoupa and Mathews 2014, have developed a strategic model based on interactions among the legislature, the agency, and the administrative court in developed coun-

---

[4] The opposite occurs under unified governments: the legislature and the executive can coordinate against the judiciary.

tries. The results of those interactions are based on variations of political and institutional arrangements such as concentration (or not) of power, selection of judges, and life tenure, among others. All these studies have found that the balance of power between government branches affect judicial independence.

Most studies of independence in Mexican and Latin American judiciaries have focused their attention on the issue of fragmentation of power. Several studies of Argentina, Brazil, and Chile (Brinks 2011, Bill Chávez 2007, Helmke 2003, Iaryczower et al. 2002, and Leiras et al. 2009, Scribner 2011, Leiras, Tuñón, and Giraudy 2015) have found support for the hypothesis that political fragmentation creates incentives between the executive and legislative branches to generate independent judicial systems. The reason is that under a fragmented government condition, it is more difficult to override judicial decisions.

In Mexico, both Magaloni (2003) and Ríos-Figueroa (2007) have developed arguments along the lines of Helmke's (2003), which sees fragmentation of power at the federal level as promoting judicial independence. Similarly, Beer (2006) and Ingram (2009) argue that political competition has a positive effect on judicial independence in the Mexican States. They demonstrate that executive's lack of majority in the legislature enhances judicial independence at national and state levels.

Studies on Argentine and Mexican state courts have emphasized the role of turnover[5] and political fragmentation[6] (Leiras, Tuñón, and Giraudy 2015, Ríos and Soto 2017). Specifically, the former analysis stresses that these two variables are two different components of political competition and that they should be evaluated. The authors analyze the Argentine state courts from 1984 to 2008 and test if there is judicial autonomy under four different scenarios: a) concentration of power and high executive turnover, b) fragmentation of power and high executive turnover, c) concentration of power and low executive turnover, and d) fragmentation of power and low executive turnover. The results find support for a) and d): ". . . when power is concentrated only the expectation of turnover may protect judicial autonomy, and, conversely, when turnover seems unlikely, only fragmentation should prevent interferences on the judiciary" (Leiras, Tuñón, and Giraudy 2015:185).

Another factor that appears to affect judicial independence is judges' career stability. In the case of Japan, Ramseyer and Rasmussen (2001) analyze the relationship between the careers of 400 judges and their rulings in cases involving the government. The authors demonstrate that judges who decided in favor of the Liberal Democratic Party (LDP), which was the incumbent party for nearly fifty-five years since 1955, did better in their judicial careers. Similar to Japan, Mexico had a unique

---

[5] Defined as the rotation in the exercise of power by members of different political organizations (Leiras, Tuñón, and Giraudy 2015:177).

[6] Defined as a situation in which different agents decide over an issue and they have different political goals (177).

party ruling for seventy-one years in which the lack of alternation in power of the executive branch established a system of incentives in which judicial turnover was common and judges usually looked for better paid and more prestigious political positions (Domingo 2000).

Most recent studies focused on Latin America and Eastern Europe have examined the effect of career stability (through life tenure) and appointment mechanisms on judges' decisions. Examples of such investigations are those of Helmke (1998, 2002), Herron and Randazzo (2003) and (Helmke and Sanders 2006). These analyses focus on national courts in post-communist countries and in Argentina. Whereas Herron and Randazzo incorporate judges' terms as a component of their judicial independence variable, Helmke tests the effect of career instability on judges' decisions. Her main findings underline that once the incumbent government starts to lose power, judges who lack institutional security are motivated to rule against the government to distance themselves.

Interestingly, Garoupa, Gili and Gómez-Pomar (2012) find no support for the hypothesis that political insulation by career judges enhances independence. In other words, their evidence suggests that career judges abandon their disposition preferences in favor of policy goals[7] (formalism, consensus, and dissent avoidance). Garoupa et al. also find that judges behave strategically as a result of changes in government. Thus, these analyses show mixed evidence about the career stability hypothesis.

Concerning selection mechanisms, several articles focused on U.S. state courts have demonstrated that there is an association between method of judicial selection and judges' decision-making (Hall 1987, 1992, Hall and Brace 1989, Brace and Hall 1990, 1995, 2001, Cohen, Klement, and Neeman 2015, Lindquist 2017). Within Latin America, Argentina, Chile, and Brazil there are interesting examples on this matter. Scribner's (2011) results show that in both Argentina and Chile judges that are not appointed by the sitting president are more likely to check presidential use of exceptional power than their colleagues who were appointed by the current president. Carroll and Tiede (2011) find that changes in the appointment mechanisms of judges in the Chilean Constitutional Tribunal influence the likelihood of finding laws unconstitutional. Brinks (2011) shows that in Brazil, judges' method of selection varies according to the degree of political control in judicial choices and unity of veto players who participate in the process. For instance, in some cases, rules grant the executive and the legislatures a great deal of freedom to select the judges, whereas in others they require these branches to choose from lists created by unelected agents (i.e., Supreme Courts, bar associations, or judicial councils). Some

---

[7] According to Garoupa et al. policy preferences are associated with the court's opinion, whereas dispositional preferences are associated with an ideal position associated with the judge's opinion.

appointment mechanisms require the cooperation of two or more actors, such as in the U.S. case where both the president and a majority of the Senate are involved in the selection process. Another case in point is Colombia, where justices of the constitutional court are appointed by the President, the Supreme Court, and the Council of State. Each of them nominates a third of the justices of the Constitutional Court (Brinks 2011). Although the literature has highlighted the crucial role of political fragmentation, career stability, and the method used to appoint judges on judicial independence, the influence of these factors on judges' behavior at the subnational level remains unexplored. Undertaking this analysis is important because scholars specialized in Mexico have also emphasized the strong influence of the executive in the national and state arenas (Beer 2006, Domingo 2000, Ríos-Figueroa 2007, Ingram 2009, and Magaloni 2003). In the case of Mexico, governors have been defined as powerful actors who not only have control within the state legislatures, but also have the power to influence the decisions of state judiciaries. Even though analyses highlight how prominent governors are, research on the decisions of state judges in Mexico is scant.

Judges' Features: Attributes, Social Background, and Policy Preferences

Observable characteristics of judges may influence their judicial decisions. Abundant literature of judicial behavior has explored the relationship between judges' characteristics and their decisions in the court. In particular, scholars have explored the effect of judges' seniority, age, gender, professional and academic background, appointing official and party identification on their judicial choices (Boyd, Epstein, and Martin 2010, Brace and Butler 2001, George 2001, Tiede, Carp and Manning 2010).

Seniority

Scholars have identified seniority as one of the judges' characteristics associated with judicial decision making (Bonneau, Hammond, Maltzman, and Wahlbeck 2007, Brace and Butler 2001, Brace and Hall 1993, Dorf and Brenner 1992, Goldman 1966, 1975, Hall and Brace 1992, Ulmer 1970, 1973). Ulmer's studies on the relationship between social background and dissent behavior emphasize that judges' decisions are contingent to a great extent on social background predictors, which reflect the way judges develop, mature, and become socialized (Ulmer 1970).

More recent studies by Brace and collaborators have included seniority as a factor in their models of judicial decision making. For instance, Brace and Hall (1993), measure seniority with the number of years served on the state court by the justice casting the vote. They find that seniority has a statistically significant effect on the probability of voting with the majority coalition in death penalty decisions. Another study by Brace and Butler (2001), which describes the Project of the State Supreme

Courts, presents descriptive statistics about justices' seniority. The average seniority in approximately half of the states is less than ten years, while the typical length of service for an Oklahoma justice is 19 years. The authors also present descriptive statistics about justices' dissents, justices as a part of the majority, and justices that did not participate. Even though their article does not test a statistical relationship between these variables, it underlines the theoretical and empirical utility of the data. It shows that there is substantial variation across the state supreme courts in these and other variables incorporated in their project.

Other scholars have focused on the freshman status of justices (Dorff and Brenner 1992, Bonneau et al. 2007).[8] The hypothesis is that justices serving their first term on the court are more likely to be influenced by the majority at the final vote. The explanation is that freshman justices are probably less confident than senior judges, and, therefore, the former are more likely to conform to the majority. In short, length of service of the judges seems to matter when examining judges' votes.

Age

Academic explanations about the theoretical link between the age of the judges and their decisions are based on the idea that appointed younger judges will have longer tenure than older judges. However, the latter will likely show greater information on their legal views to the appointing official (i.e., executive or legislature). Other scholars (George 2001, Sidney 1973) have posited that people become more conservative over time. Correspondingly, older judges will tend to be more conservative than others. As a case in point, Goldman's (1975) influential study of courts of appeals decisions finds support for this hypothesis. However, one weakness of his analysis is that there is not a control variable for political party identification. This is important because age is likely to be correlated with party affiliation, a robust predictor of judges' votes.

In another prominent study on the effect of age, Tate (1981) shows that judges' age, measured in years and cohorts, does not have a statistically significant effect on judges' decisions after controlling for party identification and other attributes of the judges. Thus, there is mixed evidence about the effect of age on judges' votes.

Gender

One of the most explored judges' attributes on their decisions is gender. The findings of studies focused on gender have shown mixed evidence. Whereas some have found significant effects of gender on judicial choices, others have encountered contrasting results. For instance, Brudney, Schiavoni and Merritt (1999), Crowe

---

[8] These scholars probably name their variable based on Howard's (1968) pioneering study about judicial choice.

(1999), Davis, Haire and Songer (1993), find that on judicial cases regarding employment discrimination cases, and unfair labor practices suits involving unions, women judges tend to make more liberal decisions on the bench than men. Unlike those studies, Ashenfelter, Eisenberg, and Schwab (1995), Gryski, Main, and Dixon (1986), Segal (2000), Sisk, Heise, and Morriss (1998), and Walker and Barrow (1985) do not find a significant relationship between judges' gender and judicial decisions.

A recent study by Boyd et al. (2010), which covers 13 areas of law,[9] focuses on whether male and female judges decide cases in a different manner and in what ways serving with a female judge causes male judges to make different decisions. The analysis is innovative because not only do they test individual effects, but they also consider panel effects. Moreover, they use statistical methods not used by earlier research to robustly demonstrate the association between gender effects and judges' decisions. Using semiparametric matching (which stems from a formal framework of causal inference) the authors find that this relationship is significant only in sex discrimination cases. That is, the probability of a judge who decides in favor of the party claiming discrimination decreases when the judge is a male. Similarly, when a woman judge serves on a panel with men judges, the latter are more likely to vote in favor of the plaintiff.

Tiede et al.'s (2010) work addresses sex and judicial behavior in sentencing decisions in U.S. federal district courts. The authors argue that the effect of gender on judicial decisions is conditional on the partisan affiliation of the presidents that appoint them. They propose a statistical model that interacts gender and partisan affiliation of the president and find that female judges appointed by Republican presidents are less likely to favor defendants.

Education and Academic Experience

Are judges who previously served as law professors more likely to vote according to their policy preferences? For several scholars, the answer to this question is yes (George 2001, Schwartz 1988, Goldman 1987). George's (2001) article argues that law professors will be more likely to vote according to the appointing president's policy preferences. The explanation is that presidents select them because it is easier "[. . .] to confidently discern the content of professors' legal philosophies and their commitment to those views from a published record." (George 2001:39). In other words, presidents appoint those individuals who have intellectually given support to their programs.

---

[9] Abortion, Americans with Disabilities Act (ADA), Affirmative Action, Campaign Finance, Capital Punishment, Contract Clause, Environmental Protection Act (EPA), Federalism, Piercing the Corporate Veil, Sex Discrimination in Employment (Title VII), Sexual Harassment, Takings Clause, Race Discrimination (Title VII).

Judges' education appears to be weakly associated to their voting behavior. George (2001), Nagel (1974), and Tate (1981) have evaluated this relationship and found inconsistent evidence across different issue areas. However, Sisk et al.'s (1998) work has found support for the link between education and judges' decisions in district courts. More specifically, judges who attended prestigious schools appear to be more likely to adopt practical reasoning to support their sentencing guidelines decisions (George 2001:28).

Professional Experience

Copious research has explored the link between U.S. judges' careers and their judicial behavior. However, there is no conclusive evidence about the significance of this relationship.

On the one hand, some studies find support for the association between professional careers and judges' decisions. For example, some studies have shown that judges who previously served as attorneys tend to vote in favor of liberal claims, such as discrimination and bias, more often than those that did not (Tate 1981, Tate and Handeberg 1991). However, other works have shown that those types of judges tend to be more conservative in their decisions (Tate and Johnston 1976).

On the other hand, there are other studies that have failed to find a significant association between judges' professional experience and their decisions. George (2001) points out that courts of appeals and district court analyses do not find an effect of judges' experience on their rulings. Ashenfelter et al. (1995) find that judges' judicial background is unrelated to their decision making in district courts. Brudney, Schiavoni, and Merrit (1999) focus on votes in favor of unions in circuit courts and find similar results. Goldman (1975) does not find a significant relationship between prior judicial experience and more liberal or conservative votes in circuit courts. Thus, it appears that professional experience may have a limited effect on judicial decision making.

Party of Appointing President

Partisanship is often a powerful predictor of political behavior. In contrast to legislators, most judges tend not to make their party preference known unless running in a partisan election. However, some scholars have argued that a proxy for judges' partisanship is the party of the appointing president. This approach has been well substantiated in the literature across several areas (Brudney, Schiavoni, and Merrit 1999, Carp, Manning, and Stidham 2009, Cross and Tiller 1998, George 2001, Gotschall 1986, Tiede et. al. 2010, Schanzenbach and Tiller 2007, 2008, and Stidham 1996). These studies have examined upper and lower courts and shown that there is a significant association between party of the appointing president and judges' decision making.

Hypotheses

Assertive and independent judiciaries[10] are essential institutions to developing democracies. Their role of checking the other branches of government represents an enormous contribution in emergent democratic countries where legislatures and civil society tend to be more passive and the executive the dominant actor (VonDoepp 2006). The performance of judiciaries in new democracies is crucial for the preservation of these regimes and the public's perception of courts as legitimate and powerful actors that can check historically strong executives.

My main argument is that judges' seniority, as well as the political and institutional context in which judges make their decisions, influence judicial independence. The following five hypotheses make this argument precise.

Based on the surveyed literature, seniority (also called length of service) plays a crucial role in the way judges vote in a case. That is, judges' decisions are contingent on this type of background predictor that mirrors the manner judges develop and socialize in the court. Senior judges are more confident and experienced than freshman judges, and consequently the former are more likely to vote against the executive. Derived from this theoretical argument, I expect to find similar results for state administrative judges in Mexico.

H1: Judges who have served in a state court for a longer period should be less likely to vote in favor of the state executive than those judges in state courts who have served for a shorter period

Judicial scholars have focused their analyses on judges' behavior and the factors that might influence the way they make their decisions. One of those factors is related to strategic judicial behavior. That is, the behavior of judges is contingent on political factors (such political fragmentation) that "inform the strategic calculations of judges." (VonDoepp 2006). The logic is that concentration of power in one actor or several actors with the same preferences make judges less likely to vote against the government because they do not want these other actors to coordinate in sanctioning them. On the contrary, if power is fragmented, retaliation will be less likely, and, therefore, justices will be less constrained and better able to decide cases more autonomously (VonDoepp 2006).

On this point, abundant research shown in the literature review section argues that *political fragmentation* tends to favor judicial independence in the United States and Latin America (Iaryczower et al. 2002, McNollgast 1995, 2006, Scribner 2011). Authors who analyze Mexico at federal and state levels have arrived at the same conclusion. Derived from these studies I focus on states and expect that the rela-

---

[10] Kapiszewski (2012) proposes an interesting approach of judicial assertiveness and independence definitions.

tionship indicated in the first hypothesis will be weaker by state in a context in which the governor's party has a legislative majority.[11]

H2: Under state legislative majority governments, the state variation effect of H1 will be weaker.

As noted earlier, career stability has been associated with judicial independence (Castagnola and Pérez-Liñán 2011; Helmke 1998, 2002; and Herron and Randazzo 2003). The main argument is that more stable judicial careers lead to higher levels of autonomy. Because Mexico has been ruled for seven decades by the same party, reelection and life tenure have always been viewed as a way to embrace and retain power at all levels of government. As a consequence, many Mexican state constitutions have limited the period in which a person can hold the position of justice in a state supreme court whereas others maintain life tenure. Thus, how does this factor influence judicial independence in the Mexican states? Do justices without life tenure tend to favor the Executive? What occurs with those justices that possess life tenure during the period they begin working and the moment they are ratified by the Executive?

As the literature on career stability shows, Mexico and Japan had one party rule for several decades, but they differ in that the latter country put in place a system that created career rewards for judges that favored the government in their decisions (Ramseyer and Rasmusen 2001), but the former did not.[12] Judges in Japan tend to pursue a judicial career whereas in Mexico career instability seems to be the norm. However, it appears that in both countries judges who favor the government tend to obtain benefits. Based on the surveyed literature, I expect life tenure to enhance independence. Thus, the relationship described in the first hypothesis will be stronger by state when local regulations establish career stability through tenure.

H3: Under state courts with life tenure rules, the state variation effect of H1 will be stronger.

As the previous section indicates, another type of institutional rule investigated at the national level by scholars of judicial politics in the United States and Latin America is appointment mechanism. Following prior works, I expect executive involvement in the appointment process to decrease judicial independence. Studies of the United States, Argentina, Brazil, Chile, Mexico, and Latin America have evaluated the relationship between a judge's method of selection and judicial independence. Derived from the literature that has examined this relationship at the structural and individual levels, I argue that differences in the contextual appointment

---

[11] This term means that the governor's party holds the majority (more than 50% of the seats) in the legislature.

[12] Magaloni (2003) explains that the president had great control over judges' nominations and dismissals despite formal rules about tenure.

mechanism used by state affect judicial independence in the Mexican state administrative courts. Therefore,

H4: Under state regulations that allow the state executive to participate in judicial appointment, the state variation effect of H1 will be weaker.

Based on recent findings in state courts in Argentina by Leiras, Tuñón, and Giraudy (2015), it seems reasonable to test if the hypotheses on political competition[13] that stand in Argentina show similar results in the Mexican state administrative courts.[14] Therefore, I expect the combination of state turnover of the governor's party and majority in the legislature to increase judicial independence in the Mexican courts. I also expect that reelection of the governor's party and fragmentation of power in the legislature will increase judicial autonomy in the administrative courts. The goal is to test not only whether the effect of divided power (political fragmentation) has an effect on judicial independence, but also but divided time (turnover) in the state courts in Argentina.[15]

H5a: Under state turnover of the governor's party and concentration of power in the legislature, the state variation effect of H1 will be stronger.

H5b: Under no state turnover of the governor's party and fragmentation of power in the legislature, the state variation effect of H1 will be stronger.

State Administrative Courts in Mexico[16]

State administrative courts[17] have not been sufficiently analyzed even though they hear a great number of cases with important policy ramifications. These courts

---

[13] According to Leiras, Tuñón, and Giraudy (2015), political competition is composed of political fragmentation and turnover.

[14] In contrast to Argentina, in Mexico there is no reelection of the state executive. Therefore, the analysis focuses on the rotation of the state executive party.

[15] —[this footnote was left blank by the author.]

[16] The information described and presented in the figures and tables come from different sources: data on the operation of courts within the judiciary, political competition, institutional characteristics of the courts, judge's attributes, and method of appointment derive from Fierro and García (2010), the state executives, the state legislatures, and the state administrative courts through request of information from each state institute of information access.

[17] The analysis of state administrative courts is crucial because they have the power to check government actions to avoid abuse of power. In other words, these subnational courts protect individuals against unlawful government actions and supervise their own agents through their decisions on administrative acts challenged by individuals or entities. The oversight tasks of the state courts have been recently enhanced as a consequence of political competition at the national and subnational levels. Therefore, these courts have greater incentives to assert their roles in generating policy.

exhibit significant variation along the variables discussed in the prior section. Eleven Mexican state administrative courts belong to judiciaries of each state. They are found in the following states: Aguascalientes, Baja California Sur, Campeche, Chiapas, Hidalgo, Jalisco, Morelos, Quintana Roo, Tlaxcala, Veracruz, and Zacatecas. These states follow the common law system in which the administrative courts operate within the judicial branch (Fierro and García 2010, López-Ayllón, García, and Fierro 2015).

Given that the goal of this chapter is to investigate independence of the judiciary from the executive branch, only state courts that are part of the judicial branch are included and only administrative cases where the government is always a party are examined. The rest of the Mexican state courts belong to the executive branch. Figure 1 illustrates in gray the Mexican states in which administrative courts work within the judiciary.

Figure 1. Mexican States in which Administrative Courts Operate within the Judiciary. Gray states are those where administrative courts operate within the state judiciary. White states are those where administrative courts operate within the state executive.

Following Brace and Butler (2001), the analysis presented here offers a description of the institutional and political structures of the eleven state administrative courts in Mexico. These courts show substantial variation in terms of method of appointment, court size, length of tenure, and political fragmentation.

Table 1 provides a description of political fragmentation in the government in these eleven states for the period 2006-2008. It provides information on the party of the governor, whether there was a majority party, and whether there was divided government. Among this group of states some show variation within their state. For instance, in Aguascalientes, Chiapas, Quintana Roo, and Veracruz there was divided government and majority party in each of the two legislative periods explored. This table also indicates that there is variation on the type of government (majority or divided government). Aguascalientes, Chiapas, Jalisco, Quintana Roo, Veracruz, and Zacatecas are some examples of such variation. A similar situation occurs in the column labeled as *Governor Party*. Governors are members of different parties between the states. Thus, the variation among the states provides an excellent opportunity to test the effect of political fragmentation on judges' decision making.

Statistics from the late 90's to 2016 show rotation of the executive's party in nine out of the eleven evaluated states (Campeche and Hidalgo do not show variation in this respect).[18] Therefore, these differences among the states can be tested to

State	Region	Governor Party	MP in Legislature	Divided Government	Turnover of Governor's Party
Aguascalientes	Center-West	PAN	PAN	No	Yes
		PAN	PRI	Yes	
Baja Californis Sur	North	PRD	PRD	No	Yes
		PRD	PRD	No	
Campeche	South	PRI	PRI	No	No
		PRI	PRI	No	
Chiapas	South	PRD	PRD	No	Yes
		PRD	None	Yes	
Hidalgo	Center	PRI	PRI	No	No
		PRI	PRI	No	
Jalisco	Center-West	PAN	None	Yes	Yes
		PAN	None	Yes	
Morelos	Center	PAN	PAN	No	Yes
		PAN	PAN	No	
Quintana Roo	South	PRI	None	Yes	Yes
		PRI	PRI	No	
Tlaxcala	Center	PAN	PAN	No	Yes
		PAN	PAN	No	
Veracruz	South	PRI	None	Yes	Yes
		PRI	PRI	No	
Zacatecas	North	PRD	None	Yes	Yes
		PRD	None	Yes	

Table 1. Political Fragmentation and Turnover in 11 Mexican States

---

[18] Testing turnover of the governor's party requires an increased time frame of analysis.

demonstrate whether there is a relationship between turnover of the governor's party and judge's judicial autonomy.

Table 2 shows the different appointment processes and judges' length of tenure for each state administrative court. Some states provide life tenure whereas in others a person can occupy the position of judge in the state supreme court for only a limited period of time. The appointment processes are dominated by governors. Court size and the number of years since their creation show variation as well. This variation among the states in terms of method of appointment, length of tenure, court size, and court age provide a great opportunity to examine the relationship between these institutional rules and judges' judicial independence.

Table 2. Institutional Characteristics in Eleven State Administrative Courts in Mexico, 2006-2008				
State	**Method of Appointment**	**Life Tenure**	**Court Size**	**Court Age**
Aguascalientes	Executive participation	No	1	3
Baja Californis Sur	Executive participation	No	1	4
Campeche	Executive does not participate	Yes	3	11
Chiapas	Executive does not participate	No	7	1
Hidalgo	Executive participation	No	3	26
Jalisco	Executive does not participate	No	6	24
Morelos	Executive does not participate	Yes	3	8
Quintana Roo	Executive participation	No	1	5
Tlaxcala	Executive does not participate	Yes	3	6
Veracruz	Executive participation	No	6	19
Zacatecas	Executive does not participate	No	1	8

Along with the structural variations in the political and institutional variables presented in the previous section, the justices that serve in the administrative courts exhibit differences in their attributes (gender, seniority, professional preparation, and academic and professional experience). For instance, in the period 2006-2008 the number of women judges varies in the state administrative courts of Chiapas, Hidalgo, Jalisco, Morelos, and Tlaxcala. States such as Aguascalientes, Baja California, and Campeche have no female judges during the examined period. In terms of professional preparation, there are also differences within each state court; some judges hold a master's degree and others just hold a law degree. Judges' length of service and seniority also show variation across the states. Some judges serve for one term, others for one or more terms.

Judges' professional experience varies greatly in state administrative courts. In Campeche, Jalisco, and Morelos states judges' earlier experience ranges from serving in other courts within the judicial branch to serving in the executive or legislative branches. Academic experience among judges varies as well. For example, in states like Chiapas, Jalisco, and Tlaxcala some judges were law professors before they were appointed. In Jalisco, there is a sharp contrast between the judges that have only served for one year in the court and a judge that has served for ten years. Tables 3 to 7 present examples of judges' characteristics in Campeche, Chiapas, Morelos, Jalisco, and Tlaxcala.

Table 3. Judge's Attributes, Campeche (2006-2008)					
Judge's Name	Gender	Seniority	Professional Preparation	Academic Experience	Professional Experience
José Enrique Adam Richaud	Male	5	*Abogado**	None	Several positions in different state courts
Iván Cabañas González	Male	10	*Abogado*	None	No governmental positions
Juan Antonio Renedo Dorantes	Male	2	*Abogado*	Law Professor	Official in the state executive

*Abogado in Mexico is equivalent to Juris Doctor in the United States.

Table 4. Judge's Attributes, Chiapas (2006-2008)

Judge's Name	Gender	Seniority	Professional Preparation	Academic Experience	Professional Experience
Jorge Chanona Pérez	Male	1	*Abogado*	None	State executive official and several positions in different state courts
Genero Coellio Pérez	Male	1	*Abogado*	Law Professor	State executive official and several positions in different state courts
Miguel Reyes Lacroix Macosay	Male	2	*Abogado*	Law Professor	Several positions in different state courts
María de Lourdes Morales Urbina	Female	2	*Abogada* and Master in Law	Law Professor	State executive official
Susana Sarmiento López	Female	1	*Abogada*	None	Several positions in different state courts
Julio Serrano Castillejos	Male	1	*Abogada*	Law Professor	Several positions in different state courts
Noé Miguel Zenteno López	Male	1	*Abogado*	None	State executive official

Table 5. Judge's Attributes, Jaslisco (2006-2008)

Judge's Name	Gender	Seniority	Professional Preparation	Academic Experience	Professional Experience
Alberto Barba Gómez	Male	1	*Abogado** and Master in Law	None	High-profile state official in the executive cabinet and several positions in the court
Eleuterio Valencia Carranza	Male	10	*Abogado** and Master in Law	Law Professor	State executive and legislature official and several positions in different state courts
Victor Manuel León Figueroa	Male	1	*Abogado*	None	High-profile state official in the executive
Armando García Estrada	Male	1	*Abogado** and Master in Law	Law Professor	Several positions in different state courts
Horacio León Hernández	Male	1	*Abogado** and Master in Law	Law Professor	No public previous positions
Patricia Campos González	Female	1	*Abogada*	NA	Several positions in different state courts

Table 6. Judge's Attributes, Morelos (2006-2008)

Judge's Name	Gender	Seniority	Professional Preparation	Academic Experience	Professional Experience
Carlos Iván Arenas Ángeles	Male	2	*Abogado* and Master in Law	Law Professor	Official in the state executive
Martin Jasso Diaz	Male	2	Abogado	Law Professor	Several positions in the court
Orlando Aguilar Lozano	Male	2	Abogado	None	High-profile state official in the executive cabinet and justice of the state court

Table 7. Judge's Attributes, Tlaxcala (2006-2008)

Judge's Name	Gender	Seniority	Professional Preparation	Academic Experience	Professional Experience
Alicia Fragoso Sánchez	Female	2	*Abogada*	Law Professor	Several positions in different state courts
Rafael Juárez Castañeda	Male	3	*Abogado*	Law Professor	Several positions in different state courts
Silvestre Lara Amador	Male	6	*Abogado*	High School Teacher	Several positions in different state courts
Pedro Molina Flores	Male	1	*Abogado*	Law Professor	Several positions in different state courts
Mariano Reyes Landa	Male	6	*Abogado*	None	Several positions in different state courts

Table 8. Method of Appointment: Appointing Governor and Party Affiliation of Appointing Governor (2006-2008)

Judge's Name	State	Appointing Governor	Party of Appointing Governor	Date of Appointment	Governor Term
Alfonso Román Quiroz	Aguascalientes	Luis Amando Reynoso Femat	PAN	14-Mar-06	12/01/04 - 11/30/10
Francisco J. Amador Soto	Baja California Sur	Narciso Agúndez Montaño	PRD	3-Nov-05	04/05/05- 04/04/11
Humberto Montiel Padilla	Baja California Sur	Leonel Cota Montaño	PRD	1-Mar-05	04/05/99- 04/04/05
Igancio Bello Sosa	Baja California Sur	Narciso Agúndez Montaño	PRD	16-Jun-05	04/05/05- 04/04/11
Jesús Ángeles Contreras	Hidalgo	Guillero Rosell De la Lama	PRI	10-Dec-82	04/01/81- 03/31/87
Osctaviano Chávez Bustos	Hidalgo	Humberto Lugo Gil	PRI	2-Mar-99	10/29/98- 03/31/99
Percys Susana Cravioto Luna	Hidalgo	Miguel Ángel Osorio Chong	PRI	19-Apr-05	04/01/05- 03/31/11

Variation among state judges is not limited to gender, seniority, and professional and academic backgrounds. There are also differences between and within the states concerning appointing governors and their party affiliation. Table 8 illustrates these variables in three states: Aguascalientes, Baja California Sur, and Hidalgo.

Table 9. Method of Appointment: Legislature and/or Judiciary			
Judge's Name	State	Method of Appointment	Date of Appointment
José Enrique Adam Richaud	Campeche	State Supreme Court & confirmed by State Legislature	24-Apr-03
Iván Cabañas González	Campeche	State Supreme Court & confirmed by State Legislature	11-Jan-97
Juan Antonio Renedo Dorantes	Campeche	State Supreme Court & confirmed by State Legislature	11-Jan-97
Jorge Chanona Pérez	Chiapas	State Administrative Court	6-Oct-08
Genaro Coello Pérez	Chiapas	State Supreme Court	4-Dec-07
Miguel Reyes Lacroix Macosay	Chiapas	State Legislature	24-Jul-07
María de Lourdes Morales Urbina	Chiapas	State Legislature	20-Dec-07
Susana Sarmiento López	Chiapas	State Supreme Court	4-Dec-07
Julio Serrano Castillejos	Chiapas	State Legislature	20-Dec-07
Noé Miguel Zenteno López	Chiapas	State Legislature	20-Dec-07
Carlos Iván Arenas Ángeles	Morelos	State Legislature	18-May-06
Martín Jasso Díaz	Morelos	State Legislature	18-May-06
Orlando Aguilar Lozano	Morelos	State Legislature	18-May-06
Alicia Fragoso Sánchez	Tlaxcala	State Legislature	8-Mar-05
Rafael Juárez Castañeda	Tlaxcala	State Legislature	15-Jan-02
Silvestre Lara Amador	Tlaxcala	State Legislature	15-Jan-02
Pedro Molina Flores	Tlaxcala	State Legislature	13-Jan-08
Mariano Reyes Landa	Tlaxcala	State Legislature	15-Jan-02

There are differences across states in the party affiliation of appointing governors. In Aguascalientes, the appointing governor during the examined period, Luis Armando Reynoso Femat, is affiliated to the National Action Party (PAN). The governor of Baja California Sur, Narciso Agúndez Montaño, is a member of the Party of the Democratic Revolution (PRD), and the governor of Hidalgo, Miguel Ángel Osorio Chong, is affiliated with the Institutional Revolutionary Party (PRI). There is also variation within the states. For example, in Baja California Sur, different governors have appointed the state administrative judges. Governor Narciso Agúndez Montaño appointed Judges Francisco Amador Soto and Ignacio Bello Sosa, and Governor Leonel Cota Montaño appointed Judge Humberto Montiel Padilla.

Table 9 presents judges' appointment method between and within state administrative courts. In terms of differences between states, the Supreme Court of Campeche appoints judges and the legislature confirms them. In Morelos and Tlaxcala, the state legislature appoints judges. In Chiapas, the method of appointment is different within the court because some judges are selected by the state supreme court and others by the state legislature. The table also shows that the date of appointment varies between and within states. The only exception is Morelos: the state legislature appointed judges serving during the period under study in the same date.

A Quantitative Analysis of Six State Administrative Courts (2006-2008)[19]

Given institutional and resource limitations, I was able to use both aggregate and individual level data of six Mexican state administrative courts that belong to each state judiciary to preliminarily test the first four hypotheses: Aguascalientes, Campeche, Chiapas, Hidalgo, Morelos, and Tlaxcala.[20] Because the goal of this work is to investigate independence of the judiciary from the executive branch, I include those state courts that are part of the judicial branch. The rest of the Mexican state courts belong to the executive branch. I examine administrative cases because the government is always a party. The types of cases covered by the administrative disputes include contracts, bidding processes, liability of officials, public safety/police enforcement, urban development, and access to information/transparency, among others.

The unit of analysis is a judge's decision. The purpose of this analysis is twofold: 1) to understand how state-court level variables affect judges' decisions; and 2) to better explain judicial decisions by analyzing individual and state-court level variables. In other words, judicial choice is viewed as a nested game (Brace,

---

[19] This section is a part of the quantitative chapter of my Ph.D. dissertation.

[20] State administrative courts of Jalisco, Quintana Roo, and Veracruz are part of the judicial branch as well, but there is no information collected from the number of sampled files in the CIDE dataset used for this analysis. Baja California Sur and Zacatecas did not provide information requested on judges' attributes.

Hall, and Langer 1999) in which judges consider external arenas that constrain their behavior when making a decision.

Some studies (Beer 2006, Ingram 2009) have gauged judicial behavior in the Mexican state courts using aggregate data. Specifically, Beer operationalizes judicial independence with a measure of judicial spending. In contrast, my research gauges judicial independence with judges' decisions at both aggregate and individual levels. Thus, the votes that judges cast allow me to determine the extent to which they favor the state executive (i.e., governor, a public official, or the state government).

Data and Measures

To test the first four hypotheses of my argument, I systematically examine judicial decisions made in a sample of the six previously mentioned state administrative courts during the period 2006-2008. I employed both aggregate and individual-level data from two principal sources. First, I used recent data from a survey of administrative court decisions conducted by a team of Mexican scholars from CIDE (López-Ayllón et.al 2010). Second, I searched for individual judge level data by accessing each state judicial council website. This institution monitors the activity of all judges, and it is supposed to gather background information of the judges. Finally, I gathered aggregate information related to political fragmentation in the state congresses from Infomex (a government website that provides information access) and institutional rules from different state regulations.

Concerning the sources of the institutional data, I collected information from the state constitutions and statutes which establish, for instance, the type of judicial selection and the judges' life tenure. Examples of such rules for each state are: political constitution, procedural administrative regulation, organic law of the judicial branch, and administrative court regulation (*Constitución Política, Ley de Procedimiento Contencioso Administrativo, Ley Orgánica del Poder Judicial,* and *Reglamento del Tribunal de lo Contencioso Administrativo).*

Once I collected all this information, I created a new dataset with both aggregate and individual level data that includes all the variables previously mentioned. The panel data on judicial decisions in the six selected courts during the period 2006-2008 (Aguascalientes, Campeche, Chiapas, Hidalgo, Morelos, and Tlaxcala) allow me to analyze whether states, institutional rules, and political competition constrain judges' decisions. The analysis of these data also helps to identify general patterns of judicial behavior across a broad range of cases in state administrative courts.

Judges' decisions in a case can be classified in the following different categories: 1) nullification of the administrative act (*nulidad*), 2) validity of the government administrative act (*validez*), 3) dismissal *(sobreseimiento),* and 4) declaration of no standing (*desechamiento*). These decisions occur in different stages of the administrative act process. More specifically, this process is divided in two stages.

In the first stage, judges perform a procedural analysis and make a decision: 1) If judges reject a case based on procedural grounds, then the outcome is a declaration of no standing, 2) If judges accept the case, then it is evaluated on the merits. In this second stage, judges decide whether the administrative act is null, valid, or if the case is to be dismissed.

Because I am interested in measuring judicial independence through likelihood of deference to the executive, the dependent variable is judge's vote in a case, and it is coded 1 if a judge decided in favor of the executive and 0 otherwise. From the data on judges' decisions, I created two dependent variables. In each case, the dependent variable is coded 1 if a judgment favors the executive and 0 otherwise. Specifically, the first variable *vote in favor of the executive on the merits* is coded 1 if the decision of a judge considers the administrative act as valid[21] and 0 if a judge nullifies the administrative act. The second variable *vote in favor of the executive all categories* is coded 1 if a judgment on the administrative act was considered as valid, dismissed, and declared as of no standing and 0 if the administrative act was nullified by a judge. This variable includes decisions for procedural reasons.

The main reason for choosing to divide decisions on the merits and decisions that also include procedural grounds is that judges' decisions on the merits and procedure are different in nature: the decisions based for procedural reasons do not require substantive considerations; they are based on technical points that make them to be less overseen. Procedural decisions are made based on statute of limitations, conflict of interests, jurisdiction, and subject matter, among others. In contrast, the decisions on the merits consider substantive considerations, which may make such decisions to be easily accessed and evaluated by people and the media.

Several studies recognize that judges may decide cases on procedural reasons to avoid deciding on the merits (Bickel 1961, Hart 1960, Peresie 2005, Prott 1973-1976). In particular, Prott (1973-1976) argues that judges try to avoid resolving controversial constitutional issues on the merits if they can solve them by procedural techniques. The reason is that the Court does not want to face criticism for a substantive decision. Although Prott examines the International Court of Justice, he also illustrates his argument with decisions made by the U.S. Supreme Court on civil liberty cases during the 1950s. Those decisions generated "considerable right-wing criticism on the Court" and the Congress considered impeaching the Chief Justice. According to Prott (1973-1976), this confrontation coincided with a dramatic drop in the number of civil liberties cases pronounced on by the Court.

In Mexico, Staton (2006) evaluates the Supreme Court decisions made on the merits based on media coverage and the selective promotion of case results by the Supreme Court. That is, the selective promotion of cases may generate media attention when it is useful and at the same time guarantee accurate communication of

---

[21] Declaration of the legality of the administrative act.

jurisprudence when the media covers a decision. This analysis of selective promotion of case results contrasts to Vanberg's (2001) study, which does not incorporate as a variable the selective promotion of cases when examining the decisions of the German Constitutional Court. One of the implications of Vanberg's model, according to Staton (2006), is that the public is better able to oversee when the media covers a conflict. However, when there is no media coverage, "courts may be forced to strategically defer to political interests." The difference between the models of these two studies is that Vanberg's (2001) assumes that the public will be informed about inter branch conflicts as exogenous, whereas Staton's (2006) considers it as endogenous.

In Mexico, federal judges seem to have substantial freedom to decide cases for procedural grounds and several scholars have argued that they have employed these rules strategically (Rubio, Magaloni, and Jaime 1994, Staton 2006).

The study analyzes four independent variables, one individual and three contextual: 1) *length of service* (years served by a judge in a state administrative court), 2) *legislative majority* (coded 1 if the current governor's party obtained more than 50 percent of the seats in a state chamber of deputies, 0 otherwise), 3) *life tenure* (coded 1 if the regulations of a state allow judges to serve for life, 0 otherwise), and 4) *method of appointment* (coded 1 if the regulations of a state allow the governor to participate in judges' appointment, 0 otherwise). According to several judicial studies reviewed earlier, I also include in my analysis six individual control variables based on judges' background and attributes: *professional background, age of decision, law professor, graduate degree, years in judiciary,* and *gender*.

Methodological Approach

Because the dependent variable is binary, and the specific focus of this analysis is about the effects of individual (length of service) and contextual (legislative majority, life tenure, and method of appointment) variables on judge's decisions between six states from 2006 to 2008, I employ a multilevel logistic model, specifically, random intercept and coefficient models. The advantage of the multilevel technique is that it allows testing models that combine unit and group-level data: the unit-level data (judges' decisions) provides higher number of observations, and the use of group data allows knowing whether some of the variance in the judge's decision model is also explained by the difference between and within states in a period of time.

Preliminary Results

The hierarchical statistical analyses provide important findings. First, the negative relationship between judges' length of service and judges' decisions in favor of the executive is statistically significant when analyzing the dependent variable for all categories, as expected. In other words, judges who have served a higher number of years in a state administrative court are less likely to vote for the executive than those judges who have served for a lower number of years.[22] Second, state contextual variables make a difference in judicial judgments as well. Legislative majority, life tenure and method of appointment appear to explain the context under which the relationship between years of service and judges' decisions takes place in the majority of the state administrative courts analyzed.[23] Chiapas seems not to always behave as expected. The reason may be that judges' length of service in Chiapas is much longer than the other non-life tenure states, which may hinder the influence of this contextual variable on the relationship between length of service and vote in favor of the executive.

In the analysis, which only considers votes for the executive on the merits, neither individual variables (key predictor and control variables) nor contextual variables are significant at conventional levels. These unexpected results may reflect the fact that it is easier for a judge to decide in favor or against the executive for procedural reasons than on the merits, because, in the former, judges' behavior is not as observed as in the latter. Notice that decisions on the merits provide judge's discussion of substance and consequently people and media can easily monitor and evaluate his reasoning and how he applies laws and regulations.

In sum, the findings in these six states provide preliminary evidence that the individual and contextual variables examined make a difference when explaining judicial independence.

Conclusion

This chapter has reviewed some of the recent literature that examines judicial independence in the United States, Latin America, and Mexico, and presented five hypotheses. It highlights some of the main explanatory variables of this strand of research: political competition, length of tenure, and method of appointment. This work proposes an integrated approach to analyze judicial behavior, which involves evaluating both institutional and individual variables. The point is to examine struc-

---

[22] Specifically, the results from a multilevel logit analysis shows that judges who have one more year of service are 6.5 percent less likely to vote in favor of the executive (in *all the categories* dependent variable).

[23] I found statistical support for the contextual hypotheses in *all the categories* dependent variable:
1. The state effect of *legislative majority* was weaker on the relationship between length of service and vote for the executive.
2. The state effect of *life tenure* was stronger on the relationship between length of service and vote for the executive.
3. The state effect of *method of appointment* was weaker on the relationship between length of service and vote for the executive.

tural variables gauged with aggregate data (courts), as well as judges' characteristics with individual data.

The chapter has also offered descriptive evidence that there is considerable variation in the structural and individual variables of the state administrative courts and judges in Mexico. There are significant differences between states in terms of the incidence of divided government, turnover of the executive party, the method of selecting judges, and the length of their tenure. States such as Chiapas, Jalisco, and Morelos are examples of individual differences between judges in terms of seniority and other control variables such as gender, professional, and academic experience. The cases of Aguascalientes, Baja California Sur, Chiapas, and Hidalgo show contrasts between and within the state administrative courts. Therefore, these data provide a valuable source from which to start evaluating both microlevel and macrolevel patterns to better understand judges' choices and judicial outcomes.

The preliminary quantitative evidence seems to show that not only the individual variable (judge's length of service), but the contextual variables (legislative majority, life tenure, and method of appointment) have a significant effect by constraining the individual relationship between judges' length of service and their decisions in the state administrative courts.

The preliminary analysis of this chapter may help to better understand the nested influences of judicial independence in subnational courts not only in Mexico but in other emergent democracies and identify new avenues for research. The first is to extend the quantitative analysis to the rest of the states that are part of the judicial branch and collect data to increase the time frame to test the turnover hypothesis with survival models.

Another avenue is to complement the study with a qualitative examination based on elite interviews. Face to face interviews with scholars, judges, public officials, and attorneys would provide additional information of the incentives' system by which a judge might favor the state executive government. Theoretical expectations that are not considered in the quantitative analysis may arise from these conversations.

To explore judicial independence and their sources in subnational administrative courts in the Mexican democracy represents a substantial contribution to justice, especially if the ultimate goal is to ensure fair and impartial justice in new democracies.

References

Beer, Caroline C. 2006. "Judicial Performance and the Rule of Law in the Mexican States." *Latin American Politics and Society* 48(3):33-61.

Benesh, Sara C. and Malia Reddick. 2002. "Overruled: An Event History Analysis of Lower Court Reaction to Supreme Court Alterations of Precedent." *Journal of Politics* 64(2):534-50.

Berkowitz, Daniel, and Karen Clay, 2006. "The Effect of Judicial Independence on Courts: Evidence from the American States," *Journal of Legal Studies* 35:399-440.

Bill Chávez, Rebecca. 2004. *The Rule of Law in Nascent Democracies: Judicial Politics in Argentina.* Stanford: Stanford University Press.

____. 2007. "The Appointment and Removal Process for Judges in Argentina: The Role of Judicial Councils and Impeachment Juries in Promoting Judicial Independence." *Latin American Politics & Society* 49(2):33-58.

Bill Chávez, Rebecca, John Ferejohn, and Barry Weingast. 2011. "A Theory of the Politically Independent Judiciary: A Comparative Study of the United States and Argentina." In *Courts in Latin America*, eds. Gretchen Helmke and Julio Ríos-Figueroa. New York: Cambridge University Press.

Bonneau, Chris, Thomas Hammond, Forrest Maltzman, and Paul Wahlbeck 2007. "Agenda Control, the Median Justice, and the Majority Opinion on the U.S. Supreme Court." *American Journal of Political Science.* 51(4): 890–905.

Boyd, Christina L., Lee Epstein, and Andrew D. Martin. 2010. "Untangling the Causal Effects of Sex on Judging." *American Journal of Political Science* 54(2):389-411.

Brace, Paul, and Kellie Sims Butler. 2001. "New Perspectives for the Comparative Study of the Judiciary: The State Supreme Court Project." *The Justice System Journal* 22(3):243-58.

Brace, Paul, and Melinda G. Hall. 2001. "'Haves' Versus 'Have-Nots' in State Supreme Courts: Allocating Docket Space and Wins in Power Asymmetric Cases." *Law and Society Review* 35(2):393-418.

____.1995. "Studying Courts Comparatively: The View from the American States." *Political Research Quarterly* 48(1):5-29.

____.1993. "Integrated Models of Judicial Dissent." *Journal of Politics* 55(4):914-35.

____.1990. "Neo-institutionalism and Dissent in State Supreme Courts." *Journal of Politics* 54.

Brace, Paul, Melinda Gann Hall, and Laura Langer. 1999. "Judicial Choice and the Politics of Abortion: Institutions, Context, and the Autonomy of Courts." *Albany Law Review* 62(4):1265-130.

Brinks, Daniel M. 2011. "Faithful Servants of the Regime: The Brazilian Constitutional Court under the 1988 Constitution." In *Courts in Latin America*, eds.

Gretchen Helmke and Julio Ríos-Figueroa. New York: Cambridge University Press.

Brudney, James J., Sara Schiavoni, and Deborah J. Merrit (1999). "Judicial Hostility toward Labor Unions? Applying the Social Background Model to a Celebrated Concern." Ohio State Law Journal 60(5):1675:1772.

Cameron, Charles, Jeffrey Segal, and Donald Songer. 2000. "Strategic Auditing in a Political Hierarchy: An Informational Model of the Supreme Court's Certiorari Decisions." *American Political Science Review* 94:101-16.

Carroll, Royce, and Lydia Tiede. 2011. "Judicial Behavior on The Chilean Constitutional Tribunal." *Journal of Empirical Legal Studies* 8(4):856-77.

Castagnola Andrea and Aníbal Pérez-Liñán. 2011. "Bolivia: The Rise (and Fall) of Judicial Review." In *Courts in Latin America*, eds. Gretchen Helmke and Julio Ríos-Figueroa. New York: Cambridge University Press.

Cohen, Alma, Alon Klement, and Zvika Neeman. 2015. "Judicial Decision Making: A Dynamic Reputation Approach." *Journal of Legal Studies* 44(1): 133-159.

Cooter, Robert, and Tom Ginsburg. 1996. "Comparative Judicial Discretion: An Empirical Test of Economic Models." *International Review of Law and Economics* 16:295-313.

Davis, Sue, Susan Haire, and Donald R. Songer. 1993-1994. "Voting Behavior and Gender on the U.S. Courts of Appeals." *Judicature* 77(3):129-33.

Domingo, Pilar. 2000. "Judicial Independence: The Politics of the Supreme Court in Mexico" *Journal of Latin American Studies* 32 (3):705-35.

Dorff, Robert H. and Saul Brenner 1992. "Conformity Voting on the United States Supreme Court." Journal of Politics 54(3):762:75.

Epstein, Lee, Valerie Hoekstra, Jeffrey A. Segal, and Harold J. Spaeth.1998. "Do Political Preferences Change? A Longitudinal Study of U.S. Supreme Court Justices." *Journal of Politics* 60(3):801-18.

Epstein, Lee, and Jack Knight. 1998. *The Choices Justices Make*. Washington, D.C.: Congressional Quarterly Press.

Eskridge, William N., Jr. 1991a. "Overriding Supreme Court Statutory Interpretation Decisions." *Yale Law Journal* 101(331-450).

____.1991b. "Reneging on History? Playing the Court/Congress/President Civil Rights Game." *California Law Review* 79:613-84.

Feld, Lars P., and Stefan Voigt.2004. "Making Judges Independent-Some Proposals Regarding the Judiciary."CESifo Working Paper Series1260.CESifo Group Munich.

____. 2003. "Economic Growth and Judicial Independence: Cross Country Evidence Using a New Set of Indicators", *European Journal of Political Economy*, vol. 19, 497- 527.

Ferejohn, J., F. Rosenbluth, and C. R. Shipan. 2007. "Comparative judicial politics." In C. Boix and S. Stokes, eds. *Oxford Handbook of Comparative Politics*. Oxford: Oxford University Press.

Ferejohn, John. 1999. "Independent Judges, Dependent Judiciary: Explaining Judicial Independence." *Southern California Law Review* 72:353-84.

Fierro, Ana Elena, and Adriana García. 2010. "Design Matters: The Case of Mexican Administrative Courts." Working Paper 48. CIDE.

García Adriana, and Alejandro Tello.2010. "Salaries, Appellate Jurisdiction and Judges' Performance: The Case of Mexican Administrative Courts." CIDE Working Paper Series 49. CIDE Law School.

Garoupa, Nuno, and Matthews Jud. 2014. "Strategic Delegation, Discretion, and Deference: Explaining the Comparative Law of Administrative Review." *American Journal of Comparative Law* 62(1):1-34.

Garoupa Nuno, Marian Gili, and Fernando Gómez-Pomar.2012. "Political Influence and Career Judges: An Empirical Analysis of Administrative Review by the Spanish Supreme Court." *Journal of Empirical Legal Studies* 9(4):795-826.

Gely, Rafael and Pablo T. Spiller. 1990. "A Rational Choice Theory of Supreme Court Statutory Decisions with Applications to the State Farm and Grove City Cases." *Journal of Law, Economics, and Organization* 6(2):263-300.

George, Tracey E.2001. "Court Fixing." *Arizona Law Review* 43:9-62.

Gibson, James L., and Gregory A. Caldeira. 2003. "Defenders of Democracy? Legitimacy, Popular Acceptance, and the South African Constitutional Court." *Journal of Politics* 65:1-30.

Gibson, James L., Gregory A. Caldeira, and Vanessa A. Baird. 1998. "On the Legitimacy of National High Courts." *American Political Science Review* 92:343-59.

Gryski, Gerard, Eleanor C. Main, and William J. Dixon. 1986. "Models of State High Court Decision Making in Sex Discrimination Cases." *Journal of Politics* 48(1):143-55.

Gretchen Helmke and Mitchell Sanders. 2006. "Modeling Motivations: A New Technique for Inferring Judicial Goals." *Journal of Politics* 68(4): 867-878.

Hall, Melinda G. 1992. "Electoral Politics and Strategic Voting in State Supreme Courts." *Journal of Politics* 54: 427-46.

___. 1987. "Constituent Influence in State Supreme Courts: Conceptual Notes and a Case Study." *Journal of Politics* 49: 1117-1124.

Hall, Melinda Gann, and Paul Brace. 1992. "Toward an Integrated Model of Judicial Voting Behavior." *American Politics Quarterly* 20 (April): 147-168.

Hall, Melinda G., and Paul Brace. 1989. "Order in the Courts: A Neoinstitutional Approach to Consensus in State Supreme Courts." *Western Political Quarterly*. 42(3):391-407.

Hart, Henry Jr. 1959-1960. "The Supreme Court 1958 Term. Foreword: The Time Chart of the Justices." *Harvard Law Review* 73:84-239.

Hansford, Thomas G., and James F. Spriggs II. 2006. *The Politics of Precedent on the U.S. Supreme Court*. Princeton and Oxford: Princeton University Press.

Helmke, Gretchen. 2003. "Checks and Balances by Other Means: Strategic Defection and the 'Re-Reelection' Controversy in Argentina." *Comparative Politics* 35(2):213-28.

____.2002. "The Logic of Strategic Defection: Court-Executive Relations in Argentina Under Dictatorship and Democracy. *American Political Science Review* 96(2):291-304.

____. 1998. "Toward a Formal Theory of an Informal Institution: Insecure Tenure and Judicial Independence in Argentina, 1976-1995." Paper presented at the 1998 Annual Conference of the Scientific Study of Judicial Politics.

Herron, Erik S., and Kirk A. Randazzo.2003. "The Relationship Between Independence and Judicial Review in Post-Communist Courts." *Journal of Politics* 65(2):422-38.

Howard, J.Woodford. 1968. "On the Fluidity of Judicial Choice." *American Political Science Review* 62(1):43-56.

Iaryczower, Matías, Pablo T. Spiller, and Mariano Tommasi. 2002. "Judicial Independence in Unstable Environments: Argentina 1935-1998." *American Journal of Political Science* 46(4):669-716.

Ingram, Matthew C. 2009. "Crafting Courts in New Democracies: The Politics of Subnational Judicial Reform in Brazil and Mexico." Doctoral Dissertation. University of New Mexico.

Diana Kapiszewski. 2012. *High Courts and Economic Governance in Argentina and Brazil*. New York: Cambridge University Press.

Kapiszewski, Diana and Matthew M. Taylor. 2008. "Doing Courts Justice? Studying Judicial Politics in Latin America" *Perspectives on Politics* 6 (4):741-67.

Johnson, Charles. 1987. "Law, Politics, and Judicial Decision Making: Lower Federal Court Uses of Supreme Court Decisions." *Law and Society Review* 21(2):325-40.

Lane, Lord Baron. 1985. "Judicial Independence and the Increasing Executive Role in Judicial Administration. "In *Judicial Independence: The Contemporary Debate*, eds. Shimon Shetreet and Jules Deschenes. Dordrecht:Martinus Nijhoff.

Leiras, Marcelo, Guadalupe Tuñón, and Agustina Giraudy. 2015. "Who Wants an Independent Court? Political Competition and Supreme Court Autonomy in the Argentine Provinces (1984-2008)." *The Journal of Politics* 77(1):175-187.

Lindquist, Stephanie A. 2017. "Judicial Activism and States Supreme Courts." *Stanford Law and Policy Review* 28(1): 61-108.

López-Ayllón Sergio, Adriana García, and Ana Elena Fierro. 2015. "A Comparative-Empirical Analysis of Administrative Courts in Mexico." *Mexican Law Review* 2(2): 3-34.

López-Ayllón, Sergio, Ana Elena Fierro Ferráez, Adriana García García, and Dirk Zavala Rubach. 2010. *Diagnóstico del Funcionamiento del Sistema de Impartición de Justicia en Materia Administrativa a Nivel Nacional.*

Luke, Douglas A. 2004. *Multilevel Modeling.* California: Sage Publications.

Magaloni, Beatriz. 2008. "Enforcing the Autocratic Political Order and the Role of Courts: The Case of Mexico." In *Rule by Law: The Politics of Courts in Authoritarian Regimes*, eds. Tom Ginsburg and Tamir Moustafa. New York: Cambridge University Press.

___. 2003. "Authoritarianism, Democracy, and the Supreme Court: Horizontal Exchange and the Rule of Law in Mexico." In *Democratic Accountability in Latin America*, eds. Scott Mainwaring and Christopher Welna. Oxford: Oxford University Press.

McNollgast. 2006. "Conditions for Judicial Independence." *Journal of Contemporary Legal Issues* 15(1):105–27.

___. 1995. "Politics and the Courts: A Positive theory of Judicial Doctrine and the Rule of Law." *Southern California Law Review* 68: 1631-83.

Mena-Mora, Amalia. 2013. "Judicial Independence of State Administrative Courts in Mexico." Ph.D. diss. University of Houston.

Moreno, Erika, Brian F. Crisp, and Mathew Soberg Shugart. 2003. "The Accountability Deficit in Latin America." In *Democratic Accountability in Latin America*, eds. Scott Mainwaring and Christopher Welna. Oxford: Oxford University Press.

Peresie, Jennifer L.2005. "Female Judges Matter: Gender and Collegial Decision-making in the Federal Appellate Courts." *Yale Law Journal* 114(7):1759-90.

Prott, Lyndek V. 1973-1976. "Avoiding a Decision on the Merits in the International Court of Justice." *Sidney Law Review* 7:433—51.

Ramseyer, J. Mark and Eric B. Rasmusen. 2001. "Why Are Japanese Judges So Conservative in Politically Charged Cases?" *American Political Science Review* 95 (2):331-44.

Ríos, Julio, and Luis Fernando Soto. 2017. "Instituciones judiciales subnacionales en México, 1917-2014." *Colombia Internacional* (91): 243-263. DOI: https://dx.doi.org/10.7440/colombiaint91.2017.08

Ríos-Figueroa, Julio and Jeffrey K. Staton 2008. "Unpacking the Rule of Law: A Review of Judicial Independence Measures." CIDE Working Paper Series 21. Department of Political Science.

Ríos-Figueroa, Julio. 2007. "Fragmentation of Power and the Emergence of an Effective Judiciary in Mexico, 1994-2002." *Latin American Politics and Society* 49(1):31-57.

Ríos-Figueroa, Julio, and Matthew M. Taylor. 2006. "Institutional Determinants of the Judicialisation of Policy in Brazil and Mexico." *Journal of Latin American Studies* 38(4):739-66.

Rodríguez-Raga. Juan Carlos. 2011. "Strategic Deference in the Colombian Constitutional Court, 1992-2006." In *Courts in Latin America*, eds. Gretchen Helmke and Julio Ríos-Figueroa. New York: Cambridge University Press.

Rubio, Luis, Beatriz Magaloni, and Edna Jaime. 1994. *A la Puerta de la Ley: El Estado de Derecho en México*. México, D.F.: Cal y Arena.

Scribner, Druscilla. 2011. "Courts, Power, and Rights in Argentina and Chile." In *Courts in Latin America*, eds. Gretchen Helmke and Julio Ríos-Figueroa. New York: Cambridge University Press.

Segal Jeffrey. 1997. "Separation of Powers Game in the Positive Theory of Congress and Courts." *American Political Science Review* 91:28-44.

Shapiro, Martin. 1981. *Courts: A Comparative Political Analysis*. Chicago: University of Chicago Press.

Shetreet, Shimon. 1985. "Judicial Independence: New Conceptual Dimensions and Contemporary Challenges." In *Judicial Independence: The Contemporary Debate*, eds. Shimon Shetreet and Jules Deschenes. Dordrecht:Martinus Nijhoff.

Sisk, Gregory C., Michael Heise, and Andrew P. Morriss. 1998. "Charting the Influences on the Judicial Mind: An Empirical Study of Judicial Reasoning." *NYU Law Review* 73(5):1377-1500.

Staton, Jeffrey K. 2006. "Constitutional Review and the Selective Promotion of Case Results." *American Journal of Political Science* 50(1):98-112.

Tiede, Lydia, Robert Carp, and Kenneth L. Manning. 2010. "Judicial Attributes and Sentencing-Deviation Cases: Do Sex, Race, and Politics Matter?" *The Justice System Journal* 31(3):249-72.

Tiede, Lydia Brashear. 2006. "Judicial Independence: Often Cited, Rarely Understood." *Journal of Contemporary Legal Studies* 15:129-61.

Ulmer, Jeffrey T., and Brian Johnson. 2004. "Sentencing in Context: A Multilevel Analysis." *Criminology* 42(1):137-77.

Ulmer, Sidney S. 1973. "Social Background as an Indicator to the Votes of Supreme Court Justices in Criminal Cases: 1947-1956 Terms." *American Journal of Political Science* 17(3):622-30.

____. 1970. "Dissent Behavior and The Social Background of Supreme Court Justices." *The Journal of Politics* 32(3):580-98.

Vanberg, Georg. 2001. "Legislative-Judicial Relations: A Game Theoretic Approach to Constitutional Review." *American Journal of Political Science* 45(2):346-61.

VonDoepp, Peter. 2006. "Politics and Judicial Assertiveness in Emerging Democracies: High Court Behavior in Malawi and Zambia." *Political Research Quarterly* 59(3):389-99.

Villarreal Corrales, Lucinda. 2007. "La Justicia Administrativa, el Proceso Administrativo y la Responsabilidad Patrimonial del Estado." In *Justicia Administra-*

tiva, eds. Germán Cisneros Farías, Jorge Fernández Ruiz Miguel, and Alejandro López Olvera. México, D.F: UNAM.

Whittington, Keith E. 2003. "Legislative Sanctions and the Strategic Environment of Judicial Review." *I.CON: The International Journal of Constitutional Law* 1(3):446-74.

CHAPTER 14

WHAT SHOULD IMMIGRATION LAW BECOME?[1]

By Geoffrey A. Hoffman[2] [3]

Introduction

This essay addresses the future of immigration law. What should it become in light of the recent drastic changes that have impacted the field?[4] The question's importance at this time cannot be overstated or ignored. Given the state of affairs

---

[1] Note that the present essay was written in 2020 before the changes to immigration policy were implemented by the current Biden administration,

[2] Clinical Professor and Director, University of Houston Law Center Immigration Clinic. The author would like to thank Ira J. Kurzban, Michael A. Olivas, Jessica L. Roberts, R. Parker Sheffy, Shoba S. Wadhia. The views expressed are the author's and not necessarily those of the University of Houston. Institution for identification only.

[3] This essay is dedicated to Professor Steve Zamora. It is on a subject he would have enjoyed discussing and debating. Steve and Lois warmly welcomed my family and me when I first came to Houston, in 2009, to head the immigration clinic at the University of Houston Law Center. I remember him hosting an outing at an Indian restaurant and having us over for a pool party at his home. I frequently saw Steve riding his bike, exercising, laughing, and engaging with everyone he met. We saw each other frequently at the Rec Center, where he encouraged me to swim more. He visited my office to drop in and give me "chotskies" from his frequent trips. His great expertise in international law and NAFTA meant that his interests overlapped with mine, and as a result we discussed the latest developments in immigration law and policy. I enjoyed my talks with Steve. I will always miss him and his kind demeanor, warm personality, and welcoming spirit!

[4] This is a prescriptive project. Given that fact, I want to state my presuppositions up front. In these introductory remarks, I make clear that immigration law in my view should be premised on humanitarian considerations and, most especially, the protection of vulnerable populations and people. It is important to note this is not antithetical to those who wish to protect American citizens and foreign nationals alike. The current state of affairs, I argue, shows that the current paradigm has been based on anything but this premise of protection and indeed has been overshadowed by a more nationalistic, isolationist, and restrictionist agenda premised on bigotry and ignorance. While there can be genuine debate about the appropriate starting point for any field, it should not be objectionable or even controversial that protecting others should be an important goal in any legal regime.

before the 2020 election, and in view of the devastating events for immigrants of the last several years, a re-evaluation of the entire field is in order.[5] While the aspirations of any field may be underappreciated or undervalued, immigration law's goals and objectives are often mired in confusion and undertheorized. Given the complex and confusing nature of the immigration laws, disparate and conflicting interests have taken hold.[6] Practicing lawyers, those most conversant with immigration law's problems, and by extension the possible solutions, find it difficult to effectuate change. In recent years, when change happens it may be through piecemeal litigation and not comprehensive reform. While important and even essential to progress, the changes brought about by individual or class-based representation many times are incremental, not to mention subject to reversal by the U.S. Attorney General and courts.[7]

---

[5] In addition to the political turmoil of the last several years, it bears mentioning that the COVID-19 pandemic itself has exacerbated the problems with the immigration system, leading to monumental changes to immigration adjudication and enforcement. Those changes include the recent travel bans, bars to entry, and further restrictions on asylum-seekers. These changes have been used as a pretext under the guise of "protecting" public health. *See, e.g.,* "The Impact of COVID-19 on Noncitizens and Across the U.S. Immigration System," available at: https://www.americanimmigrationcouncil.org/research/impact-covid-19-us-immigration-system, and Immigration-related Executive Actions During the COVID-19 Pandemic, available at: https://immigrationforum.org/article/immigration-related-executive-actions-during-the-covid-19-pandemic/. *See also* for a good overview of the changes under the Trump Administration, Migration Policy Institute, "Dismantling and Reconstructing the U.S. Immigration System: A Catalog of Changes under the Trump Presidency" available at: https://www.migrationpolicy.org/research/us-immigration-system-changes-trump-presidency. In addition, Professor Lucas Gutentag at Stanford Law School is currently working on a project with his students relating to cataloguing the various changes.

[6] The complexity and Byzantine nature of immigration law is widely recognized. *See, e.g.,* Mežo v. Holder, 615 F.3d 616, 621 (6th Cir. 2010); Padilla v. Kentucky, 559 U.S. 356 (2010) ("Immigration law can be complex, and it is a legal specialty of its own."); Scialabba v. Cuellar de Osorio, 573 U.S. 41, 75 (2014) ("Confronted with a self-contradictory, ambiguous provision in a complex statutory scheme"). Cf., a discussion in a recent co-authored article, R. Parker Sheffy & Geoffrey A. Hoffman, "Appellate Exceptionalism?" U. of Illinois L.R. Online (2020) at https://illinoislawreview.org/online/appellate-exceptionalism/.

[7] The Attorney General has exercised enormous powers under the current administration to literally shape immigration adjudication by certifying certain cases directly to himself. Although this power existed under previous administrations it was rarely used. *See, e.g.,* Matter of Compean, 24 I&N Dec. 710 (A.G. 2009) ("Matter of Compean I"), that decision was vacated less than six months later in Matter of Compean, 25 I&N Dec. 1 (A.G. 2009). In a series of recent cases, the Trump administration's Attorney General certified cases to himself, overturning previous precedents on a number of different issues. *See, e.g., Matter of A-B-,* 27 I&N Dec. 316 (A.G. 2018); *Matter of L-E-A,* 27 I&N Dec. 581 (A.G. 2019); *Matter of Castro-Tum,* 27 I&N Dec. 271 (A.G. 2018).

Practitioners had to contend with oppressive rules and restrictions issued by the former administration on a daily basis.[8] Others, such as anti-immigrant factions and the voices of those then in power, attempted to obfuscate policy, as a strategy to prevent what they perceive as an expansion of immigrants' rights and forms of relief. A cadre of immigration restrictionists or those who support a reduction in immigration have greatly altered the field.[9] Their changes have been wide-ranging, surgically targeted, as well as subtle, and not-so-subtle. Unfortunately and sadly, the measures were effective in eroding legal protections for immigrants.[10]

The first step in beginning to think about a recalibration of the field is to reframe the overarching "paradigm"—the framework of a discipline or field—and to determine the assumptions of that paradigm. The underlying presuppositions of a field must necessarily prefigure and pervade any ensuing analysis, as well as the perception of the field as a whole. The paradigm must encompass those on the "inside," i.e. those whose lives are impacted and altered by immigration law, as well as those on the "outside," those bystanders who may never have represented an immigrant but often voice their intense feelings and thoughts upon which scaffold their arguments.

---

[8] For a good discussion of changes needed with respect to employment-based immigration and a good proposal surrounding the caps on various categories of visas, *see* the Durbin-Leahy bill, entitled the *Resolving Extended Limbo for Immigrant Employees and Families (RELIEF) Act,* that would help keep American families together by classifying spouses and children of LPRs as immediate relatives and exempting derivative beneficiaries of employment-based petitions from annual green card limits, protect "aging out" children who qualify for LPR status based on a parent's immigration petition, and lift country caps. *See* this website for further information on the bill: https://www.durbin.senate.gov/newsroom/press-releases/durbin-leahy-introduce-new-legislation-to-increase-number-of-green-cards-available-eliminating-the-backlog.

[9] *See* https://www.nytimes.com/2020/04/24/us/politics/coronavirus-trump-immigration-stephen-miller.html; https://www.newyorker.com/magazine/2020/03/02/how-stephen-miller-manipulates-donald-trump-to-further-his-immigration-obsession; *see also* https:// americasvoice.org/blog/kris-kobach/.

[10] I am thinking here of very specific changes dealing with the rules, procedures, and policies affecting areas of immigration law, such as asylum, H1-B visas, student visas, DACA, etc. versus the system-wide more passive and less-publicized changes that have impeded the ability of immigrants to obtain relief, such as the executive orders of President Trump in the early days of his presidency fundamentally changing the priorities of immigration enforcement, the over 1 million court backlog, the delays in adjudications by USCIS, such as relating to U visas, Special Immigrant Juveniles, naturalizations, and more. In some cases, litigation has been (partially) successful in meeting head-on these changes, such as with developments in the *Flores* litigation, recent COVID-related student visa rules, and an injunction against the public charge rule. *See, e.g.,* https://www.clearinghouse.net/detailResource.php?id=2116; https://news.harvard.edu/gazette/story/2020/07/u-s-abruptly-drops-new-visa-rules-for-international-students/; and https://www.law.com/newyorklawjournal/2020/08/04/2nd-circuit-blocks-trump-administrations-public-charge-rule-but-limits-scope-of-injunction/?slreturn=20200724124748.

If we cannot agree, as a polity, as a people, as a society, and as political parties, on an initial starting point, then we are talking past one another. In such a case, as we have seen for decades, no progress, no legislative change is possible.

In thinking about a starting place for immigration law, one can and should begin with human rights, ensuring international norms and protections are met, providing the most vulnerable urgent protections, as well as responding to humanitarian crises and concerns. In addition, and also simultaneously, immigration law can be viewed as a facet or subset of national security law, administrative law, or constitutional law, and at times all these sources acting at once upon a particular immigrant or set of immigrants. Other areas also of course impact the field.[11] In reality, all these paradigms pull immigration law in different directions simultaneously, sometimes with disastrous consequences. That immigration law is pulled in so many directions is not surprising, as many fields of law can be similarly described.[12] However, the number of passionate voices doing the pulling is so great in this field that it feels special, with frustrating and frequent revisions to existing restrictions.

---

[11] Increasingly, for example, environmental law and the rights of environmental refugees will need to be factored into the equation. *See, e.g.*, http://www.globalization101.org/environmental-refugees/#:~:text=%E2%80%9CEnvironmental%20refugee%E2%80%9D%2C%20a%20term,seriously%20effects%20the%20quality%20of; https://www.un.org/sustainabledevelopment/blog/2019/06/lets-talk-about-climate-migrants-not-climate-refugees/. Other areas such as health law, public benefits law, technology, artificial intelligence, machine learning and many other issues will shape the future of immigration-related relief and enforcement. *See* Stuart Anderson, *Top Legal Scholar: Trump Team Radically Restricted Immigration,* FORBES (Sept. 8, 2020) (https://www.forbes.com/sites/stuartanderson/2020/09/08/top-legal-scholar-trump-team-radically-restricted-immigration/#7c80d08a764c) (discussing among other things the connections between immigration law and other fields).

[12] Fundamental tensions of course exist within every legal field. Consider proponents of law and order and their goals of punishment, retribution, deterrence, or restoration within the criminal law versus the goals of rehabilitation and effectuating a positive reentry into society for those convicted of crimes. Consider intellectual property law which aims to protect inventors' and authors' rights while at the same time encouraging innovation, experimentation and progress. Consider the tension in evidence law, which must balance the goal of seeking the truth through discovery and at trial against privacy rights and protecting claimants from overly burdensome or requests for production. All these fields have found ways to proscribe rules that allow for an agreeable balance. Immigration law has yet to find its solution or balance.

Another way of asking the same question is: *How do we begin to explore imaginative possibilities at fixing the broken immigration system?*[13] In determining what immigration law should become, this essay examines the possibilities inspired by three distinct "buckets" or categories: (1) Supreme Court decisions; (2) proposed and, thus far, unsuccessful legislation, including the immigration plan of President Joe Biden; and (3) remedies and approaches inspired by other fields of law. These buckets are chosen with the recognition that we will not be changing the system in a vacuum. In other words, the system, although broken has a history, numerous processes, and practices which will not be and cannot be changed instantaneously. We should build on the good and throw out the bad.

Moreover, former President Trump and his administration's efforts at restricting immigration also must be considered. What the former president did in terms of changing the immigration system is unprecedented. It is therefore obvious that any template for future change and for remedying current injustices requires grappling

---

[13] Given the pandemic, the Trump administration exacerbated the situation, seizing on the opportunity to formulate breathtaking new policies and restrictions. Instead of expanding protections administratively, such as through DACA and other policies during the Obama era, including the use of prosecutorial discretion, the Trump administration worked incessantly in an opposite direction. It used its powers to reinterpret and re-implement the immigration laws in a variety of new ways. The resulting morass includes a series of largely unlawful asylum-related bans, executive orders banning certain groups of lawful immigrants, resting on the success of President Trump's previous travel ban (in 2018), as well as other disastrous policies such as for international students studying under F-1 visas as mentioned above. Some of these attempts have been struck down, or stayed. Some have been upheld. However, most recently the Supreme Court in the DACA rescission case of June 18, 2020, through the opinion of Chief Justice Roberts issued a very clear admonition that the government must consider legitimate "reliance interests" of vulnerable immigrants. The Supreme Court announced unequivocally that the agency acted "arbitrarily and capriciously" in attempting to rescind DACA. It has been forced to go back to the drawing board and start anew. Even the census has been politicized. *See* Why a Shorter Census Timeline Hurts Immigrant Communities. President Trump signed an order in July 2020 stating that he would not count undocumented immigrants as "persons" in the census data he presents to Congress. Several lawsuits were filed challenging the legality of the policy. Recently, the government was the subject of a motion seeking a contempt ruling in the *Casa De Maryland v. DHS* DACA remand case, 8:17-cv-02942-RWT (D. Md.), given the way it has handled the aftermath of the DACA rescission decision from the Supreme Court, because it has failed, among other things, to allow for new applications despite the striking down of the DHS' rescission attempt in 2017. *See* https://www.caribbeannational weekly.com/legal-news/court-may-hold-trump-administration-in-contempt-for-failing-to-process-new-daca-applications/. In a class action, in federal district court, dealing with special immigrants, the court held the government in civil contempt recently, *see J.L. v. Lee Francis Cissna* (5:18-cv-04914) (N.D. Calif.); civil contempt order is available at: https://www.justsecurity.org/wp-content/uploads/2020/02/ImmigrationOrder-Granting-contemptagainstgovt officials.pdf.

with and remedying the many obstacles to immigration, as well as the restrictions to adjudicatory review over immigration decisions of the Trump administration.[14] That said, we must also not make the mistake of working solely at a project of piecemeal "fixes" concerning the changes brought about by the Trump administration, but instead (in my opinion) we should begin anew with a more robust conception of what we are trying to achieve: the protection of others, by effectuating humanitarian relief and considerations.

One further consideration before moving to categories as sources for change, as they inform our thinking about immigration law's future. During the COVID-19 pandemic, immigration law took a backseat to the enormous public health "emergency powers" of the president. While using public health as a justification for enacting restrictions is not unprecedented, the ways that President Trump used the pandemic as a pretext for furthering political ends should not go unnoticed. For example, virtually all asylum seekers were blocked at the border under the pretext of "protecting" Americans from the pandemic. Student visa holders would have been forced to leave the country if their schools had transitioned to on-line classes, despite a previous policy allowing them to stay. The new policy was fortunately partially abandoned due to the effective use of litigation by Harvard and MIT, in federal district court.[15] Other attempts to politicize and weaponize the immigration system can be found in the widespread delays in naturalization, as well as immigration court backlog both of which have been well-documented.

Finding Sources for Change in Supreme Court and Other Court Cases

Although the history of immigration law has reflected blatant racism and prejudice, the Supreme Court cases can be scoured for effective ideas underpinning

---

[14] Professor Lucas Gutentag at Stanford started a project with his students cataloguing the changes from the Trump administration. *See also* MPI Report, available at https://www.migrationpolicy.org/research/us-immigration-system-changes-trump-presidency.

[15] For the complaint, *see* https://www.harvard.edu/sites/default/files/content/sevp_filing.pdf; *see also*, https://www.nytimes.com/2020/07/08/us/harvard-mit-trump-ice-students.html; https://www.thecrimson.com/article/2020/7/15/harvard-mit-ice-lawsuit-student-declarations/; a settlement was reached in July 2020. For a discussion of the lawsuit and the settlement, see the following: https://arstechnica.com/tech-policy/2020/07/trump-admin-caves-to-harvard-and-mit-wont-deport-online-only-students/

immigration reform.[16] Courts have come a long way (some cases—to be sure—prove the opposite) since the grandfather of all immigration cases, "The Chinese Exclusion Act" case, *Chae Chan Ping v. United States*, 130 U.S. 581 (1889). There, the justices expressly relied upon racial stereotypes toward Asian immigrants and their families. The Supreme Court at that time enunciated a "Plenary Power Doctrine" held by Congress over immigration. The court upheld and justified the exclusion of Mr. Ping, despite the fact that when he left the United States he had a valid re-entry permit, and it was not until he was outside the country that the laws were changed to prohibit his return. With an expansive reading of Congressional power over immigration regulation and enforcement, the source of the immigration power is grounded in national sovereignty. There was not one specific plenary power over all immigration which was identified in the Constitution.

The plenary power doctrine is an *implied* power derived from the structure of the Constitution as opposed to explicitly stated. It can be cobbled together from the working together of different Constitutional provisions, such as, the "Take Care" Clause, which requires the president to obey and enforce all laws, though the president retains some discretion in interpreting the laws and determining how to enforce them;[17] several possible other sources have emerged in subsequent case law, e.g., the Naturalization Clause, the interstate Commerce Clause, as well as the necessary and proper clause and the spending power. These all have been implicated as a possible source of Congressional power over immigration.[18]

It is essential to reiterate the amorphous nature of the immigration power. The fact that it does rely on so many different sources strengthens the argument for latitude and leeway with regard to the implementation and administration of Congressional mandates. This is most relevant when considering the well-entrenched exis-

---

[16] Examples of the racist history in the United States are found in a number of immigration programs, laws and cases before the Supreme Court. *See, e.g.*, https://network advocates.org/recommittoracialjustice/impact/; *See also* https://www.youtube.com/watch?v =6yiQAmgI5s4. For a recent discussion of equal protection and immigration, *see* Justice Sotomayor's opinion concurring in part, and dissenting in part in the 2020 DACA rescission decision, in *Regents v. DHS*, available at: https://www.supremecourt.gov/opinions/19pdf/18-587_5ifl.pdf.

For further discussion about issues surrounding racial injustice and immigration law, *see* the scholarship of Gabriel Jackson Chin, at https://papers.ssrn.com/sol3/cf_dev/Abs ByAuth.cfm?per_id=201529. Also the scholarship of Frank H. Wu, at https:// papers.ssrn.com/sol3/cf_dev/AbsByAuth.cfm?per_id=1704741, among others.

[17] *See* Congressional Research Service (CRS) Report, "The Take Care Clause and Executive Discretion in the Enforcement of Law," at https://fas.org/sgp/crs/misc/R43708.pdf.

[18] *See* discussion of plenary power and its sources in the leading immigration law textbook, STEPHEN LEGOMSKY & DAVID THRONSON, IMMIGRATION AND REFUGEE LAW AND POLICY (University Casebook Series) (7th ed. 2019).

tence of "prosecutorial discretion" as a tool for enforcement policy.[19]Another important consideration is that the plenary power over immigration resides with Congress and not the president. Although Congress has delegated authority to the federal executive to act through its agencies to implement the immigration laws, the executive is not unlimited and is bound by Constitutional constraints in the ways it administers its power.[20]

The June 2020, Deferred Action for Childhood Arrivals (DACA) rescission decision, *Regents of the University of California v. DHS*,[21] is instructive. There, the Supreme Court was not considering the former president's ability to promulgate DACA in the first instance (that was not the issue before the court), but rather the ability of the president to rescind the enforcement policy. Chief Justice Roberts in his decision self-consciously refused to opine on the "soundness" of DACA but had much to say about the lack of a reasoned consideration for rescission. Most essentially, the court found that the Department of Homeland Security (DHS) acted "arbitrarily and capriciously" in failing, among other things, to consider the "legitimate reliance interests" of those currently with DACA. At the same time, Chief Justice Roberts gave us a roadmap forward for a possible future for DACA.[22]

Prosecutorial discretion is a facet of several Supreme Court cases, in addition to the recent DACA rescission case. Other connections to important cases in the history of immigration jurisprudence include *Arizona v. United States* 567 U.S. 387 (2012). That case considered a state's ability to enforce immigration law. The court largely rejected the state's power to do so with a limited exception for a state officer asking about one's immigration status during a lawful stop. In their discussion, the justices relied on the fact that the federal government has the ability to exercise pros-

---

[19] For an excellent recitation of the history of prosecutorial discretion, see the letter to President Trump relating to the legality of DACA by law professors and scholars, with principal author as Professor Shoba S. Wadhia, Penn State Law School, available at: https://pennstatelaw.psu.edu/sites/default/files/documents/pdfs/Immigrants/LawProfLetter-DACAFinal8.13.pdf.

[20] A lot has been written about a lack of rights for immigrants at the border and also while residing abroad. *See, e.g.,* https://www.aclu.org/other/constitution-100-mile-border-zone. While it is true that immigrants may have significantly fewer rights outside the United States, i.e. extraterritorially, it must be emphasized that in the interior of the United States where most enforcement action is being directed, immigrants enjoy many rights, including under the 5th Amendment due process and other protections, the 4th Amendment and 1st Amendment. While their claims may be limited by case law, *see Reno v. American-Arab Anti-Discrimination Committee*, and other cases, it is incorrect to allege that immigrants lack Constitutional rights.

[21] *DHS v. Regents of the University of California,* 140 S. Ct. 1891 (2020).

[22] *See, e.g.,* my recent online article in Yale J. on Regulation Notice & Comment blog which is available here: https://www.yalejreg.com/nc/chief-justice-roberts-gave-us-a-roadmap-for-a-way-forward-on-daca-by-geoffrey-a-hoffman/.

ecutorial discretion. The prime example of a population most deserving of this discretion, according to the justices, are students. As expressly pointed out by Justice Kennedy, in *Arizona v. United States*, removal from the United States "is a civil, not criminal, matter . . . [and a] principal feature of the removal system is the broad discretion exercised by immigration officials."[23] The majority also recognized that the ability to enforce immigration law without federal oversight could lead to the "unnecessary harassment of some aliens (for instance, a veteran, college student, or someone assisting with a criminal investigation) whom federal officials determine should not be removed."[24]

Another obvious connection to prosecutorial discretion that exists toward those who may have valid future claims for relief is *Plyler v. Doe*, 457 U.S. 202 (1982), where the Supreme Court struck down the State of Texas' attempt to withhold funds from local school districts for children who were not "legally admitted" into the United States, while authorizing the districts to deny enrollment to such children. The high court found such a state statute violated the Equal Protection Clause of the Fourteenth Amendment.

Plyler has had the most impact in recognizing the fact that undocumented immigrant children may be subject to deportation but also may have relief. There are possibilities for remedies in the Immigration and Nationality Act (INA), whether through future claims for potential relief, or possibilities for future lawful re-entry to the United States with an approved waiver, if required. As noted by the court, to bar this vulnerable population from an education necessarily leads to the creation of an underclass, a "shadow population," without rights and lacking voting power. As eloquently stated by former Justice Sandra Day O'Connor, "The existence of such an underclass presents most difficult problems for a Nation that prides itself on adherence to principles of equality under law."[25]

Even in the so-called "Travel Ban," also known by plaintiffs and advocates as the "Muslim Ban" case, *Trump v. Hawaii*, where the Supreme Court found the statute, INA 212(f), 8 USC 1182(f), "exuded deference," the court still recognized that the president's power was *not* unlimited.[26] In that case, as in the DACA rescission case, *Regents v. DHS*, the government argued for no judicial review over its decision to restrict immigration, or in the case of *Regents*, no review of the discretionary decision to rescind a previous president's immigration enforcement policy. The Supreme Court rejected an unlimited right or "plenary power" over immigration asserted by the executive. It was most clearly rejected in *Regents*, where Chief Justice Roberts relied on the basic presumption of judicial review under the Adminis-

---

[23] *Arizona v. United States*, 567 U.S. 387 (2012).

[24] *Id.*

[25] *Plyler v. Doe*, 457 U.S. 202 (1982).

[26] 138 S. Ct. 2392 (2018).

trative Procedure Act (APA) and noted that the APA "requires agencies to engage in 'reasoned decision making.'"[27]

Trump v. Hawaii also is noteworthy in that the Supreme Court did not reject outright immigrants' right to seek redress under the First Amendment. Although their claim was ultimately rejected, the Chief Justice's opinion considered it and applied the very deferential "rational basis" test for the Establishment Clause, finding in the end that the present administration's rationales of national security were sufficient and he did not credit plaintiffs' allegations that the president was motivated by religious animus toward Islam. The government has argued that immigrants were not even entitled to raise such a First Amendment claim, a position rejected in prior cases such as *Kleindienst v. Mandel*, 408 U. S. 753 (1972).

As a leading immigration textbook has described it, the "plenary power" doctrine has been "chipped away" at by subsequent cases in the Supreme Court.[28] Although admittedly there are many "bad" cases that have attempted to stifle the rights of immigrants, such as the recent *Thuraissigiam v. DHS*,[29] limiting habeas jurisdiction over expedited removal proceedings under INA 242(e), 8 USC 1252(e), as one example, there are also numerous other "good" cases. Those include cases standing for due process, equal protection, as well as (at least in the interior of the United States) the fact that immigrants enjoy an array of Constitutional protections, even if those protections are routinely violated where no legal counsel is around to ensure their client's rights are protected.

As far back as the 1880s, there have been Constitutional cases finding in favor of immigrants' rights. In the famous *Yick Wo v. Hopkins*,[30] in 1886, the high court applied the Equal Protection Clause of the Fourteenth Amendment to strike down a racially discriminatory law. The city of San Francisco enacted a rule making it illegal to operate a laundry in a wooden building without a permit. The problem there was that most laundries were operated by Chinese people but only one permit was granted to any Chinese owner. Virtually all non-Chinese applicants however were afforded a permit. Justice Matthews wrote, "the guarantees of protection contained in the Fourteenth Amendment to the Constitution extend to all persons within the territorial jurisdiction of the United States, without regard to differences of race, of color, or of nationality."

That racially discriminatory laws cannot be allowed to stand, whether enacted through local ordinance, state legislatures or Congress itself should not be in question. Indeed, in 1983, the Supreme Court made clear in *INS v. Chadha*, "Congress can exercise its plenary power over immigration only if it 'does not offend some

---

[27] *Regents v. DHS*, J. Roberts Op., at 9.

[28] *See supra* note 18.

[29] *See* https://www.supremecourt.gov/opinions/19pdf/19-161_g314.pdf.

[30] 118 U.S. 356 (1886).

other constitutional restriction.'"[31] However, the ability of former President Trump to make questionable policy (and some would say, overtly racial, religious or national origin-based discriminatory policy) suggests the Supreme Court has been unable to reign in abuses of presidential power. Indeed, as we saw in *Trump v. Hawaii*, the government's arguments and assertions of national security were enough to circumvent the clear mandate in the INA itself against non-discrimination.[32]

The first obvious needed reform, therefore, is the addition to the Immigration and Nationality Act of a provision that *expands* and clarifies that the nondiscrimination provision in section 1152(a) applies to all decisions, policies, and practices, by the government surrounding immigration, and not just the allocation of "immigrant visas." Indeed, Chief Justice Roberts observed in *Trump v. Hawaii*, "Had Congress instead intended in §1152(a)(1)(A) to constrain the President's power to determine who may enter the country, it could easily have chosen language directed to that end."[33] This seems like a much needed and possibly important legal foothold for future litigation attempting to prevent former President Trump (and future presidents) from violating immigrants' rights.

Other protections for immigrants' due process rights should not be ignored or forgotten. The rules surrounding access to legal counsel, use of language interpreters in cases where the immigrant does not understand English, or even where their native language is not Spanish (such as for some indigenous respondents, who may speak Quiche or other language) may be honored more in the breach than in the observation.[34] Nevertheless, it is important to work into future immigration reform efforts provisions that strongly support such rights to ensure due process is satisfied. Also, the future provisions must have "teeth" or punishment imposed against agencies where immigrants' rights are violated. Now, the statute and attendant regulations have a weak privilege to counsel of one's choice, as well as interpreters, but no

---

[31] *Id.*, 462 U.S. 919, 941 (1983); *see also Almeida-Sanchez v. U.S.*, 413 U.S. 266, 272 (1973) (no act of Congress can authorize a violation of the Constitution); *Wong Wing v. U.S.*, 163 U.S. 228 (1896) (Congress cannot criminally penalize aliens without due process).

[32] *See* 8 U.S.C. §1152(a)(1)(A) (providing that "no person shall receive any preference or priority or be discriminated against in the issuance of an *immigrant visa* because of the person's race, sex, nationality, place of birth, or place of residence") (emphasis added).

[33] 138 S. Ct. 2392, 2415 (2018).

[34] I have personally observed particular immigration courts struggle and fail to accommodate such respondents in a manner consistent with due process and fairness, often with disastrous results for the respondents.

consequences are built-in to the rules and regulations ensure that these important rights are protected.[35]

Finding Sources for Change in Proposed Legislation

Just as the current cases relating to immigration law have a lot to offer in terms of providing insight for a better possible future for immigration law, another important source of ideas for change is found in past efforts at proposed legislation. A full recitation of the multitude of legislative proposals surrounding comprehensive immigration reform could take volumes. In addition, President Biden has his own agenda and proposal. Suffice it to say, the recent (partially successful but ultimately failed) attempt at such comprehensive reform, S.744, was in 2013, and had many commendable aspects.[36] Many of these could be replicated to lead to a reorientation or reframing of current immigration law. Although the bill represented a "merits-based" attempt at reform and was soundly criticized as failing to protect family-based immigration, many provisions in the bill, such as the inclusion of a DREAM Act-type mechanism, protections for asylees, victims, and others should be highlighted and replicated.

For example, S.744, entitled the "Border Security, Economic Opportunity, and Immigration Modernization Act," provided for a mandated right to appointed counsel at no cost to the immigrant for certain "vulnerable" populations. In the version ultimately passed by the Senate, the bill would have authorized counsel in certain circumstances, provided immigration judges the opportunity to make more discretionary, case-by-case determinations relating to removal, and streamlined the asylum program. The bill contained the following language providing for counsel (at the expense of the government "if necessary") in the following cases: (1) "to represent an alien in a removal proceeding who has been determined . . . to be an unaccompanied alien child," (2) "is incompetent to represent himself or herself due to a serious mental disability . . . [under] section 3(1) of the Americans with Disabilities Act of 1990 (42 U.S.C. 12102(1)), or (3) "is considered particularly vulnerable when

---

[35] *See* 8 USC §1362 (Right to counsel. "In any removal proceedings before an immigration judge and in any appeal proceedings before the Attorney General from any such removal proceedings, the person concerned shall have the privilege of being represented (at no expense to the Government by such counsel, authorized to practice in such proceedings, as he shall choose"). In addition, there is a regulation that provides that "any person acting as an interpreter in a hearing shall swear or affirm to interpret and translate accurately, unless the interpreter is an employee of the United States Government, in which event no such oath or affirmation shall be required." 8 CFR 1003.22; *see also* 8 CFR 1240.5.

[36] Another example pointed out by Prof. Shoba S. Wadhia is S. 2611, titled, the "Comprehensive Immigration Reform Act" that passed the full Senate in 2006. Prof. Wadhia, now at Penn State, worked during her time on the Hill significantly on this bill.

compared to other aliens in removal proceedings, such that the appointment of counsel is necessary to help ensure fair resolution and efficient adjudication of the proceedings." S.744, section 3502.[37]

Advocates have raised legitimate questions as to whether this provision goes far enough. It does not. The laudatory goal of providing representation to "vulnerable" populations of immigrants leaves many questions unanswered. Potentially, the definition of "vulnerable" could be interpreted so narrowly as to limit the class of noncitizens so that almost no one could qualify for appointed counsel. Even if one were to fall within one of the three categories, there is the problem of navigating the panoply of immigration remedies on one's own without counsel that any indigent respondent faces. As argued by Matt Adams in his insightful article, "Advancing the 'Right' to Counsel in Removal Proceedings," although the majority of respondents are unrepresented, the current "morass" of immigration laws is difficult to navigate even for those fortunate enough to be able to afford counsel or receive pro bono assistance. Mr. Adams makes compelling arguments for a right to counsel in the immigration context based on analogous Supreme Court cases such as *Lassiter v. Department of Social Services*, 452 U.S. 18 (1981), *Mathews v. Eldridge*, 424 U.S. 319 (1976), among others.

Another important aspect of S.744 was its attempt at revising certain current asylum procedures. The one-year bar to asylum was rescinded. In addition, the bill eliminated some of the barriers to family reunification and authorized USCIS officers to conduct full asylum interviews at or near the border and also to grant such cases. Such a streamlining of the process is a much-needed development, as we now face historic backlogs both in terms of asylum affirmative applications as well as in the immigration courts. In addition, the president may designate certain persecuted groups with common characteristics refugee status. Unfortunately, since 2013, there has been a variety of attacks on the asylum process perpetrated by the former administration, including but not limited to the Migrant Protection Protocols (MPP) which would have asylum seekers await their hearings in Mexico, despite passing a credible or reasonable fear interview, as well as 3rd country transit bar, not to mention the bars to entry placed on virtually all asylum seekers under the pretext of COVID-19.

Other aspects of S.744 would have strengthened protections for those suffering from workplace abuse and human trafficking. The provisions in this regard of the bill expanded the availability of the U-visa for certain victims of crime to those who were victims of workplace abuse, slavery, or other serious violations of workers' rights. The bill also would increase penalties for violations of human smuggling and includes a pilot program to combat child trafficking. The bill also provided for protections for J-visa recipients (exchange visitors), as well mandated disclosures to

---

[37] This section is entitled, "IMPROVING IMMIGRATION COURT EFFICIENCY AND REDUCING COSTS BY INCREASING ACCESS TO LEGAL INFORMATION."

immigrants of the terms of their employment, bonds, and audits of exchange programs. All of these are much-needed reforms. They evidence a step in the right direction to reorienting the immigration laws to protect the people coming to the United States, enable and effectuate enforcement against those who prey on immigrants, and allow for greater efficiencies and streamlining of the immigration process.

In evaluating proposals for legislation, it is important also to be aware of President Biden's "Plan for Securing our Values as a Nation of Immigrants."[38] In his plan, several points deserve special recognition. The first is the "reassertion" of America's commitment to asylum-seekers and refugees. The plan provides for a surge of asylum officers who will effectively review the cases of recent border crossers and keep cases with positive credible fear determination within the Asylum Division of USCIS, so they are not referred directly to immigration judges. This provision mirrors the proposal in the 2013 bill and also is important to prevent duplication and inefficiencies in the system, streamline the process, and deal with the over 1 million case backlog we currently are experiencing. Importantly, the Biden plan "restores asylum eligibility to domestic violence survivors," as a way to take on head-on the partisan ruling of former Attorney General Sessions which put roadblocks in the way of such claims through his partisan decision in *Matter of A-B-*, 27 I&N Dec. 316 (A.G. 2018), among other cases.

In addition, Biden's plan proposes to double the number of immigration judges, court staff and interpreters.[39] He also proposes ending "for-profit" immigration detention centers and increasing the number of refugees we welcome into the United States.[40] The plan also includes much needed expansion of the rights of farmworkers and domestic workers, although the details are unclear. In addition, the plan expands protections for undocumented immigrants reporting labor violations, as well as increasing the availability of visas for domestic violence survivors.[41]

The "Biden-Sanders Unity Task Force Recommendations"[42] is another document that outlines changes to immigration law and puts us on a path to a more humane, efficient, and rights-oriented immigration system. It is a 110-page document that does not solely relate to immigration, but a number of sections relate directly to our question, "What Should Immigration Law Become?" and address head-on how the law should be changed to deal with specific restrictions and policies perpetrated by the former president's administration. In a section entitled, "Undoing the Harms of the Trump Administration and Righting the Wrongs," the

---

[38] https://joebiden.com/immigration/

[39] *Id.*

[40] *Id.*

[41] *Id.*

[42] https://joebiden.com/wp-content/uploads/2020/08/UNITY-TASK-FORCE-RECOMM-ENDATIONS.pdf.

document proposes several beneficial steps in the right direction. To highlight just a few, the document proposes to maintain Deferred Action for Childhood Arrivals (DACA), and support the American Dream and Promise Act, as well as streamline the process for DACA recipients.

It is beyond the scope of this article to discuss every proposal in the Biden-Sanders plan, but it is important to emphasize that the plan seeks to formulate reform measures in terms that address the changes perpetrated upon the field by the Trump administration. This approach is needed because wholesale change in the future will not be possible if it does not recognize ways to undo and redo the Trump administration's immigration restrictionist goals and polices, for example, the Border Wall, the Travel Ban, asylum, and refugee restrictions, curtailing lawful immigration, use of the Attorney General to restrict claims, to name just a few.

The Biden-Sanders plan also is most important in its recognition of the need for an Article I immigration court, as opposed to the then-current state of affairs, which provides that immigration judges are merely Department of Justice employees and thus under the direct control of the Attorney General. The Federal Bar Association, for example, has endorsed transitioning to an Article I immigration court, arguing that establishing such a court would "substitute for an overstaffed, bloated bureaucracy a new structure, modeled on the federal courts, their case management expertise, and their demonstrated record for delivering prompt, effective justice. Cheaper, faster, better justice is possible through an Article I immigration court."[43] Other groups, such as AILA, the ABA, and even the immigration judges' union have been staunch proponents for such a change.[44]

Finding Sources for Change in Other Fields of Law

A final category to utilize in thinking about much-needed changes to immigration law concerns other fields, their remedies, and procedures. Any discussion of other fields must be connected to the introductory remarks at the beginning of this article regarding the "paradigms" or inherent starting presuppositions behind any conception of immigration law. The most obvious development has been the focus on administrative law, and specifically the APA, as a source of remedies against federal agencies that act arbitrarily and capriciously, contrary to law, in violation of the Constitution or in other ways that violate the rights of immigrants. Other sources of law also have special relevance to immigration law. Criminal law and its procedures and protections may be instrumental in providing important ideas for arguments to

---

[43] https://www.fedbar.org/government-relations/policy-priorities/article-i-immigration-court/.

[44] https://www.aila.org/infonet/aila-calls-for-independent-immigration-courts; https://www.americanbar.org/advocacy/governmental_legislative_work/publications/washingtonletter/july_2019_washington_letter/immigration_article_0719/.

expand immigrants' rights. Scholars have made connections between the two fields and argued for a greater applicability of criminal protections on the theory the consequences of deportation and detention are just as (and may even be more) severe than a criminal sentence.[45] In addition, the U.S.' international legal obligations are already binding under certain circumstances on immigration agencies, especially as they relate to asylum and other persecution-based forms of relief. The recent emphasis upon ("turn to") administrative law in cases such as *Regents v. DHS* and *Trump v. Hawaii*, among others, should be noted. Some would argue that immigration law itself is a sub-species of administrative law, but such an assumption is inherently misleading. It may be surprising that immigration judges are not Administrative Law Judges (ALJs) and thus not subject to the APA, at least according to case law rejecting such claims. In addition, as noted by several immigration scholars, the government has used Administrative Law principles to attempt to shield agency decisions from judicial review, under cases such as *Chevron U.S.A., Inc. v. Natural Resources Defense Council, Inc.*, 468 U.S. 837 (1984), and *Heckler v. Chaney*, 470 U.S. 821 (1985)[46] Justice Kennedy in a recent case about cancellation of removal and the definition of a Notice to Appear, in *Pereira v. Sessions*, 138 S. Ct. 2105 (2018), wrote a powerful concurrence which focused on *Chevron*. In that concurring opinion, he lambasted certain circuit courts of appeals for their "unreflexive deference" and predicted in the future that *Chevron* would be "reconsidered."[47]

Perhaps the most effective way to expand rights of immigrants is based on the insight, as recognized in a variety of Supreme Court cases, that deportation certainly may be viewed by some as a "punishment" or even banishment from the United States, and with dire consequences for many of the immigrants involved, including in some cases death, injury and/or family separation. As the high court noted in the Sixth Amendment right to effective counsel case, *Padilla v. Kentucky*, "We have long recognized that deportation is a particularly severe "penalty," . . . but it is not, in a strict sense, a criminal sanction."[48] Although removal proceedings are civil in nature,

---

[45] *See e.g.*, the excellent scholarship of Alina Das, Christopher Lasch, César Cuauhtémoc García Hernández, Bill Ong Hing, Hiroshi Motomura, Daniel Morales (at the University of Houston Law Center), among others, such as Matt Adams, at the Northwest Immigrant Rights Project.

[46] https://www.nyulawreview.org/issues/volume-90-number-1/unshackling-habeas-review/; *see also* https://www.yalejreg.com/nc/immigration-law-is-torn-between-administrative-law-and-criminal-law-by-michael-kagan/#:~:text=Notice%20%26%20Comment-,Immigration%20Law%20Is%20Torn%20Between%20Administrative,Criminal%20Law%2C%20by%20Michael%20Kagan&text=Share%3A&text=As%20Alina%20Das%20has%20observed,immigration%20decisions%20from%20judicial%20scrutiny.

[47] *Pereira v. Sessions*, 138 S. Ct. 2105, 2120-21 (2018).

[48] *See* Padilla v. Kentucky, *supra* note 6, (citing Fong Yue Ting v. United States, 149 U. S. 698, 740 (1893)).

as the court recognized in the Fourth amendment suppression case, *INS v. Lopez-Mendoza*, deportation is nevertheless "intimately related" to the criminal process.[49] Other ways that criminal law protections can be applied to immigration proceedings, include scholars' efforts to apply "cruel and unusual punishment" Eighth Amendment protections, strengthen the minimal due process Fifth Amendment right to counsel which currently exists by making it more analogous to the stronger Sixth Amendment right, and recognize that the use of civil detention is a deprivation of "life, liberty and property" as those terms are conceived of in the Fifth and Fourteenth Amendments.

Finally, the use of immigration law as a source is at once essential to immigrants and deeply problematic. We have as a landmark precedent, *The Paquete Habana*, 175 U.S. 677 (1900), standing for the proposition that "international law is part of our law, and must be ascertained and administered by the courts of justice of appropriate jurisdiction as often as questions of right depending upon it are duly presented for their determination."[50] In that case the Supreme Court opined that "resort must be had to the customs and usages of civilized nations," even in those circumstances where there is no treaty in effect.[51] But the effect of *The Paquete Habana*, is tempered by other considerations, one of which is that some justices have been reluctant to apply international legal norms to actors in the United States. In addition, not all treaties are "self-executing," but require the passage of implementing domestic legislation, such as the Refugee Act of 1980, for the international legal norms to be applied as a remedy in the United States.

That the United States is not a member of several important treaties related to migration and migrants' rights need not hamper efforts at legislative reform, if (as is possible) Congress takes note of these protections and incorporates them into proposed legislation. For example, the United States is not a signatory of a 1990 treaty, the International Convention on the Protection of the Rights of All Migrant Workers and Members of Their Families.[52] But this instrument contains many provisions which should be and can be incorporated into Comprehensive Immigration Reform. Other examples, include the Domestic Workers Convention (2011); as well as the Convention on the Elimination of All Forms of Discrimination against Women (1979).

The United States is a member of other important treaties that could be much better implemented in more effective and powerful ways by domestic legislation. Examples of this group include: the 2002 Optional Protocol to the Convention on the

---

[49] *Id.*, 468 U. S. 1032, 1038 (1984). *See also Padilla,* citing *Lopez v. Mendoza.*

[50] *Id.*

[51] *Id.*

[52] https://www.ohchr.org/EN/ProfessionalInterest/Pages/CMW.aspx.

Rights of the Child (U.S. is a state party); the 1987 U.N. Convention Against Torture ("CAT") (same); as well as the 1967 Protocols relating to the Status of Refugees (same). Other examples of important treaties that can be reviewed for further ideas about ways for protections would include: the 1969 International Convention on the Elimination of All Forms of Racial Discrimination (U.S. does not accept competence under Art. 14), and the 1976 International Covenant on Civil and Political Rights ("ICCPR", ratified by the United States but with a number of reservations).

Conclusion

This essay has discussed some ways the former administration has transformed the field of immigration law, and ways that these changes may be fixed (and reimagined) in a new administration. Necessarily, this is not an exhaustive study. This essay took as its starting point several of the most visible (and a few not so-visible) changes in the last few years. The legal landscape has been twisted in ways that attorneys and advocates could scarcely have recognized five or ten years ago. Some of the changes were anticipated. But the extent of the damage to immigrants' rights and protections has been so pervasive that it could not have been predicted.

Given my thesis *ab initio* that protection of others is the natural starting point, I offer the following proposal for a new system of adjudication in the immigration courts. Track 1 would encompass immigrants without any criminal records and would also be expanded to include no one with any "serious" misdemeanors (e.g., no violent crimes) nor felonies. In addition, there should be some kind of statute of limitations on older convictions to allow for cases where the convictions happened years ago and rehabilitation has been accomplished. Track 1 respondents would not be subject to detention. This "serious" misdemeanor language will be familiar to everyone from the DACA requirements. Because the vast majority of immigrants are law-abiding and good people, many can be prioritized for relief (and many will qualify for relief available and which we already have with universal competent counsel assisting them to present their claims).

Track 2, on the other hand, could encompass those with violent felonies and/or "serious" misdemeanor convictions. Again, DACA can be a guiding template here. Based on my experience, I believe only a small proportion of all immigrants would fall into Track 2. Therefore, scarce judicial resources will be preserved. By dividing the cases this way, justice will be better served. Right now, there is a de facto but poorly run and conceived of track 1 and track 2 "division of labor" driven by a mismanaged system of detained versus non-detained dockets.

By re-slicing the pie in a way that honors the fact that the vast majority of immigrants are good people, a better and more humane system can be implemented. This new proposed Track 1 and 2 division also should satisfy those who are concerned with the protection of society from violent offenders, as well as those concerned with the protection of immigrants' rights. It is not much different than the thrust behind the Obama-era prioritizing of enforcement in terms of ICE and other agencies. This proposal, however, would extend the prioritization (with a thumb on the scale for expediting relief for those "track 1" immigrants) to the immigration courts. Of course, whom to place in which track will be an important and difficult issue, as well as where to draw the line. But with clear rules we will gain a lot more traction over the 1 million-plus cases backlogged, at the moment, and find ourselves granting a lot more much-needed relief to many immigrants and their families.

I will end with a reference to one of my favorite books on legal analysis, Roberto Mangabeira Unger's pivotal work, *What Should Legal Analysis Become?* There, Professor Unger seeks to reconceptualize "legal analysis" as a whole, and thus his project is necessarily more abstract and generalized than the specific question before us.[53] But his approach is nevertheless instructive. When approaching what any particular field of law should become it is essential to recognize ways that "legal analysis" itself entrenches outmoded ways of thinking. In the present context, we must clarify what the goals of immigration law should be in a way that protects immigrants' rights and people's rights, writ large. They should be founded upon the core values toward immigrants that our nation holds dear: justice, fairness, weighing the equities, allowing for discretion in appropriate cases, family reunification, protecting asylees and other vulnerable groups, ensuring due process, equal protection under law, and allowing for the intelligent and humane use of prosecutorial discretion.

---

[53] Roberto M. Unger, What Should Legal Analysis Become (Verso 1996). As a starting point, Unger focuses our attention on the concept of "rationalizing legal analysis" which can be utilized and questioned to broaden our "institutional imagination" to create a more just and fair legal system. As he says, "[t]he initial step is to show how the original genius of contemporary law. . .has remained caught within the constraints imposed by institutional structures and superstitions." (p.2) Unravelling those "institutional structures and superstitions" therefore is key to determining how to proceed to revolutionize immigration law and address its deficiencies, current limitations, and inequities. What he says next about legal analysis generally could not be more apt to the plight of immigration law at the moment: "A summary statement of our troubling predicament . . . is that we no longer have available to us a credible account of structural change." (p.3). Unger champions a kind of "democratic experimentalism" (p.7) which is lacking from views about reform and efforts to change or reinterpret the law. For him, "[o]ne of the enemies of democratic experimentalism is institutional fetishism." (p.7). In many fields of law, I am sure we would find it easy to catalogue instances of such "institutional fetishism," but in immigration law especially lately we find ourselves more and more mired in such fetishism, resulting in the miasma of human rights abuses, due process violations, and a lack of concern for humanity.

CHAPTER 15

A COMPARATIVE ANALYSIS OF THE DISPUTE SETTLEMENT MECHANISMS OF NAFTA AND THE NEW USMCA

By Gabriel Cavazos Villanueva[1]

Dedicated to the memory of Stephen Zamora, my colleague, friend, and mentor.

Introduction

The purpose of this paper is to analyze some of the most salient differences and similarities of the dispute settlement mechanisms of the former North American Free Trade Agreement (NAFTA)[2] with respect to its replacement, the United States-Mexico-Canada Agreement (USMCA).[3]

When NAFTA came into force in 1994, it created a large integrated market that increased the levels of trade and investment in the region.[4] However, since his political campaign, President Donald J. Trump promised to renegotiate NAFTA or take

---

[1] Attorney-at-Law admitted to practice in Mexico. Master of Laws (Toronto, 1997), Master of Laws (Tulane, 2001), Doctor of Philosophy (Tulane, 2008).

[2] North American Free Trade Agreement, signed on December 17, 1992: published at the "Official Daily of the Federation" in Mexico on December 20. 1993; came into force on January I, 1994 (Hereinafter NAFTA).

[3] USMCA, Official Text available at: https://ustr.gov/trade-agreements/free-trade-agreements/united-states-mexico-canada-agreement/agreement-between.

[4] *See, i.e.*, an assessment of the NAFTA achievements made by the Mexican Secretariat of Economy, available at: https://www.gob.mx/se/prensa/tlcan-inicia-el-ano-26-de-su-entrada-en-vigor.

the United States out of the Agreement.[5] In this context, on July 17, 2017, the United States Trade Representative (USTR) released the "Summary of Objectives for the NAFTA Renegotiation," which contends *inter alia* that since NAFTA came into force ". . . trade deficits have exploded, thousands of factories have closed, and millions of Americans have found themselves stranded, no longer able to utilize the skills for which they had been trained. For years, politicians promising to renegotiate the deal gave American workers hope that they would stop the bleeding. But none followed up."[6]

An initial renegotiation concluded in a brand-new Agreement that replaced NAFTA, and which, in the words of President Trump ". . . is a great deal for all three countries, solves the many deficiencies and mistakes in NAFTA, greatly opens markets to our farmers and manufacturers, reduces trade barriers to the United States and will bring all three Great Nations together in competition with the rest of the world."[7] The USMCA was ratified by the legislative bodies of the three countries and finally came into force on July 1st, 2020.

The USMCA embodies an important paradigm towards a more unilateral and nationalist approach in international trade agreements. In the case of the United States, the Agreement is a representation of the "America First" international economic policy espoused by the Trump administration.[8] Although the USMCA is a three-party agreement, its negotiation was bilateral in nature, because the United States first reached a "preliminary agreement" with Mexico in August 2018 and then struck an agreement with Canada.[9]

Although the USMCA retains the three most important NAFTA dispute settlement mechanisms,[10] their preservation was subject to a permanent debate. In this context, it is important to mention that in contrast with NAFTA, the USMCA does not explicitly reference dispute resolution as an objective.[11]

This paper briefly analyzes some of the relevant provisions of Chapters 11, 19 and 20 of NAFTA, as compared to USMCA Chapters 10, 14 and 31. In the first section, the Investor-State dispute settlement mechanism of NAFTA Chapter 11 is ana-

---

[5] Summary of Objectives for the NAFTA Renegotiation, OFFICE OF THE US TRADE REPRESENTATIVE (July 17, 2017), https://ustr.gov/sites/default/files/files/Press/Releases/NAFTAObjectives.pdf at 2.

[6] *Id.*

[7] OFFICE OF THE US TRADE REPRESENTATIVE webpage, https://ustr.gov/usmca.

[8] Thomas J. Schoenbaum, *The Art of the Deal and North American Free Trade: Advantage for the United States?* 14 OHIO ST. BUS. L.J. 100, at 106, (2020).

[9] *Id.* at 102-103.

[10] The USMCA does not contain specific dispute settlement mechanisms for environmental and labor disputes as the ones provided by the NAFTA side agreements in these matters.

[11] *Cf.* NAFTA Article 102(1)(e) and the USMCA Preamble.

lyzed as compared with USMCA Chapter 14 and specifically Annex 14-B. A second part of this paper briefly compares the NAFTA Chapter 19 mechanism for the settlement of anti-dumping and countervailing duty (AD/CVD) disputes, with the USMCA relevant provisions of Chapter 10 on Trade Remedies. Finally, this article compares NAFTA Chapter 20 with its successor, the USMCA Chapter 31 as the general dispute settlement mechanism.

Investment Disputes

NAFTA Chapter 11 has been an important source of international investment law jurisprudence, specifically, Chapter 11-B that provided the so-called Investor-State Dispute Settlement mechanism (ISDS). In its substantive part, NAFTA Chapter 11 provided investors and their investments with protection against nationalization and expropriation, including actions "tantamount to expropriation" or indirect expropriation.[12] This Chapter also provided standards of investment protection such as national treatment,[13] and most-favored-nation treatment,[14] a guarantee of "fair and equitable treatment," and "full protection and security" for foreign direct investment (FDI), to the extent required under international law and protection against performance requirements.[15] If the standard of treatment afforded to the foreign investor is consistent with the requirements of customary international law, it must also be no less favorable than the standard of treatment afforded to host country nationals, if that standard exceeds the requirements of international law.[16]

NAFTA Chapter 11 reflected an ideological approach that assumed that FDI is essential for the development of capital-importing countries, and in this context, foreign investors deserved the maximum level of legal protection, especially in countries like Mexico with a "tradition" of nationalizations and expropriations throughout its 20th century history.[17] The NAFTA Chapter 11 ISDS mechanism was severely criticized by different stakeholders and non-governmental organizations. The critiques were mainly based on the fact that this mechanism did not provide a fair balance between legitimate local public policy interests and the interests of the foreign

---

[12] NAFTA, Article 1110.

[13] *Id.* Article 1102.

[14] *Id.* Article 1103.

[15] *Id.* Article 1105.

[16] *Cf.* NAFTA Articles 1101 and 1105. *Cited by* Gabriel Cavazos Villanueva and Luis F. Martínez Serna, *Private Parties in the NAFTA Dispute Settlement Mechanisms: The Mexican Experience*, 77 Tul. L. Rev., 1017, 1026-1027 (2002).

[17] *See generally*, Gabriel Cavazos Villanueva, *The Fair and Equitable Treatment Standard in International Investment Law: The Mexican Experience* (VDM Verlag DR. Müller- Särbrucken,2009) Chapter 2.

investors.[18] The modified ISDS mechanism under the USMCA apparently has considered these critiques, because it provides for a narrower interpretation of the various FDI protection standards, with a perceived wider capacity of the host-state to implement domestic regulations that, in the case of an arbitration, are not going to be necessarily deemed as violations to international investment law.

As has been stated, Chapter 11 was incorporated into NAFTA as an essential part of the Agreement mainly as a result of U.S. demands fearing future expropriations of American investments in Mexico. Paradoxically, an often-cited report suggests that under NAFTA Chapter 11, Canada has been sued forty-one times, resulting in payouts of more than $219 million and $95 million in legal costs. The frequency for suits against Canada was higher than either Mexico or the United States.[19] In the case of the United States, the Head of the USTR, Robert Lighthizer, basically stated that protecting American companies against the risks of investing abroad is effectively providing them with an unfair subsidy.[20] In this context, the opposition against ISDS under the USMCA came from both Canada and the United States, not from the Mexican negotiating team; not even when the then president-elect Andrés Manuel López Obrador team got involved in the final stages of the negotiation process.[21]

As a consequence of the above-mentioned factors, the most significant changes to dispute settlement under the USMCA are the withdrawal of Canada from ISDS,[22] and the expansion of the conditions precedent to submitting a claim for arbitration.[23] In sum, the USMCA eliminates Canada's use of investor-state dispute resolution, reduces the scope of the remaining provisions, and expands the range of institutions and rules under which an investor may submit a claim for arbitration.[24]

---

[18] *See i.e.*, PUBLIC CITIZEN, *More Information on Investor-State Dispute Settlement Mechanism*, https://www.citizen.org/article/more-information-on-investor-state-dispute-settlement/.

[19] *See* Canadian Centre for Policy Alternatives, Canadas Track Record under NAFTA Chapter 11 (2018), available at https://bit.ly/2PyohMm.

[20] *See* Phil Levy, *Critique Of NAFTA Provision Highlights Team Trump's Misconceptions On Investment Abroad,* FORBES (October 23, 2017), https://www.forbes.com/sites/phillevy/2017/10/23/should-team-trump-encourage-investment-in-mexico/#1bbd3a1a70b4.

[21] *See generally*, Alberto Nájar, *Cómo el "efecto AMLO" destrabó la difícil renegociación del TLCAN entre México y el gobierno de Trump*, BBC NEWS, available at: https://www.bbc.com/mundo/noticias-america-latina-45326897.

[22] *See generally* USMCA Annex 14-D, *Mexico-United States Investment Disputes*, which excludes Canada from the ISDS mechanism.

[23] *See generally* USMCA Annex 14.D.5: *Conditions and Limitations on Consent.*

[24] *See* USMCA Annex 14-D. 3(3) (d). "The claimant may submit a claim referred to in paragraph 1 under one of the following alternatives: (a) the ICSID Convention and the ICSID Rules of Procedure for Arbitration Proceedings provided that both the respondent and the

With respect to the scope of some of the essential provisions in USMCA Chapter 14, it is important to note that the normative content of the concept of minimum standard of treatment is more clearly defined under the USMCA than under NAFTA Chapter 11.[25] In this context, its application for the ISDS mechanism is narrower. In the case of expropriation, Annex 14-B specifies that "The determination of whether an action or series of actions by a Party, in a specific fact situation, constitutes an indirect expropriation, requires a case-by-case, fact-based inquiry. . . ." Moreover, "[n]on-discriminatory regulatory actions by a Party that are designed and applied to protect legitimate public welfare objectives, such as health, safety, and the environment, do not constitute indirect expropriations, except in rare circumstances."[26] Such a narrow definition would have probably resulted in a different outcome in NAFTA Chapter 11 cases such as *Metalclad*.[27]

The USMCA extends protection to those investments made under NAFTA, with the broader standards of the former Agreement. In this context, Annex 14-C defines "legacy investment" as "an investment of an investor of another Party in the territory of the Party established or acquired between January 1, 1994, and the date of termination of NAFTA 1994, and in existence on the date of entry into force of [the USMCA]." In this context, the USMCA recognizes that parties will have three years after the termination of NAFTA to bring legacy investment disputes under NAFTA

Party of the claimant are parties to the ICSID Convention; 24 (b) the ICSID Additional Facility Rules, provided that either the respondent or the Party of the claimant is a party to the ICSID Convention; (c) the UNCITRAL Arbitration Rules; or (d) if the claimant and respondent agree, any other arbitral institution or any other arbitration rules."

[25] *See* USMCA Article 14.6 1. "Each Party shall accord to covered investments treatment in accordance with customary international law, including fair and equitable treatment and full protection and security. 2. For greater certainty, paragraph 1 prescribes the customary international law minimum standard of treatment of aliens as the standard of treatment to be afforded to covered investments. The concepts of "fair and equitable treatment" and "full protection and security" do not require treatment in addition to or beyond that which is required by that standard, *and do not create additional substantive rights*. The obligations in paragraph 1 to provide: (a) "fair and equitable treatment" includes the obligation not to deny justice in criminal, civil, or administrative adjudicatory proceedings in accordance with the principle of due process embodied in the principal legal systems of the world; and (b) "full protection and security" requires each Party to provide the level of police protection required under customary international law. 3. A determination that there has been a breach of another provision of this Agreement, or of a separate international agreement, does not establish that there has been a breach of this Article. 4. For greater certainty, the mere fact that a Party takes or fails to take an action that may be inconsistent with an investor's expectations does not constitute a breach of this Article, even if there is loss or damage to the covered investment as a result." (Emphasis added).

[26] USMCA Annex 14-B.3 (b).

[27] *See generally*, Cavazos, *supra* note 17, at 100-109. Providing a detailed analysis of *Metalclad v. United Mexican States*, ICSID Case No. ARB (AF) /97/1.

Chapter 11. However, USMCA Annex 14-C provides that investors may not submit a dispute to arbitration as a legacy investment where the dispute qualifies as a "covered government contract."[28]

In contrast with NAFTA, the USMCA distinguishes between disputes arising from government contracts in "covered sectors" and those arising from the traditional breaches of duty. According to Annex 14-E, a covered sector includes activities in oil and natural gas, power generation services, telecommunications, transportation, and infrastructure. Disputes relating to a government contract in one of these sectors have specific requirements for submitting a claim to arbitration. In general, Annex 14-D provides that investors may submit a claim to arbitration where they have suffered a breach of the duties of national treatment, most-favored-nation treatment and direct expropriation.[29] However, these standards of investment protection do not apply to the establishment or acquisition of an investment and to cases of indirect expropriation.[30] As has been stated, indirect expropriation has a much narrower scope under the USMCA as compared with NAFTA, which includes indirect expropriation as a breach of duty. Nevertheless, neither NAFTA nor the USMCA specifically define indirect expropriation.

Annex 14-E of the USMCA contains specific provisions with respect to arbitrations related to "covered government contracts," i.e., those concerning the above-mentioned covered sectors. In this case, an investor does not have the limitations imposed by Annex 14-D. Therefore, "the claimant, on its own behalf, may submit to arbitration under Annex 14-D (Mexico-United States Investment Disputes) a claim: (i) that the respondent has breached *any obligation* under this Chapter."[31] The reference to *any obligation* means that an investor bringing a claim related to covered government contracts can make a claim that the host-country has breached an obligation to accord fair and equitable treatment or that it has made an indirect expropriation. Because many of the allegations in previous NAFTA Chapter 11 arbitrations were based on breaches to the minimum standard of treatment or indirect expropriations,[32] it seems that the purpose of this exception for covered government contracts is to limit the number of arbitrations to those related to the most "sensitive" sectors.

---

[28] USMCA Annex 14-C Footnote 21: "Mexico and the United States do not consent under paragraph 1 with respect to an investor of the other Party that is eligible to submit claims to arbitration under paragraph 2 of Annex 14-E (Mexico-United States Investment Disputes Related to Covered Government Contracts)."

[29] USMCA Annex 14-D.4.

[30] *Id.* Annex 14-D.3 (a) (i) (A) and (B).

[31] *Id.* Annex 14-E.2 (a) (i) (Emphasis added).

[32] *See generally* Cavazos, *supra* note 17, Chapter 3, for an analysis of the different cases involving Mexico as a disputing party.

One of the most salient differences of the USMCA with respect to NAFTA in ISDS is the requirement of exhaustion of domestic remedies. Under NAFTA, an investor must wait six months from the events which gave rise to the claim before submitting it to an arbitration. Also, investors who submit a claim to arbitration waive their right to initiate or continue their case before the relevant domestic tribunals.[33]

In contrast, the USMCA requires that investors first initiate a proceeding before a competent court or administrative tribunal of the respondent. Then, the investor must wait 30 months from when it first initiated the proceeding or for a final decision from a court of last resort of the respondent.[34] This provision reflects the change of paradigm mentioned in the introduction of this paper; a shift toward a more nationalist approach that emphasizes the respect of state sovereignty by affording an opportunity to redress disputes through domestic tribunals before commencing an international arbitration.

The USMCA requirement of exhaustion of local remedies is not absolute. Investors need not rely on domestic remedies in cases in which these remedies are "obviously futile or manifestly ineffective."[35] Of course, the burden of proof is for the investors. It is important to highlight that these restrictions do not apply for covered government contracts. Investors in the covered sectors need not exhaust local remedies before pursuing an arbitration.[36] Again, it seems that the USMCA creates an incentive for arbitration almost exclusively in those sectors deemed as the most important ones for geopolitical reasons.

Transparency requirements represent important changes in the USMCA. Article 14.D.8:2 provides that "[t]he tribunal shall conduct hearings open to the public and shall determine, in consultation with the disputing parties, the appropriate logistical arrangements." Also, "[t]he tribunal shall make appropriate arrangements to protect [protected] information from disclosure which may include closing the hearing for the duration of the discussion of that information." Given the nature of the investment arbitration cases, it was expected that transparency would be an important element in the USMCA, in contrast with the limited requirements in this respect under NAFTA.

Finally, other provisions that demonstrate the shift toward an approach that gives more control to governments in ISDS cases are the ones that regulate the role of the Free Trade Commission (FTC) in these cases. The FTC is the most important governing body of the USMCA as it was under NAFTA. For investment disputes, it has the authority to issue Notes of Interpretation of the relevant provisions which, at

---

[33] *See* NAFTA, Article 1121 (1) – (2).

[34] USMCA Annex 14-D, Art. 5.1(a)-(b).

[35] *Id*. Annex 14-D Art. 5.1(b) fn. 24.

[36] *Id*. Annex 14-E Art. 4(b) fn. 31.

the end of the day, are binding for the arbitral tribunals. USMCA Article 14.D.9:2 provides that "[a] decision of the [Free Trade] Commission on the interpretation of a provision of this Agreement under Article 30.2 (Functions of the Commission) shall be binding on a tribunal, and any decision or award issued by a tribunal must be consistent with that decision."

In the same context, another important provision is Article 14.D.7:12, which provides that "at the request of a disputing party, a tribunal shall, before issuing a decision or award on liability, transmit its proposed decision or award to the disputing parties. Within 60 days after the tribunal transmits its proposed decision or award, the disputing parties may submit written comments to the tribunal concerning any aspect of its proposed decision or award." Although the comments cannot be deemed as a formal "challenge" to the award, the arbitral tribunal shall consider such comments when it renders its final and conclusive award. This provision somehow gives more control to disputing parties over the outcome of the controversy, which is especially important for governments.

In sum, the USMCA Chapter 14 provides a more limited protection to foreign investments and investors than NAFTA. It represents a change of paradigm toward an ISDS mechanism that certainly reduces the alternatives of foreign investors to arbitration. Under the USMCA, there will be no more investment disputes between Canada and the USA. However, Mexican and Canadian investors will still have the option to recur to the Comprehensive and Progressive Agreement for Trans-Pacific Partnership (CPTPP) ISDS chapter to file disputes against each other.[37]

Trade Remedies

In contrast with the USMCA Chapter 14, the new Agreement preserves, almost intact in its Chapter 10, the NAFTA Chapter 19 dispute settlement regime for AD/CVD. Unlike NAFTA, the USMCA includes substantive provisions regarding Safeguards in this Chapter, but the dispute settlement mechanism in Section D applies exclusively for AD/CVD disputes.

This mechanism was a source of contention between the United States and Canada during USMCA negotiations,[38] as it was when Canada and United States started the negotiations that ultimately produced the U.S.-Canada Free Trade Agreement (FTA). When the FTA came into force, there were important arguments that supported the implementation of this innovative mechanism: Canada was unwilling to abide by what it perceived to be a biased and arbitrary administration of the U.S.

---

[37] *See generally*, Chapter 9 of the CPTPP, available at: https://ustr.gov/sites/default/files/TPP-Final-Text-Investment.pdf.

[38] Gabriel Cavazos Villanueva & Paola Monzón Cadena, *An Assessment of the Chapter 19 Dispute Settlement Mechanism in the Context of the NAFTA Renegotiation*, 33 MD. J. INT'L L. 106, 121 (2018).

trade remedy laws. The United States, on the other hand, refused to exempt Canada from the administration of those laws. This is the most important rationale to explain one of the most singular characteristics of this mechanism: in reviewing an AD/CVD measure, binational panels apply domestic law.[39]

Although the mechanism had been successfully applied under NAFTA and Mexico did not have any concern about its inclusion in the USMCA, it finally agreed with the U.S. to exclude it. But, thanks to Canada,[40] and as it happened during the FTA negotiations, the binational panel review mechanism "became the 'eleventh hour' stop-gap measure of compromise.[41] Therefore, the preservation of this dispute settlement regime represents an almost *sine qua non* requirement for Canada's acquiescence to the USMCA.

In general, as has been stated, Chapter 10 of the USMCA preserves the *sui generis* characteristics of NAFTA Chapter 19: The review is conducted by a Panel established *ad hoc*, i.e., it is not a standing supranational court but a group of five specialists in international trade from the Parties involved in the particular dispute (two from one Party and three from the other). In that sense, the system differs from third party arbitration. The Panels substitute for domestic judicial review of the final AD/CVD determinations made by the competent investigative authority of the importing Party. Chapter 10 of the USMCA does not establish a substantive body of AD/CVD law; rather the Panels must apply the unfair trade law of the Party that rendered the determination. In this context, the Binational Panels are international adjudicatory bodies of domestic law that apply "the importing Party's antidumping or countervailing duty law to the facts of a specific case."[42]

The Binational Panels apply a specific domestic standard of judicial review. They can also apply, in addition to the domestic AD/CVD law, relevant statutes, legislative history, regulations, administrative practice and judicial precedents of the importing Party. The procedure involves the participation of private parties, in contrast to the dispute settlement mechanisms of NAFTA Chapter 20, Chapter 30 of the USMCA or the Dispute Settlement Understanding of the World Trade Organization, which only allow the participation of governments. Any person, who would otherwise be entitled under the law of the importing Party to commence domestic procedures for judicial review of a final determination of the importing Party's authority,

---

[39] *Id*. at 108.

[40] Katie Simpson & John Paul Tasker. "*Yay!: How the Canadians Won the Argument that Opened the Door to a NAFTA Deal,*" CBC NEWS (Oct. 1, 2018), available at: https://www.cbc.ca/news/politics/tasker-nafta-tick-tock-nafta-1.4845904.

[41] Cavazos & Monzón, *supra* note 38, at 108; citing Barbara Bucholtz, *Sawing Off the Third Branch: Precluding Judicial Review of Antidumping and Countervailing Duty Assessments under Free Trade Agreements,* 19 MD. J. INT'L L. & TRADE 175, 179 (1995).

[42] *Id*. at 109.

can request a Panel review through the respective complainant's government. A Panel resolution does not provide a relief by itself; it may only uphold or remand an administrative authority's determination. In the case of a remand, the Investigating Authority shall render a new determination in accordance with a Panel's opinion. The Panels' decisions are binding on the parties involved with respect to the particular matter. However, their decisions do not give life to any sort of precedent, and their effects are not *erga omnes,* but only *inter partes,* and do not bind other Binational Panels or the domestic courts of the Parties.[43] A Panel's decision is not appealable to a domestic court. The only recourse is an Extraordinary Challenge Committee (ECC), which may be established either in cases where a Party argues that a Panel did not apply the appropriate standard of review or in cases of gross misconduct of a panelist. Under NAFTA, the use of ECC has been limited to some very controversial cases, however the challenges have not been successful.[44]

Unfortunately, due to the "last-minute" approval of Chapter 10 of the USMCA, the negotiation did not allow the possibility of improving the mechanism. This situation was due to the fact that, initially, the Office of the USTR established in its objectives simply "Eliminate the Chapter 19 dispute settlement mechanism," without stating why or with what they planned to substitute it.[45]

At least three elements that represent perceived shortcomings of the dispute settlement regime could have been changed: the structure and role of the Secretariat, the dynamic for appointing the panelists, and the lack of a forum exclusion rule.

The tripartite Secretariat has often been seen as part of the reason for problems with the dispute settlement regime, including delays in the panel selection process and the panel proceedings themselves."[46] Much of the criticism stems from the fact that an independent trade secretariat was not created alongside NAFTA. The USMCA has kept the same decentralized system with a Secretariat located in the three capital cities of the region. The lack of importance that the administrations have given to the tripartite Secretariat has led to a diminishment of staff that often reflects in delays in the panel procedures.[47] The fact that the Secretariats are under-staffed and under-budgeted, leads to a series of efficiency problems.[48] For the moment, it is impossible to foresee an improved situation in this matter.

---

[43] *Id.* at 110.

[44] Stephen J. Powell, *Expanding the NAFTA Chapter 19 Dispute Settlement System, A Way to Declaw Trade Remedy Laws in a Free Trade Area of the Americas?,* 16 L. & Bus Rev. Am. 217, at 237-238 (2010).

[45] Cavazos & Monzón, *supra* note 38, at 122.

[46] *Id.* at 124.

[47] David A. Gantz, *Dispute Settlement Under the NAFTA and the WTO: Choice of Forum Opportunities and Risk for the NAFTA Parties,* 14 Am. U. Int'l Rev. 1025, 1090-91 (1999).

[48] Cavazos & Monzón, *supra* note 38, at 124.

The USMCA also maintains the dynamic for appointing the panelists. According to the Agreement, as it is the case with NAFTA, within thirty days of a request for a panel, each involved Party (through its Secretariat) shall appoint two panelists, in consultation with the other Party.[49] "Within 55 days of the request for a panel, the involved Parties shall agree on the selection of a fifth panelist."[50] Each Party has the right to disqualify from appointment to the panel up to four candidates proposed by the other Party.[51] In the experience under NAFTA, this provision, which should be an exception and not the general practice, has caused the formation of the panel to take several months, and in some cases, even years.[52]

Finally, it is important to emphasize that the USMCA does not include a forum exclusion clause for AD/CVD disputes. In this context, the Agreement does not avoid the possibility of a parallel litigation. The Secretariat is not the only cause of unconscionable delays in the Panel formation. According to Stephen Powell, "the largest cause of the delays is one Party or the other taking the Chapter 19 process hostage to trade demands it makes of the other Party that are unrelated to the issues involved in the NAFTA review."[53] The delay in the appointment of the panelists in the *High Fructose Syrup* Panel[54] prompted the United States to seek relief from a WTO Panel, before the NAFTA Chapter 19 Panel was actually established. The WTO Panel rendered a decision prior to the NAFTA Chapter 19 Binational Panel. Therefore, by the time the Chapter 19 Panel was able to hand out its own resolution, it decided to take into account the resolution made by the WTO Panel, in accordance with WTO law, and applied a principle of international comity to integrate the resolution of the special group into its own.[55] This situation is certainly undesirable in the context of the USMCA. Nevertheless, by the time this paper is being published, it seems unlikely to expect that the United States would bring a claim before the WTO.

As has been stated, the role of Canada in the negotiation was instrumental in maintaining a specialized AD/CVD dispute settlement regime under the USMCA. Unfortunately, the timeframe was not enough to make some necessary amendments to improve the system. For now, the binational panel review continues to be the only alternative to have an international adjudicatory system that—in the context of an

---

[49] USMCA, Annex 10-B.1 (2).

[50] *Id*. Annex 10-B.1 (3).

[51] *Id*. Annex 10-B.1 (2).

[52] Cavazos & Monzón, *supra* note 38, at 125.

[53] Powell, *supra* note 44, at 227-28.

[54] *In Re Imports of High Fructose Corn Syrup*, Secretariat File No. MEX-USA-98-1904-01 (August 3, 2001).

[55] Cavazos & Monzón, *supra* note 38, at 112.

even more protectionist political discourse—applies the relevant AD/CVD laws of the three USMCA Parties.

General Dispute Settlement

In contrast with Chapters 11 and 19, NAFTA Chapter 20 was the least used dispute settlement mechanism throughout the existence of the Agreement. For some commentators "the mechanism was inherently flawed and proved to be utterly unworkable. Unfortunately, Chapter 20's successor, the USMCA's Chapter 31, does not fix those fatal flaws."[56] In fact, NAFTA Chapter 20 established a process that begins with consultations ultimately leading to the establishment of a five-member panel that issues a determination and recommendations for resolving a controversy. At least, two shortcomings are identifiable in this regime: 1) the process to appoint panelists, and 2) the process to implement panel determinations.

Only three panel decisions were rendered in the twenty-five-year existence of NAFTA and none since 2001. A perceived lack of confidence in the mechanism is clear. One reason was because the process to appoint panelists includes a "reverse selection process" and the dependence on the good will of the Parties to update rosters of panelists. In the Chapter 20 regime, it has been very easy for Parties to refuse to appoint panelists to hear a case.[57] In this manner, the United States blocked Mexico's request to have a panel examine its claims over trade in sugar.[58] Although apparently this shortcoming has not been completely fixed in the USMCA text, at least the three USMCA Parties have already agreed on the roster of panelists for Chapter 31 disputes.[59]

Another perceived shortcoming in the operation of NAFTA Chapter 20 was the way its final resolutions were implemented (or not). This flaw was evident in the outcome of a particular dispute between the United States and Mexico. In February 2001, a panel issued its final decision in the Cross-Border Trucking Services,[60] ruling that the United States had breached its obligations under several NAFTA provisions. The panel recommended that the United States could no longer

---

[56] Jennifer Hillman, *Democrats Are Right to Insist on Better Enforcement Provisions in the USMCA,* COUNCIL ON FOREIGN RELATIONS, available at: https://www.cfr.org/blog/democrats-are-right-insist-better-enforcement-provisions-usmca.

[57] *Id.*

[58] *See generally*: Frieder Roessler, *Comment: Mexico—Tax Measures on Soft Drinks and Other Beverages (DS308) Prepared for the ALI Project on the Case Law of the WTO.* WORLD TRADE REVIEW (2009), 8: 1, 25–30. Available at: https://www.cambridge.org/core/services/aop-cambridge-core/content/view/S1474745608004163.

[59] *See: USMCA Free Trade Commission Decision No. 1, Annex IV,* available at https://ustr.gov/sites/default/files/files/agreements/usmca/AnnexIVChapter31.pdf.

[60] In re Cross-Border Trucking Services (Mex. v. US), Secretariat File No. USA-MEX 98-2008-01 (Feb. 6, 2001), available at http://www.ustr.gov/enforcement/trucking.pdf.

continue its ban on the entry of all Mexican trucks into the United States and it instructed the United States to consider granting operating authority to Mexican trucks on a case-by-case basis.[61] Despite this ruling, the United States did not comply with it immediately. In fact, the lack of compliance lasted until Mexico imposed retaliatory measures in 2009.[62]

NAFTA Article 2016 (2) provides that a panel should "present to the disputing Parties an initial report containing: (a) findings of fact, including any findings pursuant to a request under Article 2012(5); (b) its determination as to whether the measure at issue is or would be inconsistent with the obligations of this Agreement or cause nullification or impairment in the sense of Annex 2004, or any other determination requested in the terms of reference; and (c) its recommendations, if any, for resolution of the dispute." Therefore, an initial report contained a determination and a mere recommendation on how the dispute should be finally settled. In fact, once a final report had been rendered, "the disputing Parties *shall agree* on the resolution of the dispute, which normally shall conform with the determinations and recommendations of the panel and shall notify their Sections of the Secretariat of any agreed resolution of any dispute."[63] In this context, the report of a panel was a recommendation upon which the Parties should agree. It seems clear that in cases like *Cross-Border Trucking Services,* the outcome was, at the end of the day, more political.

The USMCA has somehow changed the language of the relevant provisions, but it seems that the perceived shortcoming remains. Article 31.18 of the USMCA provides that within forty-five days from receipt of a final report "the disputing Parties shall endeavor to agree on the resolution of the dispute." The same Article provides some guidelines on how an eventual resolution should look: "Resolution of the dispute can comprise elimination of the non-conformity or the nullification or impairment, if possible, the provision of mutually acceptable compensation, or another remedy the disputing Parties may agree."[64]

An important provision of the USMCA general dispute settlement regime is related to a non-binding preliminary reference mechanism preserved from NAFTA. It seems that this mechanism tries to avoid inconsistent domestic judicial interpretations of the Agreement. However, it is not clear whether this alternative is going to be actually used by domestic courts and tribunals. Article 31.20 (1) provides that "[i]f an issue of interpretation or application of this Agreement arises in a domestic judicial or administrative proceeding of a Party that a Party considers would merit its inter-

---

[61] *See generally*, Marc Sheer, *Chapter 20 Dispute Resolution Under NAFTA: Fact Or Fiction?* 35 GEO. WASH. INT'L L. REV. 1001, 1002 (2003).

[62] *See generally,* Daniel J. Ikenson, *Mexican Retaliation for U.S. Truck Ban is Proper*, CATO INSTITUTE, available at: https://www.cato.org/blog/mexican-retaliation-us-truck-ban-proper.

[63] NAFTA Article 2018 (1), *emphasis added*.

[64] USMCA Article 31.18 (2).   .

vention, or if a court or administrative body solicits the views of a Party, that Party shall notify the other Parties and its Section of the Secretariat. The Commission shall endeavor to agree on an appropriate response as expeditiously as possible."

Conclusion

As was the case with NAFTA, the USMCA dispute settlement mechanisms do not further the process of economic integration. The Parties to the Agreement do not seek the harmonization of social, political, or legal regimes. The three mechanisms broadly analyzed in this brief paper reflect the limited objectives of the USMCA. The most salient changes are contained in the Investment Chapter, mainly because of the absence of Canada in the ISDS mechanism and the narrower scope for FDI protection contained therein. Chapters 10 and 31 on dispute settlement regimes do not seem to have fixed some of the perceived flaws of their NAFTA predecessors. In sum, the success of the mechanisms, as well of that of the Agreement as a whole, will ultimately depend on the political will of the three Parties, and hopefully, on a common regional protection of the rule of law.

CHAPTER 16

HARMONIZATION OF CORPORATE LAW IN LATIN AMERICA

By Francisco Reyes-Villamizar[1]

Tribute to Professor Steve Zamora

It is a real honor to participate in this tribute to the great Steve Zamora. I had the privilege of enjoying his friendship for a long time. We met as many times as we could in the US, but also in Mexico and Colombia. One of the qualities that I admired the most was Steve's enthusiasm for finding mutual grounds for the understanding of different cultures in the Americas.

He and his lovely wife Lois were always looking for opportunities to study various features of the Latin American culture. In Steve's case, his knowledge of the Mexican—and more generally Hispanic American Law—was truly remarkable. He understood Comparative Law not as a simplistic discipline of relationships and similarities between legal systems, but as a profound exploration of culture, historic legacies, and attitudes towards the law. Steve spoke perfect Spanish. He had been able to learn it when he was part of the Peace Corps in a little town in the Colombian Coffee Region. Some years ago, he and his wife went back to the same place they had lived in their early youth and were amazed at the changes that "progress" had brought to the entire region.

---

[1] Former Chairman of the United Nations Commission on International Trade Law (UNCITRAL). He has been a Visiting Professor at the Universities of Fribourg (Switzerland), Tilburg (The Netherlands), Lyon (France), Agostinho Neto (Angola), Louisiana State University, Miami, Doshisha of Kyoto, and Stetson College and Arizona. He drafted the OAS Model Law on Simplified Stock Corporations.

Professor Zamora was well aware of the linguistic traps that are so common in legal translations. He probably shared Gustave Flaubert's insightful view that "God is in the details." In fact, in the book he co-wrote with José Roldán on Mexican Law he expressed his detailed and profound views on the legislation and domestic legal practice of that country and showed his understanding of the Civil Law tradition as it was transplanted to Latin America. He had an in-depth knowledge of cultural differences and always saw them as an advantage in terms of diversity and the diffusion of knowledge, instead of taking them as an obstacle to reciprocal understanding.

Steve was always easy going and would effortlessly adapt to all types of circumstances. I can refer here a brief anecdote in which his versatility appeared to be as smooth as evident. We had the opportunity to visit a small recording studio in Bogotá, and as soon as we got inside, we realized that there were all kinds of musical instruments, amplifiers, and microphones. Displaying an absence of shyness, Steve grabbed an electric guitar and immediately plugged it in to an amplifier. He stood up in front of a microphone and started singing a good old rock and roll song. And there he was: the same Professor Zamora that would delight his students in a Comparative Law class, acting as a true music star.

Steve and his intelligent wife, Lois, shared the love for the Latin American culture and devoted a long time to travelling around the region with curiosity and highly intellectual attitude. As already mentioned, both of them took advantage of their profound knowledge of the Spanish language to become true experts in the comparison of each one's academic fields. In the case of Steve, Comparative Law (US vis-à-vis Latin America) was a subject matter that he mastered gracefully. He had an in-depth understanding not only of the general aspects of the law, but also of the intricacies of the region's Private Law, both in theory and in practice. We had the opportunity to discuss my idea concerning the harmonization of the laws applicable to closely held corporations in Latin America and how he could help me to diffuse this concept in Mexico. Unfortunately, he could not see the impact that the OAS Model Law on Simplified Corporations would have in various Latin American countries, after its enactment in 2017. This paper, written in his honor, briefly describes the process leading to that initiative as well as the challenges on the way ahead.

Introduction

Latin America is in many respects uncharted territory. Despite the various cultural similarities (sharing the same language, religions, and certain attitudes towards the law), there are significant differences among the 22 countries that form part of this region. In a 22,222,000 square kilometer territory, there are nearly 600 million people, and 7 official languages. Varying degrees of economic development and institutional infrastructure determine heterogeneous conditions for the rule of law. However, certain features seem to be common in these countries, including a high level of formalism and legalism, government interference in business activities, relatively low judicial enforcement and, in some of the Latin American countries, a high degree of corruption. Against this backdrop, there seem to be just a few opportunities for the harmonization of the Law of Corporations or, more generally, for Business Law.

Despite the existence of multiple regional agreements, such as Mercosur, the Andean Pact or the Free Trade Agreement between Mexico and Central America countries (CISE), among others, efforts to harmonize Corporate Law were almost unknown in the region. In fact, the general approach to Business Law in the Latin American Region was one of legislative national sovereignty. Therefore, each State has retained full authority to legislate in the field of business organizations, which results in a significant disparity in terms of substantive and adjective company law.

Regrettably, the regional treaties referred to above have not contributed to harmonization in those countries' legislation in the area of business associations.[2] Instead, the prevailing approach throughout the region—similar to the European doctrine of the "real seat"—dictates that the law applicable to a business association is that of the country where it has its actual operation.[3] This approach hinders the development of a market for corporate chartering, similar to the one that exists in the United States. This situation is also one of the factors that contributes to the under-

---

[2] "The most remarkable feature of South American integration is that it is a disorderly and multiple process that permits parallel and overlapping initiatives." *See* Raúl Aníbal Etcheverry, *The Mercosur: Business enterprise organization in joint ventures*, 39 St. Louis Univ. L. J. 983, 979 (1995). Latin America has seen "the emergence of a number of economic unions patterned to some extent on the European Community. The largest of the South American regional trade associations, MERCOSUR, for example, unites Brazil, Argentina, Uruguay and Paraguay. It is still too early to gauge the success of these new economic combinations." *See* Larry Catá Backer, Comparative Corporate Law: United States, European Union, China and Japan, North Carolina, Carolina Academic Press (2002). For a comprehensive analysis of this topic, *see* Diego Fernández Arroyo, *Integración y Derecho en América Latina: Doscientos Años de Indiferencia Mutua*, in La Integración Posible: Latinoamérica Frente al Espejo de su Integración (1810-2010), Mexico City (2010).

[3] The 1889 Treaty of Montevideo sets forth a rule whereby all business associations are governed by the laws existing in the country of their domicile. "In constructing TM 89, it was decided that the law of the country where the basic elements of a company were originated and perfected was the most appropriate to regulate the existence and capacity of a corporation. Article 4 provides that the relationships between the shareholders and the company and third persons, as well as the form of the contract which gives birth to the company, are subject to the law of the corporation's domicile." *See* Beatriz Pallarés, *International Regime of Commercial Companies in Argentina and Mercosur*, 32 Stetson L. Rev. 801 (2003). The lack of corporate mobility within the region represents an obstacle for the creation of markets for corporate chartering. This lack of mobility is a result of the traditional legal requirement to set up a local corporate structure to conduct businesses in each Latin American jurisdiction.

development of Corporate Law in the region, due to a lack of competition among jurisdictions.[4] This circumstance is further exacerbated by a complete lack of concern regarding the harmonization of existing legal regimes. As a result, there is neither market-driven pressure for the enactment of modern *avant-garde* corporate regulations, nor a legal obligation to adopt uniform standards imposed by supranational entities such as the ones established under the Andean Pact.[5] Harmonization in the field of company law could be a sensible step in the context of the process of integration, particularly taking into consideration the fact that several countries throughout the region have either entered into or are in the process of negotiating free trade agreements with the United States.

Hybrid Business Forms

These types of business entities combine features of partnership law (i.e., direct management, freedom of contract, closely held ownership, etc.) with features of corporate law (i.e., limited liability, continuity of existence, legal personality, etc.). According to Larry Ribstein, "modern uncorporations borrow tricks from traditional partnerships. Uncorporate managers are, like partners, full-fledged owners of the firm, with strong incentives to act in the firm's interests. In addition, like partners, uncorporate owners can exit by getting cash directly out of the firm. . . . Uncorporations differ from corporations in terms of their ability both to choose contract terms that suit the particular firm and to modify terms to adjust to changes in the firm or its business environment. This is obviously a by-product of the uncorporation's reliance on contracting."[6] McCahery and Vermeulen also make the case for uncorporations, when asserting that, the introduction of hybrid entities "allows closely held firms to access limited liability by means of a perfunctory filing, reduce complexity and limit transaction costs, resulting in more capital being available for the actual operations of the business. The evidence shows that the introduction of new business forms provides the necessary impetus to help erode antiquated tax and burdensome mandatory legal rules."[7] As pointed out by Robert Keatinge, "it is not hard to imagine why states would want to authorize the formation of such ventures [LLCs]. Investors clearly will prefer limited liability to unlimited liability. Limited

---

[4] *See* ROBERTA ROMANO, THE GENIUS OF AMERICAN CORPORATE LAW, (Washington, D.C., The AEI Press 1993) (explaining the race for the bottom or race to the top debate).

[5] A different dynamic is evidenced by the European Council, which has promoted several directives aimed at the harmonization of Corporate Law in the European Union. *See* Adriaan Dorresteijn *et al.*, EUROPEAN CORPORATE LAW, 28 (Deventer, Kluwer Law and Taxation Publishers, 1994).

[6] Larry Ribstein, *The Rise of the Uncorporation*, 5-6 OXFORD UNIV. PRESS, (2009).

[7] Joseph McCahery, Erik Vermeulen et al., *A Primer on the Uncorporation*, 2-3 (ECGI, Working Paper Series in Law, Working Paper N°. 198/2013, 2013).

liability reduces exposure to loss, reduces insurance costs, and increases incentives for engaging in potentially profitable risk-taking."[8]

The experience of jurisdictions that have introduced hybrid business entities will illustrate some of the benefits of such legal forms particularly for Micro, Small and Medium Entities (MSMEs).

All hybrid forms, including the Simplified Corporation, are business entities endowed with a system of limited liability, simple formation proceedings and full-fledged contractual freedom. Both the Simplified Corporation, which has a French origin, and the Anglo-Saxon types of hybrid business entities such as the Limited Liability Company (LLC) or Limited Liability Partnership (LLP) are a good starting point concerning legislative reforms in the field of Company Law.

These types of entities, also referred to as *uncorporations,* have emerged within the last four decades in order to counteract the rigidities of traditional Company Law. The first of these models was introduced in the American State of Wyoming in 1977 and was referred to as the LLC.[9] After the creation of this business form, additional types were introduced in different parts of the world such as the LLP, the Limited Liability Limited Partnership (LLLP), and the *Société par Actions Simplifiée* or Simplified Corporation (SAS), introduced in France in 1994.[10]

The first successful experiment concerning the introduction of *hybrid* business forms or *uncorporations* in Latin America is the Colombian Simplified Corporation (*Sociedad por Acciones Simplificada* or *SAS*), created by Law 1258 of 2008.[11] The SAS has been a real legal revolution. It not only became the preferred business form in the first year of its existence, but it also started to erode the mandatory nature of Company Law in Colombia in general, offering online registration possibilities similar to LegalZoom and other websites that provide clients with incorporation assistance.

During the first decade after the enactment of such law more than half a million of these entities were created.[12] Rapidly, the Colombian SAS became the favorite

---

[8] Robert R. Keatinge et al., *The Limited Liability Company: A Study of the Emerging Entity,* 47 Bus. L. 375 (1992).

[9] *Id.*

[10] *See* Pierre Henri Conac & Isabelle Urbain-Parleani, La Société par Actions Simplifiée (SAS), Bilan et Perspectives 1 (Paris, Dalloz, 2016).

[11] In the United States, state legislatures have embraced hybrid business forms to improve the legal infrastructure and business environment. Interest group pressures and the competitive incentives of not losing local filings to other states have moved legislatures into hasty action. The expansion of new business forms appears to be based on compelling logic: it allows firms easy access to a range of governance structures designed to provide limited liability, reduce complexity and limit transaction costs.

[12] Until October 2018, 556,310 Simplified Corporations had already been created in Colombia (*See* Confecamaras,—Confederation of Colombian Chambers of Commerce, Bogotá, October 2018).

business form for entrepreneurs of all sizes. Certainly, this type of entity is not only useful for micro and small enterprises, but also for the largest national businesses.

As already mentioned, the Colombian SAS of 2008 was the starting point for the OAS initiative. After the great success of this business form, the initiative for a Model Law was presented before the OAS Juridical Committee in 2011. The lack of a harmonization system, similar to the one existing in the European Union, was one of the underlying reasons for the OAS initiative.

Relevance of the OAS Model Law on Simplified Corporations

The case for developing new business forms is a strong one in Latin America. Family-owned businesses and closely held companies abound in the region, creating significant demand for entities that allow parties to engage in extensive private ordering. Existing business forms have proven to be inflexible to suit the needs of family-owned and multi-owner firms. However, some Latin American legislators — much like some of their European counterparts — have been reluctant to develop new hybrid vehicles. As a general rule, there is no significant innovation regarding closely held corporation statutes in the Latin American region. Outmoded notions such as the lack of single member companies, a strict *ultra vires* doctrine, a fixed term of duration, the existence of several formalistic prohibitions supposedly aimed at the protection of shareholders, and a plethora of regulatory provisions better suited for publicly held entities than for small and medium family businesses, are only a few of the features characterizing an anachronistic regime that needs to be reformed.

Forming a regular business entity in many Latin American countries may cost hundreds of dollars and require the fulfillment of time-consuming legal formalities. Some of these proceedings are reminiscent of ancient institutions, many of which persist primarily due to pressure groups that hinder legal reform. The required participation of a notary public in the process of incorporation is an example of such widespread formalism.[13] Notaries are well-paid bureaucratic officers whose income

---

[13] *See* for Brazil, Article 997 of the Civil Code; for Mexico, Article 5 of the LGSM; for Argentina, Article 165 of Law 19.550; and for Colombia, Article 110 of the Commercial Code. Pursuant to Article 5 of the LGSM, "Companies shall be incorporated before a Notary, and modifications to their articles of association shall be made in a similar manner. The notary shall not authorize the articles when the statutes or their amendments contravene the provisions of this Law." In Colombia, Law 222 of 1995 created the so-called *empresa unipersonal*, whereby one individual or legal entity is enabled to form a separate legal entity through a private written document (*i.e.*, without the participation of a notary public). Article 22 of Law 1014 of 2006 extended this benefit to all new companies with a capital that did not exceed 500 monthly minimum wages, and which employed no more than 10

is primarily associated with the "public faith" that is given to contracts and other instruments once their authorized stamp and signature have been affixed onto a document. Aside from notaries, other professionals—such as attorneys and certified accountants—may also play a role in the process of incorporation, not to mention the requirement to obtain certain governmental authorizations, as well as to publish excerpts of the articles of incorporation in official gazettes.

This formalistic approach represents a significant obstacle to the establishment of business enterprises—particularly because the corporate scene throughout Latin America is dominated by small and micro enterprises. Empirical evidence demonstrates that the most flexible legal systems are more likely to attract investment and, accordingly, to obtain higher income arising from the registration of new companies. It has been held that the citizens of Delaware pay comparatively less income taxes due to the significant amounts that are contributed by foreign corporations in the form of registration fees. In fact, franchise taxes represent nearly a fifth of the overall revenue gathered by the State of Delaware. Naturally, there are several factors that characterize the institutional framework that is needed to manage such a successful corporate law jurisdiction. It is not only the substantive regulations that make Delaware attractive to corporations; the specialized judiciary and even the specialization within the local state bar also play a significant role.[14]

Increasing entrepreneurial demand for reform has only recently spurred several initiatives within the region. Such statutory enhancements are currently being outmatched by the introduction of the Simplified Corporation.[15] Even though it draws upon the French SAS, this entity closely resembles the hybrid business entities that

---

workers. It was only with the creation of the SAS in 2008 that this formality was abolished for a company type, irrespective of its size and capital. Paradoxically, formalism increases informality. According to Norman Loayza, "informality arises when the costs of belonging to the country's legal and regulatory framework exceed its benefits. Formality entails costs of entry—in the form of lengthy, expensive, and complicated registration procedures— and costs of permanence—including payment of taxes, compliance with mandated labor benefits and remunerations, and observance of environmental, health, and other regulations." *See* Norman Loayza, Luis Servén & Naotaka Sugawara, *Informality in Latin America and the Caribbean* (March 1, 2009), World Bank Policy Research Working Paper Series, available at SSRN: http://ssrn.com/abstract=1372965 (last accessed April 7, 2011).

[14] For an explanation concerning franchise taxes in Delaware and the percentages that they represent with respect to the total amount of taxes collected by that state, *see* Roberta Romano, *supra* note 3, at 6-12. *See also*, ALAN PALMITER & FRANCISCO REYES, ARBITRAJE COMERCIAL Y OTROS MECANISMOS DE RESOLUCIÓN DE CONFLICTOS SOCIETARIOS EN ESTADOS UNIDOS 77-87 (Bogotá, Cámara de Comercio, 2001).

[15] *See* Colombian Law 1258 of 2008.

have been set in place in the United Stated and the United Kingdom during the last several years. By providing a mixture of corporate and partnership-like components, the SAS allows for significant contractual flexibility, while still preserving the benefits of limited liability and asset partitioning.

The basic framework for the SAS's Model Act is based upon the following five pillars: (i) Full-fledged limited liability; (ii) Simple incorporation requirements; (iii) Contractual flexibility; (iv) Supple organizational structure; and (v) Fiscal transparency.[16]

The already mentioned Model Act on Simplified Stock Corporations for Latin America is not intended to serve as a partial amendment to be introduced to traditional business forms regulated in national codes and statutes.[17] Instead, it is recommended that its enactment take place in separate legislation that could be linked to the existing system.[18] In this manner, the SAS should have to compete with other types of business forms.

Contents of Model Law

On June 20, 2017, the Organization of American States' General Assembly adopted the Model Law on Simplified Corporations. This initiative, originally presented before the OAS in 2011, and totally based on Colombian Law 1258 of 2008, was intended to foster harmonization of Corporate Law within the region.[19] And, in

---

[16] *See* MODEL ACT ON THE SIMPLIFIED STOCK CORPORATION, et seq., *infra* the Annex.

[17] Such as Commercial Codes and Corporate Law statutes existing in different countries in this region.

[18] *See* Joseph McCahery, Eric Vermeulenet *et al.*, *The New Company Law - What Matters in an Innovative Economy?* 20 (ECGI - Law Working Paper No. 75/2006, 2006).

[19] "Many states in the Americas continue to use outdated corporate and commercial codes that were inherited from the 19th century and that have not been updated. Cognizant of this situation, during its 78th regular session held in 2011, the CJI included onto its agenda the topic of simplified companies. During its 79th regular session, the CJI heard the report prepared by Dr. David Stewart, rapporteur for the topic, and from Professor Francisco Reyes Villamizar, primary author of the Law of Simplified Companies that had been adopted in Colombia. During its 80th regular session held in 2012, the CJI approved unanimously a resolution that approved the report of the Rapporteur, to which was annexed the Model Law on the Simplified Corporation, which had been drafted largely on the basis of the Colombian law. The CJI resolution was transmitted to the OAS Permanent Council, which in turn referred the matter to its Committee on Political and Juridical Affairs ("CAJP"). To assist the CAJP with its deliberations, presentations were made in 2014 by Drs. Stewart and Reyes and again in 2016 by Dr. Reyes and a DIL representative. In March 2017, the CAJP agreed upon a draft resolution, which was first approved by the Permanent Council and ultimately

fact, it has started to yield fruitful results. Pursuant to the OAS' Department of International Law, new legislation inspired in the Simplified Corporation's Model has been enacted in various jurisdictions: "Uruguay is the latest state in the region to initiate legislative reforms to simplify incorporation. In April, the House of Representatives voted unanimously in favor of a bill entitled "Promotion of Entrepreneurs" (Promoción de Emprendimientos), which has now been sent to the Senate for approval. Title II of the bill provides for the establishment of a simplified corporation ("SAS") and, as noted in its accompanying report, the legislation has been inspired by the Model Law on the Simplified Corporation ("Model Law")."[20] Ecuador also adopted legislation to provide for the SAS and Peru is taking steps in the same direction. Both the Ecuadorian and Uruguayan initiatives were eventually enacted as laws and, thus far, have been successful experiments.

The Argentinian Simplified Corporation (enacted by law of 2017) and mostly based on the Colombian 2008 Legislation, started off as an extremely useful business vehicle, which, at least in the beginning, was well-received by businesspeople and the community at large. Unfortunately, an increasing *politization* of the legislative agenda, caused by a change in Government, has hindered the strength and initially rapid diffusion of the Argentinian SAS. The Mexican case is also a good example of a relatively failed effort to modernize Corporate Law. The legislation on SAS, enacted on September 15, 2016, turned out to be a compromise between its promoters and pressure groups, such as notary publics. As a result of these evident agreements, the SAS ended up restricted to small business units. In fact, as soon as the Mexican Simplified Corporation reaches a certain level of income, it has to be converted into a traditional business entity. As a result, the Mexican SAS has lost most of its appeal and, despite the comparative lack of official information, the Mexican SAS has lost relevance.

In any event, the Model Law on Simplified Corporations has been the first and only initiative aimed at the modernization and harmonization of Corporate Law in the region. As a first experiment its results have been, in general, beneficial for the countries that have adopted it. There are, however, many challenges ahead, including the possible adoption of the Model Law by major Latin American countries such as Brazil and the possibility of establishing a system of mutual recognition for this type of business entities across the region.

As mentioned before, the Model Law is altogether inspired in the Colombian simplified corporation law. Reference to the Colombian experience is thus crucial in

---

adopted by the General Assembly on June 20, 2017." *See* OAS, *Advancing the Model Law on the Simplified Corporation: Initial Report on Status of Reforms in the Region*, (OAS/Sec. General, DDI/doc.2, February 15, 2018 at 3).

[20] https://www.oas.org/en/sla/dil/newsletter_DDI_Recent_Advances_Law_Simplified_Corporation_May-2019.html

understanding the main aspects of the initiative. In December of 2008, the Colombian Congress enacted law 1258 of 2008, creating this new type of business. The Colombian law contains elements found in Corporate Law coming from both the Common Law and Civil Law traditions. In fact, the basic structure and contents of the law are based on the French legislation on the SAS.[21] Additionally, certain U.S. Law elements, mainly from the State of Delaware, were also included in such statute.[22] The result is a closely held corporation which resembles the so-called uncorporations that have been introduced into the United States, the United Kingdom, and some Civil Law jurisdictions.[23]

It is also noteworthy that there have been other similar laws introducing regulation on simplified, closely held corporate vehicles in Latin America. The first legislation of the sort was the Chilean Law 20.190 of June 5, 2007. According to Chilean commentator María José Viveros Bloch, this legislation was aimed at allowing the small business owner to formalize her venture.[24] On the other hand, Mexico enacted a law on December 9, 2015, regarding *Sociedades Anónimas Simplificadas* (simplified corporations). The most recent cases are the Argentinian adoption of a SAS, by Law 27.349,[25] incorporated in the law designed to encourage entrepreneurship (Title 3), and the Ecuadorian Simplified Corporation Law of 2021. There is also draft legislation on various types of similar business entities in Brazil. However, the perspectives for this Brazilian bill are still uncertain.

By providing a combination of corporate and partnership-like components, the Colombian SAS allows for significant contractual flexibility, while still preserving the benefits of limited liability and asset partitioning. As an example, some of the partnership-like features include simple formation procedures, internal flexibility and share transfer restrictions. These features allow businesspersons to better cope with agency problems within the corporations in which management has been dele-

---

[21] The original legislation of the French SAS was enacted in 1994. Several reforms followed to make it ever more flexible and simplified. For an overview of this type of business entity *see* CONAC & PARLEANI, *supra* note 10.

[22] *See* Roberta Romano, *supra* note 4.

[23] *See* Francisco Reyes & Erik Vermeulen, *Company Law, Lawyers and "Legal" Innovation: common Law versus Civil Law* (Lex Research Topics in Corporate Law & Economics, Working Paper No. 2011-3, 2011), available at https://ssrn.com/abstract=1907894 or http://dx.doi.org/10.2139/ssrn.1907894, and Larry Ribstein, *supra* note 6.

[24] *See* MARÍA JOSÉ VIVEROS BLOCH, SOCIEDAD POR ACCIONES: ANÁLISIS DE UN NUEVO TIPO SOCIAL, 44 (Santiago de Chile, Librotecnia, 2006), for the summary of the Chilean law's objectives.

[25] Published in the Official Buletin of April 12, 2017.

gated.[26] On the other hand, certain crucial corporate features like having a separate legal personality and continuity of life have also been kept.[27]

The Model Law contains a total of 44 articles regulating all stages in the corporation's life span. As with any other model law its provisions are intended to serve as a guide for legislators and policymakers alike. Therefore, they can be adapted in order to make them compatible with domestic legislation. The following is a short discussion of the main traits of the Model Law.

1. Facilitating Incorporation Procedures

It can be argued that reducing transaction costs for business may foster economic growth and trade and incentivize formal economic activity in emerging economies. Researchers have found that "informality is not single-caused but results from the combination of poor public services, a burdensome regulatory regime, and weak monitoring and enforcement capacity by the state. . . . Studies have shown that removing excessive bureaucratic formalities in the startup process has numerous benefits for both economies and entrepreneurs. Some of these gains include higher levels of firm formalization, economic growth, and greater profits."[28]

For many decades, it has been argued that migration into the formal system will produce several benefits including higher tax revenues, better regulation, social security protection and labor formalization, higher levels of transparency and disclosure, better access to credit and government services, and higher levels of investment.[29] Fully complying firms also benefit from the consequences of limited liability and asset partitioning, among others. Formalization of the business will enable more effective monitoring and supervision over the micro, small and medium sized businesses. While investors in listed corporations benefit from high disclosure standards, and complex corporate governance structures, shareholders in closely held entities require a more flexible legal framework.[30] Introducing new flexible types of

---

[26] By allowing a higher degree of contractual flexibility, parties are enabled to set up devices aimed at defining ex ante each of the corporate participants' obligations and rights. This latitude is oriented towards the completion of the corporate contract, reducing the potential for exposed disputes. For a discussion regarding the incomplete contract theory *see* Robert Scott & George Triantis, *Incomplete Contracts and the Theory of Contract Design,* 56 CASE WESTERN RES. L. REV. 1 (2005).

[27] These characteristics allow for limited liability and indefinite duration of the business enterprise.

[28] *See* World Bank Group, Doing Business 2017: Equal Opportunity for All, doc. 14 (Washington, D.C., 2017), at https://perma.cc/9ZQ8-TTBC.22

[29] *See* HERNANDO DE SOTO, EL OTRO SENDERO, LA REVOLUCIÓN INFORMAL, Ch. 3, 220 (7th ed., La Oveja Negra 1987).

[30] *See* Larry Ribstein, *supra* note 6, and Joseph McCahery et al., *supra* note 7.

business entities is thus intended to counter certain features of informality, such as a burdensome regulatory regime for business entities. It is, therefore, expected that reducing informality and encouraging firm growth by setting up an enabling environment for business could enhance economic development and provide welfare for the people of a given jurisdiction.

Following an Anglo-American approach to Corporate Law, the Model Law significantly reduces formalities for incorporation. Many of the proceedings existing in Latin American countries are reminiscent of ancient formalities that have been abandoned in other jurisdictions. Therefore, streamlining the requirements to set up the business by removing some of these cumbersome steps is not incompatible with legal certainty. Interestingly, the latter goal can be reached through a simple filing procedure before a public registry (such as a chamber of commerce).

Article 5 of the Model Law reads as follows: "A simplified stock corporation will be formed by contract or by the individual will of a single shareholder, provided that a written document is granted. The formation document shall be registered before the Mercantile Registry."

The same article also lists 7 items that normally form part of the incorporation document.[31] This requirement is not intended to create an unjustified burden on the parties, but instead is aimed at the disclosure of basic corporate information. The article contains minimum legal requirements such as the corporation's domicile, its name, and the subscribed capital, among a few others. It is basic information designed to identify the business entity, so that third parties can deal with it confidently. The same Model Law provision categorically mandates that "no additional formalities of any nature shall be required for the formation of the simplified stock corporation." Even more significant is the removal of the notary public's intervention in the process. This recommendation is geared towards the suppression of intermediaries and the reduction of unnecessary costs (including monetary and time related expenses).

Furthermore, the Model Law provides certainty as to when the legal personality arises. Article 3 states that "[u]pon the filing of the formation document before the Mercantile Registry [. . .], the simplified stock corporation will form a legal entity separate and distinct from its shareholders."[32] This simplification is intended to settle the discussion concerning the precise moment in which the legal personality is acquired. Where the law requires several different steps for the incorporation to be completed, as is frequently the case in Latin America, it becomes difficult to tell when the process has come to fruition. Under the Model Law, all incorporation formalities are reduced to a filing before the mercantile registry.[33] Such registration partly covers

---

[31] *See* the full text of the Model Law, *infra* the Annex.

[32] *Id.*

[33] This feature appears in other jurisdictions, including some in the United States whereby fil-

the functions previously served to the intervention of notary publics. Experience has shown that there is no practical need in having two sets of formal procedures (granting of a public deed of incorporation and filing before the mercantile registry) directed towards the same end. Thus, the Model Law has granted the mercantile registry with certain attestation functions over the incorporation documents filed.[34] The mercantile registry shall only provide a review of the legality of the provisions set in the incorporation documents and may only deny registration where it finds that the elements enumerated in Article 5 of the Model Law have not been included.[35]

Following the underlying concern with simplification and cost reduction, a system of online registration should be implemented. In Colombia, certain local mercantile registries have implemented an electronic system for the formation of a simplified corporation.[36] Such system requires the incorporator to have a personal digital signature that can also be acquired through an online application system.[37] All these electronic devices find solid legal grounds in Colombia, given the early adoption of the UNCITRAL Model Laws on electronic commerce, by Law 527 of 1999. Such law incorporated the principle of functional equivalence, whereby any data message is sufficient to replace paper-based formalities at least concerning so-called private documents (i.e. those that are not subject to notarization or any other form of authentication by a public officer).[38]

2. Full-Fledged Limited Liability

The Model Law reinforces the foundational principle of limited liability by including legal provisions directed at ameliorating the impact of the piercing of the

---

ing before the registry acts as a presumption as to the existence of the corporate body. *See* Revised Model Business Corporation Act SS 106.

[34] *See* Article 6 of the Model Law, *infra* the Annex.

[35] *See also* Article 8 of the Model Law, *infra* the Annex.

[36] The following web page may be accessed to incorporate the simplified corporation electronically: https://linea.ccb.org.co/SAS/index.html/ (last accessed June 7, 2017).

[37] The digital signature may be acquired by filling out the necessary forms in the following web page: https://solicitudes.certicamara.com/SSPS/Solicitudes/RecomendacionesUso.aspx (last accessed June 7, 2017).

[38] In accordance with Article 6 of Law 527 of 1999, where a legal provision requires that information be in writing, such requirement shall be complied with by means of a data message, provided that the information contained therein is accessible for its future consultation. The use of new technologies has been described by scholars as one of the factors modernizing Corporate Law: "The progressive use of new technologies has been one of the factors accompanying the process of typology renovation in the closely held corporation, with the aim of facilitating and simplifying its existence, organization and operation." Jose Miguel Embid *et al., La tipologia de las sociedades mercantiles: entre tradicion y reforma* 174 (Bogota, Grupo Editorial Ibanez, 2017).

corporate veil doctrine. Accordingly, the few exceptions to limited liability are reserved exclusively to situations where there is clear and sufficient evidence of an abusive use of the corporate form, provided that the liable party has acted wrongfully or in a fraudulent fashion.

There is an attempt in the Model Law to strike a balance between asset partitioning on the one hand, and the extension of liability to responsible parties.[39] The economic rationale for the limitation of liability and the instances for veil piercing have been broadly discussed by renowned scholars.[40] Following the mainstream approach to these principles, one of the objectives of the Model Law is to provide an appropriate remedy for grievances when the legal entity status has been severely eroded. The initiative thus intends to limit the situations in which judges can hold shareholders liable for the company's obligations. Fraud or misuse of the corporate form should be the sole events to trigger judicial intervention.[41] There appears to be no valid justification introducing so many exceptions to the principle of limited liability. There is a willingness to counteract the wholesale disregard of the legal entity in view of the many cases where the exception to the principle of limited liability becomes the rule. This is particularly true when case law is founded to a large extent upon situations unrelated to the domain of Corporate Law.

The region's writs of constitutionality (*mandado de segurança* in Brazil, *acción de amparo* in Mexico and Argentina, and *acción de tutela* in Colombia) have been used on several occasions as a mechanism for piercing the corporate veil. This type of litigation threatens the economic foundations of Corporate Law. This way, "defending weak creditors through expeditious writs (in which the true merits of each case are not carefully assessed by constitutional courts) negatively impacts certainty and reasonable reliance on these legal systems."[42] In this vein, the Brazilian experience must serve as an important warning for the region, given the precedents that have jeopardized the economic benefits arising from the principle of limited liability. In the opinion of Salama, in Brazil the trend to allow the government to become radically involved in the allocation and reallocation of corporate risks was eventually consolidated. A breakdown in former branches of legal rationality (pub-

---

[39] *See* Articles 2 and 41 of the Model Law, *infra* the Annex.

[40] *See* among many other works: FRANK EASTERBROOK & DANIEL FISCHEL, THE ECONOMIC STRUCTURE OF CORPORATE LAW, 40 (Cambridge, Harvard University Press, 1996); Henry Hansmann & Reinier Kraakman *Toward Unlimited Shareholder Liability for Corporate Torts,* 100 YALE L. J. 7 (1991); Stephen Bainbridge, *supra* note 49; Robert B. Thompson, *Piercing the Corporate Veil: An Empirical Study,* 76 CORNELL L. REV. (1991); PIERRE MOUSSERON, DROIT DES SOCIÉTÉS, 79 (2nd ed., Paris, Ed. Montchrestien, 2005); BRUNO SALAMA, O FIM DA RESPONSABILIDADE LIMITADO NO BRASIL, 26 (Sao Paulo, Malheiros, 2014).

[41] *See* Article 41, *infra* the Annex.

[42] FRANCISCO REYES, A NEW POLICY AGENDA FOR LATIN AMERICAN COMPANY LAW: RESHAPING THE CLOSELY-HELD ENTITY LANDSCAPE, 24 (Carolina Academic Press, 2013).

lic law, private, civil, criminal, etc.) seems to have taken place. As a result of that, additional legal branches were introduced to better protect the interests of certain groups. Therefore, new fields of the law appeared, such as environmental law, consumer, labor law, social security law, urbanistic law, among others.[43]

Similarly, it has been widely held that upholding the principle of limited liability is a plausible objective, particularly when facing voluntary creditors.[44] Currently there does not seem to be a major dispute on this topic. On the other hand, regarding the so-called involuntary creditors, there is an ongoing doctrinal debate as to whether the principle should also prevail in tort cases.[45] Notwithstanding the scholarly debate surrounding these topics, there is no differentiation in the Model Law concerning the situation just described. The legal entity can be judicially disregarded in the exceptions already discussed.

3. Private Ordering

The Model Law upholds the principle of freedom of contract between private parties. This marks a defining trait of modern Corporate Law, particularly regarding hybrid business forms.[46] Upon discussing the French SAS, Périn and Germain single out a distinctive feature of the simplified corporation, which lies in the possibility to adjust internal functioning, enabling shareholders to benefit from both corporate characteristics, and added flexibility: "The method of internal organization confers the SAS its originality *vis-à-vis* other types of companies. The simplified corporation is a liberalized form of moral person, which includes the financial benefits from the corporate form, with a vast autonomy to define its internal powers."[47]

The flexibility provided by the Model Law is characteristic of best practices from both the Common Law and Civil Law traditions. As noted above, a broad freedom for parties to define their legal relationships is all pervasive in American Cor-

---

[43] *See* Bruno Salama, *supra* note 40.

[44] *See* Hansmann & Kraakman, *supra* note 40.

[45] *Id.*

[46] Commenting on the Colombian SAS legislation, local scholars note: "Today, there is consensus in Colombia of the fact that the Law 1258 of 2008 is the most important reform to Corporate Law of the last decade. The SAS was created based on the pillar of corporate flexibility by incorporating, in its majority default rules." William Hernandez, *La sociedad por acciones simplificada en Colombia,* in EMBID *et al.*, LA TIPOLOGÍA DE LAS SOCIEDADES MERCANTILES: ENTRE TRADICIÓN Y REFORMA, 204 (Bogotá, Grupo Editorial Ibañez, 2017) (citations omitted).

[47] PIERRE-LOUIS PÉRIN & MICHEL GERMAIN, SAS: LA SOCIÉTÉ PAR ACTIONS SÍMPlIFIÉE ETUDES-FORMULES, 3 (3rd ed. Paris, Joly Éditions, 2008).

porate Law.[48] Likewise, the 1994 French law on SAS, along with its numerous amendments, is a good example of private ordering. According to Philippe Merle: "The novelty introduced by the SAS consists in granting absolute preponderance to freedom of contract for the shareholders, as manifested in the by-laws. The application of legal provisions may be opted out of by contracting parties."[49]

As explained above, the simplified corporation introduced by the Model Law is barred from listing its securities in a stock exchange. This is due to the need to maintain the flexibility of the Model Law regulation and to enable business persons to tailor make the corporate contract. In fact, keeping the SAS away from the securities markets removes the difficult issues concerning the protection of dispersed investors as there is a close relationship between ownership and control in the simplified corporation.[50]

The prohibition against offering securities on an exchange does not imply that the simplified corporation cannot be used to undertake large business projects, or that it is to be adopted exclusively by MSMEs. It is likely that the flexible capital structure is the most attractive element of this business entity for large firms. This flexibility allows for different types of investors, some active and some passive, and is generally regarded as adequate for large business groups and tax planning.[51]

---

[48] Noting the increasing flexibility awarded to close corporations by judges and legislators in the United States, Palmiter and Partnoy state that: "For many years, planners of the close corporation confronted judicial antagonism to special arrangements-whether embodied in the articles, bylaws, or a separate agreement if they departed too far from the traditional statutory model. Two parallel developments, starting mostly in the 1960s, have substantially loosened this judicial attitude. First, courts have become more realistic about the special demands of close corporations and have become far more tolerant of departures from the norm. Second, legislatures have recognized the unnecessary rigidity of the traditional structure and have created special rules for the close corporation," ALAN PALMITER & FRANK PARTNOY, CORPORATIONS: A CONTEMPORARY APPROACH 1005 (West, 2010). *See also*, Roberta Romano, *supra* note 3, and the Model Business Corporation Act, *infra* the Annex.

[49] PHILIPPE MERLE, DROIT COMMERCIAL. SOCIÉTÉS COMMERCIALES, 602 (5th ed., Paris, Précis Dalloz, 1996).

[50] Commenting on the approach adopted in the United States, Professor Bainbridge notes: "The regulatory regime for statutory close corporations is substantially more liberal in a variety of ways than is mainstream corporate law," STEPHEN BAINBRIDGE, CORPORATE LAW, 486 (3rd ed., St. Paul, Foundation Press, 2015).

[51] As an example of the benefits provided by this flexibility, the following is noted: "The Model Law enables the corporation to issue classes and series of shares. The distinction between these two concepts has obvious practical consequences. Share 'classes' refer to various categories of instruments that are differentiated on the basis of the inherent rights associated with them, according to the relevant regulation. On the other hand, the 'series' identify successive issues of the same class of shares, where such shares have been placed at

In the absence of the simplified corporation, Latin American MSMEs are being subject to a challenging dilemma. On the one hand, they could choose the traditional corporate form in Latin America (generally the *sociedad anónima*), benefitting from its features, but assuming the downside of stringent rules and formalities.[52] On the other hand, they could adopt partnership-like entities that provide wide flexibility, but are subject to the disadvantage of having unlimited liability. The simplified corporation combines the benefits from both types of business entities. Cozian notes the following regarding the French law on SAS: "The fundamental idea is to offer members of the simplified corporation an organizational form very similar to the 'company-contract' (*société contrat*), where the essential functioning rules are provided by agreement between the parties. This way, the rules of the corporation (*société anonyme*) may be opted out of."[53]

The initiative contains default provisions, which the parties may opt in to, or opt out of at their will. Consequently, business participants can implement almost any arrangement that they deem better suited to their business needs.[54] Some examples

---

different time periods. Finally, Article 10 of the Model Law also contemplates that the company may issue shares 'for any consideration whatsoever, including in-kind contributions, or in exchange for labor contributions pursuant to the terms and conditions contained in the by-laws.'" FRANCISCO REYES, A NEW POLICY AGENDA FOR LATIN AMERICAN COMPANY LAW: RESHAPING THE CLOSELY-HELD ENTITY LANDSCAPE, 114 (Carolina Academic Press, 2013).

[52] The French simplified corporation was partly adopted with the objective of establishing a corporate vehicle that is free from the formalities of the classic corporation (*Société Anonyme* or S.A.): "The French S.A. corporation bears the inconvenience of requiring at least seven shareholders, and having a complex system establishing the existence of a general shareholders assembly, board of directors, and director general. None of these are required in the SAS [...] to sum up, the SAS counts with all the advantages of the classic S.A. (limited liability, share transfers etc.), without the inconveniences of said entity (minimum shareholders requirement, internal organization)." JEROME BONNARD, DROIT DES SOCIETIES, 126-127 (3rd ed., Paris, Hachette Supérieur, 1999).

[53] MAURICE COZIAN *et al.,* DROIT DES SOCIÉTÉS, 365 (18th ed., Paris, Lexis-Nexis, 2005). Perin and Germain note the following regarding the French SAS: "[A]dding freedom of contract to the creation of a corporation constitutes an unprecedented privilege in French Law. For any rational agent, incorporating her firm as an SAS corresponds to the desire to increase organizational efficiency, by having it adapt to its shareholders particular needs." Perin and Germain, *supra* note 46, at 11. The same characteristic is present in the Colombian SAS whereby a decision on the internal configuration of governance organs is left to the will of the shareholder(s).

[54] Private ordering is an important feature introduced by the Colombian SAS law, into the previously rigid Colombian Corporate Law: "Naturally, the SAS' opt in approach also allows for private parties to step out of the standard provisions contained in model by laws and to draft sophisticated agreements that are appropriate for more complex undertakings. The enabling non-directory provisions of Law 1258 have fostered private ordering and sparked innovation in Corporate Law across the country. Aside from the boilerplate type of agreements that are used by most start-ups, practicing attorneys are becoming skillful at devel-

of these provisions in the Model Law are the possibility for shareholders to either fully define the main business activities of the corporation, or set up an open-ended purpose clause whereby the corporation may engage in any lawful business;[55] the possibility for the corporation to have unlimited life span;[56] freedom to organize the internal structure and operation of the corporation;[57] and the leeway to define voting majorities for a shareholders meeting,[58] among others.

The approach, based on the primacy of private ordering, assumes that contracting parties will be diligent enough either to adequately negotiate the terms of the agreement so as to suit their particular needs, or to adapt by default off the rack housekeeping rules provided in the corporate statute. Naturally, the fact that there is significant latitude for parties to define the structure of their corporation also entails a burden to prevent unintended consequences by careful negotiation of provisions at the outset.[59] For example, incorporators may wish to establish special supermajorities that differ from those contained as fallback provisions in case they desire to implement their voting arrangements. Depending on the specific circumstances, parties need to carefully design their own agreement in order to fit their needs.

4. Unrestricted Business Purpose, Perpetuity and Commercial Character

The Model Law allows for the adoption of an unrestricted business purpose for these types of corporations.[60] This characteristic coincides with the trend of advanced jurisdictions such as the United States,[61] and to a lesser extent the EU[62] and

---

oping new legal structures suitable for a more sophisticated business environment. A survey conducted with law firms and sole law practitioners in the capital city of Bogotá has allowed for the identification of several legal structures in which one or more SAS can be properly used for an unlimited number of business purposes." Francisco Reyes, *Corporate Governance in Latin America: A Functional Analysis,* 39 UNIV. OF MIAMI INTER-AMER. L. REV. 2 (2008).

[55] *See* Article 5(5) of the Model Law, *infra* the Annex.

[56] *See* Article 5(4) of the Model Law, *infra* the Annex.

[57] *See* Article 17 of the Model Law, *infra* the Annex.

[58] *See* Article 22 of the Model Law, *infra* the Annex.

[59] *See* STEPHEN BAINBRIDGE, CORPORATION LAW AND ECONOMICS, 9 (New York, Foundation Press, 2002).

[60] *See* Article 5(5) of the Model Law, *infra* the Annex.

[61] Palmiter and Partnoy explain the evolution and fallout of the *ultra vires* doctrine in the United States: "In the nineteenth century, the law of corporations was mainly devoted to the resolution of disputes arising under the ultra vires doctrine. Today the issue rarely arises. Clearly, the original purpose of the doctrine to curb the powers of large corporations has failed, largely replaced by expanded fiduciary duties." *Supra* note 48, at 171.

[62] Commenting on the First European Company Law Directive, it has been asserted that:

the UK.[63] By means of this provision, the anachronistic *ultra vires* doctrine that still exists in some Latin American countries is altogether left behind. Said doctrine is supposed to protect shareholders from the presumed excess of powers that managers may sometimes arrogate upon themselves by acting beyond the terms of their mandate. According to this view, establishing limitations to the capacity of the corporation ensures that the entity will only be liable for acts that are explicitly provided for in the corporate documents.

However, modern Corporate Law across the board tends to disregard the usefulness of this doctrine. It has been asserted that the prohibition of *ultra vires* acts may be deemed too formalistic and even detrimental to entrepreneurial activity.[64] This doctrine may even tend to create more legal uncertainty, as it subjects third contracting parties acting in good faith, to the nullification of contracts with the corporation.

The trend against this doctrine may also take into consideration the ownership structures prevailing in Latin America. As already explained, closely held family enterprises, with no separation between ownership and control, are common in the region. This may render the *ultra vires* doctrine useless, given that shareholders may assert direct control over the day-to-day running of the company.[65] On the other hand, the ample flexibility contained in the Model Law allows shareholders to either choose an unrestricted business purpose, or to introduce limitations thereto.

Additionally, the Model Law introduced the perpetuity of existence theory, which runs contrary to many Latin American legislations. Most Corporate Laws in the region have maintained a "French type of" provision whereby a company should

---

"Even though this directive notes that the corporation's legal capacity is defined by the purpose clause as set forth in the relevant articles of incorporation, it also underscores that innocent third parties are protected vis-à-vis the validity of *ultra vires* business transactions to which they were a party — provided they did not know that the corporation lacked sufficient capacity to undertake such a transaction. Pursuant to the same directive, bad faith will not be presumed solely on the grounds that the relevant party had access to a certificate issued by the relevant company registry, in which the purpose clause is described." Francisco Reyes, *supra* note 50, at 32.

[63] *See* the United Kingdom Company Law Act of 2006, s. 31(1).

[64] *See* FRANCISCO REYES, DERECHO SOCIETARIO, 299 (3rd ed. Bogotá, Editorial Temis, 2016).

[65] Palmiter and Partnoy however hold that there is still a place for the *ultra vires* doctrine in closed corporations; *see supra* note 60, at 172. The present paper suggests quite the contrary: by having shareholders actively participating in the day to day management of the closely held corporation, their scrutiny of directors' actions renders the protection of the *ultra vires* doctrine useless.

be created for a limited duration.[66] The objective is to reduce outdated formalities and introduce more flexibility for entrepreneurs.[67]

The initiative also intends to put an end to the anachronistic dichotomy of private law present throughout the region. The Model Law mandates that the simplified corporation is to have a commercial nature—without regard to the objects or purposes set forth in the relevant incorporation documents.[68] Consequently, it becomes irrelevant to analyze whether the business association's activities have a civil or a commercial nature. This characteristic is intended to provide the maximum amount of legal certainty for shareholders and for parties contracting with the simplified corporation.

5. Freedom to Define Internal Structure

With the aim of introducing more flexibility for the benefit of businesspersons, the formation and operation of internal governance organs are also simplified in the Model Law. As well as achieving a streamlining of procedures and eliminating unnecessary bureaucracy, this characteristic arguably reduces costs for the entrepreneur.

An example of this leeway can be seen in the board of directors regulation contained in the initiative. Under the Model Law there is no statutory obligation to create a board of directors.[69] Even though the importance of said body for the management of corporations is acknowledged, regulatory restrictions have been loosened to the point where shareholders may even decide if they require such board or not. For instance, small business ventures may find benefits in excluding the board altogether. This feature specifically responds to the already analyzed fact that most companies in Latin America are closely held, and thus do not reflect the idea of a separation between ownership and control.[70]

In the event the incorporators determine that there will not be any board of directors in the corporation, both the management and direction shall be entirely allocated on the legal representative and any of her subordinates. In accordance with Article 25 of the Model Law, "in the absence of a provision requiring the operation of a board of directors, the legal representative appointed by the shareholders assembly shall be entitled to exercise any and all powers concerning the management and

---

[66] Article 1865 of the French Civil code established that the corporation would be terminated by the expiration of the term for which it was contracted. The Law of July 24th, 1966 contained a provision whereby corporations could not be formed for a term exceeding 99 years.

[67] *See* Article 5(4) of the Model Law, *infra* the Annex.

[68] *See* Article 1 of the Model Law, *infra* the Annex.

[69] See Article 25 of the Model Law, *infra* the Annex.

[70] *See supra* note 51 and accompanying text.

legal representation of the simplified stock corporation." At the moment of incorporation or at any point during the corporation's life span, additional organs may be created such as management, audit, or other committees.

This flexibility is not restricted to the creation of governance organs, but also to the applicable rules for their operation. There is thus ample freedom for shareholders to determine aspects such as calling of meeting, quorum, voting majorities, and shareholders' representation, among others.[71]

This flexibility will be particularly beneficial for MSMEs because their owners will have leeway to decide whether a useful corporate organ, such as the board of directors, is excluded instead of having to set up mandatory corporate bodies with the only purpose of complying with cumbersome legal ritualism.

6. Rules On Capital

New provisions on capital and classes of stock are also included. The capital structure of the simplified corporation allows for any imaginable form of equity financing. Rules are introduced, for example, to set up either ordinary or dual classes of voting shares, including multiple voting rights. Contributions in kind or in labor are also permitted in the simplified corporation. The flexibility afforded by the Model Law is in sharp contrast with formalistic restrictions on capitalization in the region. Article 9 of the SAS Model Law contains rules that are a departure from what has typically been included in commercial codes throughout Latin America. Specifically, Article 9 enables business parties to define the amounts for the corporation's authorized, subscribed and paid-in capital. Furthermore, the term provided in the Model Law for the payment of any capital contributions can be made within the following two years, from the moment in which the shares of stock were subscribed.[72]

An additional feature that is closer to the partnership regime than to Corporate Law relates to transfer restrictions that can be included in the corporation's by-laws. In this sense, shareholders may be required to submit any transfer of shares to rights of first refusal. Additional limitations, such as the inability to convey the shares of stock for a fixed period of time can also be stipulated. Likewise, preemptive rights for the issuance and subscription of new shares can also be included in the by-laws.

---

[71] For example, it has been noted that this freedom of determination would benefit different types of shareholding configurations. When two incorporators wish to have shared management and direction: "A single-member board may prove helpful, particularly when the manager is different from the sole director. Such a system enables shareholders to divide the direct management of the corporation by granting binding authority to the legal representative and oversight powers to the single board member. In corporations with two shareholders and symmetrical capital contributions, this may be a suitable structure because it allows the exercise of reciprocal controls." Reyes, *supra* note 50, at 125.

[72] Reyes, *supra* note 51, at 113.

All these contractual devices are particularly important in the context of family-owned businesses, whenever shareholders wish to keep the entity as closed as possible. By setting up these types of clauses, third parties are, normally, denied access to ownership.

7. Protection Mechanisms

The SAS Model Law contains significant protection mechanisms, which are more sophisticated and effective than those normally contained in traditional Corporate Law across the Latin American region. As stated before, the Model Law provides significant leeway to business participants. Thus, most *ex ante* legal devices containing restrictions to freedom of contract or setting forth prohibitions imposed upon directors, officers, and shareholders, are not included in such Model Law. By means of this approach, directory regulations are replaced with default provisions, which are only applicable in the absence of specific contractual provisions.

To prevent the misuse of the corporate form, the Model Law contains legal standards aimed at the protection of shareholders and creditors. For example, as noted above, third parties are entitled to bring actions for piercing the corporate veil where there is an abusive or fraudulent use of the business entity. Additionally, minority shareholders are protected by certain causes of action intended to reduce tunneling and abuse of right.

The point of departure for this legal approach is the well-known presence of agency problems[73] existing between controlling and minority shareholders (as opposed to the traditional dichotomy that confronts the interests of management *vis-a-vis* those of shareholders as a class). As a result of the significant capital concentration across the region, controlling shareholders are enabled to extract private benefits of control. If this situation remains unharnessed, non-controlling shareholders may be expropriated.[74] Consequently, the Model Law contains provisions designed to counteract potential abuse of rights.[75] This theory of abuse of rights has been

---

[73] For a detailed discussion on agency problems *see* Hansmann & Kraakman, *supra* note 40.

[74] Commenting on the several notions of corporate governance, Donald Clarke notes that the following regarding protection of minority shareholders: "This concept is concerned with issues of finance and agency costs and has a policy component: the prevention of the exploitation of those who supply the money by those who control it. It centers on the relationship between stockholders, the board of directors, and senior management, and in effect asks, with Schleifer and Vishny, '[H]ow can financiers be sure that, once they sink their funds [into a firm], they get anything but a worthless piece of paper back from the manager?'" Donald C. Clarke, *Nothing But Wind? The Past and Future of Comparative Corporate Governance*, 59 AMER. J. COMP. L. 79 (2010), and (GWU Legal Studies Research Paper, GWU Law School Public Law Research Paper No. 583, 2011).

[75] *See* Article 42 of the Model Law, *infra* the Annex.

widely developed in vaious jurisdictions, particularly when dealing with abuse of shareholder's decisions.[76] The institution of abuse of rights (*abus de droit*) has become an important mechanism for protecting shareholders in close corporations in countries belonging to the Civil Law tradition, which generally lack the equity remedies present in the Common Law.

Article 42 of the Model Law states that "[s]hareholders shall exercise their voting rights in the interest of the simplified stock corporation." In this vein, when there is evidence of decisions rendered by a corporate body undertaken for the sole benefit of controlling shareholders, or aimed at purposes different from the corporate interest, the affected parties may seek judicial redress. Motives that constitute abuse of righst may include inflicting harm or damages upon other shareholders or the corporation, or unduly extracting private gains for personal benefit, among others

The abuse of rights theory is applied to three different instances, depending on the facts of the case: abuse of majority, abuse of minority and abuse of equal shareholdings (i.e., dual ownership on a 50% - 50% distribution). By adopting these protection mechanisms, the provisions of the Model Law introduce to Latin American Corporate Law the important developments on this field, spearheaded by French courts. Barthélémy Mercadal has noted on this regard that: "[V]oting rights may not be used in a discretionary manner. Courts will often temper voting liberty through the application of the abuse of right doctrine. Thus, they will penalize any and all decisions responding to an abusive exercise of voting rights, i.e., those votes issued in contradiction to the corporation and cast with the sole purpose of benefitting the majority (or minority) shareholders to the detriment of their counterparties."[77] The action for abuse-of-right provided under the Model Law allows the plaintiff to claim damages and rescission of an abusive act.

8. Restructuring Transactions

The rules on restructuring transactions in the Model Law are more flexible as compared to traditional corporate law prevailing in the Latin American region. For instance, Article 33 of such model act includes the so called "short form merger." This transaction may take place within a corporate group and consists of a merger of a subsidiary entity onto its parent. For this transaction to proceed, it is necessary that the parent entity of the simplified corporation own at least 90% of the outstanding shares of its subsidiary. In this event, the latter can be merged with the former, after a decision taken by the directors or managers of both entities. The short-form merg-

---

[76] In the United States the language used is that of "oppression" instead of abuse. *See* Matter of Kemp & Beatley Inc. 473 N.E. 2d 1173 (N.Y. 1984).

[77] BARTHÉLÉMY MERCADAL, SOCIÉTÉS COMMERCIELES, MEMENTO PRACTIQUE, 584 (Paris, Éditions Francis Lefebvre, 1995).

er is an exception to the general rule, whereby the shareholders meeting is the only corporate body entitled to make decisions regarding structural changes.[78]

The Model Law also contains a specific provision concerning the sale of all or substantially all assets of the corporation.[79] In this type of transaction, the selling entity may receive either cash or shares of the purchasing entity as consideration. The Model Law defines it as the event where "a simplified stock corporation purports to sell or convey assets and liabilities amounting to 60% or more of its equity value." In this event, the selling corporation does not cease to exist immediately, as is the case of a merger transaction. In fact, in order for it to be extinguished it is necessary to wind up the corporation through the distribution of its remaining assets. The sale of all or substantially all assets, which obviously takes place outside of the ordinary course of business, requires majority shareholder approval.

Additional provisions are included to protect the rights of minority shareholders in restructuring transactions of simplified corporations, including the applicability of dissenter rights and appraisal remedies under certain circumstances.[80]

9. Dissolution and Winding Up

It is as important to consider the legal framework for the formalization of business entities, such as the rules relating to their dissolution and winding up. Therefore, it is useful to thoroughly regulate the entire cycle of a business, so that it can be formalized at the outset in accordance with up-to-date legal provisions and also be able to close its operations and resolve all relations with creditors and shareholders at the end of such a cycle. This is particularly relevant in light of the obvious fact that many of the business entities will not be successful and, therefore, will need to close their operations and resolve all outstanding legal situations before extinction. In that sense, it is useful to provide a few suggested rules to govern its dissolution and liquidation.

The Model Law contains three articles devoted to the dissolution and winding up of the simplified corporation. These rules are particularly useful for corporations that have gone out of business, but need not resort to an insolvency proceeding to close their operations and resolve all situations with creditors and shareholders. This situation frequently takes place in MSMEs, in cases in which the corporation's liabilities do not exceed the value of available assets after dissolution. In these situations, it is necessary for those responsible for the business venture to provide pub-

---

[78] The short-form merger was first introduced by Anglo-American company law. Section 253 of the Delaware Code contains the relevant provisions. For a detailed discussion, *see* Francisco Reyes, *supra* note 51, at 132.

[79] *See* Article 32 of the Model Law, *infra* the Annex.

[80] *See* Article 30 of the Model Law, *infra* the Annex.

licity concerning the state of liquidation, appoint liquidators, prepare inventories and other financial statements, sell corporate assets, pay liabilities according to legal priorities and eventually return any remaining assets to the shareholders.

Article 34 of the Model Law contains the events of dissolution. There is an attempt in the Model Law to simplify the processes of dissolution and liquidation in order to make them expeditious, less ritualistic, and more in tune with contemporary business needs. The causes of dissolution for the simplified corporation will become effective as of the date in which the shareholders' decision to wind up the business entity, or the acknowledgment of the relevant legal cause for dissolution, is filed before the commercial registry. There is no need for further proceedings or decisions rendered by any third party. The only exception to the above-mentioned rule relates to such cases in which the term of duration has elapsed (if expressly included by the shareholders in the company's by-laws). In this case, the corporation will be dissolved automatically.

Furthermore, dissolution does not take place in events related exclusively to the reduction of a minimum number of shareholders, or the increase of shareholders above a predefined number. The absence of provisions setting forth plurality requirements or caps concerning the amount of shareholders effectively excludes any mandatory winding up events resulting from such circumstances.

Article 35 of the Model Law contains provisions aimed at curing the events of dissolution. The inclusion of these methods responds to the fact that, whenever materially possible, it is deemed to be less costly to preserve the business, instead of allowing for its dissolution. Consequently, the Model Law establishes that dissolution events may be cured by adopting any and all measures available to that effect, provided that such measures are adopted within one year following the date in which the shareholders' assembly acknowledged the cause of dissolution. Furthermore, in order to incentivize the conversion of other business entities into simplified corporations, and with the aim of furthering Corporate Law beyond the present state of formalism, the Model Law contains an additional provision intended to avoid dissolution. In fact, whenever there is a business entity, organized under any form for which an event of dissolution consists of the reduction of the minimum number of shareholders, partners or members, such instance may be cured by conversion into a simplified corporation. Article 35 of the Model Law mandates that for this event to take place, a unanimous decision must be rendered by the holders of all issued shares, or by the will of the surviving shareholder, partner, or member.

10. Dispute Resolution

According to comparative legal theory, the adoption or transplantation of substantive rules of a foreign origin may have a limited impact on the receiving jurisdiction, if the transplanted rules are not adequately accompanied by an effective institutional framework aimed at facilitating their enforcement.[81] Consequently, the Model Law contains provisions concerning dispute resolution mechanisms, which are oriented towards the efficient application of the law in the event of disputes among business parties.

The rules on this topic include the well-known methods of arbitration and mediation. The adoption of these mechanisms responds to the frequent lack of expeditious judicial enforcement mechanisms throughout the region.[82] The Model Law also contains an additional dispute resolution system, which relates to the assignment of adjudication powers to specialized judicial or quasi-judicial courts. This proposal is intended to counteract the general absence in Latin America of specialized judicial tribunals in charge of Commercial or Corporate Law matters.

The Colombian experience in this regard is noteworthy. In this jurisdiction, a short-term solution to the lack of specialized courts has been the introduction of a quasi-judicial, decision-making body within a governmental entity (i.e., Superintendence of Companies). This type of court has been in place in that country during the last ten years—an experiment that has proven highly successful.

The technical quality of specialized corporate law judges has been recognized as a crucial factor for the development of Corporate Law.[83] It is obvious that having well trained expert adjudicators results in better decisions. In the Colombian case, the Superintendence has a higher level of technical qualification and, consequently,

---

[81] *See* John C. Coffee, *Law and the Market: The Impact of Enforcement* (Columbia Law and Economics Working Paper No. 304, 2007). "The imposition of foreign rules without concern for local conditions (i.e. demand for law, pre-existing political and social arrangements, institutional background) is usually a recipe for failed legal transplants. Under this view, the principal effect of the program mentioned earlier was to increase the disparity between the law in the books and the law in action without significant improvements in the actual protection of outside investors." Katharina Pistor further illustrates the point: "Without ensuring complementarities between the new law and preexisting legal institutions, harmonization may distort rather than improve the domestic legal framework." *The Standardization of Law and Its Effect on Developing Economies*, 50 AMER. J. OF COMP. L. 98 (2002).

[82] For example, under the Chilean law on simplified corporations, arbitration is mandatory in all instances. This effectively bars parties from taking disputes related to or under the simplified corporation to State judges. *See* Article 441 of the Chilean Commercial Code as modified by Law 20.190 of 2007. Although this solution may seem drastic, it is merely a natural response to the dramatic situation of judicial backwardness experienced throughout the region.

[83] *See* Luca Enriques, *Off the Books but on the Record: Evidence from Italy on the Relevance of Judges in the Quality of Corporate Law, in* GLOBAL MARKETS, DOMESTIC INSTITUTIONS: CORPORATE LAW AND GOVERNANCE IN A NEW ERA OF CROSS-BORDER DEALS 258 (New York, Columbia University Press, 2003). *See also,* Francisco Reyes, *supra* note 42: "The underlying rationale for bypassing ordinary courts has to do with the notion that cases should be heard by highly-qualified officials with specialized technical and professional knowledge of corporate law."

a better understanding of complex corporate issues, as compared to the ordinary judges. Furthermore, the degree of predictability, legal certainty and expeditiousness of this specialized court is much higher than that of the regular judiciary.

Article 39 of the Model Law also limits the possibility of appealing the first instance decisions rendered by this specialized tribunal. This is an attempt to curtail the common practice of endlessly appealing processes to higher judicial instances. This will produce greater legal certainty as litigating parties will avoid being subject to protracted litigation.[84] The additional safeguards for litigants in Latin America, such as appeals for the violation of due process, can be achieved through writs of constitutionality that are commonplace in Latin America (*amparo, tutela* and *mandado de segurança*).[85]

Conclusion

Empirical data clearly demonstrates the success of Colombian Law 1258 — with over 500,000 SASs established within a mere decade following the enactment of the new legal framework. A similar phenomenon has taken place in other Latin American countries where this type of business entity has been adopted (such as Argentina, Uruguay, and Ecuador). This clearly suggests that businesspersons prefer flexibility to antiquated and misguided paternalism. The goals advanced by the OAS Model Law on Simplified Corporations match contemporary policies that give preference to flexibility, simple incorporation proceedings and broad contractual freedom as compared to traditional business entities. The adaptability of so-called hybrid business forms, which can be used as all-purpose vehicles, has led to their successful introduction into both common-law and civil-law jurisdictions around the world.

Annex to Chapter 16—Model Law on Simplified Corporations
MODEL ACT ON THE SIMPLIFIED STOCK CORPORATION (MASSC)

CHAPTER I— GENERAL PROVISIONS

ARTICLE 1. NATURE.—The simplified stock corporation is a for profit legal entity by shares, the nature of which will always be commercial, irrespective of the activities set forth in its purpose clause.

ARTICLE 2. LIMITED LIABILITY.—The simplified stock corporation may be formed by one or more persons or legal entities. Shareholders will only be responsible for providing the capital contributions promised to the simplified stock corpora-

---

[84] *See* Article 39 of the Model Law, *infra* the Annex.

[85] *See supra* Section 2 on Full-Fledged Limited Liability.

tion. Except as set forth in Article 41 of this Act, shareholders will not be held liable for any obligations incurred by the simplified stock corporation, including, but not limited to, labor and tax obligations. There shall be no labor relationship between a simplified stock corporation and its shareholders, unless an explicit agreement has been executed to that effect.

ARTICLE 3. LEGAL PERSONALITY.—Upon the filing of the formation document before the Mercantile Registry [include the name of corresponding company registrar's office], the simplified stock corporation will form a legal entity separate and distinct from its shareholders.

ARTICLE 4. INABILITY TO BECOME A LISTED ENTITY.—The shares of stock and other securities issued by a simplified stock corporation shall not be registered within a stock exchange, nor traded in any securities market.

CHAPTER II—FORMATION AND PROOF OF EXISTENCE

ARTICLE 5. CONTENTS OF THE FORMATION DOCUMENT.—A simplified stock corporation will be formed by contract or by the individual will of a single shareholder, provided that a written document is granted. The formation document shall be registered before the Mercantile Registry [include the name of corresponding company registrar's office], and shall set forth: 1. The name and address of each shareholder; 2. The name of the corporation followed by the words "simplified stock corporation" or the abbreviation "S.A.S."; 3. The corporation's domicile; 4. If the simplified stock corporation is to have a specific date of dissolution, the date in which the corporation is to dissolve; 5. A clear and complete description of the main business activities to be included within the purpose clause, unless it is stated that the corporation may engage in any lawful business; 6. The authorized, subscribed and paid-in capital, along with the number of shares to be issued, the different classes of shares, their par value, and the terms and conditions in which the payment will be made; 7. Any provisions for the management of the business and for the conduct of the affairs of the corporation, along with the names and powers of each manager. A simplified stock corporation shall have at least one legal representative in charge of managing the affairs of the corporation in relation with third parties. No additional formalities of any nature shall be required for the formation of the simplified stock corporation.

ARTICLE 6. ATTESTATION.—The Mercantile Registrar [include the name of corresponding company registrar's office] shall attest to the legality of the provisions set forth in the formation document and any amendments thereof. The Registrar shall only deny registration where the requirements provided under Article 5 have not been met. The decision rendered by the Registrar shall be issued within three days after the relevant filing has been made. Any decision denying registration will only be subject to a rehearing conducted by the Registrar. Upon the approval of a formation document by the Mercantile Registrar, challenges will not be heard against the existence of the simplified stock corporation and the contents of the formation document will constitute the simplified stock corporation's by-laws.

ARTICLE 7. ASSIMILATION TO PARTNERSHIP.—Where a formation document has not been duly approved by the Mercantile Registrar [include the name of corresponding company registrar's office], the purported corporation will be assimilated to a partnership. Accordingly, partners will be jointly and severally liable for all obligations in which the partnership is engaged. If the partnership has only one member, such member will be held liable for all obligations in which the partnership is engaged.

ARTICLE 8. PROOF OF EXISTENCE.—The certificate issued by the Mercantile Registrar [include the name of corresponding company registrar's office] is conclusive evidence as regards the existence of the simplified stock corporation and the provisions set forth in the formation document.

CHAPTER III—SPECIAL RULES REGARDING SUBSCRIBED, PAID-IN CAPITAL AND SHARES OF STOCK

ARTICLE 9. CAPITAL SUBSCRIPTION AND PAYMENT.—Capital subscription and payment may be carried out under terms and conditions different to those set forth under the Commercial Code or corporate statute [include the name of the relevant Code, Decree, Law, or Statute]. In any event, payment of subscribed capital shall be made within a period of two years to be counted from the date in which the shares were subscribed. The rules for subscription and payment may be freely set forth in the by-laws.

ARTICLE 10. CLASSES OF SHARES.—The simplified stock corporation may issue different classes or series of shares, including preferred shares with or without vote. Shares may be issued for any consideration whatsoever, including in-kind contributions or in exchange for labor, pursuant to the terms and conditions contained in the by-laws. Any special rights granted to the holders of any class or series of shares shall be described or affixed upon the back of the stock certificates.

ARTICLE 11. VOTING RIGHTS.—The by-laws shall depict in full detail the voting rights corresponding to each class of shares. Such document shall also determine whether each share will grant its holder single or multiple voting rights.

ARTICLE 12. SHARE TRANSFERS TO A TRUST.—Any shares issued by a simplified stock corporation may be transferred to a trust provided that an annotation is made in the corporate ledger concerning the trustee company, the beneficial owners, and the percentage of beneficial rights.

ARTICLE 13. LIMITATION ON THE TRANSFERABILITY OF SHARES.— The by-laws may contain a provision whereby the shares may not be transferred for a period not to exceed ten years, to be counted from the moment in which the shares were issued. Such term can only be extended by consent of all the holders of outstanding shares. Any such limitation on share transferability shall be described or affixed upon the back of the stock certificate.

ARTICLE 14. AUTHORIZATION FOR THE TRANSFER OF SHARES.— The by-laws may contain provisions whereby any transfer of shares or of any given class of shares will be subject to the previous authorization of the shareholders' assembly, which shall be granted by majority vote or by any supermajority included in the by-laws.

ARTICLE 15. BREACH OF RESTRICTIONS ON NEGOTIATION OF SHARES.—Any transfer of shares carried out in a manner inconsistent with the rules set forth in the by-laws shall be null and void.

ARTICLE 16. CHANGE OF CONTROL IN A CORPORATE SHAREHOLDER.—The by-laws may impose upon an incorporated shareholder the duty to notify the simplified stock corporation's legal representative about any transaction that may cause a change in control regarding such shareholder. Where a change in control has taken place, the shareholders' assembly, by majority decision, shall be entitled to exclude the corresponding incorporated shareholder. Aside from the possibility of being excluded, any breach of the duty to inform changes in control may subject the concerned shareholder to a penalty consisting of a 20% reduction of the fair market value of the shares, upon reimbursement. In the event set forth in this article, all decisions concerning the exclusion of shareholders, as well as the determination of any penalties, shall require an approval rendered by the shareholders' assembly by majority vote. The votes of the concerned shareholder shall not be taken into account for the adoption of these decisions.

CHAPTER IV—ORGANIZATION OF THE SIMPLIFIED STOCK CORPORATION

ARTICLE 17. ORGANIZATION.—Shareholders may freely organize the structure and operation of a simplified stock corporation in the by-laws. In the absence of specific provisions to this effect, the shareholders' assembly or the sole shareholder, as the case may be, will be entitled to exercise all powers legally granted to the shareholders' assemblies of stock corporations, whilst the management and representation of the simplified stock corporation shall be granted to the legal representative. Where the number of shareholders has been reduced to one, the subsisting shareholder shall be entitled to exercise the powers afforded to all existing corporate organs.

ARTICLE 18. MEETINGS.—Meetings of shareholders may be held at any place designated by the shareholders, whether it is the corporate domicile or not. For these meetings, the regular quorum provided in the by-laws will suffice, pursuant to Article 22 hereof.

ARTICLE 19. MEETINGS BY TECHNOLOGICAL DEVICES OR BY WRIT-
TEN CONSENT.—Meetings of shareholders may be held through any available
technological device, or by written consent. The minutes of such meetings shall be
drafted and included within the corporate records no later than thirty (30) days after
the meeting has taken place. These minutes shall be signed by the legal representative or, in her absence, by any shareholder that participated in the meeting.

ARTICLE 20. NOTICE OF MEETING.—In the absence of stipulation to the
contrary, the legal representative shall convene the shareholders' assembly by written notice addressed to each shareholder. Such notice shall be made at least five days
in advance to the meeting. The agenda shall in all cases be included within any
notice of meeting. Whenever the shareholders' assembly is called upon to approve
financial statements, the conversion of the corporation into another business form,
or mergers or split-off proceedings, shareholders will be entitled to exercise information rights concerning any documents relevant to the proposed transaction. Information rights may be exercised during the five days prior to the meeting, unless a
longer term has been provided for in the by-laws. Any notice of meeting may determine the date in which the Second Call Meeting will take place, in case the quorum
is insufficient to hold the first meeting. The date for the second meeting may not be
held prior to ten days following the first meeting, nor after thirty days from that same
moment.

ARTICLE 21. WAIVER OF NOTICE.—Shareholders may, at any moment,
submit written waivers of notice whereby they forego their right to be convened to
a meeting of the shareholders' assembly. Shareholders may also waive, in writing,
any information rights granted under Article 20. In any given shareholders assembly
and even in the absence of a notice of meeting, the attendees will be deemed to have
waived their right of being summoned, unless such shareholders make a statement
to the contrary before the meeting takes place.

ARTICLE 22. QUORUM AND MAJORITIES.—Unless otherwise specified in
the bylaws, quorum to a shareholders' meeting will be constituted by a majority of
shares, whether present in person or represented by proxy. Decisions of the assembly shall be taken by the affirmative vote of the majority of shares present (in person or represented by proxy), unless the by-laws contain supermajority provisions.
The sole shareholder of a simplified stock corporation may adopt any and all decisions within the powers granted to the shareholders' assembly. The sole shareholder
will keep a record of such decisions in the corporate books.

ARTICLE 23. VOTE SPLITTING.—Shareholders may split their votes during
cumulative voting proceedings for the election of directors or the members of any
other corporate organ.

ARTICLE 24. SHAREHOLDERS' AGREEMENTS.—Agreements entered
into between shareholders concerning the acquisition or sale of shares, preemptive
rights or rights of first refusal, the exercise of voting rights, voting by proxy, or any

other valid matter, shall be binding upon the simplified stock corporation, provided that such agreements have been filed with the corporation's legal representative. Shareholders' agreements shall be valid for any period of time determined in the agreement, not exceeding ten (10) years, upon the terms and conditions stated therein. Such ten-year term may only be extended by unanimous consent. Shareholders that have executed an agreement shall appoint a person who will represent them for the purposes of receiving information and providing it whenever it is requested. The simplified stock corporation's legal representative may request, in writing, to such representative, clarification as regards any provision set forth in the agreement. The response shall be provided also in writing within the five days following the request.

SubArticle 1.—The President of the shareholders' assembly, or of the concerned corporate organs, shall exclude any votes cast in a manner inconsistent with the terms set forth under a duly filed shareholders' agreement.

SubArticle 2.—Pursuant to the conditions set forth in the agreement, any shareholder shall be entitled to demand, before a court with jurisdiction over the corporation, the specific performance of any obligation arising under such agreement.

ARTICLE 25. BOARD OF DIRECTORS.—The simplified stock corporation is not required to have a board of directors, unless such board is mandated in the by-laws. In the absence of a provision requiring the operation of a board of directors, the legal representative appointed by the shareholders' assembly shall be entitled to exercise any and all powers concerning the management and legal representation of the simplified stock corporation. If a board of directors has been included in the formation document, such board will be created with one or more directors, for each of whom an alternate director may also be appointed. All directors may be appointed either by majority vote, cumulative voting, or by any other mechanism set forth in the by-laws. The rules regarding the operation of the board of directors may be freely established in the by-laws. In the absence of a specific provision in the by-laws, the board will be governed under the relevant statutory provisions.

ARTICLE 26. LEGAL REPRESENTATION.—The legal representation of the simplified stock corporation will be carried out by an individual or legal entity appointed in the manner provided in the by-laws. The legal representative may undertake and execute any and all acts and contracts included within the purpose clause, as well as those which are directly related to the operation and existence of the corporation. The legal representative shall not be required to remain at the place where the business has its main domicile.

ARTICLE 27. LIABILITY OF DIRECTORS AND MANAGERS.—All Commercial Code [include the name of the relevant Code, Decree, Law, or Statute] provisions relating to the liability of directors and managers may also be applicable to the legal representative, the board of directors, and the managers and officers of the simplified stock corporation, unless such provision is opted out of in the by-laws.

SubArticle 1.—Any individual or legal entity who is not a manager or director of a simplified stock corporation that engages in any trade or activity related to the management, direction or operation of such corporation shall be subject to the same liabilities applicable to directors and officers of the corporation.

SubArticle 2.—Whenever a simplified stock corporation or any of its managers or directors grants apparent authority to an individual or legal entity to the extent that it may be reasonably believed that such individual or legal entity has sufficient powers to represent the corporation, the company will be legally bound by any transaction entered into with third parties acting in good faith.

ARTICLE 28. AUDITING ORGANS.—A simplified stock corporation shall not, in any case, be legally mandated to establish or provide for internal auditing organs [include the name of corresponding auditing entity, e.g. fiscal auditor, auditing committee, etc.].

CHAPTER V—BY-LAW AMENDMENTS AND CORPORATE RESTRUCTURINGS

ARTICLE 29. BY-LAW AMENDMENTS.—Amendments to the corporate by-laws shall be approved by majority vote. Decisions to this effect will be recorded in a private document to be filed with the Mercantile Registry [include the name of corresponding company registrar's office].

ARTICLE 30. CORPORATE RESTRUCTURINGS.—The statutory provisions governing conversion into another form, mergers and split-off proceedings for business associations will be applicable to the simplified stock corporation. Dissenters' rights and appraisal remedies shall also be applicable. For the purpose of exercising dissenters' rights and appraisal remedies, a corporate restructuring will be considered detrimental to the economic interests of a shareholder, inter alia, whenever: 1. The dissenting shareholder's percentage in the subscribed paid-in capital of the simplified stock corporation has been reduced; 2. The corporation's equity value has been diminished; or 3. The free transferability of shares has been constrained.

ARTICLE 31. CONVERSION INTO ANOTHER BUSINESS FORM.—Any existing business entity may be converted into a simplified stock corporation by unanimous decision rendered by the holders of all issued rights or shares in such business form. The decision to convert into a simplified stock corporation shall be registered before the Mercantile Registry [include the name of corresponding company registrar's office]. A simplified stock corporation may be converted into any other business form governed under the Commercial Code [include the name of the relevant Code, Decree, Law, or Statute] provided that unanimous decision is rendered by the holders of all issued and outstanding shares in the corporation.

ARTICLE 32. SUBSTANTIAL SALE OF ASSETS.—Whenever a simplified stock corporation purports to sell or convey assets and liabilities amounting to 60%

or more of its equity value, such sale or conveyance will be considered to be a substantial sale of assets. Substantial sales of assets shall require majority shareholder approval. Whenever a substantial sale of assets is detrimental to the interests of one or more shareholders, it shall give rise to the application of dissenters' rights and appraisal remedies.

ARTICLE 33. SHORT-FORM MERGER.—In any case in which at least 90% of the outstanding shares of a simplified stock corporation is owned by another legal entity, such entity may absorb the simplified stock corporation by the sole decision of the boards of directors or legal representatives of all entities directly involved in the merger. Short-form mergers may be executed by private document duly registered before the Mercantile Registry [include the name of corresponding company registrar's office].

CHAPTER VI—DISSOLUTION AND WINDING UP

ARTICLE 34. DISSOLUTION AND WINDING UP.—The simplified stock corporation shall be dissolved and wound up whenever: 1. An expiration date has been included in the formation document and such term has elapsed, provided that a determination to extend it has not been approved by the shareholders, before or after such expiration has taken place; 2. For legal or other reasons, the corporation is absolutely unable to carry out the business activities provided under the purpose clause; 3. Compulsory liquidation proceedings have been initiated; 4. An event of dissolution set forth in the by-laws has taken place; 5. A majority shareholder decision has been rendered or such decision has been made by the will of the sole shareholder; and 6. A decision to that effect has been rendered by any authority with jurisdiction over the corporation. Whenever the duration term has elapsed, the corporation shall be dissolved automatically. In all other cases, the decision to dissolve the simplified stock corporation shall be filed before the Mercantile Registry [include the name of corresponding company registrar's office].

ARTICLE 35. CURING EVENTS OF DISSOLUTION.—Events of dissolution may be cured by adopting any and all measures available to that effect, provided that such measures are adopted within one year, following the date in which the shareholders' assembly acknowledged the event of dissolution. Events of dissolution consisting of the reduction of the minimum number of shareholders, partners or members in any business form governed under the Commercial Code [include the name of the relevant Code, Decree, Law, or Statute] may be cured by conversion into a simplified stock corporation, provided that unanimous decision is rendered by the holders of all issued shares or rights, or by the will of the subsisting shareholder, partner, or member.

ARTICLE 36. WINDING UP.—The simplified stock corporation shall be wound up in accordance with the rules that govern such proceeding for stock corporations. The legal representative shall act as liquidator, unless shareholders appoint any other person to wind up the company.

CHAPTER VII—MISCELLANEOUS PROVISIONS

ARTICLE 37. FINANCIAL STATEMENTS.—The legal representative shall submit financial statements and annual accounts to the shareholders' assembly for approval. In the event that there is a single shareholder in a simplified stock corporation, such person shall approve all financial statements and annual accounts and will record such approvals in minutes within the corporate books.

ARTICLE 38. SHAREHOLDER EXCLUSION.—The by-laws may contain causes by virtue of which shareholders may be excluded from the simplified stock corporation. Excluded shareholders shall be entitled to receive a fair market value for their shares of stock. Shareholder exclusion shall require majority shareholder approval, unless a different procedure has been laid down in the by-laws.

ARTICLE 39. CONFLICT RESOLUTION.—Any conflict of any nature whatsoever, excluding criminal matters, that arises between shareholders, managers or the corporation may be subject to arbitration proceedings or to any other alternative dispute resolution procedure. In the absence of arbitration, the same disputes will be resolved by (include specialized judicial or quasijudicial tribunal). The decisions rendered by the tribunal are final and shall not be subject to appeals before any court.

ARTICLE 40. CHOICE OF JURISDICTION.—Any contracts entered into by a simplified corporation with foreign natural or legal persons may include an agreement that any dispute arising on account of said contracts shall be resolved through international arbitration. In this case, the parties shall be free to determine the substantive and procedural rules under which the arbitrators shall settle the dispute. Any arbitration award handed down shall be enforceable and fully and directly valid, without any need for an official approval, exequatur, or any other procedure.

ARTICLE [41]. SPECIAL PROVISIONS.—The legal mechanisms set forth under Articles 13, 14, 38 and 39 may be included, amended, or suppressed from the by-laws only by unanimous decision rendered by the holders of all issued and outstanding shares.

ARTICLE [42]. PIERCING THE CORPORATE VEIL.—The corporate veil may be pierced whenever the simplified stock corporation is used for the purpose of committing fraud. Accordingly, joint and several liability may be imposed upon shareholders, directors, and managers in case of fraud or any other wrongful act perpetrated in the name of the corporation.

ARTICLE [43]. ABUSE OF RIGHTS.—Shareholders shall exercise their voting rights in the interest of the simplified stock corporation. Votes cast with the purpose of inflicting harm or damages upon other shareholders or the corporation, or with the intent of unduly extracting private gains for personal benefit or for the benefit of a third party shall constitute an abuse of rights. Any shareholder who acts abusively may be held liable for all damages caused, irrespective of the judge's ability to set aside the decision rendered by the shareholders' assembly. A suit for damages and nullification may be brought in case of: 1. Abuse of majority; 2. Abuse of minority; and 3. Abusive deadlock caused by one faction under equal division of shares between two factions.

ARTICLE [44]. CROSS-REFERENCES.—The simplified stock corporation shall be governed: 1. By this Law; 2. By the formation document, as amended from time to time; or 3. By statutory provisions contained in the Commercial Code [include the name of the relevant Code, Decree, Law, or Statute] governing stock corporations.

PROMULGATION.—This Act shall be effective as of the date of its promulgation, and it repeals any and all statutes, acts, codes, decrees, or provisions of any nature that are inconsistent with this Act.

CHAPTER 17

ECONOMIC SOVEREIGNTY AND OIL AND GAS LAW: ESSAY ON THE NORMATIVE INTERACTIONS BETWEEN INTERNATIONAL LAW AND CONSTITUTIONAL LAW

By Aubin Nzaou-Kongo[1]

Introduction

The principle of permanent sovereignty over natural resources is intended to solve problems that historically transcend the framework of its emergence and affirmation.[2] It was first at the core of the United Nations General Assembly's debates on the promotion and financing of economic development in underdeveloped countries, which led to the adoption of the Resolutions of January 12, 1952 and December 21, 1952. It then acquired its real momentum with the adoption, by the same body, of the Resolution of December 12, 1958. The latter created the Commission for Permanent Sovereignty over Natural Resources, which the General Assembly charged with carrying out a thorough investigation into the situation of the right of

[1] Ph.D. in international law, Research Fellow, Center for U.S. and Mexican Law, and Environment, Energy and Natural Resources Center (EENR), University of Houston Law Center (US). Assistant Professor of Law, University of Jean Moulin Lyon 3 (France), and formerly Assistant Professor of Law, University of Nîmes (France). I'm grateful to Ruby Bimpolo for her valuable comments on earlier drafts of this paper that I had the pleasure to present at the conference convened by the African Institute.
This research is funded by the European Union's Horizon 2020 research and innovation program, under the Marie Skłodowska-Curie grant agreement n° 845118.

[2] Georges Abi-Saab, *La souveraineté permanente dans les ressources naturelles, in* DROIT INTERNATIONAL. BILAN ET PERSPECTIVES 639 (Paris, Pedone ed., 1991).

permanent sovereignty over natural wealth and resources, considered to be a fundamental element of the right of peoples and nations to self-determination. On December 15, 1960, the General Assembly was able to adopt Resolution 1515, which laid out that the sovereign right of states to dispose of their natural wealth and resources should be respected. Resolution 1515 referred to the principle of economic sovereignty as an "inalienable right" of any state that could guarantee its economic independence and national interests.

Yet, a decisive turning point was marked with the adoption of Resolution 1803 (XVII) of December 14, 1962. This resolution definitively established—in international law—the principle of permanent sovereignty. From the outset, its preamble affirms that the consolidation of their economic independence depends substantially on the exercise and strengthening of the permanent sovereignty of states over their natural wealth and resources. It is worth noting—at the outset—that the formula used in this resolution is that of "the right of peoples and nations to permanent sovereignty over their natural wealth and resources."[3] The compromise reached in Resolution 1803 aims to recognize the developing countries' economic sovereignty as a necessary attribute of their sovereignty. As a complement to political sovereignty, economic sovereignty must then be exercised in the exclusive interest of national development and the well-being of the population of the state concerned. These elements were then consolidated by Resolution 3281 (XXIX) of December 12, 1974, in the Charter of Economic Rights and Duties of States, adopted within the framework of a New International Economic Order (NIEO).

The principle of economic sovereignty was subsequently incorporated into many constitutions and internal statutes. Since then, many developing countries, particularly in Africa, have attempted to emphasize the legal consequences of such a principle in the context of the exploitation of their oil and gas, and mining resources. Essentially, these constitutions seek to emphasize that it is the people who have the right of free disposal of their wealth and natural resources. In this sense, this right is destined to be exercised in the exclusive interest of the population. From now on, this principle is an instrument for the elimination of attempts and acts of spoliation, as well as all forms of foreign economic exploitation resulting from new forms of economic colonization. In domestic law, there can be no doubt that the way in which the rules have crystallized around this principle is reflected in constant normative interactions between international and domestic law, primarily with regard to the holder of this economic sovereignty, and then with regard to the various characteristics attached to this principle.

---

[3] *See* G.A. Res. 1803 (XVII), *Permanent Sovereignty over Natural Resources,* (14 December 1962), point 2.

I. Normative Interactions Related to the Holder of Economic Sovereignty

The holder of economic sovereignty should be identified initially, since it remains the same as soon as the concept of sovereignty is mobilized. The reference to the holder of sovereignty, both in a constitutional and economic order, is now classic. In various forms, written constitutions, and particularly in French-speaking Africa, use the formula that national sovereignty belongs to the people who exercise it through their representatives.[4] This formula appears in Article 5 of the Congolese Constitution;[5] Article 3 of the Gabonese Constitution of March 26, 1991;[6] Article 3, paragraph 1, of the Angolan Constitution;[7] and Article 2, paragraph 1, of the Cameroonian Constitution,[8] all of which establish the holder and the modalities of exercising sovereignty. Apart from the fact that the expression is—in itself—a statement of compromise, which it is not for us to develop here, it appears that the people are the entity to which African constitutions acknowledge to be the holder of the right to economic sovereignty.

The African constitutional practice, therefore, basically retains two means of exercising universal suffrage: election of representatives and referendum. The latter is essentially based on the revolutionary postulate that "the nation has the enjoyment of sovereignty; it delegates its exercise [. . .]."[9] From then on, the meaning and significance that the constituent power gives to it can be better understood by the beginning of the Preamble of the Congolese Constitution, for example, with the words

---

[4] *See e.g.,* CENTRAL AFRICAN CONSTITUTION, March 30, 2016, art. 26.

[5] *See* Article 5, CONGOLESE CONSTITUTION: "La souveraineté nationale appartient au peuple qui l'exerce au moyen du suffrage universel, par ses représentants élus ou par voie de referendum [. . .]."

[6] *See* Article 3, GABONESE CONSTITUTION as amended by the law of January 12, 2011: "La souveraineté nationale appartient au peuple qui l'exerce directement, par le référendum ou par l'élection, selon le principe de la démocratie pluraliste, et indirectement par les institutions constitutionnelles (L.1/94 du 18 mars 1994). Aucune section du peuple, aucun groupe, aucun individu ne peut s'attribuer l'exercice de la souveraineté nationale."

[7] *See* Article 3 (1), ANGOLAN CONSTITUTION: "La souveraineté, une et indivisible, appartient au peuple qui l'exerce par la voie du suffrage universel, libre, égal et direct, secret et périodique/régulier, du referendum et des autres formes prévues par la Constitution, notamment pour l'élection de ses représentant."

[8] *See* Article 2 (1), CAMEROONIAN CONSTITUTION: "La souveraineté nationale appartient au peuple camerounais qui l'exerce soit par l'intermédiaire du Président de la République et des membres du Parlement, soit par voie de référendum. Aucune fraction du peuple ni aucun individu ne peut s'en attribuer l'exercice."

[9] *See* MAURICE HAURIOU, PRÉCIS ÉLÉMENTAIRE DE DROIT CONSTITUTIONNEL, 18 (Paris, Sirey ed., 1930).

"the Congolese People [. . .]."[10] An evolving and variable formula, which first appeared in the revolutionary Congolese Constitution of December 8, 1963,[11] it took the form of "We, the Congolese people, mindful of [...]," under the Constitution of March 15, 1992; after being relegated to the back shelf of the political realm by the Constitution of January 20, 2002,[12] it is reaffirmed directly, with some emphasis, in 2015.[13] Although it seems to have no apparent impact, it still allows us to discern the holder of sovereignty at first.

All the aforementioned African Constitutions specify *ab initio* this principle. Public authorities are the creation of the people. This is a constitutional tradition that has been largely forged in principle, and which does not allow for any confusion between the primary sovereign and the delegate of sovereignty.[14] In this regard, it is accepted that the holder of sovereignty is "original, prior to the Constitution and the State [which the Constitution] enshrines, and it is this quality more than any other that makes [the State] sovereign inasmuch as it derives from nothing or no one in the order of law."[15] In fact, it is the creation of no one but itself, subsequently proceeding by self-institution. Basically, the constitutions can merely notice, acknowledge, and even recognize the existence of this holder. Such a situation thus makes it possible to grasp the origin of the sovereignty that is conferred by derivation on the constitutional organs. In this respect, the people are the entity from which the will expressed in the Constitution emanates and which is binding on the established authorities and the citizens. Such a process is driven by the idea of the State as a "contractual phenomenon." Therefore, it is both the product and the outcome of a delegation, which is no less than an agreement of will.

---

[10] For example, there are various formulations that open the many African constitutions: "The People of Cameroon (. . .)" (CONSTITUTION of January 18, 1996); "We, the Representatives of the People in the National Assembly (. . .)" (Constitution of March 9, 1992); "We, the People of Rwanda (. . .)" (CONSTITUTION of May 26, 2003); "The People of Gabon (. . .)" (CONSTITUTION of March 26, 1991, including all amendments up to 2010); "Chad (. . .)" (CONSTITUTION of May 4, 2018); "We, the Togolese People (. . .)" (CONSTITUTION of May 15, 2019); "We, the Sovereign People of Niger (. . .)" (CONSTITUTION of May 12, 1996; CONSTITUTION of November 25, 2010); "The People of Sovereign Senegal (. . .)" (CONSTITUTION of January 22, 2001); "Dahomey (. . .)" (CONSTITUTION of December 11, 1990).

[11] *See* CONSTITUTION of December 8, 1963, JORC, December 31, 1963, p. 1039. *See* Alexis Gabou, LES CONSTITUTIONS CONGOLAISES, 185 (Paris, Ed. LGDJ, 1984).

[12] *See* CONSTITUTION of January 20, 2002, 1 JORC (special issue, February 2002).

[13] *See* Article 2, Constitution of March 2, 1961; Article 2, CONSTITUTION of December 8, 1963; Article 2, CONSTITUTION of December 31, 1969; Article 2, CONSTITUTION of June 24, 1973; Article 2, CONSTITUTION of July 8, 1979; Article 4, CONSTITUTION of March 15, 1992; Article 3, CONSTITUTION of January 20, 2002, and CONSTITUTION of November 6, 2015.

[14] *See* Olivier Beaud, *Le souverain*, POUVOIRS, 38 (n° 67, 1993).

[15] *Id.*

In support of these various considerations, African constitutions, such as the Central African[16] and Cameroonian constitutions,[17] also state that no fraction of the people, or any individual, can appropriate the exercise of such sovereignty. The Congolese constitution adds to the formula that "no state body" can appropriate such an exercise.

However, this caveat—relating to the indivisibility of power—stems from a twofold observation.

In the first, the people are not a mechanical grouping of individuals. Nor is it an isolated individual. It is indeed an indissociable and indivisible whole. Its literal translation, when it comes to the management of natural resources, is that the holder of economic sovereignty is the people as a whole, whether Chadian, Senegalese, Rwandan or Congolese (DRC). Since domestic public law has not established a precise conception of the people, it seems appropriate to draw—from this gap—elements of a general understanding. It should be pointed out that African public rights are now part of a continental context, which has sometimes allowed or supported the construction, emergence or even consecration of new or classic concepts. This context is that of the African Union. Over the years, this context has been conducive to the most unsuspected interactions of the African Union's legal order with state or internal orders. Subsequently, it turns out that any tentative to construe the term of people in Africa inescapably leads to search its consistency in the frame of reciprocal or mutual influences between the African Charter on Human and Peoples' Rights of June 27, 1981, and African constitutions is quite naturally necessary.

The African Charter on Human and Peoples' Rights provides a dual conception of the people, which is adapted, at least formally, to the notion of economic sovereignty as it appeared in international law before penetrating African constitutions and certain legislations. The initial conception of the people is national. It is based on essentially ethnic, cultural, and linguistic aspects. It is opposed by the so-called territorial conception, which dominates contemporary international law. The latter, unlike the former, identifies the people with the population as it appears in modern constitutions. Either firmly to the entire population of a State, or—to a certain extent—to the existence of infra-state human groups.[18] It is regrettable—in this regard—that the preparatory work for the 1981 African Charter on Human and Peoples' Rights, in which Article 20, paragraph 1, enshrines the right of peoples to exist

---

[16] *See* CENTRAL AFRICAN CONSTITUTION, *supra* note 4, at art. 26, para. 2.

[17] *See* CAMEROON CONSTITUTION, art. 3.

[18] This double approach is predominant in the provisions of the Universal Declaration of the Rights of Peoples known as the Algiers Declaration of July 4, 1976. V. *See* MUTOY MABIA-LA, LE SYSTÈME RÉGIONAL AFRICAIN DE PROTECTION DES DROITS DE L'HOMME, 36 (Brussels, Bruylant, 2005). *See also* FATSAH OUGUERGOUZ, THE AFRICAN CHARTER ON HUMAN AND PEOPLES' RIGHTS. UNE APPROCHE JURIDIQUE DES DROITS DE L'HOMME ENTRE TRADITION ET MODERNITÉ, 146 (Paris, Ed. PUF, 1993).

and their right to self-determination, was not available, as it would have shed some useful light here.[19]

The absence of such work, it would seem, has not led to any form of abstention on the part of the African Commission on Human and Peoples' Rights, which took a bold and unbending stand when they felt they had to formulate some guidelines necessary for a nuanced interpretation of the Charter. The apparent difficulty has now been resolved.[20] The African Commission has repeatedly been called upon under Article 45, paragraph 3, of the Charter to interpret its provisions, and on each occasion, they have pointed out that the people—within the meaning of the Charter—are the holders of a political right, which they refer to as "sovereignty." In many ways, this position confirms a long-standing general trend that the Congolese revolutionary movement tried to influence—in early 1960s—in order to establish definitively the popular sovereignty.[21] Above all, it is worthwhile to notice that the African Commission on Human and Peoples' Rights has endorsed a very broad interpretation of what should be designated as the people.

It is also worth noting that the practice of the Commission has attached three meanings to the concept of people. The Commission identifies foremost the people with the population living in a well-defined territory.[22] In this sense, they refer to the entire population of a State.[23] In so doing, the Commission goes further when it con-

---

[19] *See* KÉBA MBAYE, LES DROITS DE L'HOMME EN AFRIQUE, 43 (Paris, Ed. Pedone, 2002).

[20] *See* Aubin Nzaou-Kongo, L'exploitation des hydrocarbures et la protection de l'environnement en République du Congo. Essai sur la complexité de leurs rapports à la lumière du droit international, 51 (2018) (unpublished Ph.D. thesis collection (on file with University of Lyon 3 Library System).

[21] Michel Troper, *L'évolution politique et constitutionnelle de la République populaire du Congo*, in CORPUS CONSTITUTIONNEL, 560 (Vol. 2, Part 2, 1979).

[22] The Commission recalled, on the occasion of the *Congrès du Peuple Katangais v. Zaire* case, that the invocation of self-determination of the Katangese people was impertinent (para. 53). According to her, self-determination could only concern and be envisaged for the people of Zaire. This decision followed a communication (75/92) introduced in 1992 by Mr. Gérard Moke, President of the Congress of the Katangese People, on the basis of Article 20 (1) of the Charter. The communication was essentially aimed at three demands: to recognize the Congress of the Katangese People as a liberation movement, to recognize the independence of Katanga, and to help the Katangese people obtain the evacuation of Zaire from its territory. *See* ACHPR, *Congrès du Peuple Katangais c. Zaire,* decision of 22 March 1995, 298, §1 RADH (2000). Having become constant, the Commission has had occasion to reinforce such an approach on the occasion of the *Constitutional Rights Project and Other v. Nigeria* and *Jawara v. Gambia* cases. V. Respectively ACHPR, *Constitutional Rights Project and Other v. Nigeria,* Decision of 31 October 1998, ACHPR *2000*, p. 193, § 51 and 52 and ACHPR, *Jawara v. The Gambia,* Decision of 11 May 2000, *ACHPR 2000*, p. 109, § 73 and 75.

[23] *See* FATSAH OUGUERGOUZ, LA CHARTE AFRICAINE DES DROITS DE L'HOMME ET DES PEUPLES, 135 (Ed. PUF, 1993).

siders that the people are an indivisible whole, which in view of this condition should not suffer any rupture of equality.[24] Moreover, the Commission concluded that the concept of peoplehood is closely linked to the exercise of collective rights.[25] This last point and to the premise that presided over the consecration in international law of the right of peoples to self-determination are interrelated.[26] Thus, it should be remembered that the people correspond to the population of a State.

The central feature of the analysis here is that all African constitutions have traditionally deployed the effects of the African Charter with respect to the legal situations they enshrine. On this matter, the seat—or more specifically the siege—of such influence is even today in paragraph 6 of the Preamble of the Congolese Constitution of November 6, 2015, which declares the African Charter on Human and Peoples' Rights to be an "integral part" of it. Similarly, the landmark it represents is rolled out across many African Constitutions, for example in point 2 of the Preamble of the Gabonese Constitution; point 9 of the Preamble of the Rwandan Constitution; and point 1 of the Preamble of the Senegalese Constitution.

Secondly, most of the African Constitutions have enshrouded—the authority attached to the holder of the economic sovereignty—in a substantive matter. As

---

[24] The Commission therefore clarified that the concept of people also incorporates sub-state communities in *Malawi African Association et al v. Mauritania*. Called upon to rule on a violation of Article 19 of the Charter, the Commission specified that: "At the heart of the abuses alleged in the various communications is the question of the domination of one section of the population by another. The resulting discrimination against, those who had been awkwardly called, the Negro Mauritanians would, according to the petitioners (cf. in particular communication 54/91), be the result of the denial of the fundamental principle of equality of peoples set forth in the African Charter and would constitute a violation of its Article 19. The Commission must, however, admit that the information made available to it does not allow it to establish with certainty the violation of Article 19 of the Charter in the forms alleged here. It has, however, identified and condemned the existence of discriminatory practices against certain sections of the Mauritanian population (para. 164)." *See* ACHPR, Malawi African Association and Others v. Mauritania, Decision of 11 May 2000, AIHR 2000, p. 148, § 142.

[25] These are the rights provided for in Articles 19 to 24 of the Charter: the right of peoples to self-determination, the right to natural wealth and resources, the right of peoples to peace, the right to economic development and the right of peoples to a satisfactory environment. These rights can only be exercised - in the words of the Commission - by a people which is bound by ". . . *its historical, traditional, racial, ethnic, cultural, linguistic, linguistic, religious, ideological, geographical, economic and other identities and affinities.*" The Commission was able to draw certain conclusions, including "(. . .) The first is that the African Charter seeks to provide for group or collective rights, namely: a set of rights that can theoretically only be enjoyed collectively, such as the right to self-determination, independence or sovereignty." *See* ACHPR, *Kevin Mgwanga Gunme et al v. Cameroon,* Decision 27 May 2009, para. 170.

[26] *See* Georges Abi-Saab, *Cours général de droit international public*, 337 RCADI 207 (1987).

such, it is proclaimed that the people do not delegate this sovereignty to any state body, but to the State itself. The aforementioned reservation makes sovereignty a right that the State, through the government, its institutional component, exercises on behalf of the people according to the terms of the preambles cited above. In that regard, the formula of the Senegalese Constitution is unequivocal: "Natural resources belong to the people. They are used for the improvement of their living conditions."[27] This boils down to the fact that the population, notably the human component of the State, delegates its right to procure conditions for national well-being to the institutional component. Therefore, this right takes the form of a power, a comcompetence, a prerogative, that the government exercises on behalf of the population. For the peaceful enjoyment of this prerogative, Article 21, paragraph 1, of the African Charter on Human and Peoples' Rights stipulates that it is—hence—up to the state to exercise this economic sovereignty in the exclusive interest of the people. As early as 1952, the two important resolutions of the United Nations General Assembly, which set out—for the first time in international law—the fundamental tenet of sovereignty over natural wealth and resources, notably Resolutions 523 (VI) of January 12 and 626 (VII) of December 21, 1952, specified that "Member States . . . shall exercise their right to use and exploit freely their wealth whenever they deem it desirable for their economic progress and development."[28]

This approach was—after a short amount of time—reinforced by Resolution 1515 (XV) of December 15, 1960, in which the United Nations General Assembly recommended that the right of each State to dispose freely of its natural wealth and resources should be considered, whereas its national interests and economic independence will be respected. The ever-increasing importance attached by the General Assembly to the economic development and the strengthening of the economic independence of developing countries could therefore justify its affirmation in Resolution 1803 (XVII) of December 14, 1962, of "the right of peoples and nations to permanent sovereignty over their natural wealth and resources." A fundamental element of the right of peoples to self-determination, this right of sovereignty—as set out in the resolution—could then only be implemented within the framework of the internal legislation of States.[29] Indeed, it is argued that Resolution 3281 (XXIX) of December 12, 1974, on the Charter of Economic Rights and Duties of States, adopted within the framework of a New International Economic Order (NIEO), decisively expanded the role of the State in the implementation of economic sovereignty. As

---

[27] *See* SENEGAL CONSTITUTION, art. 25-1.

[28] *See* G.A. Res. 523 (VI), *Integrated Economic Development and Trade Agreements,* (12 January 1952), para. 1 Preamble. *See* G.A. Res. 626 (VII), *Right to the Free Exploitation of Natural Wealth and Resources,* (21 December 1952), para. 1.

[29] *See* G.A. Res. 1803 (XVII), *Permanent Sovereignty over Natural Resources,* (14 December 1962), points 3 and 4.

stated in its Article 2, "Each State shall have and freely exercise full and permanent sovereignty over all its wealth, natural resources and economic activities, including possession and the right to use and dispose of them." Therefore, one can ascertain why this clause was taken up *in extenso* by Article 9 of the Congolese Constitution of March 15, 1992, which added—however—that the "State guarantees the freedom of private initiative in the exploitation of natural resources."

Indeed, the Charter's ambition, which seemed among other things to achieve greater prosperity in all countries, a higher standard of living for all peoples and to promote particularly economic and social progress for developing countries, placed the State at the heart of the new international economic order it wanted to establish upfront. In this sense, the Charter noted that the free choice by the State of its political, economic, social and cultural system, in accordance with the will of its people and without external interference, pressure or threat, constituted a sovereign and inalienable right.[30] In order to grasp its true significance, it is necessary to consider the logical and potentially conflicting relationship between the respective roles of the people and the State, as Dominique Rosenberg has put it: "[to the people] the non-transferable right to enjoy natural resources and [to the State] the sovereign right to implement this principle in accordance with national interests."[31]

International law has emerged—in the case of economic sovereignty—as the basis for the national affirmation of an attribute or a fragment of sovereignty as it is understood by law today, but it has also favored a definitive anchoring of the general characteristics of this sovereignty to economic situations, or even more specifically to the exploitation of hydrocarbons.

II. Normative Interactions Related to the Characteristics of Economic Sovereignty

The assertion of a principle of economic sovereignty is not enough—*per se*—to guarantee its effectiveness, so it is various elements, among which are the characteristics we are going to discuss, that will contribute to its definitive anchoring. Characteristics constitute the central pillars of economic sovereignty. In this regard, reference can be made here to Article 21 of the African Charter on Human and Peoples' Rights, which is likely to shed light on their meaning and legal scope beyond the simple statement adopted in general international law in the early 1950s. This provision underscores the importance of these characteristics, in that it highlights the right of free disposition exercised by states, but also determines and aims to sanction

---

[30] *See* Charter of Economic Rights and Duties of States, art. 1.

[31] *See* Dominique Rosenberg, *Article 21, §1 in* LA CHARTE AFRICAINE DES DROITS DE L'HOMME ET DES PEUPLES ET LE PROTOCOLE Y RELATIF PORTANT CRÉATION DE LA COUR AFRICAINE DES DROITS DE L'HOMME. ARTICLE-BY-ARTICLE COMMENTARY 523 (Brussels, Ed. Bruylant, 2011).

various situations that may affect the management of natural resources in Africa: "the case of spoliation of national resources and wealth [. . .] forms of foreign economic exploitation, particularly that practiced by international monopolies. . .."[32]

These specific characteristics of the notion of economic sovereignty are well established in international law.[33] As a result, a dual character derives from the incorporation of economic sovereignty into domestic law: economic sovereignty is designated as a permanent right, on the one hand, and as an inalienable right, on the other.

First of all, economic sovereignty should be examined as a permanent right. The *prima facie* reference for such a right is Resolution 1803 of 1962. Its wording is taken up almost *in extenso* by several African constitutions. The Congolese Constitution is a case in point. Similarly, it should be noted—at the outset of this reflection—that some constitutions, such as the Ivorian and Beninese constitutions, merely state the principle without mentioning its characteristics.

It is common ground now that economic sovereignty is a permanent right and its meaning is twofold. In furtherance of this characteristic, economic sovereignty is solemnly affirmed as a right. Such a statement is now customary in some African constitutions and can be found in all Congolese constitutions since 1992[34] and—most notably—in Article 6, paragraph 2, of the 1992 Cape Verdean Constitution, as amended in 2010. This right reflects the clear fidelity of these instruments to the text of Resolution 1803 (XVII) of December 14, 1962, which states, in its first paragraph, a "right of sovereignty."

The overarching dimension of this right can be determined from a double standpoint.

The first is the prerogative of the enjoyment of the benefits that the exploitation or management of national wealth and natural resources is likely to bring to the people.[35]

It is therefore a right of the people, whose interpretation can easily be supported based on Article 54 of the Constitution of March 15, 1992: "The Congolese people have the right [. . .] to enjoy their natural wealth and resources." While it is accepted that a constitutional tradition has gradually developed around the meaning of economic sovereignty in Congolese law, its formulation has meanwhile been relatively clearly disaggregated, as the Constitution of 2015 clearly shows. Despite the conceptual variations observed as a result of changes in usage and permanent changes in constitutions, the conception of this right of the people remains almost

---

[32] *See* African Charter on Human and Peoples' Rights, art. 21.

[33] *See* Nzaou-Kongo, *supra* note 20, at 53. *See also*, ALAIN PELLET, DROIT INTERNATIONAL DU DÉVELOPPEMENT, 108 (Paris, Ed. PUF, 1987).

[34] *See* Preamble, CONGOLESE CONSTITUTION, para. 6.

[35] *See* Rosenberg, *supra* note 31.

intact, as it was presented *ab initio* in paragraph 3 of the Preamble of Resolution 626 (VII) of December 21, 1952 and point 1 of Resolution 1803 (XVII) of December 14, 1962. In that matter, the permanent character of this right lies in the fact that its enjoyment belongs to the people. Consequently, it can only be envisaged in the interest of national development and the well-being of the population of the State concerned. This approach is reinforced by Articles 1 and 2, which are common to the two 1966 United Nations Covenants.[36] Such an approach is relatively reinforced by the wording chosen by the drafters of the African Charter on Human and Peoples' Rights, of which Article 21, paragraph 1, predicates — in referring to sovereignty over natural resources — "This right shall be exercised in the exclusive interest of the populations." From this perspective, as one can observe, the prerogative derives irreducibly from the right of peoples to self-determination.[37]

The prerogative conferred on the State to implement and apply the principle in accordance with the national interest represents another item. Here again, Article 9 of the Congolese Constitution of March 15, 1992, already affirmed that "The State exercises sovereignty [. . .] over all its natural wealth and resources." Although the current Constitution of 2015 does not use this formulation, it can — however — be considered inherent to the notion of sovereignty, as it results from the relevant international instruments and as used by the Republic of Congo. It is on behalf of the people that the State is called upon to exercise economic sovereignty. This prerogative takes on various modalities relating to the exercise of the State's territorial competences,[38] its right to regulate and its control over the management of national activities.[39] These three modalities will be largely developed afterwards.

Nevertheless, it seems appropriate — at this stage of the analysis — to indicate that the African Commission on Human and Peoples' Rights has had the opportunity to specify how the state should exercise this right in two Resolutions adopted in 2012 and 2015. The first one relates to a human rights-based approach to natural resource governance,[40] in which the Commission reaffirmed that in accordance with

---

[36] As of December 16, 1966, one relates to civil and political rights, while the other relates to economic, social and cultural rights.

[37] *See* Charles Chaumont, *Recherche du contenu irréductible du concept de souveraineté internationale de l'État, in* HOMMAGE D'UNE GÉNÉRATION DE JURISTES AU PRÉSIDENT BASDEVANT, 150 et se. (Paris, Pedone, 1960). *See also* André N'Kolumbua, *L'ambivalence des relations entre le droit des peuples à disposer d'eux-mêmes et l'intégrité territoriale des États en droit international contemporain,* in MÉLANGES OFFERTS À CHARLES CHAUMONT, 445 (Paris, Ed. Pedone, 1984).

[38] *See* Abi-Saab, *supra* note 26.

[39] *See* Jean Touscoz, *Dominique Rosenberg: Le principe de souveraineté des États sur leurs ressources naturelles, Paris, Ed. LGDJ, 1983, 395 pages,* INCD 900 (No. 4, 1984).

[40] ACHPR/ Res. 224, Resolution on a Human Rights-Based Approach to Natural Resource Governance, of May 2, 2012.

the principle of state sovereignty over natural resources, the state is the primary guarantor of natural resource management. This management must involve participation and be carried out in the interest of the people. This conclusion is all the more necessary given that the Banjul Commission[41] recalls that this is a mission that must undertake in accordance with international human rights law and standards. As for the second Resolution, relating to the obligation to guarantee the right to water,[42] the Commission, while recalling its connection with Resolution 224 (LI) of 2012 on the governance of natural resources, which includes water resources, insists on water governance based on sovereignty over natural resources with the participation of the populations. These resolutions go beyond the initial management framework and put into perspective the need for an energy democracy, although the term is not expressly used.

The right of economic sovereignty is moreover permanent. This second characteristic, which is decisive for understanding the previous one, reflects the faithfulness of the drafters of the Chadian Constitution to the terms of Resolutions 1803 (XVII) of December 14, 1962, point 1, and 3281 (XXIX) of December 12, 1974, on the Charter of the Economic Rights and Duties of States, Article 2. In this regard, the adjective is used to indicate the imprescriptible status of this right. This has a variety of legal implications. Whatever the conceptual variable used, "permanence," "permanent right," or "permanent sovereignty," it seems appropriate to indicate that this right can in no case be "taken away from peoples who [in return] can always and under any circumstances claim it."[43] In support of this approach, Article 21, paragraph 1 of the Constitution of the Republic of Guinea refers to an "imprescriptible right over [the] wealth"[44] and, in the same vein, Article 6, paragraph 3, of the Cape Verdean Constitution clearly states that "The State may not alienate any part of the national territory or any of the sovereign rights it exercises over it."

As a result, the government—whoever it might be—manages national wealth and resources, which—despite changes due to political, social, or economic circumstances—could not break the regular exercise of this right of the people over their natural wealth. In support of this argument, it is sustained that this right can be exercised at any time, regardless of any international commitments previously made[45] or actions aimed at plundering the people and guaranteeing the avaricious interests of those in power. On this point, voices related to this interpretation have been able to emphasize that "For states [such as those in Africa], the 'permanence' of their sov-

---

[41] Capital of The Gambia where the headquarters of this institution is located.

[42] ACHPR/Res. 300 (EXT.OS/XVII) 20, Resolution on the Obligation to Guarantee the Right to Water, of 28 February 2015.

[43] *See* Rosenberg, *supra* note 31, at 526.

[44] *See* REPUBLIC OF GUINEA CONSTITUTION, May 10, 2010.

[45] *See* Abi-Saab, *supra* note 26.

ereignty means that they are free, where appropriate, to modify or denounce instruments[46]" particularly in the case of colonial mining concessions, or even various forms of administrative arrangements with multinational corporations, which were initially considered as part of the legal succession of states, and which in almost all cases were a real obstacle to economic development.

The imprescriptible nature of this right also resides in the fact that this right cannot be abandoned for a long period of time, nor can it be subject to interrupted enjoyment. In this respect, economic sovereignty remains a permanent and continuous conquest of the State, which cannot transfer its exercise to another entity in a lasting manner.[47] Practice has shown that, with a view to resolving situations of state succession originally involving foreign individuals and their retention of acquired rights, the accession of a new state to independence has, in many cases, conferred only a truncated sovereignty mortgaged by decisions that it had not taken, but which had serious consequences on its economic policy.[48] The perpetuation of colonial mining concessions has long been a topical illustration of this. From then on, these problems continued to arise, even long after independence, given the economic fragility of many African states, which did not prevent them from continuing to "dispose certain rights, by convention or contract."[49] These operations regularly proved pernicious in the context of the economic development of many new states. It is this situation that is strongly stigmatized by the famous UNGA Resolution 2625 of October 24, 1974 on the Declaration on Principles of International Law concerning Friendly Relations and Cooperation among States in accordance with the Charter of the United Nations.

In addition to the general considerations often set out, it should be noted that the analysis of the development of hydrocarbon law in Congo and Gabon reveals the constant difficulty of achieving a real exercise of this sovereignty. Such a situation is common to several French-speaking African states. On the one hand, in 2019, Gabon was summoned, because of its chronic dependence on aid granted by international financial institutions, to repeal its Hydrocarbons Code of 2014 and to adopt another one, drafted by foreign experts and deemed less binding. On the other hand, the Republic of Congo, which adopted its last Hydrocarbon Code on October 12, 2016,[50] has attempted to move closer to this sovereignty by implementing a rela-

---

[46] *See* Pellet, *supra* note 33, at 110.

[47] *Id.* at 109.

[48] *Id.*

[49] *Id.* at 110.

[50] *See* Benjamin Boumakani & Aubin Nzaou, *Les nouveaux aspects de la protection de l'environnement dans les codes des hydrocarbures des pays d'Afrique subsaharienne*, *in* DROIT, HUMANITÉ ET ENVIRONNEMENT 569 (MÉLANGES STÉPHANE DOUMBÉ-BILLÉ, Ed. Larcier, 2020).

tively diffuse, underlying, and creeping nationalization, which was immediately— and fundamentally—inhibited by the country's economic and financial context. It has been argued that the adoption of this instrument was intended to remedy the deficiency of the previous legal framework, but this is not *de facto* the case. Apart from the simple inference drawn from the granting of exclusivity to the national company for the conduct of upstream activities,[51] the provisions of the new code do not have the necessary authority to achieve an assumed nationalization. The principle of economic sovereignty—in itself and without taking sociological considerations into account—tends to support the direct and effective expression of this national competence. In the Congolese context it cannot be denied that the influence of both the revolution of the 1960s, and the African Union's advocacy of the aforementioned Charter (art. 20) revealed that the principle of self-determination militates in favor of removing the stench of economic or political foreign domination.

Nor should there be any misunderstanding about the true scope of the terms of Article 7 and the following articles of the Congolese Hydrocarbon Code that envelop this initiative. Indeed, they do not confer any greater authority to this nationalization, which suffers from a double consubstantial infirmity: the material impossibility of its realization due to a multiplicity of reasons—namely quasi-monopoly situation of the multinationals, laws drafted abroad, etc.—on the one hand, and the chronic dependence on oil revenues that the discourse on diversification has not appreciably diminished, on the other hand. If these circumstances lead above all to denounce the government's lack of audacity, the timid rules that relate to it will presumably see their apparent pre-eminence supplanted in the more or less distant future by the conditions set by the international financial institutions.[52]

The economic sovereignty that underpins the priority economic action of African countries in hydrocarbon exploration, exploitation and trade is based on "the right to choose one's economic system," which is an element of the sovereign equality of states. Going further, the Charter of Economic Rights and Duties of States also attempted to rectify this state of affairs, starting in 1974, in the perspective, and innovative in international law for developing States, of a New International Economic Order (NIEO).[53] In particular, it emphasizes that "Each State shall have and freely exercise full and permanent sovereignty over all wealth, natural resources and economic activities, including possession and the right to use and dispose of them."[54] It

---

[51] *See* CONGOLESE HYDROCARBON CODE, art. 7.

[52] *See* Nzaou-Kongo, *supra* note 20, at 57.

[53] *See* G.A. Res. 3201 (S-VI), Declaration on the Establishment of a New International Economic Order, 1 May 1974, and G.A. Res. 3202 (S-VI), Programme of Action on the Establishment of a New International Economic Order, 1 May 1974. *See also* MOHAMED BEDJAOUI, POUR UN NOUVEL ORDRE ÉCONOMIQUE INTERNATIONAL, 271 (Paris, Ed. Unesco, 1979).

[54] *See* Charter of Economic Rights and Duties of States, art. 2, para. 1.

is, therefore, clear—particularly as Professor Abi-Saab points it out—that econom-ic sovereignty is the rule here and any limitations it may suffer are indeed only an exception.[55] In this sense, the exercise of economic sovereignty must be continuous, except that various circumstances must not contribute to hindering it. Consequently, Abi-Saab writes, the "limits imposed [on this sovereignty] are necessarily transitory and circumscribed in scope and time."[56]

Economic sovereignty then takes on the character of an inalienable right. Its for-mulation is of great interest for the present reflection because it allows this charac-teristic to be exposed and its declinations to be studied. As it was originally formu-lated in the UNGA resolutions, the term "inalienable sovereignty" could be confused with "non-transferable sovereignty." It soon becomes clear that the distinction is more nuanced than it seems.

In the first place, the inalienable character of economic sovereignty seems fun-damental. It is based on the imperative need, put forward by developing countries, to effectively control national wealth and natural resources and their exploitation. It was particularly in reaction to the colonial oil and mining concessions that the need for this character to be based on the principle to be adopted by the UN General Assembly was ardently defended.[57] In this regard, it is understandable that this con-trol—an emanation of the inalienable character—had to be exercised by the state, even when a previous colonial regime had contracted ownership rights over natural resources.[58] Thus, it could be considered that only "inalienable sovereignty" could justify the freedom of action of the new states. This freedom of action is notably reflected in the capacity of the host state to amend or cancel the initial negotiation of oil and mining concessions.[59] As Professor Fatouros has written, the term "inalienable sovereignty" has become an important qualification.[60] If it had been accepted that developed countries were producers, for some, but above all large consumers of fossil fuels, for a large part, the interest in affirming such a necessity could hardly have been foreign to them. However, the priority that such an interest could represent for these countries was not the same as for developing countries.[61]

---

[55] *See* Abi-Saab, *supra* note 26, at 336.

[56] *Id.*

[57] *See* Arghyrios Fatouros, *An International legal framework for energy*, 388 RCADI 332 (2008).

[58] *Id.*

[59] *Id.*

[60] *Id.*

[61] The formulation of Professor Arghyrios Fatouros perfectly reflects the reality of developing countries and dependence on hydrocarbon resources as follows: "*To begin with, the pro-duction and export of natural resources, while sometimes quite important for the economy of developed countries, is not generally as crucial for it as it is in the case of the develop-*

Important as it is, such a justification does not preclude an even broader consideration of the term.

Second, the inalienable nature of economic sovereignty lends itself to a broad interpretation. It means that the right of sovereignty cannot be alienated, nor can it be ceded, either free of charge or against payment, nor can it be encumbered with rights *in rem*. Whether in its present formulation or in that of Article 54 of the Congolese Constitution of March 15, 1992, the right of the people to enjoy their natural wealth and resources is a substantive right. There is no doubt about the rule here. It is strictly forbidden to deprive the Congolese people of their right of sovereignty, but also to plunder wealth and natural resources. In this regard, the Congolese State or the government representing it may not, at any time, alienate definitively or momentarily, neither in whole or in part, the right of sovereignty over the wealth and resources located on its territory or its dismemberments to foreign public or private interests.[62]

A dual justification explains the inalienable character of economic sovereignty. First and foremost, the need to protect the State against its own weaknesses or deficiencies.[63] This reason is undoubtedly the one that best explains the link between economic sovereignty and the rights of the people.[64] Although its consequences are legal, their economic scope is hardly questionable.

The Congolese constitution, for example, specifies that certain behaviors constitute the "crime of pillage." These are acts, agreements, conventions, administrative arrangements, or any other facts aimed at depriving the Nation in whole or in part of its own means of existence within the meaning of Article 44. The only means in question here are drawn from national wealth and natural resources. Given that the Republic of Congo remains dependent on economic development for nearly 85% of its wealth and resources, this constitutional provision of a criminal nature is particularly aimed at acts of corruption and, as a result, the impediments to better public governance, transparence or even the moralization of public life. The term "livelihood from its natural resources or wealth" refers directly to the financial means and

---

ing countries, many of which entirely depend on the export of one or two primary products. In the second place, developed countries usually possess the administrative expertise and capability to protect themselves against overreaching by private, especially foreign, companies. Thirdly, economic control over or the management of natural resources in developed countries is generally not as skewed in favour of foreign-owned investors and enterprises as it is in the developing countries." See Fatouros, *supra* note 57, at 389.

[62] *See* Justine Diffo Tchunkam, *Article 21, §5, in* La Charte africaine des droits de l'homme et des peuples et le protocole y relatif portant portant création de la Cour africaine des droits de l'homme. Article-by-article commentary, 571 (Brussels, Ed. Bruylant 2011).

[63] *See* Fatouros, *supra* note 57, at 389.

[64] Abi-Saab, *supra* note 26, at 336-337.

gains, even if fiscal, derived from the management and exploitation of natural resources and wealth.

The vigorous affirmation that appears in the Preamble of the Congolese Constitution confirms—in a relevant manner—the importance and interest that the Nation gives them as the main means of existence. In doing so, it is appropriate to see this crime of plunder as a real economic crime that hinders the development of the country. The constituent not only incriminates the aforementioned acts, but also calls into question the attempt to do so.[65] The constituent then resorts to the practice of the punishable attempt, which allows here to consider that the responsibility of the perpetrator of the crime of looting must be retained, when it is noted that the beginning of execution has been established, although it is suspended by circumstances beyond the control of the perpetrator. That said, it is not necessary that results with serious and pernicious consequences be observed. The identification of the perpetrators of this type of behavior seems to us necessary. Incidentally, it appears from Article 45 of the Constitution that these acts can be carried out by the constituted authorities; depending on the case, one will speak of the crime of looting or an act of forgery. This provision has the advantage of designating public authorities as possible perpetrators of this type of act, but the use by the constituent of the formula "if committed by a constituted authority" suggests that it may be committed by organizations or individuals. As such, organizations or individuals authorized to contract on behalf of and for the State can be clearly targeted, particularly those involved in the management of national resources, such as oil and gas companies or their agents, thus echoing the idea that every citizen, whether charged with a public responsibility or elected to public office, has a duty to carry it out conscientiously. In this sense, the stated purpose of such reprehensible actions must be to promote the personal enrichment of the one, Nation, organization or group or even of foreign individuals, who commit the crime.

This prohibition is then justified by the fact that economic sovereignty is inseparable from territorial sovereignty. As Professor Fatouros has written, "The principle reflects the general and well-established principle of territorial sovereignty, which has always been understood as including sovereignty over natural resources in the territory's subsoil."[66] It is clear from the outset that the alienation of economic sovereignty would entail *ipso jure the* alienation of territorial sovereignty. However, this concept can be more nuanced because, as Article 2 of the Charter of Economic Rights and Duties of States provides, this sovereignty also includes the right to "dispose" of natural wealth and resources. Consequently, it seems necessary to specify that the right to "dispose" of natural wealth and resources does not apply directly to them. It concerns in particular the "direct or indirect" products of the

---

[65] *See* CONGOLESE CONSTITUTION, *supra* note 5, art. 45.

[66] *Id.* at 388.

exploitation of national wealth and natural resources.[67] It is thus observed that the State disposes of part of the hydrocarbons extracted from the deposits, under the Cost Oil title, while it can hardly sell to any entity an offshore deposit discovered and whose exploitable potential would be the least bit important.

The non-transferable nature of sovereignty, which is often encountered, is at stake here. There is no longer any doubt that the State is led to concede rights to search for and exploit hydrocarbons to foreign and national investors or groups. This situation, which has gradually evolved, corresponds to what one legal scholar had called "the assignment by convention or contract of certain rights due to the economic weakness of developing countries."[68] This transfer of research and exploitation rights must be limited in time and space. On the one hand, the time of exploitation must be defined in the operating license that is granted for this purpose. In this way, control can be exercised—from the end of the mining concessions—over the time of execution of the research and exploitation work, which takes place on any site. Professor Georges Abi-Saab did not fail to refer to this temporal limitation as the "reasonable [exploitation] time," which makes it possible to foresee the time required to carry out the work, "for reasons similar to those which inspire the rule prohibiting perpetuity provisions in domestic law."[69] Could he rightly consider economic sovereignty to be a right of the people, given that its raison d'être "is to protect the State against its own weakness or deficiencies"?[70]

---

[67] *See* Abi-Saab, *supra* note 26, at 337.

[68] *See* Pellet, *supra* note 33, at 110.

[69] *See* Abi-Saab, *supra* note 26, at 337.

[70] *Id.*

CHAPTER 18

BILATERAL COOPERATION BETWEEN MEXICO AND THE UNITED STATES ON INFORMATION EXCHANGE AND ASSET RECOVERY

By Tony Payan and Rodrigo Montes de Oca Arboleya

Center for the United States and Mexico, Rice University's Baker Institute for Public Policy & Universidad Autonoma de Ciudad Juárez

Introduction

In today's globalized world, the movement of capital knows no boundaries. Although globalization has meant huge economic, technological, political, social, and cultural benefits, organized crime has taken advantage of it, engaging in illicit activities. It has also brought with it a new level of money laundering. Illegal transactions that used to take place within a country, leading to repercussions only in that country, are no longer constrained by borders. Criminals have created transnational corporations that allow them to use the financial system to move their capital from one country to another. They have thus diversified their assets through different financial instruments and spread out their earnings so much that there is no trace of them for authorities to find.

This new level of organized crime is a huge challenge for governments of all nations—individually and collectively. The fight against corruption and organized crime has become a global business, where the authorities must use new judicial and technological tools to identify the illegally based transactions. Moreover, this challenge entails the development of international and asset-attack prevention systems that have efficient enough communications channels for information to be shared, as well as adequate procedures for asset recovery that can make amends for the damage caused to the affected country through acts of corruption.

In Mexico, the fight against corruption is President Andrés Manuel López Obrador's flagship policy, and one of the main reasons why he won the election by a wide margin. Since the beginning of his term, President López Obrador decided to enhance the use of financial intelligence to investigate possible acts of corruption. Almost two years in, we have seen that this method has been the basis for investigating different cases, ranging from the theft of hydrocarbons and human trafficking to cases against former high-level government workers from past administrations for misuse of public office. Most allegations of corruption against former government workers that have been reported by the media come from investigations into their finances and assets carried out by the Financial Intelligence Unit of the Ministry of Treasury (FIU). For example, the cases against Rosario Robles, the former minister of Social Development (Sedesol, in Spanish) and Agrarian, Territorial, and Urban Development (Sedatu, in Spanish) (El Financiero, 2019-2021), and against Emilio Lozoya, the former director of Petróleos Mexicanos (Pemex) (El Financiero, 2020)—both very high-level officials in President Peña Nieto's administration— came from investigations by the FIU and allegations it then submitted to the federal Attorney General (*Fiscalía General de la República*, FGR, in Spanish).

Beyond the media impact that these cases have had, if we compare the FIU's work in the first half of President López Obrador's government (2019-2021) with

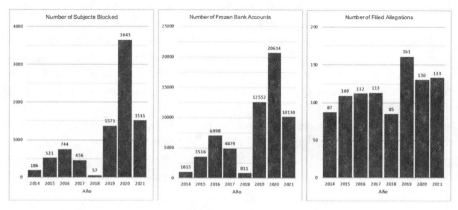

Figure 1. Indicators of activity by the Financial Intelligence Unit (2014-2021).
Source: UIF Informe de Actividades. Enero-diciembre 2021. Secretaria de Hacienda y Crédito Público, Gobierno de MéxicoGobierno de México.

the last four years of Peña Nieto's (2014–2018), we find a significant increase in the number of subjects blocked, frozen bank accounts and of allegations filed.

Yet some scholars on the topic have begun to question the use of these tools for political gain. There is, therefore, a need to study in detail each of the cases to find out how feasible they are in fighting corruption. Also, it is too soon to determine whether the strategy is proving successful because there has not yet been any criminal sentencing, which will show how well the investigation files were put together and if they are solid enough to stand up against the defense's arguments about who was likely responsible, and against judicial scrutiny. Furthermore, there has been no news of a significant recovery of assets lost to corruption that makes amends for the damage caused to the public treasury. As long as such does not occur, the country's impunity rates will continue to climb.

A key aspect to the success of the anti-corruption strategy is its internationalization, and a first step to achieve it is to focus on how the exchange of information and the recovery of assets lost to corruption and other crimes are regulated between Mexico and the United States. We have chosen to focus on cooperation between Mexico and the United States with good reason. It is difficult to find two countries with closer cooperation ties on such wide-ranging topics. Another plus to this analysis is that this cooperation is formalized and institutionalized through different instruments of international law (treaties, agreements, interinstitutional agreements, and others) that allow for a permanent cooperation among the different levels of government (federal, state, and local), independent from political actors in power. Mexico is the United States' main trading partner. The two countries share a common border more than 3,100 kilometers long that fosters trade but also creates several "gray zones" that transnational organized crime takes advantage of (Green, 2015).[1] Moreover, in the "transactions reports" published monthly by the FIU, the United States is constantly shown as the country where more international transfers are made and originate for amounts equal to or greater than $1,000.00 (U.S.). The US dollar is the most-used money for buying and selling foreign currency in Mexico.[2] This data is proof of the geographic, economic, political, and social interdependence between the two countries, and shows the need to work together in the fight against complex phenomena such as corruption and organized crime.

Considering this panorama, this text is based on a bilateral international approach to analyze the legal framework, the authorities and international entities, and the

---

[1] In the "gray zones" there is ambiguity, since the jurisdictions of each country are not clear. Green defines them as, *"a zone of ambiguity that severely challenges pervasive polarities (. . .), that can be both a concrete geographical space or object and also an analytical approach to understanding a given area or situation marked by ambiguity or porous boundaries."*

[2] Reports reviewed: from January 2019 to December 2021. Retrieved from https://www.gob.mx/uif.

procedures for actions and interoperability that govern two very specific issues—information exchange and asset recovery between Mexico and the United States.

Two Broad Topics to Cover

The use of financial intelligence is a complex topic, with different aspects. As a method of investigation, financial intelligence includes the following stages: (a) the reception of reports of suspicious financial activities from notifying entities,[3] (b) the investigation and analysis of the transactions, (c) the creation of intelligence products, and (d) information exchanges between different actors with the goal of fighting money laundering, terrorism financing, and other crimes (International Monetary Fund, 2004). In this chapter, we focus on stage (d), information exchange, which, for this research, is understood as the sending of and asking for financial, economic, and estate data from individuals or legal entities that are relevant or essential to an investigation. This information can also include administrative data from the government and from public registrars that could be useful to investigators when elaborating intelligence products that enhance the evidence presented at trial (International Monetary Fund, 2004). Not to minimize the importance of other states, we believe that the exchange of information includes a strong aspect of international cooperation that, as we have noted, will be analyzed considering bilateral relations between Mexico and the United States.

The other concept we will cover is asset recovery linked to corruption and organized crime between Mexico and the United States. Forfeiture mechanisms seek to repair the damage caused to the state's public treasury and to take from the criminals the product of their illegal activities. On the international arena, asset recovery consists of seizing and confiscating the illegal assets produced by corrupt foreign leaders or by members of organized crime, and returning them to their country of origin (U.S. Department of State, 2010).

The Complexity of the Issue

This research shows that there is an unequal evolution in the processes of information exchange and asset recovery. Information exchange has a broader development in judicial, academic, and practical terms, when compared to asset recovery. The international community has concentrated on creating international bodies and regulation of the standards for the exchange of information between authorities, without highlighting the procedure for making restitution for damages caused once it has been proven that embezzlement from a country's public treasury took place. It

---

[3] Notifying entities are usually credit institutions, but they can also be casinos, car agencies, notaries, and others.

would appear that the state's interest comes to an end when the person responsible is imprisoned, and no effort is put into making amends for the damage caused by this illegal behavior. In consequence, the judicial and institutional development of asset recovery is in its early stages.

Even though the two issues have evolved differently, they have several aspects in common. For example, the general legal framework that regulates them at the international level, and specifically between Mexico and the United States, is found in the same international treaties and agreements. Many of the same authorities and private subjects intervene in the two procedures. Likewise, asset recovery can be seen as a stage that follows information exchange among authorities during the investigation and verification stages. In other words, when the investigation of a corrupt foreign leader is strengthened through the exchange of information between the two countries, and this investigation leads to the seizure and confiscation of an asset obtained through money stolen in another country, the next stage would be for the affected country to ask for those assets to be repatriated so its public treasury could be reimbursed. This cycle must go through all the stages if a case against corruption or organized crime is to be considered as successful.

Another aspect to highlight is that the bilateral international approach makes federal governments more relevant to both issues, although the importance of state efforts is growing—so long as the governor in turn has the political will. Still, this essay is limited to the federal level, leaving for another project the analysis of actions by states and local governments. In Mexico, the current local environment is relatively limited in these issues, especially when there is no collaboration between the federal and state levels or between the state and local levels, due to political or administrative issues or to deficiencies in the infrastructure and capabilities to take part in these processes.

General Discussion

The following table shows the structural approach of this analysis. It is important to clarify that this layout is the result of an attempt to make the functioning of each process more understandable. Meanwhile, it does not ignore the multiple interconnections between the processes, which are critical to how they function.

Legal Framework: Information Exchange

There is a solid international legal framework that facilitates information exchange between the two countries. It is made up of international instruments in which Mexico and the United States are participating nations. Article 27 of the United Nations Convention against Transnational Organized Crime, on cooperation on matters of law enforcement, establishes that the Participating Nations must cooperate with each other to carry out inquiries and to improve the communications chan-

Table 1. Analysis Roadmap			
Topics	**Aspects**		
	Legal Framework	*Authorities and International Organizations*	*Procedures*
Information Exchange	The international legislation that regulates the exchange of information between Mexico and United States	The authorities and international organizations that take part in the exchange of information between Mexico and the United States	The procedures put in place for the exchange of information between Mexico and the United States
Asset Recovery	The international legislation that regulates the recovery of assets between Mexico and the United States	The authorities that take part in the recovery of assets between Mexico and the United States	The procedures put in place for the recovery of assets between Mexico and the United States

nels between their authorities to facilitate the safe, rapid exchange of information. Likewise, articles 14, 37, 43, and 46 of the United Nations Convention against Corruption establishes the obligation of the Participating Nations to adopt the necessary measures to cooperate and share information in the national and international arena.

Mexico and the United States have more than 50 signed bilateral international instruments on different issues that are currently in force.[4] Some of the most notable bilateral instruments are the Treaty for Cooperation between the United Mexican States and the United States of America for Mutual Legal Assistance, which in article 4 establishes that this assistance includes information exchange. Meanwhile, in the other signed bilateral agreements between the two countries there are some that can be applied depending on the information requested, such as the Mexico–United States Agreement for Information Exchange on Money Transactions Made through Financial Institutions to Fight Illegal Activities, the Mexico–United States Agreement for the Exchange of Tax Information, and the Mexico–United States Agreement on Cooperation in Combatting Narcotics Trafficking and Drug Dependency.

The effectiveness of these international instruments is complex. Legal practitioners must be familiar with aspects of international law and make them coincide with aspects of domestic law to substantiate their claim correctly. In other words, they

---

[4] These international instruments can be consulted with the Ministry of Foreign Relations, at https://aplicaciones.sre.gob.mx/tratados/consulta_nva.php.

must have ample knowledge about the legal systems in both countries. They must be clear about what they are going to ask for, and for what they are going to use it, when it depends on the use of the regulatory instruments. Unfortunately, not many of our authorities are able to link these concepts, which means that much of the information asked for is held up or even rejected for not being duly substantiated.

Legal Framework: Asset Recovery

As noted earlier, the two topics often overlap in this aspect. The general legal framework is contained within the same international instruments, with the difference being that their regulation is found in different articles. Articles 12, 13, and 14 of the United Nations Convention against Transnational Organized Crime regulates seizure and confiscation, international cooperation for confiscation, and the forfeiture of the product of the confiscated goods, respectively. Likewise, the United National Convention against Corruption dedicates Chapter V exclusively to asset recovery, establishing that the restitution of assets is one of the main principles of the convention, so the Participating Nations agree to broader cooperation and mutual assistance in this area.

Meanwhile, the Treaty for Cooperation between the United Mexican States and the Unites States of America on Mutual Legal Assistance is the main basis for carrying out a formal petition between the two countries regarding asset recovery (later we shall detail the differences between formal and informal requests for assistance). Other specific agreements that could be applied include the United States–Mexico Treaty on the Execution of Criminal Sentences and the United States–Mexico Agreement for the Recovery and Return of Stolen Vehicles and Airplanes or Matters of Confiscation of Illegal Proceeds.

One aspect to point out is that the U.S. Department of Justice has the Kleptocracy Asset Recovery Initiative, whose main objective is to recover assets to benefit people in the country affected by the abuse of public service positions, through transparent, responsible means (U.S. Department of State, 2010).

Even though there is a solid legal framework on this issue, both countries engage in the practice of asset recovery sparingly. It is often due to the complexity of identifying the assets generated through criminal acts. An analysis of experiences shows us that the government's main interest is for the person responsible for the crime to go to jail, which loses sight of the fact that the case should be closed with the repatriation of the assets to the affected country, thus making amends for the damage caused to the victim, which in many cases is the state itself. Losing sight of this final step fosters impunity because criminals can analyze the cost–benefit, which means they can go to prison for a few years without losing the assets or goods they gained from the crimes committed.

Another point is that the lack of petitions to restitute the state assets affected could encourage some countries to opt for lax legislation on money laundering. These countries could then benefit if nobody claims the assets once the criminal has been apprehended, which is common in cases of organized crime. Further, a lack of petitions leads to courts not generating jurisprudence or precedents for the issue, which would facilitate the interpretation and use of the legislation in future cases.

Authorities: Information Exchange

Each country has its own agency specialized in the sharing of financial data. In Mexico, there is the FIU. According to article 15 of the Interior Norms of the Ministry of Treasury, the FIU is the central national authority in charge of receiving reports about financial operations and notifications from those who engage in vulnerable activities. It also analyzes financial and economic transactions and shares intelligence reports and other useful documents with national and international authorities in order to detect transactions likely linked to money laundering and terrorism financing, and, when required, turns complaints over to the proper authority. The FIU's main tasks consist of implementing and following up on prevention detection mechanisms, omissions, and transactions that might somehow favor or help in the carrying out of crimes or transactions with illegal proceeds and financing of terrorism (Reglamento Interior de la Secretaria de Hacienda y Crédito Público, 2017).

The United States has the Financial Crimes Enforcement Network (FinCEN), an agency within the US Department of Treasury charged with protecting the financial system from illegal usage and with countering money laundering. It also fosters national security by collecting, analyzing, and making public financial data for the proper national and international authorities to use. FinCEN's main task consists of receiving and serving as a repository for financial transactions. It further analyzes and shares data for research and law enforcement and cooperates globally with its counterparts in other countries and with international organizations (FinCEN, 2020).

These two financial intelligence agencies are members of the Egmont Group, an international organization that brings together 164 financial intelligence units. Its goal is to act as an international forum and as a platform for the secure exchange of financial intelligence to combat money laundering and the financing of terrorism between member nations. For this group, information exchange is the cornerstone to counter money laundering and terrorism financing at the global level (Egmont Group, 2020). This international cooperation on information sharing between like-minded institutions should be carried out according to the international principles of reciprocity and mutual agreement. Information exchange among members of the Egmont Group is done through the Egmont Secure Web system (ESW).

We can see that authorities in both countries in charge of information exchange in financial and economic matters are perfectly identified. It means that authorities know for certain who their counterpart on the other side of the border is, which makes the procedure faster and more efficient. Information exchange also has an international organization in charge of supporting, emitting guidelines, providing a technology platform for information sharing, and offering technical assistance to its members so that the information shared is useful in investigations led by countries into money laundering and the financing of terrorism.

The information exchange experience between Mexico and the United States should serve as a roadmap to develop these same capabilities and relations with other countries. It should also be replicated throughout Mexico. The great challenge for the FIU is to support the federative states and the municipalities in building their own asset and economic intelligence units (UIPE, in Spanish), and to bring them into the sharing of information. By doing so, the FIU will enhance its own intelligence products with the information obtained from the states and municipalities, who will in turn obtain more information to enhance their local investigations.

Authorities: Asset Recovery

Unlike the clarity in information exchange, especially regarding authorities, asset recovery is muddled. In Mexico, the authorities that intervene in the recovery process are the Office of the Attorney General (*Fiscalía General de la República*), as the governing authority; the Ministry of Foreign Affairs, which provides the pertinent diplomatic channels, and the Ministry of Treasury (*Secretaría de Hacienda y Crédito Público*), through the Institute to Return to the People What Was Stolen (formerly the Administration and Divestment of Goods, SAE, in Spanish), which is in charge of managing all assets seized and confiscated while awaiting the conclusion of the pertinent legal processes.

In the United States, the situation is more complex because of the many federal ministries and agencies involved. The Department of Justice intervenes through two sections. The first is the Money Laundering and Asset Recovery Section (MLARS), the main entity dealing in asset recovery related to corrupt foreign leaders (U.S. Department of State, 2010). It also offers assistance with requests from foreign jurisdictions in recovering assets taken through corruption and other crimes. The U.S. government recommends that other countries contact it first if they need support in recovering an asset. The second section is the Office of International Affairs (OIA), which is the main U.S. authority on reciprocal legal assistance. Foreign governments must send all formal requests for legal assistance to this office (U.S. Department of State, 2010).

Meanwhile, the Federal Bureau of Investigation (FBI) has an international corruption unit, headquartered in Washington, D.C., and agents in other key U.S. cities. The Department of Homeland Security includes the Office of Homeland Security Investigations (HIS), which has a highly specialized investigations unit, with financial investigators assigned specifically around the world (U.S. Department of State, 2010).

Both the FBI and the HIS work with agents from the Internal Revenue Service (IRS). They also both have representatives in U.S. embassies around the world. These representatives can facilitate and help to governments that seek to make a request of U.S. authorities.

As this information shows, several agencies take part in the process, which leads to difficulties in finding the correct counterpart. A good first step may be approaching the embassies, but even then, inside embassies, such as the U.S. embassy in Mexico, there are also many officials and agencies represented, and this situation is simply at the federal level. The problem grows exponentially when we move to the state level. We must not forget that in countries such as the United States and Mexico, the federal nature of the government entails some unique conditions for these processes to function, unlike in countries with centralist structures where there is a clearer link between counterparts. In federalized nations, the federal authorities cannot access local material unless their interventions are justified, and in the local areas we find property registration, car registration, and even local banks governed by state authorities, like those in the United States. Therefore, the authorities must be prepared and willing to go from the federal to the local level to find the correct entity.

The huge challenge for both countries is to work together on this issue to find a faster, more efficient way to strengthen interoperability and information exchange regarding ill-gotten assets.

Procedures: Information Exchange

The procedures for information sharing can be divided into formal and informal. Formal procedures are needed when obtaining information requires a coercive measure according to the laws in the country where collection is to take place. Formal procedures are based on mutual legal assistance agreements and are used when the investigation has reached a point at which legal actions can begin before the proper courts and authorities (U.S. Department of State, 2010). Formal requests must comply with certain legal requirements, usually imposed by the country providing the information. The guidelines created for these procedures recommend contacting the foreign authority before sending the request, because often these offices have areas that offer assistance in filling out the requests (U.S. Department of State, 2010). These preliminary steps can exponentially speed up the reciprocal legal assistance process.

On the other hand, informal procedures provide access to public sources that do not require coercive investigation techniques. These procedures are used to carry out intelligence and investigation work when building a case. These informal contacts are made through public servants from both countries who usually have contacts in their counterpart institutions. For Mexico and the United States, it is very common for authorities to form task forces groups to exchange information on a particular case or for there to be a confidential exchange of information between them.

The advantage in information exchange is that it can use the Egmont Group platform, where 160 financial units from different countries share information in a safe and timely manner. Egmont Group publishes a document called "Principles for Information Exchange between Financial Intelligence Units." It establishes that FIUs should be able to share information freely with other FIUs, in reciprocal or mutually agreed upon conditions and according to the procedures agreed to by both parties. The exchanges, whether requested or spontaneous, must facilitate this information, including the people or consortiums implicated, which may be relevant to the analysis or investigation of financial transactions. This document also notes the obligations of the FIU making the request and the obligations of the FIU receiving it (Egmont Group, 2013).

It should be noted that identifying the agencies specialized in information exchange in both countries makes the procedures clearer and simpler, although they can still vary by case and crime being investigated. Likewise, having an international organization that brings together 160 financial intelligence units and provides a platform for information exchange in a safe and timely manner is extremely significant, since it strengthens trust and reciprocity between countries, both of which are essential to the efficient exchange of information at the international level.

Procedures: Asset Recovery

There are five steps that are required to recover assets lost to corruption or other crimes: (1) identify the facts and admissible evidence to establish the presence of criminal behavior (crime); (2) identify and locate the assets to be confiscated; (3) show with evidence the causal link between the assets and the criminal behavior; (4) seize or freeze assets; and (5) repatriate the confiscated assets (U.S. Department of State, 2010). Like with the issue of information exchanges, there are formal and informal procedures for recovering assets. Formal measures are needed when a coercive measure is required and enough evidence has been gathered to go to trial. U.S. law requires formal requests for the following: (a) requests for registrations of bank accounts or electronic bank transfers; (b) requests for registrations of companies or third parties when the person or entity refuses to provide them voluntarily; (c) the confiscation of properties, computers, or other electronic devices; (d) telephone, text, and/or email registries; (e) the application of a freeze order or a foreign confiscation order; and (g) pressuring or ordering of someone to give a legal testimony when that person refuses to do so (U.S. Department of State, 2010).

A formal written request for an evidence search or for coercive assistance usually requires mention of: (a) the name of the international instrument backing the request; (b) the name of the authority who will carry out the investigation or criminal prosecution; (c) a summary of the facts of the case, where the assets in question linked to the illegal behavior are mentioned; (d) crimes for which the accused may be responsible; (e) the objectives of the investigation or accusation and the names of other entities linked to the criminal activity; (f) an explanation of the assistance requested and its relevance to the investigation or procedure that is the basis for the request; and (g) any special requirements, such as confidentiality and urgency (U.S. Department of State, 2010).

Meanwhile, informal procedures are carried out among public servants, frequently at the same level and affiliated with counterpart institutions, in other words, between attorney general and attorney general, permit holder and permit holder, or police officer and police officer. This communication can be direct, and at times support is requested for routine investigation procedures. For example, Mexico may have some information about properties obtained illegally in the U.S. and ask U.S. authorities to verify them. The United States can carry out this task through routine investigations measures such as witness questioning, visual surveillance, and searches of public registrars, such as real estate (U.S. Department of State, 2010). It is highly recommended that an informal request be used first because it can help avoid errors when completing a formal request. For this reason, it is very important to develop relationships between authorities of the same rank in the two countries, allowing for trust, cooperation, and joint efforts to combat international corruption and organized crime.

This procedure can be very complex in practice, since legal practitioners deal with two different legal systems. It means that the burden of proof is different in each court, and even certain legal institutions such as "property" have different frameworks, values, and weight in each society. Likewise, terms such as seizure, asset freezing, assurance, and confiscation are labelled and understood differently in each country's legislation. Often the public servant is unable to recover assets, becoming trapped in a labyrinth of legislation, authorities, and procedures across the two countries. Some countries have opted to hire private law firms to help and to represent the federal and state governments during these procedures (Southeast Texas Record, 2018).

Conclusion

This chapter shows that the information exchange and asset recovery processes in Mexico and the United States have not evolved equally. Information exchange has a solid legal framework, the authorities involved in it are perfectly identified, and it has an international organization that acts as a supervisor, standardizing procedures for information exchanges between countries. This has helped nurture investigations with key information to obtain positive results. Its main challenge is to link the other levels of government in the two countries—for Mexican local authorities to be able to exchange information with U.S. authorities quickly and efficiently. It would be beneficial, especially in the border states, since it would strengthen security at the border crossings.

Meanwhile, the topic of asset recovery has not evolved much, due mainly to the number of authorities involved and the complex procedures. Even though there is a solid legislative framework, institutions are left unable to develop the necessary capabilities to work on these processes. Another repercussion of the lack of a legislative framework is a lack of jurisdictional criteria to help understand and interpret the legislation for future cases. The procedures are truly complex because both countries have domestic laws that regulate assumptions differently or even contradictorily, and something that is prohibited in one country may be permitted in another. Also, several topics reach beyond the administrative sphere, requiring intervention from judges and magistrates. The existing framework needs to be reformed in both countries, to simplify and accelerate procedures. Moreover, the role of task forces and international organizations must be strengthened, as they were for information exchange, to standardize rules and procedures and to provide confidence for the actors involved.

This essay is an approach to analyze the topics of information exchange and asset recovery between the two countries. The next stages will include an analysis of successful cases that can help us to understand the best roadmaps and procedures. Also, this structural analysis could serve to create a manual or practical guide for federal entities to learn about their areas of opportunity in both topics.

References

Egmont Group. About. 2020. https://egmontgroup.org/en/content/about

Egmont Group. "Principles for Information Exchange Between Financial Intelligence Units." 2013. https://sic.gov.lb/sites/default/files/international-standards/EG%20Principles%20for%20Information%20Exchange%20%282013%29.pdf

El Financiero. "UIF prepares two more complaints against Rosario Robles. 5 Sept., 2019. https://www.elfinanciero.com.mx/economia/uif-prepara-dos-denuncias-mas-en-contra-de-rosario-robles

El Financiero. "Finance Intelligence reveals cases of deviations for $83 million pesos in Pemex during Lozoya's management." 30 Jan. 2020. https://www.elfinanciero.com.mx/economia/inteligencia-financiera-revela-nuevos-casos-de-desvios-en-pemex-que-ascienden-a-83-mdp

Financial Crimes Enforcement Network (FinCEN). "What we do?" 2020. https://www.fincen.gov/what-we-do

Green, S. "Making grey zones at the European peripheries. Ethnographies of Grey Zones in Eastern Europe: Relations, Borders and Invisibilities," 173. 2015.

International Monetary Fund. "Unidades de Inteligencia Financiera: Panorama General. Washington DC." 2004.

Naciones Unidas. "Convención de las Naciones Unidas contra la Corrupción." New York, 2004. https://www.unodc.org/documents/mexicoandcentralamerica/publications/Corrupcion/Convencion_de_las_NU_contra_la_Corrupcion.pdf

Naciones Unidas. "Convención de las Naciones Unidas contra la Delincuencia Organizada Transnacional y su Protocolos." New York, 2004. https://www.unodc.org/documents/treaties/UNTOC/Publications/TOC%20Convention/TOC ebook-s.pdf

Reglamento Interior de la Secretaria de Hacienda y Crédito Público. 2017. https://www.gob.mx/cms/uploads/attachment/file/299882/Reglamento_Interior_de_la_SHCP_DOF_27_de_septiembre_2017.pdf

Southeast Texas Record. "Buzbee files lawsuit on behalf of Mexican state, court papers accuse ex-governor of stealing from treasury." 2018. https://setexasrecord.com/stories/511326646-buzbee-files-lawsuit-on-behalf-of-mexican-state-court-papers-accuse-ex-governor-of-stealing-from-treasury

Unidad de Inteligencia Financiera. "Evaluación Nacional de Riesgos: Resultados Preliminares." Secretaría de Hacienda y Crédito Público: Gobierno de México.

Unidad de Inteligencia Financiera. Informe de Actividades. Enero-diciembre 2021. Secretaría de Hacienda y Crédito Público: Gobierno de México.

U.S. Department of State. "Instrumentos y procedimientos de los Estados Unidos para la recuperación de activos: Guía práctica para la cooperación internacional. Departamento de Estado de los Estados Unidos." Washington, DC, 2010. https://star.worldbank.org/sites/star/files/booklet_-_spanish_final.pdf

CHAPTER 19

STEPHEN T. ZAMORA—A TRUE LEGAL EAGLE CREATIVITY, ADVOCACY AND DIPLOMACY— THE ZAMORA IMPRIMATUR

By Sofia Adrogué[1]

Dean Stephen T. Zamora was the paradigm legal eagle—innovating, navigating, and bridging across countries and jurisprudential systems as the consummate diplomat and negotiator, always with an emphasis on ethics and integrity. In his

---

[1] A native of Argentina, Sofia Adrogué is a seasoned trial partner (25 plus years) with Diamond McCarthy LLP, a 10 year Texas Super Lawyer & Latino Leaders "25 Most Influential Hispanic Lawyers" & "Most Powerful Women in Law." Having served on over 15 boards, she is currently a Member of the Houston First Board of Directors as well as the City of Houston Mayor's Hispanic Advisory Board and Chair of the Boards & Commissions Appointments Subcommittee. She serves as the Editor of the TEXAS BUSINESS LITIGATION treatise (5th Edition) & has published and/or spoken on over 250 occasions. She is a graduate of Harvard Business School Owner/President Management Program, an alumna of HBS (U.S. Keynote Graduation Speaker for HBS OPM 37, ostensibly the first woman, & U.S. Class Representative), and a graduate of the University of Houston Law Center, magna cum laude, & Rice University, magna cum laude, Phi Beta Kappa, both on full academic scholarships. She has received over 40 awards, including the 2021 World Affairs Council of Greater Houston Global Leader of Influence; 2020 Comcast Hispanic Heroes Award; a Greater Houston Women's Chamber "Hall of Fame" Inductee; a Houston Chronicle Channel 11 "Texas Legend" & 10 "Extraordinary Latinos" (Inaugural List); National Diversity Council "Most Powerful and Influential Woman of Texas" & one of the "Top 50 Women Lawyers"; a UH Law Center Immigration Clinic Arrival Award & a Houston Jaycees "Outstanding Houstonian"; a Texas Jaycees "Outstanding Texan"; and a U.S. Jaycees "Outstanding Young American"; among other recognitions. She serves as the Co-Host & Co-Producer of LATINA VOICES—SMART TALK. Sofia has been recognized for her public service by the City of Houston with a proclamation of July 10, 2004 & December 18, 2018, as "Sofia Adrogué Day."

Zamoraesque way, with quiet gravitas, he had the power to persuade. Having experienced a myriad of cultures, through his family roots and upbringing, as well as while in the Peace Corps early in his most formidable trajectory, he was the "change-maker" who immersed himself with other leaders, always inviting, engaging and trail-blazing.[2] Indeed, he perfected the notion that the negotiation table is thousands of kilometers long; the negotiation is not simply what is happening around the table.[3] He further understood that we must always remain vigilant and pragmatic about the present, while also cognizant of all the external factors that affect the negotiation, including, of course, the role of cultural sensitivities and norms, as well as an appreciation for the global context. He did so masterfully, strategically, and successfully, always with a moral compass.

Not surprisingly, Dean Zamora was honored with the Order of the Aztec Eagle by the President of Mexico, a monumental distinction and the highest accolade given to a foreign national in recognition for services to Mexico or humanity.[4] The decoration has several classes and has been given to such diverse leaders as Queen Elizabeth II, Nelson Rockefeller, Cesar Chavez, Bill Gates, Nelson Mandela, Walt Disney, Gabriel García Márquez, and Mario Vargas Llosa.[5]

As Prof. López de la Osa Escribano, the former Director of the Center for U.S. and Mexican Law at the University of Houston Law Center (UH Law Center), eloquently articulated with meticulous breadth and scope in his leading article, Dean Zamora's contribution to the creation and advocacy of international programs at the UH Law Center, a contribution that commenced upon Dean Zamora's arrival, was of great import and lasting effect.[6] His initiatives, spanning over thirty years, in "the understanding of Mexican laws and legal institutions in the United States, and of U.S. laws and legal institutions in Mexico,"[7] culminated in the creation of the Center for U.S. and Mexican Law. It is the only center in any U.S. law school dedicated to the independent and critical study of Mexican law and its interactions with U.S. law.[8] As the current Dean of the UH Law Center has aptly described, even after his official retirement, Dean Zamora "continued to lead the Center for U.S. and Mexi-

---

[2] Alfonso López de la Osa Escribano, *Professor Stephen T. Zamora: A Visionary and Generous Soul,* 40 HOUS. J. INTL. L. 723, 731 (2018).

[3] Deepak Malhotra, Eli Goldston Professor of Business Administration, Harvard Business School.

[4] *See* https://www.chron.com/neighborhood/heights-news/article/FACES-IN-THE-CROWD-UH-professor-receives-1854945.php.

[5] *See* https://en.wikipedia.org/wiki/Order_of_the_Aztec_Eagle; *see also* https://www.chron.com/neighborhood/heights-news/article/FACES-IN-THE-CROWD-UH-professor-receives-1854945.php.

[6] *See generally* López de la Osa Escribano, *supra* note 2.

[7] *Id.* at 728 (citing https://www.law.uh.edu/mexican-law/MissionStatement.asp).

[8] *Id.*

can Law, which is the premier institute in the country studying these issues. Steve possessed a dogged determination to advocate for stronger economic and legal relations between the U.S. and Mexico and better understanding between the lawyers of both nations. His unique voice brought clarity and understanding to these issues."[9]

Dean Zamora wholeheartedly "believed in the relevance of international law in every U.S. lawyer's education."[10] He appreciated the concept that Thomas L. Friedman coined and revolutionized in 2005: "The World is Flat."[11] Dean Zamora recognized the evolving level playing field, the ramifications of globalization in the 21st century, and the necessity of countries, corporations and individuals in a global market where historical and geographic divisions are becoming increasingly irrelevant. He certainly would not be surprised that today, "with more global issues demanding international cooperation to address, businesses are operating in a highly complex, increasingly transparent environment."[12] As Richard N. Haass, President of the Council on Foreign Relations and author of *The World: A Brief Introduction* expertly noted, "[w]e've got to expect that we're going to be in a world of greater, not less, geopolitical turbulence."[13] This is, in essence, the Zamora imprimatur, global with expansive breadth and scope, focused not just on international but on "supranational cooperation,"[14] and, most evidently, of significant benefit today.

Similarly, he advocated for years, before it was encapsulated so beautifully by Dr. Stephen L. Klineberg, that his Houston is the prophetic city—the city of the future.[15] It is egalitarian, with an entrepreneurial can-do and will-do spirit. It is an inspired city and is the nation's demographic future. In racial and ethnic composition, the Houston of today very much resembles the United States forty years hence.[16]

---

[9] *See* https://www.law.uh.edu/mexican-law/StephenTZamora.asp.

[10] López de la Osa Escribano, *supra* note 2, at 727.

[11] THOMAS L. FRIEDMAN, THE WORLD IS FLAT: A BRIEF HISTORY OF THE TWENTY-FIRST CENTURY (2005).

[12] *See* James Manyika, Co-chair and Director of the McKinsey Global Institute Interview of Richard N. Haass, President of the Council on Foreign Relations and author of *The World: A Brief Introduction* (https://www.mckinsey.com/~/media/McKinsey/Featured%20Insights/Leadership/James%20Manyika%20speaks%20with%20Richard%20Haass%20about%20businesses%20as%20global%20entities/James-Manyika-speaks-with-Richard-Haass-about-businesses-as-global-entities.pdf?shouldIndex=false).

[13] RICHARD N. HAASS, THE WORLD: A BRIEF INTRODUCTION (2020). *See also* Manyika, *supra* note 12.

[14] López de la Osa Escribano, *supra* note 2, at 728.

[15] STEPHEN L. KLINEBERG, PROPHETIC CITY: HOUSTON ON THE CUSP OF A CHANGING AMERICA (2020). (Stephen L. Klineberg is the Founding Director for The Kinder Institute for Urban Research, and the Professor Emeritus of Sociology at Rice University. *See* https://kinder.rice.edu/people/stephen-l-klineberg).

[16] *Id.*

Like a true visionary, Dean Zamora also believed you need to "shun the incremental and go for the transformative."[17] For instance, he would be ecstatic to learn that Houston received the 2026 World Cup bid to host his beloved countries—the United States and Mexico.[18] The 2026 FIFA World Cup will be the first time the competition will take place across three nations—Canada, the United States, and Mexico—united North American hosts.[19]

His passion for his cities was matched, if not surpassed, by his contributions across areas of international law (judicial review in Latin America, liability for damages in international transport, and international monetary law, among others).[20] Cognizant of the deep impact that Dean Zamora made to our jurisprudence, his principled, disciplined research and zealous advocacy also resonate within the context of complex litigation and best practices for such success in our 21st century. Indeed, litigation in the 21st century continues to be the subject of vigorous substantive debate and commensurate study. Some commentators have defined a 21st century litigator as "one who uses the court system only as a last resort if a dispute cannot be resolved outside its bounds."[21] With institutions continuing to seek a "roadmap for reform" in our 21st century civil justice system, issues of costs and length of time for resolution of matters and satisfaction with the overall process remain at the forefront of the debate.[22] Dean Zamora was masterful in delivering a resolution outside of litigation with his enhanced understanding of counsel, adverse parties, and intercultural and comparative legal and business experiences.

---

[17] Linda Applegate, Baker Foundation Professor & Sarofim-Rock Professor of Business Administration, Emerita, Harvard Business School.

[18] Mary Anderson (Author) & Sofia Adrogué (Contributor), *Houston's 2026 World Championship Soccer Bid*, RIVER OAKS LIVING (May 2019) (addressing Houston's journey of the 2026 World Cup bidding process); https://www.houstondynamofc.com/news/houston-awarded-hosting-rights-for-2026-fifa-world-cup. (Houston was selected as one of the 11 U.S. host cities for the FTA World Cup.™)

[19] *Id.*

[20] López de le Osa Escribano, *supra* note 1, at 726.

[21] SOFIA ADROGUÉ & CAROLINE BAKER, TEXAS BUSINESS LITIGATION (ALM 4th Edition 2019) (Preface). Combining 50 plus cumulative years of practice and over 20 years on a state district court bench, Sofia Adrogué and Caroline Baker envisioned a work that would serve as an encyclopedia on business litigation—from A to Z—including some of the unexpected issues that may emerge such as a bankruptcy proceeding or a criminal investigation, along with applicable ethical considerations. The "Who's Who of the Bar," legendary trial lawyers and specialists, analyze 25 business litigation topics. *See also* SOFIA ADROGUÉ & CAROLINE BAKER, Texas BUSINESS LITIGATION (ALM 5th Edition 2022).

[22] SOFIA ADROGUÉ & CAROLINE BAKER, TEXAS BUSINESS LITIGATION (ALM 4th Edition 2019) (Preface).

Another legal giant and pioneer, albeit in litigation, Steve Susman, like Dean Zamora, was years ahead of his time. He developed a set of Pretrial Agreements that his namesake firm, Susman Godfrey, proposed to opposing counsel.[23] Steve Susman's initial inspiration merits repetition as it is commensurate with Dean Zamora's approach to the business of law and international relations: "The key to the efficacy of such a Pretrial Agreement has always been to attempt to reach agreement on as many of these items as possible before discovery begins. Once you are in the heat of battle, what appears to be good for one side is often deemed to be bad for the other; therefore, it is hard to reach agreement at that point."[24]

Steve Susman's Pretrial Agreements were so effective that he evolved the concept and created a list of possible Trial Agreements,[25] which culminated in a working website appropriately named *TrialByAgreement.com*[26] where these agreements can be found and debated among trial lawyers.

Steve Susman's approach to litigation—principled, competitive, and pragmatic—epitomized Dean Zamora's approach:

I truly believe that Trial Agreements are worthy of full discussion among experienced trial lawyers and judges well in advance of pretrial. My attitude is to take whatever agreements I can get—the idea being that any such agreements advance the ball and make pretrial and trial more professional and efficient, not to mention making trial more understandable to the jury. Trial by Agreement is a way of reducing expense, stress and the uncertainty of pretrial rulings and a jury trial.[27]

Of note, it is fitting that Steve Susman's work to "keep jury trials from becoming extinct" resulted in his envisioning, founding, and funding his Civil Jury Project at NYU Law School—a "collaborative effort between law students, lawyers, judges and political bodies across the nation" to "examine the factors leading to a decline

---

[23] Sofia Adrogué & Caroline Baker, *Litigation in the 21ˢᵗ Century: The Jury Trial, The Training & The Experts—Musings & Teachings,* from David J. Beck, Lisa Blue, Melanie Gray & Stephen D. Susman, *The Advocate* (Fall 2011). *See also* https://trialbyagreement.com/category/pretrial-agreements/.

[24] *Id.*

[25] https://trialbyagreement.com/agreements/trial-agreements-made-easy/.

[26] https://trialbyagreement.com/.

[27] Adrogué & Baker, *supra* note 24.

in civil jury trials and educate the legal community and the public on methods to revitalizing the dying system."[28]

Dean Zamora, like Steve Susman, actively promoted disciplinary collaboration. Almost twenty years before creating the Center for U.S. and Mexican Law, Dean Zamora created the North American Consortium on Legal Education, whose principal objective was, and remains, the promotion of "professional cooperation and comparative legal education in North America."[29] Prof. López de la Osa Escribano further encapsulates Dean Zamora's spirit of international diplomacy. "Professor Zamora's global vision led him to build bridges, promote synergies and alliances, and seek ways to solve legal issues and controversies. He was never divisive but rather the opposite; working to get things done for the sake of the community as a whole."[30]

Such a modus operandi is similar to another quintessential luminary and visionary, a Houston legend, Hon. James A. Baker III. As the new book, *The Man Who Ran Washington: The Life and Times of James A. Baker III*, poignantly describes, in just two decades, Hon. James A. Baker III led five presidential campaigns and served three presidents in such influential positions as Secretary of State, Secretary of the Treasury and White House Chief of Staff.[31] In an interview for *Listening to Leaders*, Secretary Baker articulated the values that guide him.[32] Not surprisingly, great leaders like Dean Zamora, Steve Susman, and Secretary Baker, share great values. Specifically, when asked about how he would define great leadership, Secretary Baker stated as follows:

> I consistently go back to James MacGregor Burns, who defined it as "a commitment to values and the perseverance to fight for those values." I agree but would say it in a bit different terms: Leadership is knowing what to do and then doing it.
>
> The tough part of leadership is the "doing it" part. A commitment to values is knowing what to do. The perseverance to fight for those values is doing it.

---

[28] SOFIA ADROGUÉ & CAROLINE BAKER, TEXAS BUSINESS LITIGATION (ALM 3rd Edition 2017) (Preface). *See also* https://civiljuryproject.law.nyu.edu/.

[29] López de la Osa Escribano, *supra* note 2, at 726. Of note, as of 2018, 11 law schools in Canada, Mexico, and the United States are member institutions of NACLE. Its relevancy is evident with commensurate traction given the Center for U.S. and Mexican Law that Dean Zamora also created as articulated above.

[30] *Id*. at 730-31.

[31] PETER BAKER & SUSAN GLASSER, THE MAN WHO RAN WASHINGTON: THE LIFE AND TIMES OF JAMES A. BAKER III (2020).

[32] WILLIAM MCKENZIE, LISTENING TO LEADERS, George W. Bush Institute book (2019). https://www.bushcenter.org/publications/books/listening-to-leaders.html
See also, e.g., https://www.houstonchronicle.com/opinion/outlook/article/James-A-Baker-III-says-listening-trusting-and-14904084.php.

Too many people are not being exposed to and trained in the principles and values that have made this country great. One of those is compromise, which is a dirty word today. Compromise is how the founders arrived at agreements on things that were bitterly disputed. Sadly, we've lost that. The center is gone in politics.[33]

Just like Steve Susman advocated in his arena, and Dean Zamora exercised in his, Secretary Baker serves as the paradigm of the art and value of compromise.[34] It, like the vanishing trial, has sadly become a vanishing trait that Steve Susman, Dean Zamora, and Secretary Baker dedicated their lives and talents to preserving. A spirited debate continues about the cause(s) of the vanishing trial, as well as the best manner in which to handle and resolve complex business litigation. Success in such matters requires creativity, advocacy, and diplomacy—the Zamora imprimatur.

Of critical import, indeed a commonality shared also by Steve Susman and Secretary Baker, Dean Zamora valued and learned from his *familia*. As Prof. López de la Osa Escribano poignantly noted, Dean Zamora was married to a "mirror of him in many aspects,"[35] the other esteemed Dean Lois Parkinson Zamora. The present dean of the UH Law Center, Dean Leonard Baynes, emphasizes that Dean Zamora's "tenure as dean was notable for two reasons. First, he was the University of Houston and the Law Center's first dean of Hispanic origin; and second, at the same time, his wife, Lois, was dean of the University's College of Liberal Arts and Social Science, making them quite unique in academia."[36]

In a book by another native Houstonian, Joe Jaworski, *Synchronicity: The Inner Path of Leadership*, there is an apropos description of family that Dean Zamora firmly embraced:

If you want to make a peak climb, you've got to have a good base camp, a place where there is shelter and where provisions are kept, where one may receive nurture and rest before one ventures forth again to seek another summit. Successful mountain climbers know that they must spend at least as much time, if not more, attending to their base camp as they actually do in climbing mountains, for their survival is dependent upon their seeing to it that their base camp is sturdily constructed and well stocked.[37]

---

[33] *See* https://www.houstonchronicle.com/opinion/outlook/article/James-A-Baker-III-says-listening-trusting-and-14904084.php; *see also* William McKenzie, *supra* note 33.

[34] JAMES A. BAKER III, THE POLITICS OF DIPLOMACY (1995).

[35] López de la Osa Escribano, *supra* note 2, at 730.

[36] *See* University of Houston Law Center's tribute to Dean Zamora's life and legacy. https://www.law.uh.edu/mexican-law/StephenTZamora.asp; http://www.law.uh.edu/news/briefcase/v35n01/files/basic-html/page21.html.

[37] JOSEPH JAWORSKI, SYNCHRONICITY: THE INNER PATH OF LEADERSHIP (2011).

No doubt, with his partner in life, the other respected Dean Zamora, and his two children, Camille and Peter, he had an impenetrable base camp, always fully stocked.

Keenly aware of the 2020 annus horribilis, a McKinsey & Company acronym brilliantly defines an archetype recipe for success; Dean Zamora, the ever visionary, would have appreciated the import and relevance of **SHAPE**: **S**tart-up mindset; **H**uman at the core; **A**cceleration of digital, tech, and analytics; **P**urpose-driven customer playbook; & **E**cosystems and adaptability.[38] The constant visionary, the true legal eagle, from his arrival to the University of Houston, he mastered the need to reimagine, recalibrate, reinvigorate, and reset.[39] He succeeded beautifully, while doing so with our neighboring nation, his Mexico, engaging in Zamora-style diplomacy that reflected the legal eagle and the Aguila Azteca that he undeniably was, personifying the phrase: *L'Union fait la force.*

---

[38] *See* McKinsey & Company https://www.mckinsey.com/featured-insights/future-of-work/from-surviving-to-thriving-reimagining-the-post-covid-19-return; *see also* McKinsey & Company Covid-19 Series (Summer 2020).

[39] *See* McKinsey & Company Covid-19 Series (Summer 2020).

ADDENDUM TO CHAPTER 19

PROFESSOR STEPHEN T. ZAMORA: A TALENTED PROFESSIONAL RELATIONSHIPS PROMOTER

By Sten L. Gustafson[1]

In the fall of 1989, I entered as a first-year law student at the University of Houston Law Center, with no experience in or knowledge of anything remotely related to finance, corporations, or anything else related to business. Like many stu-

---

[1] Sten Gustafson is a highly experienced energy service industry executive, investment banker, and corporate securities attorney, and is currently the founder and CEO of Pyrophyte Acquisition Corp. (NYSE: PHYT). With over 25 years of experience in the global energy sector, Mr. Gustafson has advised on over 100 corporate transactions around the world for over $100 billion of transaction value. Following his graduation from the University of Houston Law Center, Sten was a transactional lawyer with the international law firms of Cleary, Gottlieb, Steen & Hamilton, and Baker Botts L.L.P. He spent nearly 20 years in investment banking, including as Managing Director and the Head of the Energy Group, Americas for Deutsche Bank. From 2012 to 2014, Mr. Gustafson was Chief Executive Officer and Director of Era Group Inc. (previously NYSE: ERA), where he led the successful spin out of Era from Seacor Holdings in January 2013. From 2017 to 2018, Mr. Gustafson served as a member of the Founding Steering Committee created by the Public Investment Fund of Saudi Arabia to establish a private commercial helicopter operator (The Helicopter Company) in the Kingdom of Saudi Arabia. From 2017 to 2019, Mr. Gustafson served as a director at CHC Helicopter. Since 2018, he has served as Chairman of the Board of Directors of the publicly traded Norwegian company, Golden Energy Offshore (GEOS.ME.Oslo), a fully integrated shipowner and operator of offshore service vessels for the global offshore wind industry as well as the oil and gas industry. Since 2020, Mr. Gustafson has also served as an independent director for American Rare Earths, an Australian-listed rare earth mining company (ASX: ARR), providing critical materials for electric vehicles, wind turbines, and other renewable energy technology.

dents who enter law school, I was less than certain about my eventual area of focus, and frankly, was hoping that this direction would somehow appear to guide my path. As the old saying goes, "when the student is ready, the teacher will appear." I was fortunate enough to have Stephen Zamora as my professor for Contracts for my first year, and after that first year with him, my path then became clear to me. For a topic that could easily become esoteric and tedious, he made the class intriguing, and his willingness to meet and answer questions with his open, welcoming manner truly opened my eyes to a career path that I could not have imagined otherwise. Despite never having taken a single undergraduate class pertaining to business, I felt that I had found my path, with Professor Zamora leading the way.

During our increasing dialogue outside of the classroom, I was fascinated with Professor Zamora's experiences with the World Bank, and his work in international financial transactions while at Cleary, Gottlieb, Steen & Hamilton. The summer between my first and second years of law school, I was encouraged by Professor Zamora to take a summer curriculum sponsored by the University of Minnesota at Uppsala University in Uppsala, Sweden. These classes and the overall experience were transformative for me, introducing me to international corporate and financial transactions, as well as friendships with other students and professors from all over the world, many of which I remain in contact with to this day.

My second year, I had the opportunity to take his International Financial Transactions class, which then built upon the experiences I had benefitted from just months before in Sweden. I had most certainly found my area of interest, and Professor Zamora continued to foster it, asking me to serve as his research assistant for an article he was writing. The second semester of my second year, I then worked with him closely in researching in support of his article. While working with him, he suggested that I seek a summer associate opportunity with his old law firm, the highly regarded international law firm of Cleary, Gottlieb, Steen & Hamilton. In many ways, Cleary Gottlieb represented a dream opportunity for me, as they were particularly notable for their work in international finance, particularly in innovative, developing areas. However, there was what seemed to be an insurmountable impediment—they did not interview students from the University of Houston Law Center.

Undaunted and unsolicited, Professor Zamora picked up the phone and called his old mentor and prior head of Cleary Gottlieb's D.C. office, Don Morgan, and urged him to interview me. As a testament to how highly Don Morgan thought of Professor Zamora, he agreed to find some workaround to get me involved in Cleary Gottlieb's recruiting process. Sure enough, a few days later, Professor Zamora called me to his office and let me know that Cleary Gottlieb would be interviewing at the University of Texas Law School, and if I drove over there, they would meet with me. Because Cleary Gottlieb was viewed as such a blue-chip firm, their interview schedule was, of course, completely filled with UT Law students. However, once again, because Don Morgan had such respect for Professor Zamora, he told the Cleary Gottlieb attorney conducting the interviews in Austin to find room in his schedule to meet with me. Consequently, we met during the only time he had availability—for dinner.

Serendipitously, the attorney who originally was scheduled to come to Austin ended up having a work emergency, so he was replaced by another attorney at the last minute. I had dinner with this "replacement" attorney, and we got along so well that we are still good friends twenty years later. I was elated to let Professor Zamora know that I had received an offer to work at Cleary Gottlieb's Washington, DC office (where he had worked), and I knew that I had to deliver to ensure that Professor Zamora's recommendation was warranted, as he had truly delivered for me. In fact, I was the only person from the state of Texas to receive an offer from Cleary Gottlieb that year.

When I arrived at Cleary Gottlieb's D.C. office that summer, I was greeted by Don Morgan, who said, "So you're the student that Professor Zamora speaks so highly of!" I simultaneously felt pride and pressure to deliver, because it was critically important for me to not let Professor Zamora down. He had obviously put his reputation on the line to push for me to get the interview, and now it was up to me to back it up. Thankfully, the summer went well, and I received an offer from Cleary Gottlieb.

A few years later, while a full-time associate at Cleary Gottlieb, I was working in Sweden on a creative, cutting-edge financial transaction representing Goldman Sachs in securitizing Swedish mortgages. I reflected then that I had made a round-trip of sorts thanks to Professor Zamora—back in Sweden where I had come as a summer law student at the recommendation of Professor Zamora, but now as an attorney thanks to the recommendation of Professor Zamora, working on the kinds of transactions I had never heard of until I took Professor Zamora's classes.